War, Memory, and the Politics of Humor

War, Memory, and the Politics of Humor

The Canard Enchaîné *and World War I*

ALLEN DOUGLAS

University of California Press
BERKELEY LOS ANGELES LONDON

All illustrations in this book are reproduced courtesy of *Le Canard Enchaîné*, Paris.

University of California Press
Berkeley and Los Angeles, California

University of California Press, Ltd.
London, England

Library of Congress Cataloging-in-Publication Data

Douglas, Allen, [date]
War, memory, and the politics of humor : the Canard enchaîné and World War I / Allen Douglas.
p. cm.
Includes index.
ISBN 0-520-22876-6 (cloth : alk. paper)
1. Canard enchaîné. 2. World War, 1914–1918—Humor. 3. French wit and humor—History and criticism. 4. Satire, French—History and criticism. 5. World War, 1914–1918—Press coverage—France.

D526.3 .D68 2002
940.3′02′07—dc21 2001027676

Manufactured in the United States of America

11 10 09 08 07 06 05 04 03 02
10 9 8 7 6 5 4 3 2 1

The paper used in this publication is both acid-free and totally chlorine-free (TCF). It meets the minimum requirements of ANSI/NISO Z39.48-1992 (R 1997) *(Permanence of Paper)*. ♾

To the memory of my grandfather,
Lieutenant Max H. Friedman (1889–1986),
who served in the Air Corps of the American
Expeditionary Force in France in World War I

Contents

Illustrations

Preface and Acknowledgments

My involvement with France and the First World War is a family affair. My grandfather, my mother's father, volunteered for duty in that conflict as a flyer with the American Expeditionary Force. His war was hardly typical. He made sure we knew how dangerous combat flying was, repeating the characterization of that era's planes as "flying coffins." But when my grandfather got to the front in late 1918 there was a shortage of aircraft; before he could get one, the armistice intervened. Last to come, last to go, my grandfather spent many months in postwar France. Paid as an officer, feted as a hero, he led the A.E.F. basketball team to an inter-Allied championship (he played professionally before and after the war and was inducted into the Basketball Hall of Fame). He returned with only happy stories of the Gallic republic and spoke little of the heartbreaking tragedy of the war for most French men and women. What I first learned of the war was the songs "Mademoiselle from Armentières," "The Yanks Are Coming," "We Are the Kee-Wee-Wees," and "I Wonder Who's Kissing Her Now." My grandfather sang some to me; others he sang to my mother in her childhood, and she passed them on to her own children.

When my French-speaking wife and I married in 1971, it was obvious that our honeymoon would take us to France, which neither of us had previously visited. My grandfather's advice was limited: be sure to drink Vouvray. We were happy to comply and developed an affection for the bubbly Loire white wine. (We could hardly afford Champagne in those days.)

Our next trip across the Atlantic came in 1973, when we went to Paris to work on our respective dissertation topics. Before leaving, I received advice from my professor Eugen Weber. Among his suggestions was the offhand comment that I might want to take a look at a satirical weekly newspaper, *Le Canard Enchaîné*. I began reading the paper, was quickly hooked, and eventually subscribed.

Over a decade, and many trips, later, being in Paris, I decided to renew my subscription to the *Canard* in person. By this time, my biography of Georges Valois was winding itself up, and I was casting about for a new line of research. As I left the offices of the *Canard Enchaîné*, I looked back through the door pane ornamented by one of its trademark ducks. Why not direct my research toward my favorite periodical, I thought?

Only after I began reading the back issues of the *Canard* did I understand how relevant had been my grandfather's wartime memory of Vouvray. The *Canard*, which began publishing in 1915, was intimately connected with, and had its essence shaped by, World War I. And the totem drink of this young periodical was, almost from its inception, that same bubbly white. Vouvray, the war, the *Canard* were all part of the same story—the story that became this book.

Begun in Austin, Texas, *War, Memory, and the Politics of Humor* was completed in Bloomington, Indiana. In 1992 the library of the University of Texas at Austin saved my eyes by printing out years of the French weekly from microfilm. The helpful professionals at the microfilm room at the main library at Indiana University, Bloomington, cheerfully took over this work (even purchasing a new lens) in the fall of 1992; this work was supported by a research fund provided by Dean Morton Lowengrub of the College of Arts and Sciences. Other research funds from the College of Arts and Sciences and the West European Studies National Resource Center at Indiana facilitated continued trips to Paris and the acquisition of research materials. I am appropriately grateful for the assistance and the confidence expressed through such support.

Between Texas and Indiana came five weeks at the Rockefeller Foundation Residency Site in Bellagio during the summer of 1992. I thought I had died and gone to heaven. Like my fellow residents, I was coddled by the staff at the Villa Serbelloni, and my study, "La Polenta" (a tower in the woods with a view of Lake Como), was an ideal environment in which to read years of *Canards*. I am especially grateful for this unique experience to Lynn Szwaja and the staff of the Rockefeller Foundation in New York, to Pasquale Pesce in Bellagio, and to all the other *bellagini* who shared my time there and who helped create an intellectually stimulating and supportive environment.

To work on the *Canard Enchaîné* was to have, yet again, the inestimable privilege of working in Paris. I received courteous and helpful assistance at many Paris-area research facilities, from the Archives Nationales and the old Bibliothèque Nationale on the rue de Richelieu to the new Bibliothèque de France–François Mitterrand at Tolbiac. It is a particular pleasure to salute the patient good cheer with which the often-mystified staff at the Mitterrand library struggled with the limits of a high-tech system that had not yet worked out its kinks. The librarians at the Bibliothèque de Documentation Internationale Contemporaine at Nanterre were invaluable in helping me locate crucial materials on wartime press censorship. The uniformed French soldiers at the Service Historique de l'Armée de Terre were as helpful and efficient as their smock-covered civilian colleagues at this military archive in the majestic Château de Vincennes.

The archives of the *Canard Enchaîné* for the period before 1940 were almost completely lost (as were so many other personal papers and archives) in a hasty evacuation from Paris as German troops approached in June 1940. I owe my access to the few papers that survived to the generosity of Messrs. Laurent Martin and Nicolas Brimo. Brimo, the weekly's director of public relations, put me in touch with Martin, who was preparing an in-house history of the weekly as I was preparing the present book. We shared sources (as well as food and drink), and I am grateful to him for letting me read and copy materials that I otherwise would not have been able to use.

Friends and colleagues also helped me refine my thinking by providing the stimulus of public lectures. Universities around the world allowed me to test out my ideas: Marmara and Yeditepe universities in Istanbul; Tel Aviv University; Al-Akhawayn University in Ifrane, Morocco; and Moulay Idriss University in Meknès, Morocco, on three occasions. I was also privileged to present a paper on the *Canard* at a plenary session at the national meeting of the Society for French Historical Studies in 1994, and, in that same year, I read an invited paper at a conference, "France and the Arabs," held at Princeton University.

Numerous were the friends and colleagues who aided my work through invitations, assistance, comments, and encouragement: Stéphane Audoin-Rouzeau, Annette Becker, Jean-Jacques Becker, L. Carl Brown, William Cohen, Matthew S. Gordon, Akile Gursoy-Tezcan, Patrick Hutton, Abdallah Malki, Jane Marcus, Matt Matsuda, Michael Miller, Driss Ouaouicha, and Jay Winter. To all of them, I can say only that I hope the resulting work lives up to their expectations.

My searching and constructive readers for the University of California Press greatly improved the manuscript. Without their contribution, backed by the critical support of Dr. Lynne Withey, this book would be neither what nor where it is.

But the reader has probably already guessed to whom my deepest debt is owed: to my wife, Fedwa Malti-Douglas. The companion of my life and work, she has provided tremendous patience, unflagging encouragement, advice both shrewd and searching, and the incomparable example of her own work.

NOTE ON TRANSLATION, ELLIPSES, AND EMPHASIS

All translations are my own, unless otherwise indicated. Since ellipses are so common in the writing of the *Canard Enchaîné,* I have used brackets to indicate only those ellipses that are my own. All other ellipses are in the original. In quotations, all emphases are in the original.

Introduction
War, Lies, and Newsprint

In 1924, the third of September was a Wednesday. We can easily imagine that it was sunny and mild, the kind of day when Parisians sipped their drinks and read their newspapers outside in the sidewalk cafés. Why not, then, imagine this too? A man in his early thirties has just ordered a Vouvray. He wears a Croix de Guerre in his lapel; his left leg is extended stiffly: probably a war wound. After all, the Great War has been over for less than six years. He opens his newspaper and begins to read. The article is entitled "Long Live the Courts-Martial!" But our veteran is smiling, despite the repressive reputation of these military tribunals. Let us read over his shoulder.

> One could perhaps vacillate over the designation of the being most antipathetic to the valiant Parisian population.
>
> —It is the cop, Mr. Poincaré would say, jealous of the popularity of his successor.
>
> —No, it's the concierge, a number of regular guys, who have stood in the rain awaiting the opening of a hospitable door, would argue.
>
> —Error, it's the creditor, individuals short of dough would affirm.
>
> But what if one encountered a phenomenon who united in his sole and unique person the triple quality of cop, of Cerberus, and of the lender, there would certainly be only a cry of horror against him. And we would acclaim the hero who did not fear to tackle this redoubtable trinity.
>
> This was fully understood by the second court-martial, which has just acquitted the valiant Captain Rouhier, who shot down with his revolver his concierge, the peace officer Jacquinot, who dared to insist on the repayment of the money he had lent to him.

After noting that if anyone else had attacked such a pillar of society, the jurors would surely have headed him for severe punishment, the article goes on:

> We should, therefore, be happy that the deputies of the Cartel des Gauches have still not carried out the abolition of the courts-martial, which figured, formerly, in the Republican electoral platforms. If Captain Rouhier had not been able to count on the goodwill of the justice of his comrades, without a doubt he would have hesitated to accomplish his brilliant action; and the tenants, debtors, and how many former demonstrators would have been deprived of a great joy.[1]

What is this newspaper that joyfully attacks the military and military justice while cheerfully assuming general hostility to other representatives of authority? (The inclusion of "former demonstrators" with tenants and debtors is a subtle swipe at police behavior.) And the article brings in politics, too. Raymond Poincaré is the center-right politician who has just left office after losing the parliamentary elections. But Edouard Herriot (Poincaré's more popular successor) and his left-center Cartel des Gauches also come in for ridicule—in this case for not abolishing the courts-martial as they had promised. Officers and police, politicians of the right and left, does this paper hold nothing sacred?

What periodical could play so expertly on multiple levels of irony while felicitously combining slang with the most elevated, even comically overelevated, French? Its title was *Le Canard Enchaîné,* and this was its 427th weekly issue. *War, Memory, and the Politics of Humor* explores the way this periodical, between 1915 and 1928, balanced censorship and stereotype, memory and prediction, the comic and the tragic, to construct an original discourse of the First World War.

For over eighty years the *Canard Enchaîné* has cut through the conformities of French politics and society. Founded in 1915 as a challenge to the patriotic gore of First World War journalism, the *Canard* has prospered. It is true that it printed only five issues in the year of its birth, 1915, but this duck became a phoenix when it was reborn in July 1916. With constantly expanding sales, the *Canard* held to its weekly schedule and published not only throughout the war but during the peace as well. In fact, it published without a break until the fall of France in 1940, and then it was revived at the liberation to continue until today as one of the Gallic nation's most influential organs.

This success almost partakes of historical anomaly. Small nonconformist periodicals were legion before the First World War; as the twentieth century wore on, they became increasingly rare. But this feat of the *Canard* has been combined with another. It takes no advertisements, accepts no subsidies, and does not appeal to its followers to support it through donation campaigns. Living entirely from subscription and newsstand sales, the satirical weekly has shown, with its circulation of a half million, that a newspaper can live because of, and not despite, its independence. This fact alone should be enough to commend it to our attention as one of the enduring objects of twentieth-century French culture.

WAR CULTURE

The essence of the *Canard Enchaîné*—its political positions as much as its discursive strategies, its verbal tics as much as its visual style—derives from the circumstances of the First World War. Its history is that of a wartime publication that became a successful peacetime political and satirical weekly. Hence the project of this book: investigate the *Canard Enchaîné* in the four years of war and the decade that followed the armistice. During these fourteen years, from 1915 to 1928, the *Canard* transformed the wartime division between combat soldiers and "exploiters" into an antimilitarist critique of peacetime politics and society, one in which the memory of the Great War itself was never far below the surface.

As the most durable textual institution to come out of World War I, the *Canard* has played an outsize role in what Paul Fussell, in his classic study, defined as "the Great War and modern memory."[2] And it is probably in this context of the aftermath of the "war to end all wars" that the *Canard* made its most important contribution to the evolution of French political thought and institutions. No understanding of the legacy of the war in France, or elsewhere, would be complete without an understanding of this war-born periodical.

But the *Canard* was more than a product of the war. It was intimately connected with the war experience—as reflection and as part. This book examines the *Canard* as part of war culture. As such it seeks to contribute to the cultural history of the First World War, as masterfully practiced by scholars like Jay Winter, Stéphane Audoin-Rouzeau, and Annette Becker.[3] But the satirical weekly survived the war to interpret the conflict to its compatriots. It played a major role in the process by which citizens of the Gallic republic sought to digest, to come to terms with, the war. *War, Memory, and the Politics of Humor* is, therefore, also a study of the history and politics of memory as they have been explored not only in the multivolume collection *Les lieux de mémoire* by Pierre Nora[4] but also in the work of Patrick Hutton, Matt Matsuda, Winter, and Daniel Sherman.[5] For the *Canard,* the memory of the Great War was a problem that pointed forward as well as backward. All memory is in some sense present-oriented; that of the *Canard* was also future-oriented. It is part of the cultural history of interwar France, as that has been explored, for example, by Michael Miller and Charles Rearick.[6] Finally, the satirical weekly provides a unique window on that larger question explored by scholars from Fussell and Modris Eksteins to Winter: the place of the First World War in the formation of the culture of the twentieth century.[7]

While historians of interwar France (most recently Robert Soucy) have increasingly focused on the elements of fascism and right-wing authoritarianism in its political culture (seen as foreshadowings of Vichy),[8] less attention has been devoted to the other side of the political coin. More than any other cultural product, the *Canard* took the basic elements of the World War I–front ideology—solidarity among combatants in opposition to civilians, the cult of the war dead, and distrust of politicians and profiteers, all elements that were central to the development of fascist movements—and steered them into a quintessentially Gallic, democratic antiauthoritarianism. The democratic tradition in France is in many ways quite different from that on the other side of the Atlantic, but it is equally vigorous. The *Canard* helped preserve that vigor. Though the *Canard* did not openly target communism, as it did fascism, it kept a sufficient distance from the Bolshevik system to prefigure a critique of totalitarianism. The *Canard* was a reaction to the war that also fought the most important political effects of the war.

Studies of intellectual and ideological currents in twentieth-century France (like those of Jean-François Sirinelli and Christophe Prochasson) have often relied on intellectuals.[9] Their analyses were certainly influential. But perhaps even more so were the lower-brow but equally sophisticated products of the writers and cartoonists of the *Canard.* With its off-color remarks, its learned puns, and its political wisecracks, the French satirical weekly brought together the domains of high, popular, and political culture.

High and popular culture, the political meaning of mass media, the interplay of visual and verbal: *War, Memory, and the Politics of Humor* focuses, methodologically speaking, on the *Canard Enchaîné* as a cultural object with its own distinctive discourse. How is humor developed in such a tragic environment? How are the visual and the verbal combined? What are the characteristic elements of this discourse, its rhetorical devices (taken in the largest sense), its tics and topoi? And what are the ideological implications of this mix of humor and politics? What do they say about French society? about the First World War? about war in general? These are the questions that underlie this study. *War, Memory, and the Politics of Humor* looks at plots as well as principles, at the messages of pictures alongside those of words, and, even more, at the interplay of the verbal and visual.[10] And, like most works of cultural criticism, it assumes that the unspoken is often as important as the spoken and that ambiguity or even self-contradiction are also part of cultural discourses.

The discourse of the *Canard* would not fit any conceptualization of cultural dynamics structured around the opposition of a hegemonic "discourse" and subversive "practices." The openly satirical weekly presented itself as subversive (though for its readers it could play a hegemonic, organizing role). Whether or not one adopts William Sewell's useful concept of "thin coherence," it should be obvious that cultures define themselves as much by what they choose to argue about as by what they hold unspoken (and how true this is of modern French intellectual and political culture!). And on its own level the *Canard* played the same games: assuming some conflicts as polemics and ignoring others while subsuming still others in creative tensions. Cultural systems vary in the ways and degrees to which they project conflicts outside and inside themselves. One cannot understand the *Canard*, or its success, without looking at both sides of this coin.[11]

To counter the language of war (both during the conflict and after, through memory) the *Canard* created a counterlanguage, effectively a new discourse—that is, a set of ideas concretized in expressions, slogans, images, and mental structures.[12] Obviously not all the elements of this language were new. If they had been, readers would not have been able to understand it. The *Canard* drew on the long French tradition of wit and political satire from François Rabelais to *L'Assiette au Beurre*. But the war-born weekly reorganized preexisting elements into new patterns, patterns both appropriate to the war and inconceivable without it.

A history of the elements, both formal and ideological, that the *Canard* borrowed from earlier media would undoubtedly be rewarding. But it would take us away from our principal goal—to understand the discourse of the *Canard Enchaîné* as a reaction to the war. Such a diachronic view would have the disadvantage of obscuring the synchronic functioning of the *Canard*'s discourse and especially the way this discourse carries its own ideological implications. This does not mean the elimination (or even the bracketing) of context. *War, Memory, and the Politics of Humor* is grounded in the position that the *Canard*'s discourses cannot be understood outside the context of the war. Simply, this discourse must be analyzed as a functioning system. By the same token, significant comparison with the discourses of similar periodicals in France or in other national traditions would demand a rigorous examination of those works for the same period, a task that is outside the scope of this study.

This book has a synchronic bias, at least relative to most historical writing. Not that *Canard* positions did not change or evolve. This study pays careful attention to such developments, setting what changed against what was constant. But it seems inescapable that the most important *Canard* positions remained largely constant from 1915 to 1928 and even more so within the separate periods of the war and the postwar.

This analysis of the *Canard* in war and peace thus also helps to illuminate the relationship between ideas and events. It is not that they are unrelated streams, each following its own logic. It is that the rates of evolution of the two series are sufficiently distinct that different kinds of events have different kinds of impacts on the world of representation. If the war was the great seismic event that colored everything in the paper, smaller sequels, like the ebb and flow of political and diplomatic history, changed little. We will see again and again that important *Canard* attitudes to war, disarmament, and economics were largely impervious to the dramatic political and diplomatic shifts in the first decade of peace. Most historians would divide the 1920s into a period of crisis (from 1918 to 1924, or 1926 for France) and a period of stabilization afterward. For the *Canard* the whole was a single postwar (when not also a prewar). This discourse assured the paper's success, more so than specific positions that could vary according to circumstances.

War, Memory, and the Politics of Humor focuses on a relatively neglected area in the study of World War I culture, humor. But humor makes its own methodological demands; and one cannot analyze with the traditional tools of intellectual history an object like the *Canard Enchaîné*, an object that is deliberately elusive, often but unstably antiphrastic, and that combines verbal and visual codes. Finding meaning (or more often meanings) in the *Canard* demands close attention to language, rhetoric, and the techniques of humor generation. One of the arguments of this book is that such expressions, patterns, and techniques carry their own ideological ballast, which is as important, if not more important, in the long run, than doctrinal or political statements.[13]

And in dealing with what functions as a language, one can discern its patterns only by looking at how it varies and evolves in usage. Examination of the tendency of an element to repeat, and especially examination of invariants (that is, what repeats and what remains constant), is crucial to isolating the ideologically significant aspects of the discourse. The same goes for the identification of structural elements that appear only upon examination of a large number of examples.

Some of the richest carriers of intellectual and ideological content are what I identify as *Canard* topoi. Semiotically speaking, these are semantic syntagms (remembering that *semantic* refers to carriers of meaning). The syntagms can consist of verbal or visual codes or both, and, despite their compound nature, they function as single signifiers.[14] But the associated signifieds need not be univocal; they often contain potentially contradictory propositions, and the referents of these signs are potentially highly varied. I have adopted the term *topos* from traditional rhetoric not only because of its familiarity but also to stress the way the satirical weekly turned these formulae into recognizable and repeatable markers.

Despite the importance of the *Canard Enchaîné,* it has received surprisingly little scholarly attention. The book by Laurent Martin, *Le Canard Enchaîné ou les fortunes de la vertu: Histoire d'un journal satirique 1915–2000,* appeared when my own book was already in production. Martin's work is a valuable survey and introduction to the history of the *Canard,* especially its transformation after the 1960s into a highly influential exemplar of French investigative journalism. Ample room still exists for a range of studies on the *Canard.*[15]

EXPLORING THE *CANARD*

If Athena, according to myth, emerged fully armored from the head of Zeus, one could say that the *Canard* emerged, ready for battle, from the belly of the god of war. Its principal weapon against the climate of censorship and patriotic falsehood was antiphrastic irony. Double meanings, thus, were congenital to the satirical weekly. Such ambiguities, however, did not remain limited to the domain of rhetorical devices. They sunk into the content of the paper's political and ideological positions. In many cases, the *Canard* could appear to argue both sides, or at least more than one side, of an issue. A certain ideological versatility, which often permitted the reader to choose the meaning with which he or she was most in sympathy, unquestionably broadened the newspaper's appeal and contributed to its success. Each chapter of this study, therefore, while presenting both a major subject area and a theme, often also reflects a tension between two, sometimes politically contradictory, approaches to the same issue.

The first chapter introduces the satirical weekly as it was hatched in 1915. While using visual and verbal irony to dodge the ever-active scissors of the censor, the *Canard* bobbed and weaved between patriotic support of the common soldier and ridicule of the Central Powers, on one side, and a budding antimilitarism that generally remained on the safe side of explicitness, on the other.

The *Canard*'s distinctive organization and layout form the subject of chapter 2. Carefully balanced mixtures of materials marked the weekly's style. Visually this balance went further than the inclusion of large numbers of editorial cartoons. Concretizing the newspaper's title into a visual metaphor, the cartoonist H. P. Gassier, and later Henri Guilac, created a duck-everyman who could take on a variety of guises and who was as at home on the masthead as he (or even she) was in the spaces between and within articles. The heavy use of such visual elements, which stood in a semiotically ambiguous position between ornamentation and pictorial editorializing, allowed a visual irony that could either complement or contrast with the verbal one.

The weekly also described itself as a "humorous newspaper." Mixing funny stories, off-color anecdotes, jokes, puns, and pastiches, the *Canard*'s columns were as often devoted to cackles and cuckoldry as to capitalism or communism. With traditional humor and politics on the one hand and verbal and visual games on the other, the *Canard*'s distinctive organization was also a discourse. In this type of journalism, the reader never knew on beginning an article whether it would be serious or funny in tone, ironic or direct in argument, and righteously political or snickeringly exploitative in character—or, finally, as in the paper's *pièces de résistance,* clever combinations of the above antinomies.

If the slaughter of thousands of young men was the greater tragedy of these years, another crime also caught the *Canard*'s attention: the daily massacre of the truth in the French press. *Bourrage de crâne*—skull stuffing, or eyewash in English usage—is the name usually given the combination of patriotic bombast and naively mendacious optimism that dominated the mass press. Chapter 3 chronicles the second major vocation the satirical weekly took from the Great War (and which survived that conflict)—that of critic of the French mass press. The *Canard* was especially hard on the patriotic press, relentlessly mocking how its leaders either avoided military service (Maurice Barrès) or had abandoned their earlier antimilitarism (Gustave Hervé). But the weekly also taught its readers why and how the mass press worked.

Both the satirical attack on the bellicose mass press and the alchemy that rendered humor from tragedy come out most clearly in the *Canard*'s discussion of the "tears of *L'Intran*" (chapter 4). *L'Intransigeant,* a formerly leftist, now reactionary nationalist and militarist, newspaper, specialized in moving patriotic anecdotes that invariably ended with an onlooker or participant wiping a tear of emotion from his or her eyes. The *Canard* mocked these stories and even set up pastiche contests based on them. Within a short time, the association of tears and *L'Intran* became a humorous topos that could be evoked in a variety of contexts. The *Canard* sensed that the falsely placed pathos of *L'Intransigeant*'s campaigns created the opportunity to extract laughter from tears without downplaying the tragedy of the war. Where the right-wing paper transformed suffering (tears) into militarism, the leftist one transmuted both into humor. At the same time, the paper's phony anecdotes exposed anxieties over war-caused social changes.

The attack on the verbal heroism of the mass press was part of a broader sociology (chapter 5). The wartime *Canard* divided French society into two groups. On the one hand were the fighting men, the French front-line soldiers, along with the families they had left behind. On the other was everyone else. This second group included those in uniform who did not fight—from staff officers to *embusqués* (those with soft jobs in the rear)—as well as those the paper called *mercantis:* businessmen and businesswomen who gouged the families of soldiers (and sometimes the fighting men as well) through high prices and shoddy goods. Though the *Canard*'s attack on "legitimate" business and commerce had a socialist flavor, the weekly shunned openly socialist positions, preferring instead to cast its sublimated class warfare as a struggle between self-sacrificing soldiers and exploitative noncombatants.

If the years of war marked the establishment of the *Canard Enchaîné,* its favorite themes, and its distinctive discourses, the decade that followed saw the weekly adapt both its themes and its discourse to a different journalistic climate. These years could be called those of peace since they followed the armistice of 1918, but for the *Canard Enchaîné* they were really the postwar. For the weekly it was a time for arguing over the memory of the war, waxing ironic over its effects, attacking the newer wars that followed, and laughing bleakly over the prospect of another European conflagration. Despite the evolutions of French politics (which the *Canard* followed as a predator does its prey), the principal themes and topoi of the paper's articles and cartoons remained remarkably consistent across the decade from 1918 to 1928.

Probably the most distinctive of *Canard* journalists in the decade after the war was Georges de la Fouchardière (chapter 6). His most important contribution was a weekly column that featured imagined conversations with a colorful ne'er-do-well, Alfred Bicard. As an alcoholic and compulsive gambler prone to Archie Bunker–like malapropisms, Bicard can say things that would be scandalous from a more respectable source. But he also forms the ideal vehicle for an examination of the *Canard*'s attitudes toward alcoholic beverages.

It has long been a part of the French self-image (generally accepted by foreigners) that French citizens are controlled drinkers, that they do not get falling-down drunk. That notion is called into question by reading the *Canard* for the 1920s, where drunks who see double and cling to lampposts rival prostitutes and politicians as sources of humor. But at the same time apéritifs are a symbol of life's pleasures, while wine, especially the Loire-produced Vouvray, functions as a totem-drink. And, whether those of hopeless drunks or of sophisticated imbibers, French drinking habits are especially contrasted with the stupidity of prohibition in the United States.

Peace and the slightly later abolition of the censor allowed the *Canard* to become frankly antimilitarist and only slightly less openly pacifist. The tension now was often between optimism and pessimism, as an early enthusiasm for Woodrow Wilson gave way to an increasing and remarkably precocious cynicism about the prospects for another war (chapter 7). Within a year of the peace treaty, the satirical weekly began to express its pessimism through a pun that became a topos. Playing on the two meanings of the common phrase *la dernière guerre* (the last war or simply the most recent one), the *Canard*'s writers coined the phrase *prochaine dernière guerre*, or "next last war." Again, however, there were two wings to the positions of this journalistic duck. While one wing mercilessly attacked as dangerous warmongers all those who criticized the attempts at Franco-German rapprochement and indeed all those who continued to trade in anti-German hysteria, the other wing greeted the peace offensives of Aristide Briand with a cynicism fed by the paper's reports on continuing military buildups in France and around the world.

More than anything else, however, for the *Canard* of the 1920s the Great War was a matter of memory. As I show in chapter 8, no issue was closer to the heart of this war-hatched weekly. Memory was the continuation of wartime truth telling: setting the record straight. But for France, as for most former belligerents, the memory of the conflict received its official concretization in ceremonies and monuments of commemoration, from the monuments to the dead in every village square to the great commemorations of the armistice. Sensing how such practices could be turned to militaristic uses, the *Canard* made the challenging of official modes of commemoration one of its most common topics throughout these years. However, the paper's line was not univocal. The *Canard* respected the memory of the self-sacrificing common soldier, and it criticized those who sullied commemorations with balls and jazz bands. But the satirical weekly saved its biggest ammunition for the official ceremonies associated with the cult of the unknown soldier who lay beneath the Arc de Triomphe (chapter 9). Here, the weekly savaged the exploitation of the dead soldier through the twin motifs of cannibalism and of a vengeful resurrection from the grave. Like the commemoration of the armistice, the cult of the unknown soldier provided the occasion for a critique of the very idea of the cultivation of the memory of the war.

For the *Canard Enchaîné* wars were not only in the past of memory or in the uncertain future of pessimistic predictions but in the present, and the present wars included France's colonial wars of the mid-1920s: its war (in alliance with Spain) against the Moroccan Rif and its campaigns in Syria against the Druse and other dissident groups (chapter 10). The *Canard*'s frank, and politically daring, anti-imperialism, which blended easily with its more traditional antimilitarism, led to its unequivocal condemnation of both conflicts. Yet foreign peoples, whether Arab, Berber, or other, were an irresistible source of humorous gags, and the *Canard* consistently muddied its principled antiracism with the racist exploitation of popular stereotypes—from harem girls to naked cannibals. Beyond this tension between stock humor categories and ideological positions lay the world war, whose evocation marbled the paper's accounts of France's colonial conflicts.

Chapter 11 focuses on French domestic politics as viewed by the *Canard*. The paper vacillated between two positions. The first was a left-of-center "republicanism" situated somewhere between the Radical and Socialist parties. In domestic matters this position supported laicism (including anticlerical humor), freedom of the press, and a government closely controlled by the parliament. Abroad it supported an internationalist foreign policy with a corresponding reduction in military service. Electorally, it tended toward clear hostility to politicians of the right and center, support for Radicals and Socialists, and attacks on members of either of these parties when they seemed to be straying toward the right. The *Canard* never directly supported the communists, either in France or in Russia, but the reds were the only French group never subjected to the paper's acid satire. Instead, the *Canard* satirized the way the rest of the press covered the supporters of the Third International. The satirical weekly's lack of direct support, coupled with its unrelenting critique of anticommunist repression in France, made it an odd kind of fellow-traveler.

But alongside its nonconformist but electorally recognizable leftism stood the paper's second political position, a more politically ambivalent antiparliamentarism. Starting with stock jokes about Deputies as ideologically versatile windbags (and Senators as dirty old men), the *Canard* developed a position suggesting that the entire democratic-electoral process was an exercise in futility. This position, though it had its proponents on the far left, is more usually associated with the French radical right, where it was usually linked with a cult of the war veteran. That the *Canard*'s two positions were either outside electoral politics or on the democratic left (but not the right) was shown by the paper's precocious and vigorous opposition to both Benito Mussolini and his potential imitators in France. Any fascist implications of the *Canard*'s antiparliamentarism were thus blunted by the weekly's thoroughgoing antiauthoritarianism.

Characteristic of France during the 1920s was the large role that often obscure economic and monetary issues played in national politics and national life. Reparations, war debts, inflation, and monetary crises alternately combined to dominate French politics from 1922 to 1928. The *Canard* articulated its own distinctive approach to economic affairs (chapters 12 and 13). In some ways the most remarkable aspect of the *Canard*'s approaches to economic matters was its willingness to blame others, here the internal "other" of peasants and shopkeepers. On the one hand, the weekly argued that France was impoverished by the war, as developed in its sardonic view of the "fruits of victory." On the other hand, it repeatedly blamed high prices on greedy merchants (the *mercantis* of wartime) and farmers. These French groups were shown as rapacious, duplicitous, and getting rapidly rich on the misery of their fellow citizens. On the question of war debts (whose repayment to Britain and the United States was widely unpopular), the *Canard* again combined structural explanations with finger pointing. The weekly was careful not to credit the decline of the franc to foreign speculators (preferring to blame French government action). Yet, on the subject of debts, the exploitation of stereotypes and the paper's general line came together in an attack on an avaricious, hypocritical—and dry—Uncle Sam.

Clearly, in the pages of the *Canard,* both during the war and after, humor had its politics. This book's concluding chapter carries the argument further in two ways. First, it examines the particular devices used by the writers of the satirical weekly—from bisociation (associating together items from separate series or systems of thought)[16] to antiphrastic irony, parody, and repetition—to show how the discourses of the *Canard* carried their own politics. Second, the chapter shows how the *Canard*'s humor did not merely sugarcoat its politics but in many ways was its politics. The *Canard Enchaîné* found in humor an affirmation of life and as such the most effective antidote to war, that affirmation of death. An anti-utopian *joie de vivre* linked the *Canard's* view of politics with its politics of memory.

HISTORY AND BIOGRAPHY

One reason for the *Canard's* distinctive personality is that it was conceived, fathered, and nurtured into a vigorous adulthood by one man: Maurice Maréchal. Aged thirty-seven when he founded the weekly in 1915, Maréchal had been excluded from military service by a weak heart (though he served briefly as an auxiliary). A native of Château-Chinon in the Loire valley from a petit-bourgeois background (his father was an inspector in the forest service), the young Maurice went straight from the lycée to work as a professional journalist. He wrote for a number of small leftist and pacifist periodicals while working for the radical leftist and antimilitarist Hervé and at the same time did editorial work for *Le Matin,* an organ of the conformist mass press. Maréchal threw his own modest savings into the new venture, and his wife served as secretary and general helpmate, delivering the first issues herself by bicycle. With the second launching, in 1916, the *Canard* enlisted the help of the Messageries Hachette for distribution to railway-station kiosks. Even then, resources were still tight, as can be seen by the paper's concern to keep the number of returned copies to a minimum.[17]

Maurice Maréchal was a man of words, but his new paper was as visual as it was verbal. For the world of the image he turned to Henri-Paul Deyvaux-Gassier, who signed himself H. P. Gassier. Born in 1889, Gassier drew political cartoons for a variety of left-wing sheets, including *L'Humanité* and *L'Heure,* and, like Maréchal, he had worked for Hervé and had been spared military service. Gassier's professional opportunities were apparently limited by his devotion to his anarchist convictions (though his work also appeared in conformist papers like *Le Journal*). But his willingness to work for little or nothing in the service of his convictions fit in well enough with the *Canard,* which, for many years, could offer only the most modest remuneration.[18] Gassier was responsible for the paper's visual style, and he was the first to pen its trademark ducks. After the war this role of chief cartoonist and illustrator fell to Guilac, who was able to step into Gassier's visual shoes because he shared with his predecessor a spare, open graphic style that blended well with typography.

When Maréchal brought the *Canard* back in July 1916, he had finally assembled a team. The most important addition was Victor Snell, who served as Maréchal's right-hand man and second in command as well as being the major writer for the weekly. His role was recognized in April 1921, when he was credited on the masthead with the title of editor-in-chief (alongside Maréchal as director). Snell's regular job was at *L'Oeuvre,*[19] the new daily paper founded by Gustave Téry—a paper whose witty battles with the censor made it a frequent target of disciplinary action.[20]

Many of the *Canard*'s other new voices were also associated with Téry's spunky daily, with which the weekly shared printers and, for a time, a building. Collaborators in common and a generally cordial relationship did not mean, however, that the *Canard* was unwilling to mock the new daily. If Maréchal's most useful new collaborator came from *L'Oeuvre,* so too did his most visible new journalist, Georges de la Fouchardière, who came on board with the relaunching in 1916.[21]

De la Fouchardière was known principally as a humorist. The same was true of Rodolphe Bérenger, who used the pen names Rodolphe Bringer and Roger Brindolphe; his connections were with the socialist, and later communist, daily *L'Humanité* as well as with the similarly leftist *L'Heure.* Bringer/Brindolphe, born in 1869, was excused from military service for physical reasons. The third of the *Canard*'s trio of humorists did not join the paper until after the war: René Buzelin was mobilized as an auxiliary and then discharged as physically unfit.[22] Important for contributions and editorial work after the war were Jules Rivet, who also worked for *L'Humanité,* and Pierre Bénard, who earned his keep at *L'Oeuvre.*[23]

The *Canard* was founded and run, for years, by men who had been spared combat. As the war went on, however, veterans of the butchery began to add their voices to the civilian chorus. Gaston de Pawlowski had served at the front for many months before his byline appeared in 1917. Léon Kuentz used the pen name André Dahl. A volunteer even before the war, he served from August 1914 to September 1918 at the front, where he also ran a trench newspaper. Decorated with the Croix de Guerre, he wrote for a large variety of nonconformist periodicals before and after the war, besides serving as a mainstay of the *Canard.* But in the later twenties, the most important veteran writer, and an increasingly important editor and journalist at the *Canard,* was Michel Piot, whose pen name was Pierre Scize. Also a combat volunteer, Scize took from the war decorations (the Military Medal and the Croix de Guerre), serious wounds that led to the loss of his left arm, and a lifetime's worth of righteous anger.[24]

A number of stars of postwar French letters also occasionally came within the orbit of the satirical weekly. The most important of these was Roland Dorgelès, whose byline appeared occasionally during the early twenties and who may have played a larger role behind the scenes and as a provider of anonymous copy. Dorgelès was a professional journalist, a decorated combat veteran, and a successful novelist (he was a member of the prestigious Goncourt Academy). What most distinguished Dorgelès from his *Canard* colleagues was his political position. While most at the weekly were firmly on the pacifist left, Dorgelès had worked for Clemenceau and enjoyed relationships with literary and political figures across the spectrum.[25]

Tristan Bernard was one of those whose byline appeared only occasionally but who was nevertheless credited with a role in the development of the spirit of the *Canard*. A humorist, writer, and celebrated Parisian wit, he also counted Dorgelès among his familiars.[26]

Paul Vaillant-Couturier, journalist, poet, war veteran, and then communist, also wrote for the *Canard* from 1917 without becoming a member of its inner circle. A poet before the war, Henri Barbusse became famous in 1916 by winning the Goncourt prize for his combat novel *Le feu*. After the war he continued to write, becoming a leading antiwar activist and loyal communist intellectual. The *Canard* greeted *Le feu* warmly and was honored to print the war hero's prose.[27]

Despite the variety of personalities and pen names, Maréchal worked to create a consistent product. Blurring the sense of distinct journalistic voices was the *Canard*'s habit of using a variety of pseudonyms, themselves available to more than one journalist, when not simply printing articles anonymously or under the byline "Canard." When the writer Maurice Charriat quit in a huff in 1922, he insisted that the pseudonym Maurice Coriem belonged only to him, though the weekly claimed that several of its writers had used it. But the *Canard* gave it up cheerfully, explaining that they were hardly down to their last pseudonym.[28]

As it was with writers, so was it with cartoonists. The *Canard* published drawings with pseudonyms, with illegible, phony signatures, or simply anonymously. Nevertheless, a number of cartoonists' names appeared regularly. From early in the history of the weekly, Lucien Laforge added his ducks to those of Gassier. Guilac was aided after the war by artists like Henri Monier and William Napoleon Grove. Jacques Pruvost and Paul Levain, whose pen name was Pol Ferjac, also joined during the postwar decade. The most visually distinctive new talent was Auguste Pedro de Pedrals, who used the pen name Pedro (and who also drew for the Canard's journalistic bête noir, *L'Intransigeant*). His incisive cartoons had a nervous cubist-inspired style that departed from the dominant open lines and curves Guilac had continued from Gassier.[29]

A paper needs readers, and the *Canard* found them. By July 1917, Maréchal claimed 40,000 readers. The paper's print run rose above 100,000 after the war, attaining a high of 150,000 in 1923–1924.[30] Not only had the *Canard* more readers, but these readers had more *Canard* to read. On April 27, 1921, the weekly enlarged its format, permitting five columns per page where there had been four. At the same time, it started intermittent publication on six pages, though this innovation did not stick, and the *Canard* returned to its classic four.

The weekly even played, again only for a time, with changing its name. In October 1919, as wartime censorship came to an end, the weekly changed its heading to *Le Canard Déchaîné* (the unchained, or unbridled, duck). But the journalistic fowl returned to its old name in May 1920. As its excuse, it reported a summons by an investigating magistrate (from which nothing further developed).[31]

Maréchal wavered on another *Canard* institution, only to come back to it even more firmly: the newspaper's refusal to take advertisements. In late October and early November 1924, as prices for paper were rising, the *Canard* announced its intention to start taking a few carefully selected advertisements from relatively safe sources like book publishers. On the following January 26, however, the weekly congratulated itself as it announced that it was abandoning the idea (and had not taken any advertisements in the interim) and was raising its newsstand price instead.[32]

WAR, LIES, AND MEMORY

The *Canard* survived on the loyalty of its readers. Jean Galtier-Boissière, the antimilitarist journalist who wrote for the weekly before breaking with it in the 1930s, recounts the following anecdote. After the death of Bénard, "in the mortuary chamber, near the bed where Pierre Bénard was resting, an old gentleman was sobbing. Jeanson asked his name: it was the FIRST SUBSCRIBER to the *Canard.*"[33] Loyalty could go a long way. In the words of Henri Monier, cartoonist and memorialist, there was a *Canard* "mystique" that connected the readers and their paper by "an invisible but solid tie." By 1922, *Canard* readers had begun to form their own fan clubs, which met to stage witty parties and spectacles.[34]

How did the satirical weekly earn this kind of devotion? For most observers, the *Canard* won its first, and most enduring, claims to glory during the First World War. From Monier again: "There were two miracles in the 1914–18 war: the one of the Marne, due, as everyone knows, to Saint Genevieve, and that of the *Canard Enchaîné.*"[35] What was this miracle? Galtier-Boissière, after noting that the war had "provoked, quite naturally, the hatching of the *Canard,*" explained that "this divine joker *Canard* found the way to say many truths while appearing to clown around. Was it not necessary, at this time, to borrow the mask of folly in order to be understood by a few wise persons, under the pretense of making them laugh?"[36] This was the view of a then-sympathetic war-veteran journalist. In the words of a police report: "It was much read at the front, and certain soldiers on leave in the war zone declared that the 'Canard Enchaîné' was the only periodical 'not involved in skull stuffing.' " The historian of the interwar French press, R. Manévy, stigmatized this *bourrage de crâne* as a "crime against the intellect" that from the beginning of the war had "raged in certain organs of the Parisian press with a nauseating shamelessness."[37]

Wartime censorship and moronically mendacious propaganda were the background to the creation of the *Canard.* But the problem went far beyond the Parisian press. Falsehood, or at least the occultation of the truth, seemed to have a special, even a characteristic, relationship with the First World War.

Even the inaccuracy of the mass press during the war needs to be seen in context. Scrupulous accuracy was not high on the list of priorities of the prewar press. Dorgelès, a journalist before, during, and after the war, admitted that "to speak frankly, I sold lies," and, "in sum, I have never lied so much as when I was being paid to tell the truth." Dorgelès made up incidents about famous people, guessed who was present at events. Since his inventions sometimes came to light, it was clear that he was not the only journalist to peddle fiction as fact.[38] Lying from patriotic motives did not involve too great a change of habits.

The inaccuracies of omission and commission on the part of the press (abetted but not always caused by the censor) were not appreciated by the soldiers. Even their commanders noted their skepticism. War novels also express the front-line soldier's contempt for *bourrage de crâne.*[39] But these same novels, and some memoirs, make it clear that the soldiers themselves were participants in the game of hiding the truth.

Truth was in some sense a casualty of the gulf that had developed between combatants and civilians. A soldier in Barbusse's 1916 *Le feu* explains to his comrades that no one will believe them if they try to describe what they have been through. In the same novel, two chapters later, a group of combat-weary soldiers is on leave in a French city. On two separate occasions, they make their own contribution to civilian misunderstanding. In the first incident, our soldiers are gaping in sarcastic disbelief at a store window that shows a German officer on his knees surrendering to his rosy-cheeked French counterpart. Before they can express their feelings, an elegantly dressed beauty confronts them: "Tell me, gentlemen, you who are real front-line soldiers, you have seen that in the trenches, haven't you?" "Uh . . . yes . . . yes," answer the intimidated and flattered men, while the crowd, which has been listening in, murmurs that it must be so since these soldiers have confirmed it.

The second story finds the same battle veterans in a swank café. Another fashionable lady (this one accompanied by her husband) recognizes our heroes for decorated trench fighters. Holding out an illustrated periodical, she asks whether the war can really be as horrible as that, what with the dirt, the fleas, the fatigue duty. One of the soldiers blushes as he explains that, no, it is not so bad as all that, that they are not unhappy. The lady is only too eager to take his word for it, and her response is an anthology of *bourrage de crâne.* There are "compensations." "That must be superb, a charge, huh? . . . And the little soldiers whom one cannot hold back and who yell 'Vive la France,' or who die laughing." The dispirited soldiers leave with a sense that they have failed in their duty.[40]

Did the soldiers have a duty to lie to those they left behind? In his memoirs, Dorgelès argues that they did. "To my mother, I began to lie," as he put it, claiming that he was in a noncombat zone, though he was a front-line soldier. When he read his fictional creations to his comrades, they asked why he told tales. He insisted that it was so that his mother would not worry.

> When I saw some of them, after a rough time, writing long letters, explaining in detail that it had been "a real butchery," that their best friend had been killed before their eyes, and that they had barely made it back themselves, I shamed them:
>
> —Don't you think they are unhappy enough as it is? You are torturing them with your stories. Your duty is to hide the truth from them.

The charade continued when Dorgelès's mother and sister visited him unexpectedly at the front, and an officer recounted his heroic actions to them. To reassure his womenfolk, the journalist soldier recounted the battle in a hilarious fashion "in which no one got killed." " 'Is it true that the Germans run away?' asked my mother naively." "Yes," her son answered, "as soon as they see us."[41]

These examples, which could be multiplied from the war books of other countries (and other French examples), show that the problem of truth and falsehood was far bigger than censorship, official lies, or patriotic propaganda. Something in the First World War defied honest expression.[42] The combination of unprecedented horror and unprecedented national mobilization created an apparent emotional need for falsehood—one that was widely shared. This climate was the *Canard*'s challenge, but it also was its raison d'être. If falsehood is considered the most important characteristic of the war in terms of culture and written expression, then the *Canard* becomes France's most important discursive reaction to the gigantic butchery. Among cultural products, it has certainly turned out to be the most lasting.

After the war came its memory. But what could memory be for a conflict that had been experienced as a lie—a lie given or a lie received or both? Such memory could not be a simple question of assimilation. It would have to be a contested memory, one that wrestled with the gulf already opened between events and representations. If the structure of memory in prewar France (1870–1914) was dominated by acceleration, as Matsuda persuasively argues,[43] then that of the war and postwar was molded by the gap between experience and its representations. This was a modern, not a postmodern, condition; for the conflict lay not between signifier and signified (since even in a system of lies the first still defines itself through the second) but between sign and referent.

Exploiting the connection between mendacity and memory, the *Canard* presented an unusually complex and profound critique of the memory of the war, memories that were expressed in a range of ways, from verbal texts and public ceremonies to commercial objects. One result was a radical critique of memory practices and discourses that are still with us today. A tool to probe both past and future wars, the *Canard*'s memory of the Great War was also a vision of France and the world; and the weekly's humorous style was the reply of French esprit to the new horrors of the century.

1 Satire and Censorship

Paris, September 1915: One might think this hardly the time and place for humor. France has been at war for over a year. The national territory has been invaded; several of the country's richest departments remain occupied. A year after the "miracle" of the Marne, neither the French nor their allies are having any luck in breaking, or even pushing back, the German lines. And the tragic slaughter continues as the manhood of France mixes its blood with the mud of the trenches. So where does one find humor at such a moment? And how can such humor be patriotic? A new periodical provided an answer and, while dodging the censor, created a discourse of humor that was patriotic without being militarist. It was *Le Canard Enchaîné,* number 1, September 10, 1915.

The enchained duck? There is more to it than that. Among its other meanings, *canard* is a popular, and disrespectful, French term for a newspaper—a term related to its English meaning, a false and injurious rumor.[1] *Enchaîné* (enchained) echoed Clemenceau's transformation of his *Homme libre* to *L'Homme enchaîné* in October 1914 to mock wartime censorship.[2] The title, *Le Canard Enchaîné,* thus bears a double semantic load, its name signifying both falsehood and subservience. What better way, in a climate of patriotic bombast, to stake a claim to independence and veracity?

The irony, so clear in the new paper's title, strikes again in its introduction to its readers:

> The *Canard Enchaîné* has decided to break deliberately with all the journalistic traditions established up to this day.
>
> Because of which, this newspaper certainly wishes to spare its readers, first of all, the torment of an introduction.
>
> In the second place, the *Canard Enchaîné* engages its honor not to cede, on any occasion, to the deplorable mania of the day.

> It is enough to say that it promises not to publish, under any pretext, any strategic, diplomatic, or economic article whatever.
>
> Besides, its modest format forbids this type of pleasantry.
>
> Finally, the *Canard Enchaîné* will take the great liberty to insert only, and after meticulous verification, news that is rigorously inaccurate.
>
> Everyone knows, in effect, that the French press, without exception, has communicated to its readers, since the beginning of the war, only news that is implacably true.
>
> Well, the public has had enough.
>
> The public wants false news . . . for variety.
>
> It will have it.
>
> To obtain this wonderful result, the editors of the *Canard Enchaîné,* recoiling before no sacrifice, have not hesitated to sign a one-year contract with the very famous Wolff news agency, which will transmit to them, every week from Berlin, by *special barbed wire,* all the false news of the entire world.
>
> In these conditions, we have no doubt that the public will be so kind as to grant us a warm welcome, and, in this hope, we present to them, in advance and respectfully, our most sincere condolences.

The irony of this text is obvious—starting with the introduction, which declares that there will be none. Equally clear is the attack on the veracity of the wartime French press. That truth is the first casualty of war is proverbial. But the French mass press during World War I was noted for a particular sort of pompously aggressive and shamelessly mendacious coverage that the French themselves called *bourrage de crâne* (literally skull stuffing), a phrase that carries a more dramatic punch than the English "eyewash," as it is sometimes translated. This patriotic gore was an easy target because it was particularly unpopular with the troops.[3]

Born of the Great War, the *Canard* survived by adapting its discourse to peacetime. In the years that followed the armistice, the satirical weekly made a profession of antimilitarism. But how antimilitarist was the paper during the war? The collection for 1915 through 1918 shows an apparent variety of positions on the war. But interpreting these positions demands coming to terms with the weekly's distinctive discourse and, within this discourse, with its use of irony.

Perhaps most interesting in the irony of the *Canard's* introduction is its inherent instability. The paper says that it will provide only false information. Read this declaration literally and we can deduce the opposite of whatever it prints. But if we read it literally, we are faced with the paradox of the Cretan liar. If I say that what I am going to say is a lie, that I am a liar, then what I say is the truth. Hence any statement in the *Canard* can logically be read either antiphrastically, as a reference to its opposite, or literally. And these readings are within the context of ironic interpretation. Not all the passages in the introduction beg to be read ironically. Some, like the promises to be different from other papers and to eschew strategic, economic, and diplomatic articles, seem apparently true. Hence, in its first flight, this journalistic bird exploited a prevailing climate of falsehood to create a discourse with an unusual referential flexibility.

The problem of variable believability was even exploited in the "re-introduction" in the first number of the new, 1916, series. After repeating some of the same points from the September 1915 article, the editors went on to claim:

> The *Canard Enchaîné* is also an honest newspaper. It will take, therefore, the elementary precaution of warning its readers of the degree of belief that they should accord to the items that will come under their eyes.
>
> And this in the simplest manner: doubtful news will be preceded by one star, news that is false but reasonably possible by two stars, and radically false news by three stars.[4]

Needless to say, the paper gave no such indications. There were a few occasions, over the years, when the *Canard* presented clearly nonironic claims to veracity, but they never affected more than a fraction of its prose.[5]

What better contrast to a wartime bombast that was losing its credibility? But also, what better way to deal with the censor—for French press censorship was constant throughout the Great War. Not only were facts of potential military importance censored, as one would expect, but items considered likely to affect morale could also fall under the censor's axe. As Jean-Jacques Becker notes, wartime censorship gave France's governing politicians the almost irresistible opportunity to squelch criticism.[6]

Neither the *Canard*'s claims to falsehood nor its self-description as a "humoristic newspaper" spared it the scissors of "Madame Anastasie," as the censor had long been personified in the French press.[7] The cartoon dominating the weekly's first page mocked the white spaces that marked excised articles: a newspaper covered completely with white paint is nevertheless cut to ribbons by Anastasie.[8] As late as 1917, one of the weekly's major writers, Victor Snell, joked that to make good use of the blanks one should place them in strategic spots in articles oneself, in order to communicate those things that one dared not say.[9]

The opening number of the second (1916) series featured a cartoon in a rectangular box wedged between paper title and headlines (see figure 1). It shows a hand with scissors menacing an enchained, but squawking, duck. Around the scissors are the words "Tu auras mes plumes. [You may get my feathers.] Tu n'auras pas ma peau. [You won't get my skin.]" Of course, *plumes* (feathers) also refers to the pens of writers, and *avoir la peau* signifies defeating or killing someone. Not only was this visual/verbal icon maintained without a break through early September 1918, and intermittently thereafter during the remaining weeks of the war, but, without the words, it became a visual topos that graced the newspaper's columns well into the years of peace and, thus, well after the end of formal censorship.

Censorship made a good foil, but it was also a challenge for the writers and cartoonists of the *Canard.* Many articles were cut or excised, and the paper complained amply of the censor's inconsistencies and overzealousness, as did many other wartime periodicals.[10] But the *Canard* also struck back. On December 13, 1916, and on March 14 and 28, 1917, the *Canard* explained how it had succeeded in printing, in other newspapers, articles or parts of articles refused by the censor for the weekly. On another occasion, the weekly asked its "Aunt Anastasie" why it took her four hours to read the *Canard* when it spent only two on the news dailies of the same length.[11] One can easily see why the censors might move more cautiously around this slippery bird.

The *Canard* wore the scars from its battles with the censor like white badges of honor. But how much of this sparring was hype? The official biography of Maurice Maréchal, distributed by the public-relations office of the *Canard,* interprets the military call-up of Maréchal, which interrupted the appearance of his periodical in 1915, in the following way: "It was a time when the general staff, seeking men, was scraping the bottoms of the drawers, as they said at that time, but it also seems that there was a desire to paralyze the activity of a troublemaker."[12] The suspicions of the paper's in-house historian would seem to be confirmed by the comment in a police report of 1929: "After its fourth number, the 'Canard Enchaîné' was suspended because of the attacks it directed, in a humorous style, against numerous political and military personalities."[13] (The weekly published five issues in 1915.) Whatever the case, the reborn *Canard* of 1916 experienced no breaks in publication, despite its gleeful skewering of well-placed individuals.

Did the military authorities, in and outside of the censor's offices, see the satirical weekly as a troublemaker? Only to a limited degree, if one judges from the materials in the cartons of the Service Historique de l'Armée de Terre in Vincennes, especially when these are added to the registers of the Service des Périodiques in the Bibliothèque de Documentation Internationale Contemporaine (BDIC) in Nanterre.

Figure 1. Gassier's duck and the censor's scissors (1916).

The censors, who worked under military command, were generally more concerned with the inadvertent publication of information that might serve the enemy or unnecessarily divide the French than with antimilitarism or pacifism. The *Canard* was censored no more, and in many cases less, than similar newspapers. The *Canard* was never subject to suspension or other of the disciplinary measures taken against papers like *L'Oeuvre,* which resisted the instructions of the military authorities.[14]

The general staffs of the armies and army groups kept an eye on papers read by their troops. The *Canard* was read at the front and did attract negative attention from some military watchdogs. General Henri Gouraud, commanding the 4th Army, included the *Canard Enchaîné* among three papers that were "capable of exercising a very bad influence on the morale of the troops," while complaining that he could not block its sale in the military co-ops. Yet the lists present from the 2nd, 3rd, and 6th armies do not mention the satirical weekly. The 40th Corps of the 7th Army reported all the papers being read by its men, including the *Canard,* but declared that none of these periodicals "appear to exercise a bad influence" on morale. Not only was the *Canard* missing from the lists of pacifist papers compiled by the general staffs, but the satirical weekly received far less negative attention than reputedly pacifist papers like *L'Heure* and *La Griffe* or even mainstream organs like *L'Oeuvre.* When one adds the fact that *Canard* collaborators, like Gassier, also contributed to papers that did provoke action from the military (like seizures), one can see the success of Maréchal's formula. His weekly was critical enough to excite the occasional suspicions—but not the systematic hostility—of the guardians of the press.[15]

Nor was the *Canard* seen as a threat by the civilian police, who reported to the Ministry of the Interior. Neither in the wartime reports on pacifist or defeatist activities nor in the above-mentioned postwar summary report dedicated to the *Canard* is the satirical weekly considered dangerous to the security of the country. Even the weekly's vigorous censure of the war in the Moroccan Rif in the mid-1920s[16] did not lead police agents to mention it among antimilitarist activities during that conflict.[17]

But Anastasie did cut from the wartime *Canard.* The BDIC has conserved the registers of cuts required through July 1918. These registers make it possible to see not what the *Canard* would have been without the censor, since the paper was conceived and written for an environment of censorship, but the tendencies limited by the guardians of the press.[18] In a total of 262 items,[19] the single largest concern of the censors was polemics against personalities or groups; these attacks accounted for seventy cases: twenty-seven foreign (neutral or Allied) figures or countries, forty-three French figures. The censors also objected to attacks on themselves (nine cases) and mockery of the repeated medical exams that accompanied the army's attempts to find increasing numbers of able-bodied men (seven). Fifty-eight items that could be seen as contrary to the war effort or morale were cut. Of these, thirteen were labeled pacifist, eleven pessimistic or demoralizing. Ten more cuts involved unfavorable comparisons between the front and the rear.

The censor probably modestly reduced the proportion of pessimism in the *Canard*'s mix. But most of the topics, like the length of the war and the front/rear comparisons, received ample treatment anyway (as did the medical exams). Political figures got considerable protection (as they did in all of the press), but the journalists mentioned by the censors were regularly pilloried in the weekly.

Thus, though the *Canard* played with the limits of censorship, this was at least as much a game to impress readers as an attempt to challenge Dame Anastasie. It is well known that censorship breeds a particularly searching type of reader, one always on the lookout for allusions and veiled references. The effect was to broaden the semantic registers of the journalists and their audience, to create complicity in games of encoding and decoding. And all in a newspaper that says that it does not mean what it says except, of course, when it does.

Such ambiguities also allow the reader to find what he or she is looking for, to read his or her own prejudices into the words and pictures of the *Canard.* Part of the weekly's success undoubtedly came from its ability to appeal to a modest but real variety of political positions. On the subject of the war, these ambiguities helped the *Canard Enchaîné* to combine a firm, support-our-boys patriotism with a condemnation of war that we would have to call pacifism.

Humor did not mean an absence of patriotism—at least for the *Canard.* The paper even used one to justify the other. The French needed humor, it pleaded with the censor, especially in tough times, when there was so much to be sad about. A sad French man or woman would no longer be French but would almost be a "kraut." (The cheerfulness and spirit of fun of French soldiers were almost an official value.)[20] Certainly, the *Canard* mocked France's enemies, the Central Powers. The reference in the introduction to the Wolff agency, the semiofficial news agency of the German government, as the source of false news certainly fit patriotic molds, as did accompanying examples of German dispatches reporting that the Eiffel Tower was burning. The Ottoman Empire was treated with a mixture of contempt and silliness that was not free from racism.[21] It was patriotic, certainly, to make jokes about the national enemy. But attacks on the veracity of German reports could also be understood as an attack on French exaggerations. As the war continued, the *Canard* made ridicule of the French press a major focus.[22]

The way a criticism of the French press could be combined with a nonmilitarist evocation of the fighting men can be seen in an article from July 1916. Even its title, "Spare Our Reserves," carried its burden of criticism of offensive-happy generals and journalists. The article scolded the press for its "mania" for articles about brave children who ran away from home to the front and captured German soldiers. These stupid stories were causing real children to run away, and the papers then treated them as heroes. If their fathers were fighting, the *Canard* reminded its fellow journalists, it was to spare their sons having to do the same in twenty years.[23] The optimism of this argument (the war to end all wars) would not survive the war,[24] but the hostility to facile glorifications of war would be strengthened into a distinctive form of pacifism.

Chronologically, the first set of arguments that approached pacifism appeared in a serialized story that ran in the first ten issues of the 1916 series. "La classe heureuse" (The lucky class)[25] told the story of a Frenchman who was just young enough to have missed service in the 1870 war but old enough to be spared the draft in the Great War. Mr. Hubu (shades of Alfred Jarry)[26] represents a common form of mindlessly vicarious bellicosity. He sits in the café explaining to the other customers (while drawing on the table) how he would drive the Germans back and criticizing the army's apparent reluctance to bash through the enemy lines. Safe in his "lucky class," he is a patriot and a militarist on the cheap. The situation changes, however, when our Mr. Hubu is mobilized, apparently by mistake, despite the fact that his class is supposed to be exempt. He rages at the military bureaucrats who treat him so cavalierly. Insulted by an officer, he discovers, to his silent mortification, that "one is always someone else's kraut."[27] More important, his ideas on the war begin to change. In his discussions at the café, he is less sure about the virtues of holding on until the end. Despite his attempts to hide the evolution of his sentiments, he cannot conceal his less glamorous view of war. As the author, Henry Bordelaux, put it, "He gave in to the baroque idea that speaking of peace might perhaps serve to bring it about."[28]

Not to worry, Hubu flunks his physical exam (he is too fat) and eventually returns to his old certitudes, barely softened by his brush with military service. The serial started on safe-enough ground, mocking the hypocrisy of those who indulged in purely verbal bellicosity. This was a theme that the *Canard* would exploit not only throughout the war but in the years of peace. The "baroque idea" that talking of peace might help bring it about is something else however. It actually enunciates the pacifist idea that talking of peace (in peacetime or war) is the best way to preserve it, in contrast to an oft-repeated Latin dictum: if you want peace, prepare for war. Worse (or better), it could be used to argue that the French should seek peace now (that is, in 1916), a notion that was publicly unacceptable. Certainly, had even the first point been made separately, it would likely have earned the unwelcome attentions of the censor.

Of course, Bordelaux did not say anything about seeking peace; a character in a story did, and this character was dominated by fear, hardly an admirable example. But here is where the *Canard*'s rhetorical sophistication comes into play. "He gave in to" suggests that the idea had a certain independent force or necessity. Calling the idea "baroque" is literally a criticism of it, but in context it functions as irony. To those who sympathize with it, the idea is the opposite of baroque, it is commonsensical. And even the literal meaning can be salvaged since such an idea would seem baroque only in a France gripped by war hysteria.

Peace had other, perhaps even more equivocal, defenders in the pages of the wartime *Canard*. In April 1917, one of the weekly's most talented writers (and chief anticlerical), Georges de la Fouchardière,[29] began a series under the provocative title "The Divine Tragedy."[30] In 1917 this title could have been an apt description of the war, but de la Fouchardière's series of seven "songs" deals more with extraterrestrial matters—at least in theory—with God and his angels. Broad satires on the miracles in the Bible and modern bureaucratic procedures are drawn from the fiction that heaven is organized as a series of ministries. In the last section, Lucifer is organizing his attack on the divine citadel. Why? Lucifer was fed up with the war:

> Lucifer is a pacifist, a friend of letters, of the arts, of joy, of good food, and of love, in a word of all the things condemned, as much by the churches called Protestant as by our holy Catholic, apostolic, and Roman religion.

> War is an invention of the gods, who are drinkers of blood. War is the negation of joy, the abolition of good food and love, the death of letters and of the arts. That is why Satan was fed up with the war.[31]

Anticlericalism in the service of pacifism! But the fallen angel as spokesman? The author has gone beyond anticlericalism to an attack on religion in general. But his argument is much cleverer than that used by other freethinkers during the war, that the horrors of the conflict showed the nonexistence of God.[32] The point of view of the story becomes clearer if one notices a certain similarity between de la Fouchardière's Satan and that of Anatole France in *La révolte des anges,* published in 1914. His devil is also the pacific lover of the fine arts and the good life. The reference to the gods as "drinkers of blood" irresistibly calls up Anatole France's *Les dieux ont soif*—that is, if the reader had not already noticed that the first episode of de la Fouchardière's series bore the subtitle "Les dieux n'ont plus soif," along with the allusion to Anatole France's words in the seventh song.[33] Not only was the spirit of Anatole France one of the more important predecessors of that of the *Canard Enchaîné,* but the young newspaper was appropriately proud of this connection; it repeated, for example, the anecdote in which the distinguished author reported that the *Canard* was the only paper he still read.[34] Just as Anatole France's Satan was a model character, so was he for de la Fouchardière.

But de la Fouchardière's "seventh song" ends in the middle of the action, with the "to be continued" that had ended his earlier episodes. Satan, to end the war, is organizing a series of strikes and using Jesus Christ ("leave your nets and follow me") as his organizer. The narrator's last words are "But one had not seen anything yet." The authorities, one suspects, had already seen too much, for in the spring of 1917 not only were strikes raging (and in defense industries) but many had taken on a pacifist coloring. Apparently, satires of religion and the Church, even government bureaucracies and war (mis)reporting, were acceptable safety valves. But playing with strikes and pacifism was too dangerous. And the series stopped cold.[35]

One should not think, however, that the *Canard*'s forays into pacifism were limited to fiction. Take the following literary notice:

> Mr. Julien de Narfon entitled an article "The Heresy of Pacifism." And he shows quite appropriately that to be for peace is to be against the teachings of the Church.
>
> We suspected as much.[36]

For a paper with the *Canard*'s consistent anticlericalism,[37] the implicitly positive tone of the item demands an ironic reversal. The commentary could be more direct. For example, in August 1916, the *Canard* annotated a phrase by the futurist (and future fascist) Emilio Marinetti, "War, Oh sole hygiene of the world," with the comment, "All the same, the hygiene of peace is better for living to a ripe old age."[38]

An article of February 13, 1918, combined pacifism with anti-German patriotism. As part of a series of articles with the title "Dans le 'No Man's Land,' " G. de Pawlowski noted the coming of the plague to Russia. If it had only come earlier and struck, say, Germany in 1914, it would have prevented the war. A good cholera epidemic, though much less murderous than a modern war, would have struck all the classes of the population, while a war affects only soldiers. In such a situation, no government, no matter how imperialist, would have gone to war. And the phenomenon was not limited to Germany, the author went on. Countries went to war when they were too rich and healthy.[39] The notion that countries go to war because those who make the decisions do not have to do the fighting became a leitmotif for the *Canard* after World War I. Here it is served up with a sauce that reflects the ideological ambidexterity of so much of the weekly's wartime prose. If the series began with a patriotically nasty wish for Germany and continued with a reference to the war's being started by an imperialist country (which would still be Germany), it ended by suggesting that the plague of war could be unleashed by any country. The contradiction could be rationalized if one considered Germany solely responsible for the war. Much in the *Canard* would support this position. Yet the weekly also mocked the tendency to blame one country for the war—leaving the question of war responsibility anything but closed.[40]

Not surprisingly, the *Canard*'s comments on war and peace also had a temporal aspect. By the winter of 1916–1917, the satirical weekly's good-humored support for the fighting men was increasingly mixed with an ill-concealed impatience over the length of hostilities. As a soldier-duck put it in a cartoon of December 12, 1917, "When will our torments finally come to an end?"[41] Such impatience was expressed in two major ways: by joking that the war would never end and by expressing disappointment over the nonarrival of peace. By the end of 1916 the *Canard* had begun to evoke the idea that the war might be virtually interminable. A cartoon of December 13 of that year shows a soldier on leave having his palm read by his *marraine de guerre:* these were women who wrote, from motives of patriotism, to soldiers with whom they were not previously acquainted. The woman tells him he will live a hundred years, and the soldier replies, "Chic, I'll see the end of the war."[42]

Based on public-opinion surveys taken from letters read by the postal censors, Becker concludes that the sense that the war seemed interminable but had to be put up with anyway, for patriotic reasons, came to France in late 1917 and early 1918, after the crises of the late spring and autumn of 1917.[43] The *Canard* seems to have been an opinion leader in lassitude. More to the point, the reference to one hundred years could be understood in a variety of ways. If our young soldier will live to one hundred, he will have to survive the war. But if that were the only meaning, he could have said, "Chic, I'll survive the war." Instead he seems to need the one hundred years to see the war's end. In France, such a reference could not fail to evoke the country's greatest national trial: the Hundred Years' War.

In another national context this reference could simply imply endlessness. For example, in Ernest Hemingway's 1929 *A Farewell to Arms,* the narrator-hero (an American volunteer with the Italian army) muses that perhaps no one wins wars anymore: "Maybe it is another Hundred Years War." This comment brings Hemingway's point close to the English "neverendians" discussed by Fussell.[44] In a French context the comparison is even more negative. During the Hundred Years' War the enemy occupied the national territory for decades, and the government was reduced to a "Kingdom of Bourges"—to speak in terms of the standard French national understanding of the conflict, not as we might see it in feudal terms.

This cartoon, with its implicit linkage of the Hundred Years' War and the potential endlessness of the present one, was the second part of a process of association that had begun five months earlier. In July 1916, the *Canard* published a cartoon by Gassier (based on an idea by Tristan Bernard). Entitled "During the Hundred Years' War," it showed two knights in armor before a medieval castle; one says to the other, "Do you think we will have a winter campaign?"[45] In July 1916, a reference to a winter campaign was a sign that the war would not come to a speedy end. If in this first cartoon the evocation of the medieval conflict is explicit, its link to an interminable war remains implicit. To bring that point to the fore is the job of the second cartoon. The *Canard* echoed the connection of the Hundred Years' War to the length of the twentieth-century one in the following issue, of December 20, and again in January 1917. A hundred years seemed bad enough, but the war could be simply endless. Early in 1918, one soldier said to another in a cartoon, "The end of the war? I believed in it at the beginning."[46]

Imagining an interminable war could signal a kind of pessimistic resolve. But the *Canard* went further—to lament the nonarrival of peace. Cross-species aviary politics appeared in a cartoon of January 24, 1917 (see figure 2). Under the title "The Bird of Peace," it shows a creature that appears to be a duck (from its bill) with wings spread, facing downward and carrying an olive branch in its mouth. The legend: "This dove was then only a duck [*canard*]?"[47] The duck with an olive branch would make of the weekly a bringer of peace, but here it is the signifier of falsehood that dominates—rumors of peace were just canards. A few months later, in April, the paper ran a story of a soldier who received an Easter egg with several peculiarities: it was square, it had a tricolor ribbon, and it bore the Croix de Guerre. When he opened it, out came a dove holding in its beak a card with the word "Peace." Taking this to be a divine omen, the soldier went out to celebrate with his comrades. Later, after urinating in his bed, he awoke from this dream, and when he thought about this dream, now gone, "he scratched his head sadly."[48]

These dreams of peace that evaporate with the morning, these doves that turn to ducks, speak of more than mere impatience with the frightful slaughter. They can also suggest possibilities for peace that were not adequately followed up, doves that got away. The potential connection between government policies and the continuation of the war was at least hinted at in the December 27, 1916, issue. The lead article speaks of the response that the French government will make to recent diplomatic maneuvers. Very respectfully, it begins:

> The *Canard Enchaîné* does not concern itself with giving advice to the government and to the diplomats: [. . .].
>
> It is of the opinion that each has his task—and it thinks that since the Chamber, the Senate, and the Congress of the Socialist Party have given their confidence to the government to answer the German propositions, it has but to do the same.[49]

The newspaper would seem to be sticking to its announced role of burlesquing everything and everybody, without getting involved in questions of high politics and strategy. Page 3, however, tells a different story. There, a young Breton soldier-cook receives, among a group of Christmas gifts, what passes for an olive branch. His superior, the chief cook, throws it directly into the fire. The end of the story is its moral: "And the young cook very much missed the pretty branch, which had given him more pleasure than the potato, the slice of bread, or the coal." This story casts a special light on the paper's confidence in the alacrity of those in power to respond to chances for peace.

The end of 1916 and the next year saw a number of (ultimately stillborn) political and diplomatic attempts to bring the war to the end. The

L'OISEAU DE LA PAIX

Cette colombe n'était donc qu'un canard ?

Figure 2. Duck or dove (1917).

Canard's deferred doves and consumed olive branches were the paper's mournful salutes to their failure. Rarely was the paper as blunt as in the cartoon of November 14, 1917. In the midst of a torrent of politically motivated arrests, the god of war asks, "And what if they arrested me too?"—*arrêter* here being understood as both arrest and stop.[50]

Seeking peace in 1916 and 1917 was not easily compatible with patriotism. Much of the national territory was occupied. The word for those who were willing to consider peace under these conditions, for those who did not insist on victory first was defeatists. Who were the opponents of the defeatists? The "to-the-enders," or *jusqu'au-boutistes.* The *Canard* felt free to mock the expression, with its potential for polysemy (e.g., which end? well, the right end). And, given the chance, the weekly would have gone further. The censor knocked out the legend of a cartoon that appeared in September 1916. Entitled "The Dead Parakeet," it showed a deceased bird lying on its back in a cage while a woman, her head buried in her arms, appears to be sobbing on the table in front of it. In the mid-background we see serious individuals in mournful postures. Such mourning for a bird during a time of national tragedy carried its own satirical punch, but the banned legend would have given the *coup de grâce:* "Such an intelligent animal which said *'jusqu'au bout'* all by itself."[51] The *Canard* did not, however, make equivalent fun of the so-called defeatists; instead it mocked the use of the term by their opponents.[52] This was another of the weekly's ideologically charged tricks: make fun of one side of an issue (all in play, of course) but leave the other untouched.

For a time it appeared that peace might come neither from compromise nor from victory—but from defeat. During the spring and early summer of 1918, the final German offensives (strengthened by the removal of Russia from the war) drove the Allies back to the Marne and at one point even broke through their lines. Instead of talking of peace on this occasion, however, the *Canard* departed from its normal stance of generally good-natured mockery to uncharacteristically directly defend the soldiers of France.

Number 100 (May 29) of the *Canard Enchaîné* contained an unusual statement crammed onto the front page, without any headline, in the print style of a judicial insertion:

> In general, it is a pleasure for us to compose this little newspaper, following our fantasy and that of the good friends who inspire us. It seems to us that next to the stinkers, the bellowers in slippers, and the desk-bound tacticians, we have the duty to introduce a little, just a very little, bit of French independence and irony.
>
> But, at the present moment, when all the youth of France who are our hope, when all that the nation possesses of strong and healthy men, when our dearest friends support with abnegation the most frightful struggles, we almost regret the innocent pleasantries of which this newspaper is made.
>
> But so many letters received from *over-there* have warned us in advance against ourselves, so many disinterested councils have told us to continue, that we will therefore continue.
>
> If we have our grotesque figures and our skull stuffers, it is good that, in spite of the brutal enterprises of our enemies, we keep our critical spirit, our free thought, and our good humor—that they will never conquer.[53]

A clearer defense of its attitude the *Canard* would never give. But alongside the defense of its free-spirited humor and ill-covered by the absolution it claimed from its combatant-readers lay a barely hidden guilt and an anxiety that leaked through the confidence of the conclusion. Hatched in 1915 and 1916, the *Canard* was not published during those nervous days of August 1914, when German armies approached Paris and the government evacuated to Bordeaux. The individual writers had seen those days, and the paper had no compunctions about mocking the flight to Bordeaux; but these were opinions expressed after the fact. Until the spring of 1918, the satirical weekly had lived through a war of murderous stalemate. Now faced with possible catastrophe, the *Canard* eschewed any calls for peace and fell back on the sincere celebration of the men who were defending their country. "Support our boys" supplanted "give peace a chance."

The next issue (June 4) continued this line. On the masthead, where the scissors-dodging duck had once reigned supreme, only words were present: "Confiance dans nos poilus" (Confidence in our doughboys).[54] Later in that same issue, while mocking the tendencies of Parisians to flee the capital (now subject to German bombardment), the *Canard* insisted that it was enchained by "the most faithful feelings and a patriotism that was the most sure as well as the least noisy." At the same time a tone of patriotic congratulation added itself to the paper's more traditional anticlericalism. On August 14, when the tide had clearly turned, and Allied troops were pushing the Germans back, the Gallic duck crowed like a cock, but with its own political twist: the free-thinking, republican soldiers of France showed more dignity, courage, and humanity than the pious warriors and church-going Junkers of William II.[55] Later in August, after a characteristic attack on bombastic war reporting (tank crew members who continued to maneuver with an eye shot out or a shoulder blown away), the *Canard* delivered itself of the following message: "No one in France is ignorant of what we owe to our valiant, our admirable tank crews. But why is it necessary that instead of the laurels to which they have a right one offers them the derision of these exaggerations?"[56] These articles had a new tone, an ill-concealed pride in the victories in progress. This triumphalism represented the high point of the *Canard*'s militarism.

By September the Germans were suing for peace, and the question became whether and on what conditions to give it to them. In effect, a debate was beginning that would continue after the war: whether the French should push (or should have pushed) on to Berlin rather than grant an armistice to Germany. On the twenty-fifth of this month, the *Canard* argued that if talking of peace while things were not going well could be called defeatism, that was no longer the case. "A defeatist Frenchman is now an impossibility because we are victorious."[57] A year and a half earlier, the newspaper had used, with only a contextual suggestion of incongruity, the expression "a premature peace." If the idea seemed strange in 1917, it needed little criticism in the fall of 1918. Indeed, that same September 25 issue, which had banished the idea of defeatism, led with the words "Finally! The End!" The article that followed used a typically Canardesque argument. The minister had said that classes would return in early October. Though he obviously meant school classes, the paper decided that he must have meant the military classes and that the war was thus over.[58] Beyond the joke, any reader could see the claim for the end of the conflict.

The debates over the armistice gave the weekly the opportunity for a last swat at the *jusqu'au-boutistes.* Calling antiphrastic irony into one last war service, the *Canard* pretended to agree with a Socialist deputy who called for going on to the end, or *bout.* In particular, the paper objected to those who said that France had come to the *bout.* If this was the "end," then the *Canard* claimed to want to go "further than the end" and claimed the title of "further-than-the-enders." As for the so-long-delayed dove of peace, the war-born periodical saluted it with a cartoon that made explicit the weekly's earlier hinted explanations for the tardiness of the winged messenger. As the dove streaks across the sky, one hunter says to the others in his group:, "I think that this time we have missed it." The hunters in the cartoon were the leading reactionary and militarist journalists against whom the *Canard* had been writing throughout the war.[59]

The next issue appeared two days after the armistice. It brought together the principal aspects of the *Canard*'s approach to war and peace. The feature cartoon made the now-optimistic comparison with the Hundred Years' War. Entitled "All the same, there has been progress," it showed a knight from the medieval conflict telling a now-veteran doughboy, "Lucky fellow. Me, after four years and four months, I still had ninety-five years and eight months coming." The headline (in the old duck-with-scissors place) was limited to one word: "Ouf!" If these two items expressed relief at the end of the nightmare, the lead article was borne on the other wing of the *Canard*'s attitude to war. Under the short title "Honor!" it proclaimed, "And, first of all, honor to the doughboys! Honor to the noble and good fellows who, for months, for years—those at least who lasted the whole time—showed so much admirable abnegation."[60] With the condemnation of war went the salute to the ordinary Frenchmen in uniform, who were the heroes of the *Canard*'s pacifist-tinged militarism.

The war that created the *Canard* and provoked its distinctive style also forced its pacifism into a sometimes unstable union with an equally sincere (but politically necessary) support for the fighting man. After the war, these constraints would be gone, and the satirical weekly would be free to fly boldly through the skies of pacifism and antimilitarism without abandoning its support for those who had borne the greatest sacrifices of the war.

2 Verbal and Visual, Humor and Politics

Organization as Discourse

Format is a species of content. This was especially so for the *Canard.* And format for the *Canard* meant the mixing of words and pictures, first among them pictures of ducks. The semiotic mélange of *canard*-as-duck-as-falsehood-as-newsrag-as-political-and-humorous-weekly inextricably intertwined the verbal puns with the visual one of the web-footed bird as periodical. The cutesy, partly humanized bird created by Gassier has marked the paper's pages from its first issue in 1915 and its masthead from its "resurrection" in 1916. The message of this bird? In this paper, visual and verbal define each other.

Yet the first flights of this mascot were timid, even tentative. And its basic visual form, the arrangements of lines, took time to become clear and confident through gradual definition and visual sharpening. More significant is the way the duck's role gradually became more broadly visible and better defined. While the first page of the first issue exploited the verbal presence of the bird—its now classic opening statement was entitled "Coin! Coin! Coin!" (Quack! Quack! Quack!)—the pictorial reference did not appear until page 2. There, the duck made his debut in profile and top hat with a chain pulling back from the metal collar around his neck.[1] (The headpiece defines the male gender.)

In the full-page poster advertisement that closed the maiden issue, the duck appeared again as symbol of the paper (see figure 3). But in his first materialization the cartoon animal bore a text that imbricated its symbolism in a further series of puns: "I am enchained, it's true! But I have no strings attached." The French, "je n'ai aucun fil à la patte," evoked as well the *patte,* or foot, of the duck. During 1915 the only major change in this duck-as-newspaper symbol was the gradual replacement of the top hat (probably judged too *haut bourgeois*) with a middle-class bowler.

Figure 3. Gassier's inaugural duck (1915).

A token of the flexibility of the duck character was the addition of a German cousin. In a page 3 cartoon, Gassier drew a crowing duck, with pointed helmet, astride a dead Turk. "Wolff" was written on the Teutonic bird, whose balloon said "Victory." This same page was capped by the heading "Dernière heure" (Latest news), and it offered "all the false news of the entire world transmitted from Berlin by special barbed wire." The stories that followed, like the cartoon, fit the attack in the early *Canard* on the Central Powers and their propaganda.[2] On either side of the "Dernière heure" headline were two sets of ducks with German-style pointed helmets. Like the duck in the cartoon, they evoke the paper, but they also signify *canard* as falsehood. Do the German ducks share significations with their cousins from the other side of the Rhine? The legend for the cartoon is "Cocorico." This stereotypical crowing of the Gallic cock does more than mix species. As a well-known signifier of French chauvinism, the crowing supports the idea that a critique of French official war reporting could hide behind the mockery of German lies.

Only in the *Canard*'s second start, in July 1916, did its feathered mascot land, for the duration of the war, on the periodical's masthead. This mini-cartoon depicted a pair of scissors attacking an enchained duck. Of course, others mocked the censor too and by using the same icon: scissors. But a comparison makes clear the semiotic superiority of Gassier's duck. In January 1915, Gustave Hervé, whose bellicose journalism made him a frequent target of the *Canard*, ran an anticensorship cartoon in his *La Guerre*

Sociale. As illustration for a column, "Peut-on le dire?" (Can it be said?), the paper pictured an old woman (Anastasie) holding up a huge pair of scissors so as to slice a copy of *La Guerre Sociale,* which itself is being held up by a minuscule Gustave Hervé.[3] Gassier's bird combines both the reference to the newspaper and the specific identification of the periodical (while still carrying, in reserve, the other significations of *canard).* The result is more effective: the threat to the bird is direct while that to Hervé is mediated through his newspaper. And the image has a visual logic since people do take shears (the poultry kind) to ducks and other fowl.

The comparison with Hervé's rival imagery brings out the essential qualities of the bird logo along with its advantages in a mass-media market, which demands brevity and instant recognition. The duck icon signifies at once a paper and this particular paper with far more visual efficiency than would the picture of a paper with its headline. And the duck, in most of its significations, is what semioticians call a symbol—that is, it exhibits a logical relationship between the signifier (the visual duck) and its signifieds (from newspaper to falsehood). Unlike an icon that suggests identity between the signifier (say, a photograph) and its signified (the individual or scene in the photograph), the symbol openly expresses its semiotic character; it invites the reader to be aware of the process of representation. This is a large part of the *Canard*'s role: to call attention to the way the French press was manipulating information. If such a device had been created in recent years, we would call it postmodern, but in the case of the *Canard* it is part of the paper's creative modernism.[4]

But the bird is also an animal. As such, it shares with other animal characters, from the traditional figures of the fables of Bidpai and Jean de La Fontaine to modern ducks like Donald and Daffy, the ability to combine human qualities with those of the animal species in question. The resulting cuteness (exploited in the contemporary marketing of animal characters) helped smooth the way for the *Canard*'s often nonconformist politics.

These two central semiotic qualities of economy and contextual versatility allowed our duck to become a journalistic jack-of-all-trades. He could, flowers in beak, wish his readers a happy New Year in January 1918 or salute, hat in hand, the Russian Revolution of March 1917. German when coifed with spiked helmet, he could also be the French *poilu,* honored on the occasion of the victorious armistice in November 1918.[5]

Versatile as a person, the duck could still do service as waterfowl. On the first page of its resurrected series, the weekly introduced what would be one of its longest lived journalistic devices—for it is still in existence today—the column entitled "La mare aux canards" (The duck pond). This

Figure 4. The duck pond (1916).

collection of anecdotes and commented-on citations from other newspapers was surmounted by a drawing of a group of ducks paddling around in the water (see figure 4). Not only is this a more natural situation for a duck, but the birds are here drawn in less humanized form and look like decoys in profile. The hint of humanity comes with speech. One duck has a speech balloon: "Poussez pas" (don't push).

At about the same time that the duck-and-scissors cartoon was being withdrawn from the heading of the paper, in October 1918, Gassier updated his duck pond. Now there were but three waterfowl, one entering, one in the middle, and one leaving the water muddied by the experience. Above the birds, but inside the drawing, is a text attributable to any or all of the waterfowl: "Ah! Quel jus!" This translates as "what water!" but the slang *jus* (literally, juice) suggests a vaguer and less attractive qualification of the liquid in question.[6] How appropriate that ducks who carry a semiotic burden of journalism in disrepute should frequent a less-than-pristine pond. Gassier's "Ah! Quel jus!" gives the pond of his media ducks the moral connotations of a swamp.

But the "Mare aux canards" and "Dernière heure" did not remain the weekly's only repeating columns. Gradually, across 1916 and 1917, the *Canard* added others, so that, by 1918, it displayed a strong framework of sections and titles to which a reader could look forward from week to week. Not only did many of these sections have "Canard" in their titles, but they also frequently adapted the feathered mascot to their subjects. "Les livres" (Books) had an intelligent-looking duck reading. "Le conte du Canard" (The *Canard* story) showed an enchained duck addressing a group of smaller ones in the water. Sometimes this column was labeled in the plural, "Les contes du Canard." Summer 1918 brought the vacation column "Les ca-

Figure 5. Pinel's duck mocks the Academy of Medicine (1916).

nards aux champs" (Ducks in the fields). With hats and pipes, a variety of ducks relaxed among the flowers in a bucolic scene.[7] Over the years, columns and their accompanying images evolved to add the variety of new visual and verbal games to a familiarity anchored in the exploitation of a permanent mascot.

By mid-1916, others were trying their hands at the paper's totem animal. An artist whose pen name was A. L. Pinel (or often just the initials) introduced a sort of duckling, rounder and softer than Gassier's more adult bird. The youthful fowl could express a variety of emotions, from the sadness of tears (under a discussion of censorship) to the derision signified by a biological deposit (under an article that mocked a member of the Academy of Medicine; see figure 5). Other, unsigned, ducks show the visual marks of another *Canard* cartoonist, Lucien Laforge.[8]

Gassier's helmeted German ducks also turned up on odd pages. By 1918, the *Canard Enchaîné* had become visually thick with such fowl. In an issue chosen (almost) at random, that of January 9, 1918, ducks grace every page. On page 1 two such birds stand under articles; one is kicking off a slipper, the other is smoking a pipe. The second page features two more ducks under articles. And they echo each other visually; both have their heads covered by objects—one by a cooking pot, the other by a military helmet (even this juxtaposition satirizes the military). On page 3 it is the columns "Conte du Canard" and "La mare aux canards" that carry the web-footed creations. The last page boasts the Teutonic ducks of "Dernière heure" and a set of ducklings above a column of literary news.[9] Such flocks fulfill a number of functions. One is using up space. They also contribute to giving the *Canard* a characteristic visual style. But this is a look with a content: a sense of play linked to a constant reminder of the falsehood-as-truth premise that underlay the satirical weekly.

The ubiquity of the *Canard*'s ducks highlights two distinctive aspects of the paper's use of images. First, pictures are signifiers—that is, they carry messages. But they can do so in at least two ways. As Pierre Fresnault-Deruelle puts it, they can be "self-sufficient semaphores," telling their own story without the need of text; or they can be "pre-texts" or "supplements" to the "all-powerful word" (or both).[10] The *Canard*'s freestanding ducks function both ways, as messages of their own and as commentaries on accompanying articles. As we shall see in chapter 12, they sometimes add an important new level of meaning.

Second, the ability of the *Canard*'s ducks to appear almost anywhere in the paper—from the title through the editorial cartoons and column headings to the empty spaces in and outside of articles—established an equally distinctive visual texture, one in which visual and verbal materials interpenetrated. Ordinarily one can think of the visual components of a newspaper (or at least one without advertisements) as being essentially divided between editorial cartoons and illustrations. Editorial cartoons are closed visual and verbal systems. Illustrations are meant to go with specific articles. But the *Canard*'s freer-floating ducks (and other small designs) effect a link with the birds in the cartoons and column headings, effectively creating a mixed visual/verbal discourse that invites one to judge all the verbal texts through the visual pun of the duck-as-newspaper-as-falsehood.

The frequent intercalation of visual with verbal texts and the relative openness this interpolation gave the pages of the *Canard Enchaîné* were related to another characteristic of the weekly's visual language: its economy. Before the war, political cartoonists often had Beaux-Arts training, which showed up in the detail of their caricatures in a tradition made famous by Honoré Daumier. Such drawings demanded whole pages in large formats to reproduce their professional qualities. This elaborate style could be seen, for example, in the prewar *L'Assiette au Beurre,* which functioned essentially (when not exclusively) as a showcase for large-format cartoons. As in other areas, the First World War gave a sharper focus to changes that had a number of causes, from the rise of photography as a better vehicle for mimesis to the shift in the high-art tradition to a bolder, less naturalistic treatment of line and form. As the century wore on, cartoonists tended to be less professional artists/painters and more what they are today, journalists of the rapid drawing. The *Canard Enchaîné* played a major role in the triumph of the new style; its influence was attributable, according to a later cartoonist for the weekly, Henri Monier, to the work of two of its cartoonists, Gassier and Laforge. There was an intimate solidarity between the organizational choice to scatter images throughout the pages, the new style, and the clean lines of Gassier's ducks and cartoons. Though some of the weekly's other wartime cartoonists were less spare in their strokes, Gassier's visual economy set the tone and increasingly dominated the *Canard*'s visual alphabet.[11]

The *Canard* was a pioneer among political weeklies in the importance it granted to such visual arrangements. This was just as true of the formatting of the newspaper as a whole. Superficially, the *Canard* followed the organizational patterns of other newspapers: big articles and a lead cartoon on page 1, columns and reviews of the press on subsequent pages, and service items like book reviews and recipes on the last page. But this organizational similarity hid a crucial structural principle best defined by describing its effect: the reader beginning an article in the *Canard* never knew whether what he was about to read next would be politics or just fun, serious or a joke, irony or direct argument.

Number 80 of the new series, dated January 9, 1918, is typical. Under the title *Le Canard Enchaîné* is the subtitle "Journal hebdomadaire" (Weekly newspaper). From its first number in 1915 until early April 1917, the *Canard*'s subtitle had been "Journal humoristique" (Humorous newspaper). The duality was telling. Was the *Canard* a humor periodical devoted essentially to entertainment (though at times it could certainly exploit the politics of the day) like others of this type? Or was it a weekly newspaper, which generally meant a newspaper of opinion and doctrine whose function was to illustrate and defend a point of view? It was both; and each aspect of its formula was expressed on its front page at different times.

There were no banner headlines in any issue of the *Canard*. Such headlines had been forbidden early in the war.[12] For the humor weekly, the ban permitted the articles to compete for attention with each other and with the cartoons. After the first few issues of 1915, which were organized around themes, individual numbers of the *Canard* never announced their principal preoccupations. To do so would have reduced the ambiguity, the play between jest and earnest, the potential surprise. Characteristically, the *Canard* eschewed banner headlines, even after the war, when they were permitted.

No headline, but between the address of the newspaper on the left, and the subscription prices on the right, a small box had held, since 1916, Gassier's duck-menaced-by-scissors—but not on the issue of January 9, 1918. Instead the space contains a text: "Headlines? Yes . . . but nothing is more chic than a white headline." Only the *Canard*'s earlier treatment of this space made this game possible, with its allusions to the restrictions on headlines and the white of the censor's blanks. Of course, one could then mock the mockery, and the next issue, January 16, fills this space with "It is not necessary that a headline mean something." Under the headings, the visual layout of the January 9 front page is classic: a large cartoon by Laforge in the middle, on either side large, one-column articles, and under the cartoon two smaller articles. Most issues employed slight variations on this basic layout. Sometimes the cartoon was big enough to stretch from the center columns all the way to the right (as on January 23). At other times the absence of an editorial cartoon might be compensated for by the presence of a heavily illustrated (in sketches) article (as on January 16).

To return to our number of January 9, the cartoon by Laforge is overtly political, an attack on the royalist journalist Léon Daudet. But there was no necessity in this choice. The issues of January 3, 1917, and February 6, 1918, to take but two examples with the cartoon in top center, feature essentially nonpolitical cartoons. Though both evoke the war, they do so as a backdrop for more traditional humor topoi. In one, called "The ex-doughboy at the dinner party," a distinguished-looking "Baron" refuses a proffered cup of coffee in favor of a glass of *pinard,* the cheap wine served to soldiers at the front. In the other cartoon a soldier suggests to his attractive *marraine de guerre,* or war godmother, that they take advantage of the fact that he is still of this world. The dangers and privations of the war are present but as an essentially nontragic basis for humor based on class juxtaposition and sexual innuendo.[13]

While nothing in the form of the two lead articles of January 9, 1918, signals their degree of political engagement, one of the titles contains such an allusion. "Ni vite, ni tout ou le bon truc" (Neither quickly nor everything or the good trick) mocks the "vite et tout" (quickly and everything) with which a number of journalists (including *L'Oeuvre*'s Gustave Téry) had called for quick action on the charges of antipatriotic activities against a number of leftist politicians.[14] This article, which is on the left, adopts an anticlerical pose to criticize Pontius Pilate for having had the naiveté to let the Jesus affair terminate so quickly instead of drawing it out as a form of protection against his political enemies. And the piece is signed with the comical-sounding name Simon Hégésippe.

The article on the right is by the *Canard* humorist whose pen name was Whip. Extending slightly onto page 2, it is essentially a drawn-out clever story or anecdote. A couple is entertaining their war godson (hence the title "Le filleul"). The servant cannot find any of the items that her mistress has asked for to make a good dinner for their guest. Just when it seems that all is lost, a delivery service returns (for deficient address) the packages of foodstuffs that the couple had tried to send to their protégé at the front, and all enjoy a sumptuous meal. The humor is provided by a series of devices: the man of the couple is called Mr. Phnax; he speaks without consonants and has been a subscriber to the *Canard Enchaîné* for seventy-seven years.

Politics on the left and humor on the right (of the page)? Again, not necessarily. The first issue of 1918 (January 2) gives over its left column to a mildly droll, nonpolitical set of New Year's greetings that are simultaneously legitimate greetings and also a take-off on them. A similar uncertainty reigns under the cartoon by Laforge, in the lower center of the January 9 issue. The longer of the two articles is labeled "Le jeu de trente et quarante" (The game of thirty and forty). It starts seriously enough, with an attack on the Paris municipal council for raising the price of gas without improving its quality. But after this two-paragraph complaint, itself in line with the *Canard* tendency to criticize the municipal councilors for price increases in city services, the other nine paragraphs go straight to the world of silliness. They argue that the way to save money on gas is to substitute for the current practice of charging by cubic meters one of pricing by square meters. (These, for example, take up much less space.) What started as a political article swiftly turns to nonpolitical humor.

The other piece bears the oxymoronic title "For the Civilian Doughboys." It develops a facetious argument: now that civilians are facing deprivations from the war, they should get decorations like the combat ribbons won by front-line soldiers. Before completing this spoof, however, the anonymous author works in a mockery of the oft-repeated slogan that the war will be won by the side that holds on for the "last quarter of an hour."

Like the first page, the second features a cartoon top center and ducks under articles on the right and left. A small piece is entitled "La brigade des tabacs" (The tobacco squad). It explains how a satirical story by the *Canard Enchaîné*—that the prefecture had created a special squad to police café and tobacco outlets (usually the same)—had been believed and reported seriously by other newspapers.[15] This was a wonderful occasion for the weekly to gloat (and there were others), but it was also an opportunity to repeat attacks on another favorite target, the police. In French, when officers of the law beat someone up to teach a lesson it is called *passer au tabac.*

In the middle of the page, across three columns, spreads a piece by Rodolphe Bringer, one of the *Canard*'s leading humorists. The five anecdotes of the article are all based on misunderstandings of common Parisian expressions. Characteristically, only the last has political content: it mocks a patriotic war journalist for using the expression "to leave one in peace." Did this mean he was a defeatist? A little antibellicist politics, but only after the reader has been sucked in by humor that is, at least politically, innocent.

On Bringer's right is an example of another of the genres in which the weekly excelled—the pastiche. Called "Les trois millions du *Canard Enchaîné*," it mocks the donation campaigns conducted by many political newspapers, but especially by the reactionary royalist daily *L'Action Française*. Copying the style of both the royalists' supporters and their editor, the piece pretends to be a letter of financial and political support with grateful commentary.

Most French newspapers, and virtually all those that aimed at a mass market, included among their most important features a feuilleton, or fictional serial. The *Canard* had its own; and in number 80 the bottom third of both pages 2 and 3 is given over to the weekly installment of the "Feuilleton du Canard Enchaîné." But even here, the reader could not always be sure of what was coming. Some feuilletons, like "La classe heureuse," were straightforward stories with a political moral.[16] But a feuilleton could also be as thoroughly apolitical an entertainment as "Zulaïna," a nine-part "Persian tale" that ran from March 6 to April 17, 1918.[17]

The feuilleton in the January 9, 1918, issue was the seventh episode (of nine) of a story entitled "Le flacon de gaz." The byline, Panthéon Courcelle, suggested the subgenre—feuilleton-pastiche. Panthéon Courcelle was a reference to Pierre de Courcelle, one of the better-known feuilleton writers of the mass press.[18] The story is a clever mélange of satirical overwriting and double entendres with just enough of an episodic and dramatic plot to keep the reader hanging on. It begins with a society lecturer and academician frightening his audience with a small bottle of what is purported to be a deadly new German chemical weapon. Quite by accident, a young man seeking employment as a police spy denounces (for the wrong reasons) a group of people who are actually involved in illegal trafficking in war supplies. Along the way we are treated to an unflattering portrait of the seamy sides of aristocratic, business, and political circles. The last episode ("A Premature Epilogue") veers back to open satire. The narrator-cum-author, who until now has remained almost completely invisible (and outside the story), abruptly explains that he will stop the story at this point, as he has already provided enough material for any of his colleagues (he provides names) to spin a long series from it. After disobliging references to the industrial way in which many such serials were produced (by young, badly paid ghost-writers), the author/narrator ends his story by speculating on the possible futures of his characters, combining observations on the corruption of French society with references to the literary tricks of the feuilleton trade. This exercise in meta-feuilletonism was characteristic of the *Canard*'s play with levels of discourse. But it was also characteristic of the paper's frequent critiques of the feuilletons and other aspects of France's mass press. Such play extended to the similarly plotted crime and adventure films that were making a splash in wartime France. In January 1917, the *Canard* began a feuilleton entitled "Le masque aux dents gâtées" (The mask with rotten teeth), which was a take-off on the hugely successful film *Le masque aux dents blanches* (The mask with white teeth).[19]

Page 3 of our issue number 80, above the second part of the feuilleton episode, is given over to two "duck" columns, a short article, a large cartoon, and a short advertisement for a coming feuilleton. To begin with the advertisement, it was straight: a real notice for a real feuilleton by a real and well-known author, Pierre Mac-Orlan. And there was no necessity in that either since the *Canard Enchaîné* also put in false advertisements for nonexistent feuilletons.[20]

Of the two columns, one, the "Conte du Canard," was more normally in its place on the last page of the weekly. This story is called "Flagrant délit," and it is an absolutely ordinary brief narrative of an adulterous tryst interrupted by the jealous husband, who kills his rival—except in this case the entire story is told backward, beginning with the death of the paramour and ending with the two lovers entering the hotel. A note further down the page attributes the odd narrative style to a frivolous typesetter. No politics here in the traditional sense—and love triangles were staples of *Canard* fictional narratives—but the reader was invited to solve a puzzle.

The other column, "La mare aux canards," which extended onto page 4, includes the usual mixture of anecdotes: some are off-color puns, others are attacks on deputies for doing police work or for terminal pretentiousness. At the end is a welcoming notice for a new trench newspaper, honored with the expression "canard." If "the duck pond" was characteristically mixed in content, the cartoon is openly political; it attacks rich industrialists and the clergy and royalists who pestered them for donations. Finally the short article zeroes in on the clerical exploitation of the war. Its title, "Union très sacrée" (Very sacred union), evokes *union sacrée,* the term for the patriotic unity of France at war. This piece, not without humor, exposes the case of a group of nuns in a hospital who are obliging wounded soldiers to go to mass, even if they are Muslims.

Page 4 of the issue is a busy combination of a large number of smaller columns that signaled, for the reader, the last page of the periodical. Here, too, humor and politics are devilishly mixed. "Dernière heure," by far the largest section under its German-duck heading, is dominated by a long article on "the Charles Benoist Affair." The piece, a take-off on reporting about the Caillaux Affair, is stuffed with goofy names (besides mocking the seriousness with which minor facts were being interpreted). For example, it speaks of the famous detective agency "Brother-Hétasseur." The name would be better written "et ta soeur" (and your sister), the French equivalent of "and so's your mother!" An Italian official is called Manjapolenta (eats polenta). Despite the broad humor, the point of the article is perfectly political; it defends the embattled Joseph Caillaux (long associated with attempts to reach accommodations with Germany) by satirizing the campaign against him. Politics is interlaced with ethnic stereotypes, sex, and gender. (The role of gender, like that of stereotypes, in the *Canard*'s ideological mix will be explored in subsequent chapters.) Yet, the reader could, if he or she wished, ignore the politics and simply enjoy the satire of current-affairs reporting. That, too, was an effect of the *Canard*'s mixing of humor with politics.

The entire right side of the page is taken up by a column that went back to the first issue of the new series in 1916, "A travers la presse déchaînée." *Déchaînée* (unbridled) was, of course, the opposite of *enchaîné* and was used to refer to the serious press of France (especially the mass press and the right-wing political press). When the *Canard* talked of periodicals (humorous or not) to which it felt close, it often did so under the heading "La presse sérieuse" (The serious press).[21] The "unchained" press in the issue in question is blamed for political hypocrisy and bad manners, and also for humorously sloppy writing.

This fourth, and final, page is completed by a full-size cartoon and three minicolumns. The cartoon is a snicker-worthy association of the length of women's dresses with that of the war. Of the three minicolumns, "Regards littéraires" is the most univocal, consisting of a series of comments about recent developments in the worlds of journalism and publishing. The "Petite correspondance" column was one of the most regular features of the *Canard*, both during the war and after. It satirized the mail-box features of mass newspapers, which permitted readers to correspond with each other through the semianonymity of initials. This one begins, "It is certain that if things keep going on like this we will end up with a war on our hands." Other brief messages either simply made fun of the drinking habits of the French (more on this below) or took swipes at generals, politicians, or journalists. Politics? Humor? The reader could find either or both. The last item, "Recettes culinaires," reads almost as a Marx-brothers version of a recipe book. Were there politics even here? Yes, if one counts the exploitation, in one mock recipe, of the fact that *panier à salade* (salad basket) is also French for a paddy wagon.

The potential instability of the *Canard*'s discourse, its constant wavering, and its recombination of political commentary, more-or-less political humor, and largely nonpolitical humor relied on the paper's choice and organization of materials. Not only was there always a substantial percentage of nonpolitical material (to speak more precisely, material that would not have been judged political at that time) in the tales, serials, and sexually oriented cartoons, but there was always the possibility of finding material hiding in features that seemed, at first sight, dedicated to another sort of material.

This essential quality of the *Canard*'s discourse distinguished it clearly from its competitors: the other humor periodicals of the time. *La Baïonnette,* which advertised itself as "the top satirical illustrated magazine in France," was filled with cartoons and sexual innuendo but had little else in common with the *Canard.* The same could be said of *Le Rire,* published during the war as *Le Rire Rouge,* though both this weekly and *La Baïonnette* published prose by the *Canard* writer G. de Pawlowski.[22] Even periodicals of humor and commentary with a reputation for impertinence and Parisian wit, like *Fantasio* and *Le Ruy Blas,* were, in their patriotic conformism, closer to the *Canard*'s targets than to the web-footed weekly itself. *Fantasio* sometimes went in for pastiche and satire, publishing, for example, a "Tadeblag [sic] Zeitung" with offices on "Kolossalkanardstrasse" in Berlin. But all one has to do is compare the claim that this paper "was linked by special wire to the Old German God" with the *Canard*'s reception of the false news of the world by "special barbed wire" from Berlin to see the difference in satirical vision. Other French humor periodicals did not echo the *Canard*'s newspaperlike format, its congenital antiphrastic irony, and its discursive ambivalence and instability. Need it be added that these distinctive *Canard* qualities also distanced it from the prewar satirical (and leftist) *L'Assiette au Beurre?*[23]

Add the *Canard*'s games of hide-and-seek to its truth-as-falsehood claims and the paper also functions as a puzzle, a set of tricks, allusions, double and triple entendres that the reader is invited to decipher. Since Sigmund Freud, it is well known that the sense of mastery created by problem solving (especially when combined with the recognition that accompanies a successful solution) is one of the sources of pleasure in many kinds of humor. Téry, promoting his new daily paper, *L'Oeuvre,* tried the gambit of claiming that "imbeciles do not read *L'Oeuvre.*" The *Canard,* many of whose writers also worked for Téry's organ, tried the opposite tack. Its "Reintroduction" had noted that it "would not claim that imbeciles will not read it. It is too concerned, in effect, with its broad diffusion to restrain so willingly the number of its readers."[24]

Clever satire, but everything in the *Canard*'s organization and its discourses said the opposite. It counted on its readers to decipher its allusions, to solve its puzzles, and to move with agility back and forth between multiple referential systems. Of course, the readers knew it too. They could continually congratulate themselves on having gotten the joke, having uncovered the allusion. And the multiple referential systems of the *Canard* and the mixtures of subject matter generally made this system work in only one direction. One enjoys the puzzles one has solved but, in the overwhelming majority of cases, blithely ignores the allusions one has missed. What reader would not have appreciated the combination of satire and compliment that the weekly offered in July 1917: "Imbeciles read the *Canard Enchaîné*, but they do not understand it"?[25]

This game created a collusion between readers and paper that could extend beyond loyalty to something resembling the behavior of fans. After the war, the process would only increase.[26] The strong personality given the weekly by its verbal/visual mascot also played a part in this connection. So, too, did the asides that the weekly's writers were always hiding in little notices crammed between articles, asides that incited the reader to remain alert to multiple meanings. In October 1916, already: "Attention, beware! The *Canard Enchaîné* sometimes tells the truth." Or a year later: "Ask anyone, at anytime and anywhere—at the front, in the workplace, in the street, . . . What is the most serious newspaper? You will be told, It's the 'Canard Enchaîné,' and that is the truth."[27]

3 Unstuffing Skulls

The Canard *versus the Mass Press*

Seriousness and humor were never far apart for the *Canard Enchaîné.* But one of the things it was most serious about was what the other journalists of wartime France were doing: the patriotic combination of official optimism, vulgar chauvinism, and pretentious bellicosity that went under the name *bourrage de crâne* (skull stuffing). The *Canard* was so successful in unstuffing skulls that for many observers, and for historians like R. Manévy, this was the weekly's most important contribution.[1] But the *Canard* went further than just countering war propaganda; it extended its scrutiny to a critique and exposé of the French mass press. Besides being a "serious," "humorous" periodical, the *Canard Enchaîné* functioned as a virtual anti- or counter-newspaper.

Bourrage de crâne was not the same thing as false information, as *canards.* Not only could it be technically true (even a truism), but it had to play a patriotic, militaristic role. Thus the *Canard* gave French skull stuffing its own, nonaviary, icon. The visual elements of this icon appeared for the first time in a March 7, 1917, Gassier cartoon. Entitled "The Card Not Foreseen by Mr. Herriot," it bore the legend "Carte blanche for the bourreurs de crâne."[2] The texts were a reference to the ration cards that had recently been introduced by the Radical Minister of Supply, Edouard Herriot. But the picture shows a number of well-known journalists (including Maurice Barrès and Gustave Hervé) using hammers to drive nails into the head of an unhappy man whose large bald cranium makes an easy target. Literalizing and embodying the image make it into an active, intrusive process.

A few issues later, the image settled down to periodic status, becoming an easily recognizable logo. The May 2 issue headed a column by Maréchal with an unsigned drawing of a large head (with hair) out of which hang

Figure 6. Skull stuffing visualized (1917).

large pieces of paper with the names of patriotic newspapers. Above the drawing, the heading was "Les bourreurs de cranes" (see figure 6). The issue that followed revived the missing elements of Gassier's cartoon: under the same heading, an unsigned drawing showed two journalists, each in the process of driving a peg into the head of a protesting male. To hammer or not to hammer? For the column "Les bourreurs de crâne," the *Canard* settled on the large head with protruding newspapers.[3] Though it did not appear as regularly as "La mare aux canards," the skull stuffers frequently got their own column of press citations with commentary. At times other labels were used. One, "Union sacrée," was devoted to citations of rightist papers that attacked the left. Another short-lived column celebrated especially stupid headlines.[4] In the spring of 1918, the *Canard* tried another formula: *cherrer dans les bégonias,* slang for to exaggerate or overdo it. It could also be shortened to *tu cherres.* The March 13 issue included a small column introduced by a drawing of a corpulent man treading in a flower bed (the begonias) as a duck observes, "Oh! Tu cherres." The title of this occasional column was "Dans les bégonias."[5]

BARRÈS AND HERVÉ

The first (and the most famous) of what would become a series of games for readers of the weekly was a contest to pick the "great chief of the tribe of skull stuffers." In the resurrected, first issue of 1916 the *Canard* announced that it would hold a "referendum for the election of the great chief," but the actual contest was not formally opened until the end of November. Readers were invited to defend their votes, and the resulting comments were printed in subsequent issues. And the contest, too, had its logo: a man's suit with a question mark in place of the head and a royal crown surmounted by a hammer.[6]

The results were announced in June 1917; the winner was Gustave Hervé with 5,653 votes, and, close behind him, Maurice Barrès with 5,402 (the next journalist had fewer than 3,000 votes).[7] This result should not have surprised readers of the satirical weekly. On August 30, 1916, the *Canard* offered five subscriptions (to be distributed to front-line soldiers) to the first reader to discover the "remarkable particularity" of that issue. Next week (along with fifty subscriptions for the winners) came the answer: the whole number made no mention of either Barrès or Hervé.[8] Indeed a "remarkable particularity," since the journalistic bird regularly pecked at both these Frenchmen throughout the war years.

Barrès and Hervé combined some of the most stupidly chauvinistic wartime journalism with political positions far from those of the *Canard.* In pursuing them the *Canard* could act with characteristic two-sidedness: as leftist periodical, on the one hand, and as antinewspaper and scourge of the wartime press, on the other. The "documentation" provided by the *Canard's* public-relations staff attributes the weekly's focus on Hervé to the fact that Maréchal, having once worked for, and admired, the former Socialist, was all the more disappointed by his wartime chauvinism.[9] That attitude certainly did not help Hervé, but the virtually equal obsession with Barrès, with whom the founder of the *Canard* had no special relationship, showed the weekly's ability to transcend personal considerations in the service of a global vision.

In many ways, Hervé was the easier target. Before the war a leader of the left wing of the French Socialist party, he had made a reputation for his extreme antimilitarist and antipatriotic rhetoric (e.g., "planting the flag in the manure pile")[10] and for uncompromising hostility to the existing capitalist order. Appropriately, his newspaper bore the name *La Guerre Sociale* (Class war). But with the coming of war, Hervé swiftly shifted from class to international war and from pacifism to exaggerated militarism. His *Guerre Sociale* became *La Victoire* in early 1916.[11]

Barrès had been a proponent of a vague mixture of socialism and nationalism in his youth, but he had evolved toward a conservative nationalism that led him to the Chamber of Deputies and the Académie Française. But Barrès was also a talented and successful novelist. His earlier works breathed a bourgeois individualism bordering on anarchism, but his later work celebrated religion, patriotism, and the cult of Alsace-Lorraine and made him one of the founders of the modern French nationalist movement. As leader of the League of Patriots (and a native of Lorraine), Barrès regularly led delegations to the Strasbourg statue in the Place de la Concorde, where he perorated in favor of the reconquest of the lost provinces.[12]

He preached the anti-German war but did not fight it: that was the essence of the *Canard*'s beef with the professional patriot from Lorraine. Its attitude was best illustrated by a story the weekly hung, like an albatross, around the head of the conservative nationalist. On August 8, 1914, days after the outbreak of the war, *L'Illustration* published a story on Barrès. As the journalist for *L'Illustration* put it, he encountered Barrès amid the patriotic crowds in central Paris. The deputy explained, with "a nice movement of the chin," that the hour had struck, that he was going to sign up. The crowd then respectfully parted to allow the nationalist to make his way to the Ministry of War. But Barrès, the *Canard* noted maliciously, decided not to fight. Instead he solicited from the Ministry of War permission to leave Paris as German troops approached in early September. From this time forward, anytime the *Canard* wished to evoke the contrast between words and deeds it had but to mention the "nice movement of the chin," whether or not Barrès was the subject.[13]

In his early fifties, Barrès was free from mobilization, so the *Canard* ridiculed him with examples of men in their sixties and seventies serving on the front lines.[14] The *Canard* evoked Barrès's self-preservation in a number of ways. An investigative journalist reported how at the front he had met Barrès, who had joined up under a false name.[15] In August 1918, the satirical weekly used ironic bisociation. Borrowing the dramatic descriptions of the air raid led by the famous Italian warrior poet Gabriele d'Annunzio, the *Canard* rewrote the account with Barrès as the littérateur-hero and with the raid on Strasbourg instead of Vienna. Not only did the paper mention that Barrès and d'Annunzio were the same age, but it had the politician from Lorraine drop tracts similar to his famous speeches at the Place de la Concorde. "Barrès lives his *oeuvre*," the weekly summed up pithily.[16]

Barrès could also be targeted for his membership in the Académie Française. The political and aesthetic conservatism (not to mention the wartime chauvinism) of this venerable institution made it a natural for the *Canard*. "Send in the Academy!" reads the legend of a Gassier cartoon of July 12, 1916, in which a portly German officer surrenders in front of a trench filled with Academicians in uniform. Barrès appears over the parapet orating from a copy of the newspaper *L'Echo de Paris*. The ceremonial sword that formed part of the uniform of the "immortals" (as the members of the Academy are called) hangs from his side, a symbol of the exclusively verbal bellicosity of the Academicians. In an earlier cartoon, the immortals had been pictured as donkeys. Barrès was particularly recognizable since his long nose adapted easily to the distinctive physiognomy of the academic asses.[17]

Barrès's academic sword figured prominently in a series of seven frames with accompanying dialogue by Gassier entitled "Les imprécations de Maurice." A pastiche of *Le cid* by Pierre Corneille, the text showed Barrès waving his sword and ended with him sending his son off to fight in his place.[18] If Maurice Barrès made a career of verbal patriotism, his son was another story. Philippe Barrès served with great distinction in the First World War.[19] Was not this an adequate sacrifice on the part of the elder Barrès? The *Canard* answered that whether or not the younger Barrès did his duty was irrelevant.[20] Indeed, the last frame of Gassier's strip zeroed in on what the *Canard* saw as Maurice Barrès's abuse of the situation. The elder Barrès says to his son, "Go and do *our* duty!"

The globalizing pronoun evoked an issue dear to the nonconformist weekly: the way linguistic slips covered shoddy arguments and improper assimilations. The first-person plural *(nous, notre)* and the third-person impersonal *(on)* were the biggest culprits. In "La classe heureuse," M. Hubu states that "we *[nous]* will make all necessary sacrifices" as soon as he has verified that he does not risk being called up. And the narrator explains that many honest folk conjugate in a similar way: "I have been excused at the physical, you are mobilized, he is at the front, *we* will go all the way to Cologne." Since journalists too used this grammar, the frontline soldier could read his courageous newspaperman saying, "In spite of the fearsome bombardment of our trenches *we* are holding on; and *we* are advancing with a smile on our lips."[21] The *Canard* turned the game of pronouns against Barrès by repeating a joke from *L'Oeuvre.* The daily paper had saluted his return from a propaganda tour in England by having the nationalist writer sing a slightly different version of the famous opening lines of the *Marseillaise*: "Allez! Enfants de la patrie." ("You go, children of the fatherland" for the original, "Let's go, children of the fatherland.")[22]

But these jabs at Barrès were nothing compared with the way the weekly picked on Gustave Hervé. On September 20, 1916, the *Canard* linked the issue to the point (also frequently evoked by the paper) that Hervé, like his colleague Barrès, had failed to volunteer for military service. Hervé had written, "We *[nous]*, the survivors of the bloody epic, are we going to, after the war . . . ," which earned this response: "What? No more joining up? No more charge against the barbed wire of the enemy? No more glorious death?"[23] In the early fall of 1918, as Allied troops began to push back the Germans from the northeast of France, Hervé was pilloried again for using *nous* when referring to the French advance. "And Gustave is quite nice," added the satirical weekly, "he could have said *me!*"[24]

Hervé's amalgamation of his own personality with that of the fighting men of France was particularly dangerous, or so thought the *Canard,* because of the bloodthirstiness of his advice. Hervé was a great preacher of the heroism of others, one of those who insisted on more offensives and blamed the French general staff for its (relative) timidity. In February 1917, Hervé angered the *Canard* by disagreeing with the advice of André Tardieu (journalist, politician, and serving officer) that a new offensive should await sufficient artillery preparation. "Better an offensive that fails," Hervé had written, "than a victorious defensive."[25]

The German aerial bombardment of Paris in February 1918 brought out Hervé's verbal bravado. He even argued that it had been a humiliation that Paris had been spared when London had been many times the target of air raids. After quoting Hervé directly, the *Canard* opined that, yes, "the families of the fifty-six dead felt, like the others, extremely humiliated. But now they are no longer humiliated at all. They are very happy. Like Hervé. Very happy." A funnier response to the tragedy came when the weekly put words into Hervé's mouth: "I know well," the paper had him write, "that there were victims, but they were a ridiculously tiny number. And, further, one cannot make an omelet without breaking eggs. The essential thing is to have a big cellar like mine, not to be an egg and to eat the omelet."[26]

De la Fouchardière summed it up perceptively:

> I would not dare to affirm that the Gothas [the German bombers] came specially to please Gustave. But their work must have given complete satisfaction to our candid exterminator. Please note that Gustave is not mean at all; but he loves to follow military bands and national burials; he imagines thus that everyone is looking at him. . . . Gustave is not mean; all that he asks is that people be massacred nicely around him; thus he has the illusion of being promoted to the rank of professional hero after having been for three years an amateur hero.[27]

De la Fouchardière's attack was perspicacious because, before the war, Hervé had been equally extreme in his preaching of class war. For the *Canard,* Hervé's political switch from radical leftist antimilitarism to reactionary chauvinism was treason. Thus, for example, de la Fouchardière attacked Hervé in a rare nonironic article. This "Informal Letter to Mr. Gustave Hervé, Patriot" accused the former Socialist of being worse than the other "cretins" with whom he now worked, for they had been born that way and had never known better. Hervé, de la Fouchardière argued, was a traitor worse than Judas, who betrayed Jesus but then expiated his fault. (In Hervé's case he should have died on the field of battle.)[28]

But, for the *Canard,* Hervé's ideological mobility was more than just an issue of political morality. It affected his coverage of current events and became inextricably bound up with his own brand of *bourrage de crâne.* The Russian Revolution of February/March 1917 was welcomed wholeheartedly by the *Canard,* which (without irony) invited the German people to follow suit. For the revolutionary-turned-chauvinist Hervé (who extended the same invitation) the revolution in Russia posed problems that the satirical weekly could not resist exploiting. Combining his wartime optimism with what remained of his earlier leftism, the editor of *La Victoire* celebrated the freedom of Finland and Poland, the end of the persecution of the Jews, and the release of political prisoners. The *Canard's* answer was feigned surprise. "What? All these things existed and you did not say anything about them?" Of course, as the weekly noted in this page-long review of the press, nine-tenths of the newspapers of France also shifted within hours from praise of the tsar to celebration of the revolution. But as a former revolutionary, Hervé received, literally, the last word: "At the precise moment when the Russian revolutionaries had raised the red flag over the Winter Palace in place of the imperial flag, what was citizen Gustave Hervé doing? He was hanging the imperial flag from the balcony of his newspaper!"[29]

If Barrès and Hervé had, from the point of view of the *Canard,* different sorts of political liabilities, they stood together as archetypical *bourreurs de crâne.* Both were satirized through the conventions of the paper itself. The earliest issues of the new, 1916, series included a short column, "Le point de vue du fumiste." A *fumiste* was a mystifier or practical joker, an excellent format for the *Canard's* games with veracity. The column was signed "Gustave fumiste." A pastiche of a column from *La Victoire,* "Le point de vue du plombier," was signed "Nicolas—Plombier" (Nicolas the plumber), the substitution of Nicolas for Gustave satirized Hervé's use of a pseudonym.[30] Barrès never got a column, but he had the privilege of having his name frequently mangled, as in "Boris Marrès."[31]

Barrès and Hervé lived off the heroism of others. A question, therefore, emerged: How would these two live after the war was over? Already in January 1918, when the military situation looked bleak for France, the *Canard* began to imagine the end of the war. Rodolphe Bringer proposed founding an "Association for the Protection of the Victims of Peace," chief among whose wards would be war journalists. Not only would Barrès's organization, the League of Patriots, find itself with nothing to do, but, paraphrasing La Fontaine's "The Grasshopper and the Ant," Bringer wrote, "M. Gustave Hervé va se trouver fâcheusement dépourvu quand la paix sera venue" (Mr. Gustave Hervé will be caught desperately empty-handed when peace arrives).[32] In October 1918, with a victorious peace clearly around the corner, the *Canard* imagined a number of figures contemplating the possibility of peace. Hervé and Barrès were easily recognizable from their visual caricatures. Hervé was quizzical: "So then I will have to become antimilitarist again?" Barrès was sad: "Imagine that I am still waiting for my Croix de Guerre."[33] On October 23, a Gassier cartoon, "Decidedly, It Is Really Over," showed Hervé and Barrès meeting in the street:

> —Where are you going then, my dear Maurice?
>
> —To sign up, my dear Gustave. . . .
>
> —What do you know, so am I![34]

ACTION FRANÇAISE

We saw in chapter 1 that as an armistice seemed imminent in November, Gassier pictured four journalists as hunters who had failed to shoot down the dove of peace.[35] Two of the dove haters were Barrès and Hervé, who had ornamented so many of the weekly's front pages. The other two unlucky sportsmen were Charles Maurras and Léon Daudet, mainstays of the daily newspaper *Action Française* and of the royalist league of the same name. Daudet and Maurras's right-wing, militaristic, and antirepublican journalism was more than enough to earn them the permanent ire of the left-wing paper. But Daudet's elaborate spy mania, which had developed even before the war, and his and Maurras's fanatical chauvinism further irritated the writers of the *Canard*. In some respects, Maurras and Daudet were more difficult targets than Hervé or Barrès. They displayed a greater intellectual consistency, their movement tended to be self-contained, and they were—each in his own way—highly skilled polemical journalists. Daudet had a way with words that rivaled the skills of the *Canard*'s contributors. How to attack this pair, whose influence was growing as the war progressed, despite their anticonstitutional politics? One way was to point out that though he could have fought, Daudet (like Hervé and Barrès) chose not to. A cartoon from November 1915 imagines the portly Daudet in uniform seizing an imperial flag as he slays a German officer with his sword.[36] Some criticism of the royalists zeroed in on specific characteristics of the movement. One critique addressed the contradiction between the fanatical anti-Germanism of the Action Française and the fact that the House of France (which the royalists wished to return to the throne), like most of the royal families of Europe, had heavily intermarried with German princely families.[37]

But pastiche was a more typically Canardesque response; and the distinctiveness of the *Action Française*'s style made this mode of mockery particularly inviting. The paper's title was transformed into the *Réaction Française* (French reaction), a far better description of the politics of the royalist daily. A bit later it became *L'Inaction Française,* which mocked the league's failure, felt by many royalists as well, to bring back the monarchy. (After the war the royalist daily became the *Putréf Action Française,* which devastatingly called attention to its slow decomposition.)[38]

The slogan of the league/paper was "Everything That Is National Is Ours." Commenting on an advertisement for a new syphilis remedy that contained none of the serum of the (suspect-sounding) "Ehrlich," the *Canard* terminated its note with "Everything that is national is ours, proclaims Mr. Léon Daudet."[39] This clever bisociation of politics and venereal disease effectively exposed both the potential absurdity of the Action Française claim and the silliness of anti-German hysteria.

We have already seen, in chapter 2, that the *Canard* was happy to satirize Action Française contribution drives. The article in question ended with a take-off on Maurrasian prose:

> And what a testimony to the solidity of the fiber of the branch of the tree of our race! Abandoned for more than 120 years without stable direction, subject for all this long period to the influences that alienate and decompose, what other people than ours would have thus maintained its constant structure, its hereditary plan of life, its will to persevere and to rise up again, of which my books, which are available everywhere for the price of four francs, furnish the formula and the user's guide?[40]

Starting with Maurras's typically conservative preference for organic-vegetative metaphors, this masterpiece of satire brought together Action Française doctrine with the royalist's concern to push his own works.

At times the prose of Maurras and Daudet was so idiosyncratic that it at once defied and obviated the need for pastiche. In a passage that illustrated his tendency to mix opponents together and then accuse them by association, Daudet wrote (referring to Joseph Caillaux, Louis Malvy, and Miguel Almereyda): "Willy nilly the Caillautist must, at a given moment, turn out to be Malvyst, the Malvyst Caillautist and the Caillauxmalvyst Almereydian."[41] The *Canard* writer called this a "new style" and "Daudetist," but his own attempt to turn such prose back against the royalist polemicist was less extreme, and therefore less comical, than Daudet's original elucubrations. In 1916, the weekly quoted an almost hundred-word, barely comprehensible sentence by "Maurras, prince of thinkers and master of French style," before offering a prize to whoever could figure out what it meant.[42]

STUFFING GERMAN SKULLS

Though the *Canard* attacked Barrès, Hervé, Daudet, and Maurras—all famous for their anti-Germanism—it was not about to appear as a defender of the enemy. Accordingly, besides mocking the Central Powers,[43] the *Canard* also criticized German *bourrage de crâne,* stigmatizing it as worse than the French versions of the same malady. Commenting on absurd accounts of panicking Parisians held in line by colonial troops (disguised as women!), the *Canard* explained that in German these writers were known as "Khranenburrer." And since the Germans "were always trying to make everything bigger, they have überkhranenburrer." In late August 1918, with the German army giving way before the advancing Allies, a Teutonic journalist explained to his fellow citizens that such suppleness was the true art of war and that German generals were winning defensive victories. The *Canard* awarded this writer the title of "ace of the *Deutschekranenburrergesellshaft* [sic, for the missing *c*]."[44]

The *Canard*'s patriotism meant that it too could get caught in *bourrage de crâne.* In July 1917, the *Canard* ran a cartoon about the Russian summer offensive. Entitled "Now, It Works," it had as a subtitle "The Russians Have Taken Thirty Thousand Prisoners and Have Advanced Many Kilometers." It pictures a Russian soldier pointing to a steamroller on which "Nicholas" has been crossed out and "Republic" written in its place. The soldier says, "Of course! The others had mounted it backward." The reference to the Russian steamroller put this cartoon in the finest tradition of French skull stuffing.[45] The opportunity to square patriotic optimism with support for the new Russian revolutionary government apparently created a situation that even our wily duck could not resist.

THE MASS PRESS AND SKULL STUFFERY

The *Canard* was more than just a left-wing paper, even a patriotic left-wing paper. It also saw itself as a watchdog for all the press and especially for the mass press of wartime France. One of the institutions of World War I journalism in France was the "military critic." This journalist had the unenviable job of trying to find something intelligent and reasonably optimistic to say about the meager information provided in the official communiqués, without, of course, provoking the scissors of the censor. And this feat of words had to be accomplished daily, throughout four years of largely bloody stalemate.

Every major paper had one of these war commentators. Most bore military titles, like Colonel this or General that, and many were retired officers. Some, however (as the *Canard* was quick to point out), were just pseudonyms for ordinary journalists.[46] Whether military or civilian, the "military critics" were the principal interpreters of the war to the French public.

This role also made them the principal purveyors of skull stuffing. Not surprisingly, empty platitudes often filled the commentaries of these journalists. To Lieutenant-Colonel X, who wrote for the mass daily *Le Journal,* was attributed the following truisms: "The essential trait necessary for winning a battle is to be the stronger," "an army that retreats ceases immediately to gain territory," and "the true formula for war is to achieve the maximum results with the minimum losses." The *Canard* mocked similar empty phrases from the pen of Marcel Hutin, who wrote for *L'Echo de Paris.* In February 1917, the *Canard* provided its own military commentator, Colonel Poucet (a wink at Lieutenant-Colonel Rousset, who wrote for *Le Petit Parisien*). Poucet explained the virtues of the French soldier, who was always eager to attack, and discussed how easy it would be to launch victorious offensives in virtually every sector. His article had an optimistic ending that, in early 1917, could easily be read with bitter irony: "What is certain is that this future, very close, I insist, has in store for us only the most agreeable, the most comforting, the most miraculous surprises."[47]

But the *Canard* held more than empty rhetoric against the press. Journalists' patriotic optimism had made of them bad prophets. According to the *Canard,* Lieutenant-Colonel X had said of the German action that it was "the last spasm of the ferocious dying beast" during the Battle of the Marne (in 1914), then again during the Battle of the Yser, and he was now recycling it in September 1916 during the Battle of the Somme. The *Canard* went on to mock all the war prophets (including Barrès and Hervé), who, though they were only predicting for a month to ninety days in the future, always seemed to be wrong.[48] In all fairness, few foresaw the length of the First World War, even after the opening battles.[49] And the *Canard* could see this difficulty and shift to a gentler, more indulgent, irony. In April 1917, Bringer pretended to attack the other *Canard* writers and to defend the skull stuffers: "these poor and brave people who seek to make us see the future through rose-colored glasses, to scratch us precisely where we itch." How would we have reacted, the French journalist asked, if we had been told, in 1914, how it would really turn out, that "in April 1917 the krauts will have barely left Noyon"?[50]

But if the "military critics" so consistently got it wrong, the real cause for the *Canard* was that, like the other journalists, these critics had no real knowledge of what life was like in the trenches. Accordingly, the weekly reported on a visit to the front by the most important military critics (with their names barely altered). The journalists are stunned to discover that the French and German trenches are separated from each other by lines of barbed wire—two lines since the Germans have theirs too.[51] And there were plenty of ways of underlining the nonbelligerence of these military experts. In an article on the "aces" of the press, the *Canard* claimed that General Cherfils, military expert for *L'Echo de Paris,* had "shot down his fiftieth reader." Similarly, the weekly asked, in July 1918, with mock surprise, why Lieutenant-Colonel Rousset, after four years of service "in the trenches of the rue d'Enghien," had still not been promoted to full colonel.[52]

By July 1916, patriotic journalism had become so formulaic that de la Fouchardière felt able to offer up the recipe to his readers. For the Academicians' article, he suggested that to "Teutonic barbarism" you oppose the "clear French genius nourished for many centuries by the milk of the virgin of Lorraine." For this and other typical passages, de la Fouchardière provided references to the writers and newspapers that abused these topoi. Taking a swipe at the contradictions between the ambient racist chauvinism and the multiculturalism of the Allied armies, he advised the beginner to be sure to enumerate all the "virtues of the French race. And, of course, in the French race you include also our friends the English, our heroic Senegalese infantry, and the admirable Cossacks of the Don."[53]

The *Canard* pilloried the anti-German hysteria that was challenging the traditional French reputation for good sense. Some aspects of the hysteria needed no exaggeration. In November 1916 the *Canard* reported, under the subtitle "Our Superiority," the finding of a specialist in "ethno-chemistry": German urine was one-third more toxic than French. Sometimes, however, pastiche made it easier to generalize the target. The *Canard* interviewed a Dr. Obnubile, formerly a pacifist and now converted to the virtues of "our holy and just war." After examining women who had suffered under enemy occupation, the good doctor concluded that "the Germans must have barbed foreskins, classic sign of the well-known ferocity of anthropologists." The sympathetic interviewer added that French historians were right to show how Wagner sanctioned rape and Goethe had stolen his best poems from the songs of upper Alsace; the historians thus provided a great service to "our sweet France, of which the acuteness of the critical sense and moderation in all things are the most exquisite qualities."[54]

Several techniques serve the *Canard*'s politics here. "Anthropologists" spoofs *anthropophages,* or cannibals. More significantly, the points about Wagner and Goethe, which were not outside the norm for wartime propaganda, were rendered ridiculous by their association with the sillier foreskin argument. The comment about French critical sense and moderation works both as a satire on the self-congratulatory appreciation of French culture and an appeal to these very same virtues against wartime hysteria.

The *Canard* took a dim view of imbecilic anti-Germanism, but it was not above exploiting, in a racist way,[55] the foreign origin of purveyors of patriotic palaver. One of the weekly's favorite targets (which survived the war) was a journalist for *Paris-Midi* whose pen name was Maurice de Waleffe. The *Canard* pilloried de Waleffe for the usual journalistic crimes: for abetting the assassination of Jean Jaurès, for pledging to go to war and then staying home, and for the normal patriotic bombast. But de Waleffe was Belgian, the weekly informed its readers, and his real name was Cartuyvels. Not only was the Flemish Cartuyvels much less French sounding than de Waleffe, but in later issues the *Canard* transformed it into Kartoffel, which had the advantages of being German and of carrying the less-than-noble meaning of potato.[56]

The *Canard* was an anticlerical newspaper. Its position was summed up in the phrase "religion: it is the mysterious; it is rarely good sense."[57] So the *Canard* did not like attributing important events to God and his saints. It considered such attributions a particular form of *bourrage de crâne* when those same results should, in the weekly's estimation, have been credited to more terrestrial agents—like France's heroic front-line soldiers. The weekly had no difficulty exploiting the inconsistency of the selective use many conservative Catholic writers made of the idea of divine providence. For those who thanked Saint Genevieve for saving Paris a second time at the Battle of the Marne, the *Canard* asked, And where was she at the French defeat at Charleroi?[58]

The patron saint of Paris received her funniest treatment from the pen of H. P. Gassier. In June 1918, as Allied troops were barely stopping the German offensive toward Paris while Clemenceau held the home front together, Gassier's cartoon was entitled "They Will Not Pass. Reapparition of Saint Genevieve."[59] It showed a group of German soldiers stopped by the winged figure of Clemenceau. Not only did this cartoon replace a superhuman with the appropriate worldly agency, but it mocked the Catholic saint by changing her into the old anticlerical politician. Along the way, the *Canard* was also satirizing the rallying of the Catholic right (and the French Catholic hierarchy) behind the Radical Clemenceau.[60] As often with the satirical weekly, the cartoon could be read two ways: as a patriotic salute to Clemenceau or as a spoof of the whole cult of the energetic president of the Council of Ministers.

Anti-German propaganda in World War I also made heavy use of atrocity stories. In their invasion of Belgium and northeast France, German forces had frequently acted against civilians and had burned whole villages on the flimsiest of pretexts. These "war crimes" incited the circulation of far more lurid charges. Without questioning the horrors of war (and without granting any certificates of virtue to the Germans) the *Canard* nevertheless tried to expose the mechanism by which anti-German rumors developed. In an issue (its fourth) devoted to rumors and rumor mongering, the *Canard* told of a journalist investigating the story of a little French boy who, on a visit to Germany before the war, had had his right hand cut off before being returned to his country. After following up a long chain of witnesses who each had heard the story from someone else, our writer finally finds the boy who had injured (but not gravely) his hand by pushing it through the window of a railroad car on his arrival at the Gare de l'Est.[61]

The lack of accuracy of the mass press was a central theme of the *Canard*—after all it was reflected in its name. Often, however, it was enough for the weekly to show that what the press wrote was not even possible. When *Le Matin* wrote, to show the nefarious activities of the Bolsheviks, that one of these revolutionaries was carrying five hundred thousand gold rubles to make purchases for Germany, the *Canard* wondered what Russian would be strong enough to carry 387 kilograms (about 800 pounds) of gold.[62]

The prize in the area of wartime skull stuffing went to the patriotic gore of tales of battlefield heroism. With so much improbable heroism, the *Canard* had but to choose. The judicial reporter of Hervé's *La Victoire* wrote, according to the *Canard,* of a soldier who "had lost his left arm on the Yser, his right eye in Champagne, and in the trenches of Craonne his right side was pierced." So, the *Canard* explained, "a man who had lost his left arm at the Yser was nevertheless sent (upon the advice of doctors, evidently) to the Champagne front, where he lost, this time, his right eye," and so on.[63] Then there was the one about the English soldier, reported in *La Presse,* who exclaimed "Zut" after having his lower jaw blown away. The enchained duck answered: "Try to pronounce 'Zut!' *in English* while deprived of the lower jaw."[64]

Given the kind of heroic stupidities bred by wartime journalism, finding these citations was not too difficult. Canards, in the sense of false stories, silly stories, impossible stories, there were aplenty. Sometimes, however, the satirical weekly made life just a bit too hard on the frustrated journalists of France's wartime newspapers through its habit of providing true/false news—and its habit of mixing, without warning, satire with real reporting.

What if the "serious" press took seriously a made-up story of the *Canard*? In July 1916, a page 1 story in the *Canard* purported to puncture a German bluff. A German submarine specially designed to carry cargo, the *Deutschland,* had crossed the Atlantic, and the ship was in Baltimore harbor. The *Canard* journalist explained that the sub had never crossed the Atlantic, it had been put together secretly, at night, in Baltimore harbor by German Americans. Two weeks later, in the same front-page position, the weekly explained with surprise laced with triumph that though the story was intended as a joke, several newspapers, including *La Liberté,* had reported the explanation seriously to their readers. The *Canard* reminded its audience of its promise (not kept, it is true) to provide only demonstrably false information. Later in that same issue, the *Canard* reprinted an article from *L'Oeuvre* in which de la Fouchardière explained the whole game. The original piece had been written by one of the *Canard*'s humorists, Victor Snell (it was signed Berthelier). De la Fouchardière went on to explain that Snell had wanted to write another article explaining that the submarine was blocked in the harbor by a giant sardine, but he renounced the idea for fear that the information would end up in *Le Temps,* the most respectable paper of the day.[65] There were other cases, as the war wore on, of stories by *Canard* humorists taken up as fact by other papers.[66] Nothing better illustrated the way satire and reality continually approached each other in the cockeyed world of French World War I journalism. And nothing better illustrated the aptness of the *Canard*'s rhetorical formula for navigating, and combating, that journalism.

GUIDE TO THE PRESS

A true unstuffing of French skulls demanded a more skeptical attitude to the whole press enterprise, especially that of the ostensibly neutral and accurate mass press. Thus, the *Canard* sought to expose the unreliability of contemporary journalism and to show how this unreliability, rather than being accidental or even the result of wartime constraints, was linked to the way most newspapers were put together. A counter-newspaper, the *Canard* was also what we today would call a media critic.

Being a counter-newspaper involved ridiculing standard journalistic forms. The *dernière heure,* frequently present in other papers, was one. Sometimes the satire was cleverer. The highlight of most newspapers' front page was the daily communiqué put out by the military authorities, to which many readers undoubtedly turned first. In the same format, the *Canard* put its "Communiqués de l'arrière" (Communiqués from the rear), which reported on the less than heroic activities of the civilians behind the lines.[67]

Bit by bit, the *Canard* introduced its readers to a few of the secrets of journalism. The well-known writer Pierre Mac-Orlan explained that "literary criticism and art criticism have as their first goal to show off the erudition of the critic. If space remains, one concerns oneself with the genius or the errors of the object of the criticism."[68] In the introduction, we saw Dorgelès's admission of false reporting. The journalists of the *Canard* understood too, for example, how articles were written in advance. The weekly reported that the death of the Austrian Emperor Franz Josef caught a major paper with its obituary writer absent. So a biography was pulled from the files. Only after the paper was already being printed did someone notice that this text, written before the war, treated the Hapsburg with a respect inappropriate for the ruler of an enemy nation. Hastily the edition was pulled, reprinted, and went out several hours late.[69]

Sometimes the papers were not so lucky. The major Paris papers boasted that their wire services brought them news from around the world first (satirized by the *Canard*'s "barbed wire" from Berlin). The need to meet deadlines could, however, get them into veritable Dewey/Truman difficulties. On November 8, 1916, the major Parisian papers announced the election of the Republican candidate, Mr. Hughes, as president of the United States. Better still, they had explained how this result was best for France. Two days later, they had to correct themselves and announce the victory of Woodrow Wilson. They then, however, explained that the victory of the Democrat was the better result from the point of view of the Allies. Coming to the aid of its embarrassed colleagues, the *Canard* offered them a model article; it praised the victor of the U.S. elections, called the results a victory for France and the cause of justice, and so forth, but all the while scrupulously avoided giving away the identity of the lucky candidate. And the *Canard* drew the moral for its readers: "The public wants assurances. The public wants news. That the first should be categorical, that the second should be correct, that is of no importance. And such is the explanation for the extraordinary good fortune of the *Canard Enchaîné*, which publishes, without looking twice, the true and the not true, the false and the apocryphal. In this it is like the other newspapers. But the difference is that it says so."[70]

Of course, for most U.S. elections there are only two likely results. When the traitor Bolo Pasha was executed in April 1918, the *Canard* published a systematic analysis of the coverage of this incident in the major Paris dailies. These sources agreed on nothing: the time of the execution, whether Bolo agreed to sign a paper, whether he accepted the succor of the Church, the number of shots he received, the size and composition of the execution squad.[71] The *Canard* wanted to dispose of any reputation for accuracy that still stuck to the mass press. In July 1918, our journalistic bird caught *Le Matin* with two opposing explanations of an Austrian retreat at the Piave River. On page 1 it was because the river was a swollen torrent; on page 3 the same river (at the same moment) was described as being almost completely dry.[72]

That articles were not always written by the people named in the bylines was an open secret for all journalists, though not always apparent to the average reader. When the *Canard* used made-up bylines, it was all in good fun—and many of the phony bylines were transparent jokes. The results could mislead however. If the submarine story had been attributed to Victor Snell, it might not have been taken seriously. In either case, the *Canard* treated false bylines in the mass press as another manifestation of the general dishonesty of the journalism of its day; in November 1916, it accused Charles Humbert, a skull stuffer at *Le Journal,* of taking credit for articles written by Jean Weber. Generalizing its charge a year and a half later, our weekly reported on the formation of a professional organization of journalists: "A member has already asked that journalists be obliged to 'write their articles themselves.' If this judicious proposition is adopted," the *Canard* argued, "several important bylines will disappear soon from the public sheets."[73]

ADVERTISEMENTS AND INDEPENDENCE

In one sense, nothing was more typical of the French mass press than advertisements. Not that French papers of the war years carried that many. They had always had fewer than most papers do today, and the war further restricted their ability to attract commercial notices.[74] Nevertheless, it was advertisements that allowed the mass press to exist, that underwrote its expenses, just as it was advertisers who demanded the large markets that underlay the mass press's relatively apolitical posture. Such apoliticism was only relative to the highly ideologically charged world of French journalism during the Third Republic. And the *Canard,* through its attacks on the mass press, both during and after the war, highlighted the mass press's generally conservative conformism.

Ads were as subject to pastiche as any other element of contemporary journalism. The *Canard* provided phony ads, placed exactly where real ads would be, satirizing the ads of the time along with other political and social topics.[75] But the *Canard* also attacked advertising in general. As Victor Snell put it, advertising was unstoppable, the true fourth estate (dethroning, thus, the press in general).[76]

Another *Canard* author explained the gravity of the matter when the government floated a project to tax patent remedies, the makers of which were the principal advertisers in the press of the time. "There is a parliament ignorant enough, forgetful enough of the great and ineluctable laws of History, to strike with a criminal tax the pills, Rob logs, granules, suppositories, pessaries, pomades, syrups, plasters, eyewashes, juleps, tinctures, youth potions, beauty potions, invigorating drops, and other laboratory manifestations of French science. These committers of sacrilege have, then, not seen that in meddling with these specialties they were attacking the freedom of the Press—of the mass press?—because, I ask you, what does it live on, this mass press?" The *Canard* answered its own question: "Everyone knows that if it [the mass press] has managed to dethrone the little press of opinion, still mired in the archaic rut of convictions and doctrines, it is because it has been able to organize for its service all the public urinals of France!" Thanks to syphilis, constipation, diarrhea, and other banes of existence, "it fills its pockets, its inkwells, and the skulls of its readers."[77] Strengthening the *Canard*'s satire was the bisociation of the mass press and barely mentionable infirmities. That so much of the commercial prose available to the papers during the war came from purveyors of what were often no more than snake-oil remedies only facilitated the *Canard*'s attack.

The *Canard Enchaîné* exploited the state of French journalism. World War I was something of a watershed in the evolution of the French press. After it, smaller, more ideological periodicals found it increasingly difficult to survive. But the mass press that was replacing them was still new enough to be subject to criticism, not just of its wartime exaggerations but also of its distinctive qualities and methods. Attacking the journalistic world of wartime France, the *Canard* also critiqued emerging forms of mass culture.

The commercial underpinning of the mass media is well known today—though it was certainly less evident to the average Frenchman of 1917 than the phrase "everyone knows" would imply. The *Canard*'s attack can be read as a defense of the older press of opinion, which was losing its competition with the newer, more informational, nominally more neutral mass press. But the satirical weekly was also a product of the mass press, off which it lived as surely as any parasite lives off its host. The mass press was one of the conditions without which the *Canard*, at least as we have it, would have been inconceivable.

The "enchained" weekly made a fetish of its freedom. Throughout its history it has trumpeted the fact that it has lived exclusively from its subscriptions and newsstand sales (and all the evidence suggests that it has). The *Canard*'s boasts of independence were not, however, directed only at the commercialism of the mass press. It was also well known in journalistic and political circles that France's flourishing collection of newspapers of doctrine and opinion could not survive on their sales or on the modest ad revenues that their limited circulations could justify. For the public, newspapers, as we saw, ran contribution campaigns. But the most important contributions came from rich individuals who supported the paper's positions, from economic groups who wanted to influence these positions, and from the secret funds of the French government and those of a large variety of foreign governments. The "abominable venality of the French press" eventually became a stock phrase among its critics.[78]

Thus, warring newspapers could always question each other's sources of support. The more chauvinist ones could hint at a German source for the funds of their opponents. For example, in July 1917, Hervé and a center-left journalist, Alfred Dubarry, were demanding to know each other's financial sources while refusing to unveil their own. After satirically imagining that all the papers would have to reveal their sources to Gustave, the *Canard* took the trouble to expose its own: its forty thousand readers. Of course, it might take some time to get all the names and addresses to the former antimilitarist: "Many of our readers are at the front, and if, after this month delay that I am asking of you, some of them, because they will have been killed, are no longer able, alas!, to give us their name or their address, I am counting on your great good will not to hold it against them."[79] The *Canard* was not above covering its claim of independence with the sacrifices of French soldiers. But then, its whole attack on *bourrage de crâne* and on the mass press in general always had as its background the fact that while journalists were playing with reality in their pages, men were dying in a real war.

Yet, the *Canard*'s games with truth and falsehood did not mean that it might not turn out to be the most reliable source of information. On October 25, 1916, the *Canard* boasted that it was unrivaled as a source of false news. But the weekly also reserved for itself another specialty, that of occasionally being able to affirm news that no one else in the press either had access to or would print. In this case, alone among the Parisian press, the *Canard* had announced, two weeks earlier, the coming departure of Mr. Richard as director of the powerful Sûreté Générale. Now that the event had taken place, the weekly took the occasion to mark the point.[80]

Since the 1970s, the *Canard Enchaîné* has become the premier (for a long time the only) practitioner of American-style investigative journalism in France. The far poorer *Canard* of the war and interwar years had neither the resources nor probably the desire for this kind of specialization. But already during the Great War, and with gradually increasing frequency after, the *Canard* used its much-vaunted independence to deliver little scoops, to dig out and publish what other papers would not.[81]

By its origins, its specialized readership, and its clear ideological preferences, the *Canard* belonged with the opinion newspapers, of which it has been, in a sense, the sole real survivor. But the weekly was tied to the mass press of its day. Through a characteristic irony, the *Canard Enchaîné*, which trumpeted its falsehood, put itself in a position to deliver, with maximum credibility, the truth. A left-wing paper, a counter-newspaper, the *Canard* could also be an investigative newspaper.

4 The Tears of *L'Intran*

Semiotic Hijacking and Wartime Anxieties

Tears there were aplenty in World War I France: tears of widows, tears of fiancées who would never marry, tears of now-childless mothers, tears of civilians confronted with trainloads of wounded, tears of soldiers about to go under chloroform and fearing for their limbs. And despite the better-known stories of the patriotic reaction to the mobilization, even mobilization was greeted in many towns and villages with tears of anticipation for the losses of war.[1]

The relative absence of lacrimation in the *Canard Enchaîné* is striking. In part, this lack was due to the weekly's humoristic vocation. But the *Canard's* dearth of tears went further, to a general avoidance of death and mourning. The periodical's position on the war was not the whole explanation, either. The occasional postwar *Canard* writer Roland Dorgelès, who displayed a patriotic antimilitarism similar to the *Canard's*, nevertheless exploited the sympathetic tears of civilian witnesses in his novel *Les croix de bois* (The wooden crosses). Only after an episode of civilian emotion are the combat soldiers, the work's principal protagonists, allowed to cry, though the combat they were involved in was far from their first.[2] Dorgelès's use of tears was close to the type of lachrymose activity the *Canard* attacked.

TEARS AND PASTICHE

But in one area the *Canard* not only spoke of tears but made them a major focus: the tears of *L'Intransigeant. L'Intran,* as it was more popularly known, had been founded in 1880 by the savagely brilliant radical journalist Henri Rochefort as a socialist and hence leftist and nonconformist daily. The Boulanger affair in the late 1880s brought it to clear revanchist and militarist positions so that, when it fell into new hands in 1909, the conservative nationalism it adopted was not then too out of character.[3]

The wartime *Intran* made heavy use of tears as markers of patriotic emotion. The *Canard* created from this habit a counter-discourse that hijacked the original symbol and transformed it into a signifier of journalistic overkill. In so doing, however, the weekly exposed anxieties over male disempowerment and the instability of gender roles. Shedding tears is a bodily function, and it is not surprising that the entire treatment of this issue in the *Canard* is strongly colored by issues of corporality—from those of eroticism to those of disability.

For the *Canard, L'Intran* was one of the worst purveyors of *bourrage de crâne.* The "begonias" column of June 26, 1918, featured a story from the nationalist paper about how the dietary restrictions in Berlin were so severe that children were often born without nails and even without skin.[4] Most of the *Canard*'s other anti-*bourrage* campaigns were personality driven, as with those against Barrès and Hervé. The newspapers of these journalists were pilloried essentially as the mouthpieces of those two heroes of the verbal battlefields. With *L'Intran* it was different. The *Canard* zeroed in on the paper and on its characteristic patriotic anecdotes. The focus on anecdotes, usually published anonymously, shifted attention away from the journalists who signed the longer, more important, articles. But the *Canard* singled out these anecdotes because they carried an ideologically charged manipulation of wartime tears. The satirical weekly fused tears and *L'Intransigeant* into a single humorous topos that survived well into the years of peace.

The chosen vehicle of the duck/newspaper was a pastiche contest for its readers. On July 10, 1918, the *Canard* reprinted a pastiche of an *Intran* anecdote from the pages of the leftist, antimilitarist paper *La Vérité.* The *Canard* invited readers to submit their own pastiches of *L'Intran*'s infamous anecdotes, or "echoes" as they were called.[5] Instituting this contest was clever; and not just because the *Canard* got free copy from its readers. Writing a pastiche (or reading one) is the best way to become aware of the formulaic elements in a particular discourse. Once humor has been recognized in the pastiche, it is then irresistibly called up by the model. And having the *Canard*'s readers engage in the kind of witty parody usually the province of the paper's writers reinforced the complicity that, as we have seen, was one of the paper's major appeals.[6]

The contest rules did not explicitly require tears, but they did specify that the entries should be both sentimental and "whimpering" *(pleurnichard).*[7] Perhaps more important, the *Canard* attached tears to *L'Intransigeant* even where not originally present. On July 24, two weeks after the announcement of the contest, the *Canard* presented an anecdote from another paper, the *Petit Journal,* but described this moderately conservative paper as one "that the anecdotes from *L'Intran* keep from sleeping." The story made no reference to tears, but the *Canard* provided its own in its commentary: "Moved to tears by this little story . . ." The association between lachrymose displays and the nationalist paper dictated their joint presence in this journalistic tidbit, which contained neither element in its original form.[8]

Tears or not, the *Canard*'s readers flooded their newspaper with imitation *Intran* anecdotes. Twenty-five in all were published from July 24 to October 9, 1918—a period that saw the tide of battle turn definitively and that witnessed the victorious offensives that forced Germany to ask for an armistice in November. The optimism of this last phase of the Great War might have made it somewhat easier to joke about tears, but the *Canard*'s contest was first announced on July 10, when German troops were still at the Marne and before the first of Ferdinand Foch's victorious offensives.

Not content to let its readers derive their impressions of a typical *Intran* anecdote from that paper itself, the *Canard Enchaîné* provided guides to "the real thing" during the second half of 1918. The "begonias" column of August 14 carried a teary story from the pages of *L'Intransigeant.* A colonel asks the men in his battalion to step forward, first those who have been wounded five times, then four, then three, two, and eventually those who were only wounded once. Out of six hundred men, only two have received no wounds at all. Sensing their isolation, the colonel consoles them: "Do not cry. You will get it on some coming occasion."[9] And the *Canards* of that same July 1918 that saw the contest begin offered other evidence of what an *Intran* anecdote should look like. There is the story from the *Petit Journal* that the *Canard* had likened to an *Intran* story. In this narrative, a fashionable Parisienne, descending the stairs to the Metro, breaks her high heel. In a gallant gesture, an American (the story does not say but we presume he is a soldier in uniform) puts his knee to the ground, takes off her shoe, uses the stairway to repair the heel, and puts the shoe back on the young lady's foot. Like old friends, the two go down the stairs together.[10]

Another hint could be derived from the *Intran* pastiche that had marked the birth of the contest in the issue of July 10. Here again are American males and a Parisian young woman, but the shoe is on the other foot. A *midinette,* or young female dressmaker, has just come back from the public celebration of the U.S. military contribution. She spies three U.S. soldiers and graciously gives them the three flowers remaining in her bouquet, pinning one on a lapel of each "Yank." Without warning, a fourth American serviceman appears, his heart heavy because he has not received a flower. Virtually without hesitation, our *midinette* hikes up her skirt, showing her pale skin, removes her garter belt, and presents it to the stunned American.

In the fall of 1918, after the contest was over, the *Canard* provided two last examples of *L'Intran* prose. On October 16, under the title "The Real Echoes from *L'Intran*," the paper quoted a story of a meeting attended by Marshal Joseph Joffre and the U.S. trade unionist Samuel Gompers. Though neither knew the language of the other, they understood each other perfectly, and Gompers shouted, "Vive la France" after a speech by Joffre.[11] A model story appeared under the heading "Nothing Can Beat the Real Thing" nine days after the armistice. Introducing this item (again in the "begonia" patch), the *Canard* explained that wonderful as the contest entries had been, they could not outdo the original. A U.S. soldier, seeking to participate in his own way in the victory celebration, bought an American flag and dipped it respectfully at each passing group of uniformed Frenchmen. A group of Frenchwomen who witnessed this decided to return the honor by themselves kissing the stars and stripes, an act that brought tears to the eyes of the Yankee.[12]

TEARS, SEX, AND FOREIGNERS

In the five stories just discussed—three actual *Intran* anecdotes, one *Intran*-like story from another paper, and one pastiche—the incidents vary superficially. Two thematic elements, however, stand out in the collection. The first, that of tears, shows up in two of the three *Intran* stories, while the soldier in the pastiche has "a heavy heart." These tears take the expression of sorrow and mourning, transfer it from its logical wartime place (or places), and reverse its impact from negative to positive. From signifiers of pain and loss, tears become indices of patriotic pride and the joys of communion. The reversal is probably clearest in the case of the wounded-soldiers anecdote from *L'Intran*. It is not those whose bodies have been torn by iron that shed tears, but those unfortunates who have been spared.

Yet, there is a second topos, one more ideologically ambivalent. Three of the five examples involve relations between U.S. servicemen and Frenchwomen. In some cases (like the pastiche), the sexuality of this encounter is explicit (as the lady flashes her leg); in others, like the shoe-repair story from the *Petit Journal*, it remains largely implicit. Significantly, the last *Intran* citation, the unbeatable–real thing echo, combined both elements, testifying to their centrality to the *Canard*'s image of the *Intran* echo. Did the *Canard*'s reader-contestants share these thematic foci? Eighteen of the twenty-five entries feature tears of patriotic emotion. The readers, like the editors of the satirical weekly, saw the tears as essential elements, and they, thus, participated in the *Canard*'s counter-metamorphosis of the *Intran*'s tears.

One example, published on July 24, mocked these patriotic tears by mixing species. A crowd of French men and women, their eyes moist with tears, acclaim U.S. soldiers on parade. A French dog is sad, however, because he cannot express his appreciation to these soldiers of democracy. He seizes a begonia and drops it at the feet of the marching soldiers. One of them, not seeing the canine, crushes him under his feet. "Then, under the emotion-filled eyes of the crowd, the little dog holds back the tears that are about to come and begins again to acclaim our allies."[13]

Here tears are satirized through overkill: first the crowd has tears in its eyes, then the dog holds back his, and even at the end the people have "emotion-filled eyes." Of course, dogs do not have tears to hold back, which highlights the absurdity of the situation. But a shadow hangs over this sendup of rhetorical overkill and patriotic pablum. The dog, symbol of France in its description (lively and intelligent like a French animal, not a brutal, sauerkraut-eating Pomeranian), is crushed under the heels of the foreign, albeit allied, army. The resulting ambivalence about the soldiers of democracy will appear again.

With its exaggerated teariness and its rhetorical winks to journalistic begonias, this story was quite distinct from its *Intran* forebears. Most of the other pastiches stuck closer to their models, especially in the placement of teardrops. In most cases, the tears appear among the onlookers, occasionally among the direct participants, after the event has taken place. As with the *Intran* originals, they are the visible signs of the emotion underlying the patriotic acts. Their ridiculousness stems from the situations out of which they arise. These phony anecdotes burlesque the patriotism-on-the-cheap that lay behind so much wartime propaganda. Part of the problem with these tears of civilians, and other noncombatants, was their inappropriateness to the far smaller sacrifices they were called on to make. Another entry, published on July 31, tells of a maid who has to inform her master first that there is no coffee and then that there is no milk because of the war—a joint realization that brings moisture to both pairs of eyes. Beyond the joking references to wartime shortages (a staple of *Canard* humor during these years),[14] the anecdote plays on the lack of fit between the lachrymose reaction and the sacrifice in question.

Civilians were targeted in World War I France by, among other things, the German "Big Bertha" artillery piece that shelled Paris in mid-1918.

Two pastiches echoed the campaigns that celebrated the heroism of the residents of the French capital. The ninth contest entry explains how the Parisians, rather than fleeing the shells in terror, eagerly gather up souvenir shell fragments. The police try to get them to leave by warning of another round, but this admonition only incites the civilians further, as they insist that they will then be perfectly located to collect fragments. Moved to tears, the police give in to this display of patriotic courage.[15] The comparison between civilian and military courage is more explicit in the eighteenth entry, published in September. A group of civilians assures some skeptical soldiers that they can stand up to enemy fire as well as they. Faced with the incredulity of the professionals, a fat lady runs to put herself under the impact of an incoming shell.[16] The mockery in both cases comes not only from the absurdity of comparing military to civilian courage but also from the genuine terror, leading in many cases to departure from the capital, that was the result of the German bombardment of Paris in the spring of 1918.[17]

As in the *Intran* (or pseudo-*Intran*) examples, four entries created more or less erotic encounters between Allied soldiers and attractive young Frenchwomen. Two meetings are relatively innocent. A young Parisian woman spies a British soldier (a "Tommy") who is unhappy with the gloriously worn-out state of his military greatcoat. With a characteristically Parisian gesture, the elegant young woman pulls a new greatcoat from her bag and presents it to the soldier before discretely running off.[18] In the first published echo from a *Canard* reader, a *midinette* (symbol of working-class femininity) pins her cockade on the chest of a Tommy. When he protests, she insists, explaining that her grandfather had been killed at Waterloo. But when an Italian soldier appears, she repeats her gesture, this time noting that her grandfather had "also" died at Solferino.[19] The parallel has limits (the French fought the Austrians, not the Italians, at Solferino), but beyond the absurdity of dying twice (and forty-odd years apart) is the point that these friends of France have not all always been so.

The connection is a bit more intimate in two pastiches published in the issue of August 21. In the first, a young woman runs off in her underclothes after giving her skirt to a Scots soldier whose kilt is combat-worn; in the second, another young woman passes her face powder to a Senegalese soldier.[20] The barely suppressed eroticism of these encounters manifests a concern: that Frenchwomen will mate with foreign soldiers. Anxiety about women left behind was a staple of French war writing. ("I Wonder Who's Kissing Her Now" was sung by U.S. soldiers in that conflict.) The reliance on foreign troops added a special flavor to these concerns. A Gassier cartoon in the *Canard* of March 13 showed a U.S. soldier with an affectionate young Frenchwoman on each arm. His comment evoked Wilson's diplomacy: "And they say that this is not a war of conquest."[21] The year 1918 saw a constantly increasing number of U.S. troops in France. But even then, this contest produced seven pastiches that confronted Frenchwomen with French soldiers, compared with only four that placed them with foreigners. The *Canard*'s international encounters contrast with anecdotes in competing humor periodicals, which sought to dispel any ideas of Allied soldiers consorting with Frenchwomen.[22] More important, the contest's seven Franco-French encounters, when added to the international ones and a significant number of other echoes, expose a deeper level of anxiety over the effects of the war.

SUBVERSIONS AND INVERSIONS

In many ways, these pastiches of patriotism show the war as turning French society upside down. It is doubtful that that was the intention of their authors (or of the *Canard*). Humor thrives on play, on exaggeration, and on the reversal of expectations. But it can also expose unconscious or barely conscious issues. The false *Intran* anecdotes of the *Canard Enchaîné* showed the war as reversing or upsetting traditional relations between old and young, parent and child, man and woman.

Such subversion is most evident in the two echoes from August 21, that of the Scots and that of the Senegalese soldier. In the first, the kilted soldier not only receives but puts on the skirt of the now semi-nude Parisienne. This act makes him a transvestite—unless he already was one insofar as a kilt is a type of skirt. And he has entered this world of gender bending by accepting clothing from a woman. She is the active party, he the passive one. But this observation applies to the other anecdotes in which French *élégantes* provide coats or handkerchiefs to battle-worn *poilus,* acts that give these stories at least a whiff of gender subversion.[23]

The African story ads race to gender confusion. On the train a Senegalese breathes in delicious perfume and murmurs that someone certainly smells good. A *midinette* opens her box of face powder and offers it to the soldier. Then, under the tear-filled eyes of the onlookers, the Senegalese powders his "manly visage." Not only does this African cross gender boundaries by putting on ladies' makeup, but the white face powder takes him across racial divides as well. He is whitened as he is feminized.

But are these cases not just part of the burlesquing of wartime narratives? Certainly their transvestic qualities are part of their humor (and cross-dressing accompanies other war narratives, from *Grande Illusion* to *South Pacific*). But the role shifts and feminization they suggest are reflected in more subtle ways in other anecdotes, ones where the humor is less broad. Descending the stairs to the Bastille Metro station is a richly decorated but severely injured soldier with a cane on one side and a crutch on the other. He slips and falls. Multiple hands reach out to help him, but one person insists on guiding him down the stairs: a "triumphantly, proudly pregnant" Frenchwoman. (Need we add that the onlookers are in tears?)[24] The role reversal could hardly be more complete. Not only is the woman helping the man, but this is a pregnant woman, someone who normally would receive the courtesy of seat preference or other assistance in public transportation. The man has been rendered weak and helpless, effectively feminized, by his war-begotten wounds. That echo appeared on September 11. Three issues later we are at the post office, amid "smothered sobs." Why all the emotion? Because a soldier, his head swathed in bandages, has just bought a stamp but cannot lick it. A pretty girl comes to his rescue; she sticks out her tongue so that he can wipe the stamp across it.[25]

Against these multiple stories of women helping men, there is only one where a man helps an injured soldier (in this case by passing his already-lit cigarette to a wounded veteran).[26] The replacement of soldiers by women workers was commonplace in the First World War, and it becomes associated, in these anecdotes, with the gender-role reversals caused by war injuries. In another echo, a patriotic young woman is taking tickets on the bus to replace her husband, who is at the front.[27]

With the disruption of traditional male/female relations go those based on age, as soldiers become virtual infants.[28] In an echo published on August 14, a group of soldiers marches through a newly liberated village. The locals offer them free wine (by contrast most soldiers' accounts complain of the prices charged for wine). But when a last soldier arrives behind his comrades, the archetypical French beverage has run out. A suckling infant offers the thirsty warrior his mother's breast, to which a drop of milk still clings. Later in the contest, on October 9, a gravely weakened soldier, just returned from Germany, finishes his last few drops of milk. A young woman in the same train car pushes away the child from her breast and offers her maternal fluid to the needy hero. An old man watching this scene then joins in.[29] This pastiche was particularly apt since it mocked the kind of story (of the pitiful weakness of soldiers returned by the Germans) that the commander-in-chief, General Philippe Pétain, recommended to journalists.[30]

These echoes combine erotic play with a mockery of much of the patriotic imagery, which spoke of France as mother of her people (even Marianne was sometimes represented as a mother suckling her young).[31] But like so many of the other pseudo-*Intran* pieces, it shows a world where men are disempowered as they are turned into women or children. Women are eroticized as they are denuded (from the skirtless young woman who gives her garment to the Scots soldier to the nursing mother), but in a way that, as Marina Warner has shown, makes of them at the same time representations of power.[32] The relative powerlessness of the male is further underlined. Children even usurp the rights of adults. The child of a nouveau-riche mother reacts with horror as he sees her slathering herself with lotion from a bottle marked "Eau de Cologne." He jumps up from his crib, smashes the bottle on the floor, and crushes the pieces under his naked heels.[33]

SOCIAL CLASS

But does not humor demand these inversions of roles, these dissolutions of boundaries? Often, but not always. In fact, while so many social categories are challenged in these wartime fantasies, one set of distinctions seems to emerge strengthened: those of wealth and social class, as portrayed, for example, in the anecdote of the master and servant without milk or coffee. Though the French class system is held up to mild ridicule, it is shown as stable. The master remains master, and the servant respectful and dutiful.

Two more elaborate sendups of class relations also leave social boundaries intact. Two working-class young women *(midinettes)* are desperately unhappy because family difficulties have used up all their money and they have nothing with which to buy things to send to their war godson at the front. A handsome and decorated officer hears their story and hands them a banknote, a donation that brings tears to the eye of a watchful policeman. Charity links the working-class *midinettes* with the upper-class officer while maintaining their social distance.[34]

The survival of class distinctions, even in an environment of burlesque, stands out in an echo published in September 1918. An aristocratic lady offers dinner to a common soldier. She serves him in the pantry, where servants would eat. But the soldier is too intimidated by the grande dame to touch his food. To make him more comfortable, she commits the linguistic derogation of speaking to him in working-class slang. He is moved to tears by this display and kisses the hem of her skirt in gratitude. This story provides a commentary on the naive arrogance of the nobility—patriotically inviting the soldier to dinner but feeding him in the pantry. True, the lady apparently seeks to blur the barriers between them through a comically inappropriate use of language. But the important point here is that, in a sense, she fails. By kissing her hem, the lower-class male recognizes how unbridgeable the gulf between them is. A subtle reference to the need of some officers to "talk down" to their less educated soldiers may also be present.[35] The only anecdote with any suggestion of bridging classes describes how on a cold day a rich lady gives her fur coat to a poor female newspaper hawker (selling *L'Intran* and the *Canard*). Though here the transfer of clothing takes place uniquely across class lines, the act of charity defines the class differences, as the generous party is identified as a famous philanthropist.[36]

The tears of the *Canard* echo while they subvert those of *L'Intran*. If the conservative newspaper transformed the tears of tragedy into those of patriotic feeling, the *Canard* dissolved this last emotion into laughter. But in the fantasy of burlesque this transformation replaces one set of problems or anxieties with another. The war has feminized and weakened men; it has destroyed their bodies and turned traditional hierarchies upside down.[37] Only the French class system seems intact; French soldiers or their families victimized by the war will still feel the brunt of the division of society into rich and poor.

When announcing its contest in July, the *Canard* promised a half dozen bottles of wine to the winner. Was this too in jest? In any case no winner was ever named. When the last echoes were printed on October 9, the Germans had already requested an armistice. In its second peacetime issue, on November 20, the *Canard* closed the series with its example of the unbeatable-true *Intransigeant* anecdote. But the satirical weekly could not leave this story without comment. The *Intran* echo ended, one may remember, with the tears of the U.S. soldier. The *Canard*'s writers added that a French soldier, who saw the American's emotional response, collected the tears in his helmet, "and when the helmet was full. . . ." Besides echoing miracle stories (the overflowing liquid collected in a sacred receptacle), this narrative extension brings the wartime series to a fitting end. Tears are overflowing into peacetime, but the blood for which they are in many ways a substitute has itself, at least, ceased to flow.

POSTWAR TEARS

But where did these peacetime tears go (that is, after overflowing from the helmet)? They went to two, occasionally converging, streams. The first is the theme of patriotic emotion, as exploited in the press. For example, the *Canard* of March 9, 1921, celebrated (ironically) the renewed tensions between France and Germany through an evocation of the possibility that, with another war, the country could relive the glorious hours of the last one, replete with tears of patriotic emotion. No mention is made of *L'Intran,* but the mere mention of the tears was enough to evoke the wartime genre.[38] Here, tears signify both the horrors of war and the funnier, because verbal, ones of *bourrage de crâne.*

More often, however, this tears-as-patriotic-pablum stream mixed with the second system of references, that to *L'Intransigeant* itself. A story of February 9, 1921, imagined a French Rip Van Winkle who had fallen asleep at the time of the armistice only to awaken and ask whether the "Krauts" had paid—that is, paid the war reparations. The humor comes from the fact that the Germans were avoiding (and never did really pay) the reparations demanded of them by the victorious Allies (see chapter 11). But the paper sprinkled the story with plenty of patriotic tears (which can now take on another, more pessimistic, signification: that the Germans will not pay) as well as making a direct reference to *L'Intran.* The *Canard* returned to its combination of tears, *L'Intran,* and the end of the war over a year later by linking *L'Intran* to "de la larme . . . istice," a pun on *larmes*/tears.[39]

More important, this tarring of the right-wing newspaper with patriotic stupidity through the reference to lacrimation meant that anytime any *Canard* writer wanted to mock *L'Intran* all he had to do was to mention tears—and such mentions kept going through 1928. In the last of weeks of 1923, for example, while noting that none of the major papers were covering a story that embarrassed the government, the *Canard* said that *L'Intransigeant* could have done it with one eye, while shedding a patriotic tear with the other.[40] By combining the horrors of war with the silliness of *bourrage de crâne,* the *Canard*'s tears-of-*L'Intran* topos was an eloquent symbol of the weekly's history. Techniques forged in the journalistic battlefields of the Great War gave a distinctive character to the newspaper in the years of peace.

The *Canard* continued its series of echo contests throughout the 1920s. In 1921, there were echoes of *Excelsior,* which had begun to print patriotic anecdotes similar to those *L'Intran* had created during the war. The year 1922 saw a contest of echoes from *Le Matin.*[41] But try as they might, these upstarts could never challenge *L'Intransigeant*'s position in the *Canard* as the ultimate repository of a maudlin, and ultimately dangerous, patriotic sentimentalism. At the end of January 1924, the *Canard* introduced a "new series" of *L'Intran* echoes. After invoking the new political climate, from the rise in prices to the occupation of the Ruhr, the weekly noted, "And yet *L'Intransigeant* remains unchangeable and daily (especially daily). By it the little horizon-blue flower is still cultivated, along with patriotic emotion, the mother of all tears." (French uniforms were horizon-blue.) The postwar climate permitted clearer intimation of the cause-and-effect relationship between patriotic emotions and the losses that brought tears.

And the confrontation of real and false echoes was also more openly antimilitarist. In a 1924 *Intran* anecdote, as a troop of French soldiers passes, all the men take off their hats in respect, except for a small boy. An old man lifts the hat from the child's head until the flag has passed, saying that, next time, the boy should do that himself. In the *Canard* version, as the flag passes a desperate young man cannot take off his hat because he lacks both his arms. The old man removes the head covering and tells his younger fellow citizen that the next time he should go out bareheaded.[42] The armless young man is certainly a wounded veteran and, as such, the *Canard*'s ultimate answer to the patriotic sentimentalism of *L'Intransigeant.*

More was at stake in the weekly's transubstantiation of tears into laughter than antiwar politics. Finding the humor in life (even the sad parts of life) was—along with the life-affirming celebration of pleasure—part of the *Canard*'s raison d'être. Thus, in 1924, the weekly put into the mouth of Léon Bailby, editor-in-chief of *L'Intransigeant:* "Let us rush to cry about all things for fear of being obliged to laugh about them." This was a reversal of a quote by Pierre de Beaumarchais that the *Canard* proudly placed on its own masthead of April 15, 1925: "I hurry to laugh about everything for fear of being obliged to cry over it."[43]

5 Soldiers versus Profiteers

Class War as Patriotism

In the mid-1920s, the rightist politician Georges Valois explained that, for the French Communist, the bourgeois was really the *embusqué*, the draft dodger or shirker who had gotten himself a safe job in the rear.[1] The *Canard Enchaîné* was never really Communist (though it often echoed Communist positions), but it certainly tended to amalgamate the categories of *embusqués* and bourgeois, of wartime virtue and social class.

The *Canard* had an essentially binary view of wartime French society—heroes who did their duty and slackers who did not—except that this division was doubled by another—those who lived by work and wages (including soldiers) and those who did not. This last category ranged from big businessmen to landlords and even to small shopkeepers. Some figures could unite these binarisms, like the war profiteer, who exploited soldiers, workers, and the nation while avoiding combat.[2] The great divide between front-line fighters and the rest of society that was a dominant characteristic of all the belligerents, not only during the war but for years after, marked the *Canard* as well. But, for the weekly, patriotism also functioned as an uneasy cover for class warfare or, at the least, class resentments. The two divisions, fighters versus *embusqués* and exploiters versus exploited, did not always overlap. The result was expressed by the *Canard* less as a contradiction than as another typical creative tension, one that, unlike (for example) the binarisms of those pacifists analyzed by Thierry Bonzon,[3] stayed safely within the borders of patriotism.

FIGHTERS VERSUS *EMBUSQUÉS*

The second issue of the *Canard Enchaîné*, September 20, 1915, was dedicated to the *embusqué* (or more precisely to *les embusqués*). But the *embusqué* is not the person who does not fight, the weekly was quick to explain. An *embusqué* is someone who has the duty to fight but avoids it. Railroad or factory workers, like doctors or drivers, did not belong in this category of opprobrium. Not that all forms of economic activity were equally condoned. Merchants who overcharged the government or who speculated amid wartime shortages were clearly *embusqués,* as were all those who took the place of the combat soldier and hoped he would not return. Patriotic morality transformed an originally military distinction into a more class-conscious critique of exploitation in general.[4]

For the *Canard Enchaîné,* the *embusqué,* like the *bourreur de crâne,* became a stock source of humor. An issue in November 1916 included an advertisement (phony, of course) for a product called "L'Embuskéol," guaranteed to protect against "colics and trenches" and available in all the "pharmacies of the rear."[5] The newspaper also cheerfully accepted the fundamental humanness of wanting to protect one's loved ones. A cartoon of June 1917 pictured "the bad prayer of the good father." The elderly gentleman, on his knees before the altar, pleads, "Lord, make him an *embusqué!*" A hint of class shows up even here, however, since the father shows all the signs of bourgeois prosperity, from his watch chain to the top hat. A working-class parent might not have carried a sufficient charge of opprobrium—or of ridicule; a well-off (and one assumes reactionary) parishioner better fit the *Canard*'s anticlericalism.[6]

BUSINESS IS BUSINESS

Patriotism and social justice came together most efficiently in an attack on war profiteers—the businessmen (and women) who became wealthy at the expense of the nation in arms. The weekly could not just come out and state that suppliers to the French army were overcharging, nor did it have to. In a "review of the press," the September 1915 *Canard* noted (from an Austrian socialist newspaper) how Hungarian merchants had bought up cattle cheaply and then sold them at a scandalously high profit to the army. "It is certainly not the suppliers of the French army who would act in this way," the *Canard* concluded. Irony? Well, yes, but the title of the selection was more straightforward: "Business Is Business."[7] The collusion of politicians, journalists, and munitions makers was the subject of an imagined dialogue published in the *Canard* of October 17, 1917. The conclusion of the article: the French had recently separated church and state, but they should have made a still more important separation, that between war and commerce.[8]

Since the war is so profitable, the weekly suggested, businesspeople fear the end of hostilities. Already in December 1916, in response to talk of peace, an imagined Mr. Tarte insists that he dreads the thought since he owns a munitions factory.[9] The approach of the real end of the war in October 1918 renewed the *Canard*'s exploitation of the fear-of-peace motif. The same multiple-frame cartoon that showed Hervé and Barrès nonplussed by the prospect of an end to the slaughter also pictured a war profiteer, like a caricature capitalist, corpulent and well-dressed, hugging his piled-up sacks of money. Among his comments: "Oh no! No! Not yet!" If one adds this image to the implicit claim, made two issues later, that the industrialist André Citroën had made five hundred million francs from the war, one would think that, for the *Canard,* the war profiteer was the big businessman. Certainly, also, the weekly made clear its skepticism of the attempts by the French government to regain for the collectivity some of the enormous profits made from the war.[10]

But when the *Canard* said "war profiteer" or the equally injurious *mercanti,* it could have much smaller fry in mind as well. A mid-1917 cartoon showed a distinguished-looking Parisian gentleman talking to two shopkeepers who exude a robust prosperity but whose absence of glamour betrays their modest and rural origin. They stand amid their luggage in front of their coal store. The Parisian asks, "What! You are going back to your native region for good?" Their answer: "Why yes! This winter has aged us fifteen years." But the response is written in the Auvergnat-accented French that was a stock source of humor among Parisians: "Eh! oui! Chet hiver, nous-j-avons vieilli de quinge ans!" Such Auvergnat coal dealers were so common in the French capital after the middle years of the nineteenth century that they could still be exploited humorously in the middle of the twentieth in the Astérix comic-strip album *Le bouclier arverne.* The title of the cartoon in the *Canard,* "Their Fortune Made," makes it clear that these transplanted peasants have grown rich exploiting the coal shortage (which occasioned much *Canard* humor).[11]

Price-gouging shopkeepers certainly showed up in the pages of the wartime *Canard,* though criticism of them was not as important as it would become during the postwar inflation.[12] The point is important. Attacking *les gros* was always safe on the French left, but small shopkeepers were a mainstay of the Radical party (and to some degree also of the Socialists), both before and after the war. The weekly's willingness to go after this social group reflected new, war-born tensions. Nevertheless, the *Canard*'s defensiveness on this issue reflected a continuing ideological discomfort.

On May 30, 1918, the *Canard* devoted its anticlerical column, "Saint of the Week," to Saint Pothin. The name of this saint could also be written Potin, and he was the patron saint of grocers. The reference was (among other puns) to the grocery-store chain Félix Potin (still flourishing today). But the *Canard* was also attacking the role played by an executive of the grocery chain in the Clemenceau government Directorate of Provisions. The article recommended, "If your grocer, puffed up by the sufferings of the public, refuses to provide you, at short weight, with his rancid margarine, his horsemeat sausage, good people, address yourselves directly to Saint Pothin."[13]

Such suggestions of sharp business practices were hardly flattering to the guild of grocers. The corporative organ of the grocers even reproached the *Canard*'s de la Fouchardière for his claim that a kilogram weighed scarcely more than 850 grams as far as foodstuffs were concerned. The *Canard* writer who replied chided the grocers for their sensitiveness (did the generals protest when jokes about their absence of brains went the rounds?). But the weekly went on to argue that only the wholesalers were being criticized, not the retailers.[14]

The distinction works well ideologically since it is easier to stigmatize the faceless, and presumably more prosperous, wholesaler, but it does not fit the example (or the reference to Saint Pothin) because in World War I France cheese, butter, or meat was almost always measured out by the retailer. Despite these slips, *Canard* authors did try to direct blame toward middlemen. The "Conte du Canard" for September 5, 1917, made a pastiche of Voltaire's philosophical tales and told of a rich and pacific country in India that is attacked by its neighbors. With the men at the front, prices climb steeply. A wise man discovers that the wives of the producers of foodstuffs are selling them at the usual prices and that it is the "traffickers" at the wholesale market who are pushing up the prices. When half of these are decapitated, the prices return to their normal levels.[15] Here, the middlemen are to blame. Such a conclusion fits nicely with the *Canard*'s barely expressed anticapitalism.

The immorality of war profiteers was also unpatriotic since they took advantage of the war to extract their illicit profits. The antipatriotic element was all the clearer, however, when soldiers were the victims. Two *Canard* cartoons each exposed a different aspect of the problem. The first, in 1916, shows two battle veterans, tin cups in hand, standing before a counter behind which stands a smugly healthy barman. He says to the two soldiers, "Twenty-seven months at the front, evidently, that is not bad, but, me, I have done better: I have signed up for the second war loan."[16] The title of the cartoon, "The Heroic *Mercanti,*" provides one level of commentary, juxtaposing the heroism of the soldiers with the absence of the same by the civilian. But the self-satisfied look of the barkeep makes it clear that he has been getting rich on the soldiers, presumably by selling them poor wine at high prices—a common complaint in accounts by French veterans.[17]

A similar comparison appears in the second cartoon, of August 1917. The merchant (who has the robust look of a peasant) says to the combat soldier, "And me, do you think that I do not have to take risks? What if my merchandise spoils?" He receives the answer "Alas! It is still we who will eat it!"[18] One is reminded of the comment in Jean Giono's antiwar novel, *Le grand troupeau.* Speaking of the need to slaughter a sick pig before it dies, the old farmer advises his daughter, "Don't you be concerned about the disease; it is for the soldiers."[19] Even here, however, the *Canard* stopped with the *mercantis,* the middlemen, and did not take on the rural population directly. In this it was more squeamish than some other writers, like Barbusse, whose *Le feu,* published in 1916, had a child explain innocently to a group of front-line soldiers that his rural family hoped the war would go on since they were getting rich selling to the soldiers and the army.[20]

LANDLORDS

One could argue that these were bad merchants, that not all their colleagues were under attack. But some social and economic categories, despite their distance from the war, received no quarter from the satirical weekly. First among these were landlords. Indeed, the third issue of the *Canard* was dedicated to this group.

Referred to contemptuously by the slang term *probloc,* the landlord was pictured as a sour-faced, middle-class Scrooge and was honored with the title (traditional for that group) of Mr. Vulture. The commandments of the landlord include: "Only cash shalt thou worship," and "Thou shalt permit in thy house neither dog nor cat nor even child." Fortunately, the *Canard* observed, this grasping tribe had recently met its match: the moratorium. The moratorium was a suspension of rents, for the duration of the conflict, owed by mobilized men and their families. The *Canard* imagined an investigative reporter trying to actually see the moratorium. He finally meets this mythical beast, whose chief enemy is the equally antediluvian "Vautourius-Loyeritis" (Vulturus-Rentitis).[21]

But what if the landlord were a person of modest means who depended on the rents for his sustenance? The newspaper met this objection with the story of "the good landlord." A former bakery worker, he put aside enough savings to open his own bakery; after many years at this trade he had saved a comfortable sum that, for his retirement, he invested in a rental property. Two months later, when the war breaks out, his working-class tenants, who have not heard of the moratorium, try to pay him. He refuses. But how will he live since he has put all his savings into the building? The former baker goes back to being a simple worker. "Baking again the big golden loaves, he recovered his youth. . . . He smiled and sang from morning to evening."[22] Only salaried labor is truly uplifting, this moral tale suggests; and those whose incomes are damaged by the moratorium have but to go out and do a little honest labor.

From the one-sidedness of its social analysis, one would guess that the *Canard* counted more renters than landlords in its readership; and the argument is clearly made that the ravages of greedy landlords preceded the war. Yet here, too, the patriotic division of fighting soldiers versus greedy civilians sharpens the class-based critique. Under the headline "Is It Really True?" the *Canard* reported a motion allegedly passed by the syndicate of landlords. The motion stated that, given that the Germans would certainly have burned down Paris if they had entered the city (thus ruining the property of the landlords), given that the Germans were prevented from doing so by the victory of the Marne, given that among the heroes of the Marne there were certainly far more soldier-renters than soldier-landlords, and given, finally, that rents had gone up scandalously during the previous ten years, the landlords decided to receive no rents for the duration of hostilities and, once the war was over, to reduce all rents by 50 percent. As the war continued, the *Canard* maintained its solicitude for the moratorium and hostility toward landlords, returning to the issue, for example, in August 1916 and July 1917.[23]

Since the moratorium on rents was a good thing that came out of the war, which was a bad thing, it was also an irresistible source of irony. "From extreme evil can come good," explained the *Canard*'s Victor Snell, "and under the hard necessities of the war, beneficial reforms have been instituted. Thus, experience has shown that one can live quite well without drinking absinthe [a cheap, and unhealthy, spirit] and without paying one's rent." A few months later, the weekly presented its war aims, which were nothing less than a continuation of these, and similar, social reforms. First among the *Canard*'s war aims, thus, was the abolition of rents, if not of landlords as well, followed by the regular distribution to all men of draft age of the cheap red wine called *pinard* and of strong spirits on special occasions. This was the routine in the army, where wine rations were regular and *eau de vie* was distributed before offensives.[24] To list these goals was to show their temporary nature, including that of the moratorium on rents.

LIFESTYLES OF THE RICH

The *Canard* also focused on the fact that the war (though it did create some nouveaux riches) did nothing to bridge the fundamental gulf between rich and poor. Wartime restrictions on luxury consumables would have no real effect, it argued. When the parliament considered a ban on the sale of spirits *(alcools)*, the *Canard* explained that as a duck it drank only water and a bit of *pinard*. Thus it risked nothing. But neither did the rich deputies and ministers who had cellars full of brandies. It was the common people who would no longer be able to put a drop of *eau de vie* in their coffee.[25] The rich-versus-poor topos received military coloring on the occasion of the charity auction by the Hospice de Beaune, a hospital that owns some of the most famous vineyards in Burgundy. These fine wines would not be going to the troops, the paper noted.[26]

The year 1917 brought other restrictions, including those on the ingredients of pastries, so the *Canard* interviewed a pastry chef who insists that he can make his products from substitutes but dies in convulsions after eating a chocolate éclair made with tar and powdered bricks—"another victim of the war." In a cartoon a few months earlier, occasioned by a temporary closing of pastry shops, a crowd is pursuing "the bad Frenchman." What had he done? He had eaten a chocolate éclair. But then, an anonymous *(Canard)* writer noted in May 1917, "as I write these lines, thousands of warriors are fighting, while in Paris one of the questions most occupying everyone is the suppression of pastry."[27] Thus, even the humorous exploitation of the situation could be redeemed by making the military-versus-civilian distinction. In this way the *Canard* could, ideologically at least, eat its cake (or pastry) and have it too.

The limitation of restaurant meals to two courses invited comical commentary—but here linked to a criticism of the lifestyles of the rich. After all, how many poor people had to worry about a second course in a restaurant? It was easy to have fun with the idea of the state enforcing such rules; a cartoon of February 7, 1917, shows a portly policeman lifting his baton to stop a diner from eating a third course. But the next issue showed how little such restrictions affected those who could afford to indulge their appetites. The "Petites correspondances" for that week contained the following advice: certainly one was limited to two courses, but one could stuff oneself silly with oysters and snails, whose consumption was not regulated.[28] Later that month, the *Canard* wrote of a war profiteer who got around the two-course rule by bringing two servants into the restaurant with him. The master ate five of the six courses, leaving the last for his employees.[29]

Meatless days, too, could be treated with humor, more or less. Snell wrote of a dinner he enjoyed, with Barrès, at the home of a wealthy Jewish lady who had made her way up in society by marrying a nobleman and adopting anti-Semitic ideas. In effect, she suffers from none of the wartime restrictions. Filet mignon on a meatless day? She buys her meat in advance and preserves it in an icebox. Fresh bread? She has her own baked daily in special ovens that are manufactured for bourgeois households. The same goes for her homemade pastries, thanks, among other reasons, to a large supply of sugar that she acquired before it disappeared from the market. Should it come as a surprise that the husband of this generous hostess is an *embusqué*? One can also easily imagine the degree of sacrifice of the society lady who complains, in a 1918 cartoon, that on meatless days she is obliged to feed chocolate to her dog.[30]

CIVILIANS AND SOLDIERS

Behind all these distinctions, between rich and poor, between the *embusqués* and those who did their duty, lay that between soldier and civilian. In November 1916, André Dahl, a combat soldier who contributed often to the *Canard,* explained the difference. It was not whether one wore a uniform but whether one was at the front, whether one read the communiqué or whether one lived it. All those who were not at the front were civilians, whatever it said on their clothing. And though Dahl distinguished between the civilians who profited from the war (a noisy minority) and those who suffered (the silent majority), much of his discussion effectively described the *embusqué,* the profiteer or the patriot by procuration. Picking up a verb conjugation that, as we saw in chapter 3, was also applied to journalistic *bourreurs de crâne,* he wrote of the civilian: "At first he said, 'You will get them.' He said afterward, 'One will get them.' Now he says, 'We will get them.' The war over, he will affirm, 'I got them.' " Dahl most fundamentally concludes, referring apparently to all civilians, that they will never understand what the war was really like.[31]

This notion of the unbridgeable gulf created by the experience of the trenches, an experience that could never be conveyed, became a staple in the writing of veterans of the First World War. The idea reappeared in the *Canard* as well. Citing the front newspaper *Le Bochofage* (The kraut eater),[32] the *Canard* repeated this quip: "People from the rear who imagine that they know the war because of their readings remind me of young girls who think they know what marriage is from reading novels." Another *Canard poilu*-writer, Raymond Lefebvre, put it more bitterly. Addressing a fellow soldier, he explains that, at the front when they had said that the civilians would never understand their experience, they had not really meant it; they had felt simply that those left behind would be horrified by their tales. Now, he understood that those in the rear would never want to understand, that the soldiers could never describe the war to them in a way they were prepared to hear.[33]

In the divisions of *embusqués* versus the conscientious French and of the rich (the exploiters) versus the hardworking members of the popular classes, it was always clear on which side the *Canard* situated itself and its readers. Obviously, the satirical weekly could not survive (or pretend to) without civilian readers. In contrast with the trench newspapers with which it has sometimes been compared, the *Canard* devoted most of its columns to life in the rear and carried less war material than competing humor periodicals like *La Baïonnette.* Neither the *Canard*'s frequent antimilitarism nor its antiphrastic predilections were realistic possibilities for the officer-controlled trench periodicals.[34]

Yet the weekly still wanted to speak to, and for, the mud-covered defenders of France. The *Canard* staked its claim to be a soldier's paper in a number of ways. One we have already seen: by publishing the notes of its own war-veteran journalists. The numbers of these increased as the conflict went on. Another soldier-writer, Henri Béraud, angrily refuted the charge of a hostile writer that he was an *embusqué,* noting that he had been at the front for four years (it was then July 1918).[35] The *Canard* also passed along soldierly advice, as when Béraud told civilians how to write to front-line soldiers. Do not talk of the war (of which you know nothing), he requested, but tell us about life back home.[36]

In early 1917, the *Canard* explained that the real soldier was the infantryman whose uniform was sky blue for only three weeks a year (when he got a new greatcoat). But this did not keep the web-footed weekly from printing with evident pride, a year and a half later, the letter of a soldier in the artillery who wanted the newspaper to become the godfather of his "75" (probably the best known of the French field artillery in the war). The paper happily accepted, sending subscriptions and drink to the artillery unit. Its only request was that the cannon should be dubbed the "Canard Déchaîné" (unchained), a title it judged more appropriate for a weapon.[37]

Another message from the front expressed the *Canard*'s conception of its contribution to the war effort. From military sector 130, the newspaper received the following citation in July 1918:

> CANARD ENCHAINE, first class [that is, private] canard, which, although enchained in Paris, has nonetheless continued, and this in spite of daily and nightly bombardments, to supply with jokes and good humor our admirable *poilus,* contributing thus largely to the successes of the French army.
>
> This citation includes the Croix de Guerre and six liters of *pinard.*[38]

WOMEN

The *Canard's* treatment of the largest category of civilians—that is, women—focused on the erotic and the corporal, as was visible in the battle over the *Intran* anecdotes. But when dealing specifically with the relationship of women to war, the weekly took a harsher stand, mocking female pretensions to military virtues and even making light of the rape of French women.

When Dahl, in November 1916, defined the civilian, he specifically spared women from his critique since nature had destined them for other and special purposes—from bearing children to keeping up with the fashions.[39] The gentle irony of that last quip was greatly increased by other *Canard* authors, who ignored Dahl's advice and felt free to pillory women. Dahl's suggestion might seem to excuse women since they could not fight in any case. But for the *Canard* this impossibility was used instead to make their behavior at once more ridiculous and more objectionable. Altogether typical was a cartoon that appeared in February 1917. Titled "Convalescent," it shows a soldier glowering at a society lady who has just come in from the cold. She says, "So, your feet were frozen? Poor little godson! It's just like me. I have just come in and the end of my nose is like a little ice cube." Another take on the seriousness with which women responded to the war emerged in a cartoon by Gassier. As a lady powders her face, one male says to another that if rice powder were banned, women would all be pacifists. Ridiculous in the superficiality of their femininity, women were equally ridiculous if they presumed to invade the masculine world of martial heroism. Reading the newspaper in her bath, an elegant lady exclaims, "If I were not a woman, I would already have died at the front three years ago."[40]

Certainly, women were taking over more traditionally masculine activities, as we saw with the echoes of *L'Intran.*[41] But combat? The *Canard* raised the notion in a February 1917 article entitled "A Success for the Feminists," arguing that the replacement of male "auxiliaries" by women in the offices of the Ministry of War was only a first step. Eventually, as success was added to success, women would demand, and receive, the right to perform combat duty: "It is their right! It is logical!" the article insisted.

Like most *Canard* pieces, the article was open to several interpretations. The putative author was a feminist addressing her sisters. Yet certain claims were not likely to be accepted as such by the *Canard*'s masculine readership, like the statement that women were naturally less talkative than men and would therefore work harder.[42] As for the argument that such a step was a logical continuation of feminist positions, it could be taken by those with feminist ideas as a bold suggestion, or, alternatively, it could be taken by those without such sympathies as a refutation of the whole feminist position. Either view underlines the same message: women do not risk their lives.

In wartime, women run other risks. Many were raped during the initial German invasion, and such atrocities received enormous coverage in the French press.[43] The *Canard* invoked the issue in January 1917 with a Laforge cartoon. An upper-class woman is marching across her room carrying her umbrella like a rifle. The maid explains to the man of the house that "Madame" thinks she is Joan of Arc. His answer: "Do not pay any attention, Mélanie. This happens to her every month since she was raped by an uhlan," a member of the feared Prussian cavalry. The presumably male French reader is being invited to laugh over the rape of a French woman by a German soldier. The reference to rape is more indirect in another cartoon, this one by Gassier in 1916. It shows a ridiculous and ugly "old maid" dreaming out loud in a café: "The war is so fine! I would like to be Joan of Arc. . . . A hundred uhlans would not frighten me!"[44] We have already seen that the *Canard* disliked atrocity stories; and its discussion of alleged barbed German foreskins mocked French reactions to the German rape of French women. But in these cases the weekly went further and not only made light of the real sufferings of French women but subsumed them under the category of gender transgression, of the woman who plays at being a warrior.[45]

More commonly, alleged feminine frivolity served as an extreme case of civilian nonchalance. In January 1917 the *Canard* published excerpts of an alleged "letter from a *poilu* to one of his comrades," a long indignant description of elegant Parisian nightlife. The writer salutes the "courage" of these ladies, who are "as Spartan as they are Parisian, of which nothing in their bearing or their language would allow one to suppose that someone dear to their heart is perhaps expiring, dirty, in the mud and is kissing their photograph between two cries of 'medics!' " This resentment of the entertainments of women left behind was frequent in war novels and was virtually an obsession with Roland Dorgelès. To the anger arising from unshared suffering was added the sting of sexual jealousy. But, in contrast with much war literature, the *Canard* devoted little attention to the affairs of the wives of soldiers with Frenchmen who had escaped the fighting. As we saw with the echoes of the *Intran,* the *Canard* was more concerned with Frenchwomen's relationships with foreigners than with *embusqués*.[46]

If the sexual politics of the *Canard's* attacks on feminine frivolity were usually clear, their class politics were only a bit less so. Almost all the women in these examples were of the upper classes. Their coddled selfishness was as much a product of class as of gender, the *Canard* suggested; and if such women represented the extremes of civilian self-absorption, they just as easily symbolized the vices of the idle rich. Women of the popular classes were occasionally used as a subject for humor in the satirical weekly, but never in a way that suggested either an absence of sacrifice (which would make little sense) or a lack of understanding of what France's front-line soldiers had to endure.[47] Gender politics had to fit within the class-as-patriotic-politics of the *Canard Enchaîné.*

CIVILIAN HEROISM

The importance of the civilian-versus-soldier topos meant that men—of almost any class—could also exhibit a lack of appreciation of the sacrifices of the common soldier. One such veteran of the trenches, in full gear, is rebuked by a portly male hotel employee: "Hey, *poilu!* You could wipe your feet!" To which the soldier answers, "Of what, of this mud from the Somme?"—referring to the area of a great battle.[48]

Even the unavoidable hardships of civilian life paled in comparison with those of the soldiers in the trenches. Thus, for example, in May 1918, the *Canard* published a letter (real or fictional, we will never know) from a soldier in which he explains that his comrades, moved by what they have heard about the restrictions imposed on civilians, offer to adopt one as "civilian goddaughter" and to send her some grains to help her survive and to raise her morale. Perhaps the most savage comparison appeared in a cartoon of October 1916. The husband in a comfortable, but far from elegant, bourgeois couple says to his wife, while their maid looks on disapprovingly, "Another winter campaign? How frightful! The price of butter will go up again."[49]

Behind such critiques is the reality that as these Parisians (we see the Sacré Coeur through their window) worry about their butter, men are dying. A similar lack of equivalence was developed by the *Canard* as early as September 1916 in an article following up on reports of a murder in Paris: "A Man Is Killed in Paris, Indescribable Emotion on the Front

Lines."[50] A year later, the *Canard* wrote, "Finally, the poor civilians, so painfully immobilized in the rear, are going to be able to satisfy their warlike passions because, since last Sunday, the hunting season is open." As if this disobliging comment were not clear enough, the paper published a cartoon in October entitled "Approximation." A hunter with his dog is musing, "In sum, what is the war? Instead of game, it's the krauts that you have in front of you."[51]

These examples come from 1916 and 1917. In 1918 the situation changed, for the German offensives of that spring brought Paris closer to the front lines and contributed to its regular bombardment by zeppelins and long-distance artillery. We already saw how the heroism of the Parisians figured in the *Intran* echoes of this period; and the heroism of the civilians of Paris was a major focus of the *Canard* in the spring of 1918 as well, where it was commonly ironically contrasted with the courage of the soldiers. For example, on April 3, the weekly reported a conversation between a soldier and a "beautiful woman" (of Paris, of course). He can barely get a word in edgewise as she explains how dangerous it is in Paris, between the artillery and the Gothas. She remains completely oblivious to his attempts to explain what it is like at the front. Another *poilu* wrote to the *Canard* that he had arrived on furlough as the bombardments began, that he had to go back to the front lines, but that he did not want anyone to think he was fleeing the dangers of the capital. The paper assured its readers that there was not a single soldier who was not ready to share the perils of life in Paris.[52]

The letter (presented as authentic) does more than highlight the chasm between the risks of life in Paris under occasional bombardment and those of life (or should we say death?) in the trenches. It also underlines the problem of civilians fleeing Paris for safer locations. The fact that the vacation season was not too far away (we are in late spring) gave an additional excuse for such travel (mercilessly pilloried by the *Canard*). The weekly even provided free advice to those who were having trouble getting seats on the packed trains for points south. Why not consider going to the north and east (the location of the fighting), where there was so much more room, "and six months of *campagne* in the north and east were certainly worth more than those one could spend in the south." The pun here is based on the fact that *campagne* could be translated as "military campaign" or as "the country." And the motivations of the early-season vacationers came out in the quip "to leave is to survive a little" ("partir, c'est survivre un peu"). This expression is a take-off on the proverbial "partir, c'est mourir un peu" (to leave is to die a little), which explains adequately what the soldiers are doing. Still other puns evoked the difference between fleeing Parisians and self-sacrificing soldiers.[53]

The last stage in the satirical rapprochement of civilian heroism (or lack of same) with its military counterpart was the description of the Parisians' rush southward in military terms. Already in July 1917, the *Canard,* referring to the seasonal vacationers of that year, had spoken of the "great Deauville offensive," after the beach resort of that name.[54] The year 1918 provided even better comparisons. Commenting on early vacation departures, the *Canard* reported that the trains were "literally captured by force of arms."[55] July 1918 produced a series of "Communiqués from Paris":

> The battle remains fierce at the Orsay, Lyon, Saint-Lazare, and Grande-Ceinture train stations.
>
> After a fierce struggle, leading often to hand-to-hand combat, Uncle Froussard [fearful] was able to take the train.
>
> [. . .]
>
> The civilians continue their strategic withdrawal. They are abandoning Passy, the Champs-Elysées, la Muette, the boulevard Saint-Germain, as well as the Gobelins. They are retreating to positions further south: Cannes, Biarritz, Pau, Bordeaux; their morale is excellent.[56]

The *Canard* did not push the point, but departures for the country were a privilege reserved to the middle and upper classes. Yet the treatment of this issue, like that of the reactions of civilians to the bombardments of spring 1918, concentrated on the ridicule associated with the comparison with the front, not on class differences. War-brought violence was, thus, less of a class issue than war-brought penury.

CIVILIAN DEATHS

The above cases invoked combat, and hence death, but indirectly—and with a smile. Another strand, however, also graced the pages of the *Canard Enchaîné;* it reflected clear hostility to civilians and expressed this hostility through the idea of their violent deaths. On July 19, 1916, page 4 featured a six-frame cartoon narrative of a comfortable middle-aged gentleman who reflects on the war. It really is not as bad as he had feared. After all, every day one has his little communiqué to read, and, then, many blondes look very good in black. At the cinema one has emotions [on the screen one sees that this is a war movie]. Any bad aspects? Well, he can no longer drink his absinthe. The text under the last frame adds that there are these nasty zeppelins, which should certainly leave us alone. The picture in the frame, however, tells a slightly different story. Our civilian is blown to pieces by an explosion, with his cane, hat, head, arms, and legs all flying in different directions.[57]

It is not a coincidence that this basically unacceptable wish is expressed only iconographically. By early 1918, the *Canard* soldier-writer de Pawlowski, in one of his articles in the series "Dans le 'No Man's Land,' " felt prepared to be a bit blunter. "The entire nation must take part in the war," he wrote, "and share its risks. If long months ago one had decided to guillotine each day, through a lottery, as many civilians as die at the front, operations would have been pursued, one can be persuaded of it, with a greater energy." If the war continues, de Pawlowski is suggesting, it is because those who decide (civilians) and those who die (soldiers) are two different groups. But, having made such a crude point, the author immediately softened it with irony: "But, in the rear, one has remained attached to the old formalism, to obsolete procedures; one still thinks that in order to kill someone with a rifle shot or a cannon blast it is absolutely indispensable that he be guilty. It has been a long time since this prejudice from another age has ceased to exist at the front." The philosopher and combat veteran Alain (Emile Chartier) gave a psychological explanation of de Pawlowski's ruminations. "Every soldier," he argued, "has wished at some time or other that the civilians would also take a few hits."[58]

Killing civilians hardly fit in well with either the *Canard*'s horror of war or its general good humor. But it did fit the paper's exploitation of the gulf between civilians and soldiers. Certainly the class resentments that permeated the weekly's war coverage would continue after the war. But so too would the civilian/veteran distinction that blended with it; and peace, rather than dulling this last contrast, would permit it to emerge even more clearly.

6 *In Vino Veritas*

De la Fouchardière, Bicard, and the Politics of Inebriation

"Le jour de boire n'est pas arrivé" (the day of drinking has not yet arrived), the *Canard* warned its readers in mid-October 1918. In other words, the end of the war, clearly within sight, had not yet come.[1] With this pun on the opening verse of the "Marseillaise," "Le jour de gloire est arrivé" (the day of glory has arrived), the *Canard* linked an alcoholic festiveness to the expected moment of patriotic celebration. But the French had not waited for the armistice to drink. From the wine and *eau de vie* rations of the soldiers to government-mandated restrictions on stronger spirits, alcoholic issues played their role in the France of the First World War and in the *Canard Enchaîné* of the same epoch. But the association of peace with drinking carried a message that would be borne out in the postwar *Canard,* as alcohol became increasingly important in the thematic economy of the weekly—so important that a drunk, the wise fool Bicard, could become a major purveyor of the *Canard*'s philosophy of life.

The *Canard* saw restrictions on strong spirits (like other alimentary prohibitions) as sparing the rich.[2] Yet the weekly exploited the traditional humorous figure of the drunk even during the war. On the first page of the June 4, 1918, issue, a drunk clings to a lamppost while excusing himself to the policeman who looks at him censoriously: "I'll explain it to you: I wanted to buy a packet of tobacco." The cartoon is entitled "Restrictions," and it cleverly links alcoholic excess to the difficulty of finding tobacco (a problem amply commented on in other *Canard* items).[3]

Drunks are common enough as butts of humor (Andy Capp is, in our day, one of the wittier exploitations of this topos).[4] But the Frenchman who needs the lamppost to steady himself carries other ideological baggage. No one has ever suggested that the people of France do not imbibe. It has often been an article of pride, however, that French men and women know how to handle their liquor. Not that alcoholism has not long been recognized as a problem. What the French are not supposed to do (or at least those who are well-bred) is to display the kind of inebriation that we would call falling-down drunk: unable to stand, speaking with difficulty, or losing control of bodily functions. Such gross departures from the civilized art of drinking are thought to characterize foreigners. Maurice Barrès himself supported this stereotype in his patriotic novel *Colette Baudoche.* There it is the German professor who, to the horror of the French family with whom he is staying, achieves this state of drunken stupor.[5] Yet the *Canard's* drunk as a comic figure is unmistakably French, though he remained relatively scarce during the war. Of course, Frenchness and French culture are constructs. The inhabitants of *l'hexagone* (France itself)—and the overseas territories—displayed considerable variety. Yet, the idea of a French identity and a French culture was dominant among the Parisian intelligentsia, including the *Canard,* despite the paper's willingness to play with regional or class stereotypes.

The bombardment of Paris in the spring of 1918 periodically sent its inhabitants to the relative security of their basements—which for most social classes doubled as wine cellars. Such a subject was too good to pass up. One alert, imagined by the *Canard's* Georges de la Fouchardière, finds people groping around in the dark, while someone opens a barrel of Beaujolais and floods the floor with wine.[6] But wine-cellar humor was also a good opportunity to restate the socially sanctioned relation between the war and alcoholic celebration. As an elegant-looking gentleman sits drinking on a low stool in the "cellar" (in a Laforge cartoon), his wife apostrophizes him, "See here, Nestor, if you drink all the champagne now, what will we have for the victory?"[7] In this contest between patriotism and thirst, the wife delivers the message that, indeed, the day to drink has not yet arrived.

Did victory open the spigots of the *Canard's* journalistic wine casks? Certainly, but virtually all the themes exploited during the years of peace had been at least adumbrated during the conflict itself. Indeed, the alcoholization of the paper seems a progressive function; it got stronger as the twenties progressed. When the day of glory did come, the *Canard* saluted it with a *poilu*-duck holding a bottle under his wing. Yet the first celebration of Bastille Day after the armistice, in July 1919, occasioned only a minor reference to the *jour de boire* and the suggestion that France did not want to separate its "thirst for glory" from "*pinard* and cocktails."[8]

The Bastille-Day-as-patriotic-drunkenness motif appeared again in 1921 with a small cartoon featuring two revelers losing their balance while singing "Liberty guides our steps." In July 1922 the lead article, by Victor

Snell, celebrated the "rational and commercial utilization of July 14" by the apéritif manufacturers whose advertising banners graced the traditional outdoor balls.[9] But it was not until July 1924 that the drunken reveler became the dominant symbol of the holiday. The lead cartoon on the first page of the July 16 issue showed a drunk lying unconscious in the street over the legend "July 15th" (see figure 7). Farther down on the same page, one recovering drunk (who can barely sit up) says to another (in a similar posture), "Say, ol' chum, are you sure that last year we weren't more plastered?"[10]

These exploitations of the drunk as stock character certainly did not add to the prestige of the national holiday, but they also did not speak well for alcohol. Yet the apology for (when not the glorification of) alcoholic beverages was a consistent element in the *Canard.* The defense of drink showed up, first of all, and with the least ambiguity, as an attack on the temperance movement. Even during the war, the weekly published a short, mildly satirical portrait of "the enemy of alcohol," the temperance-activist-as-boring-pest.[11]

After the war, Roland Dorgelès took up the criticism of such moralists with far greater vigor. Under the title "Alcohol Kills!" Dorgelès wrote: "After a slaughter of fifty-two months, which has cost the country a million and a half killed, and among the most healthy, some virtuous old men and women discover that the population is tending to decrease, that the birthrate is declining, and that to save France it is necessary to drink only infusions." The novelist-veteran went on to explain how, when he was recovering in a military hospital, he used to bring wounded soldiers to read a plaque on the wall that stated, "Alcohol kills as surely as a bullet" in order "to study at leisure the ravages of furious anger on the human face." And what hypocrisy when it was the military itself that provided spirits to the soldiers. "At the front, alcohol had all the virtues. Brandy warmed us up when we were cold, supported us when we were hungry, revived us when we were tired; it replaced bread, meat, coal, rest." Concluding that the million and a half men who had died since 1914 did not expire from cirrhosis of the liver, Dorgelès distilled his attack on temperance into a broader one on the horrors of war. And, equally, he was continuing the *Canard*'s wartime contrast of civilian stupidity with the real experience of combat. When, six years later, Dorgelès appeared to change his mind, the *Canard* was quick to dissociate itself from him. Dorgelès declared, "Religion is decreasing and alcoholism is increasing. Well, I prefer priests to bars." The *Canard*'s Pierre Bénard protested that "he preferred—and greatly—bars to priests."[12]

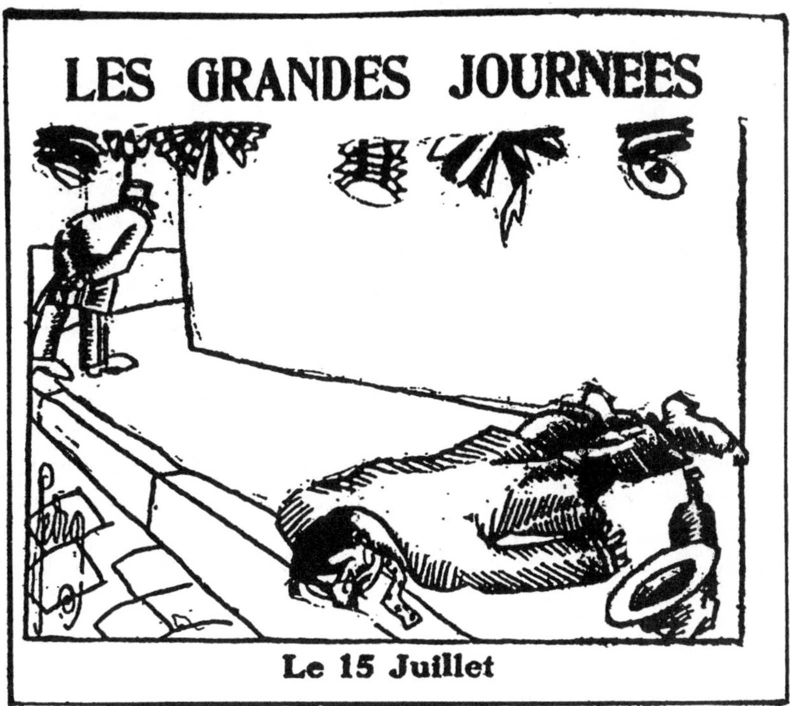

Figure 7. After the national holiday, by Pedro (1924).

Dorgelès's cocktail was laced with bitters, but that was not true of other *Canard* beverages. If military-issue *eau de vie* symbolized the life of the trenches, other drinks celebrated the joys of life and Frenchness. That wine is a "totem-drink" for Frenchmen (as Roland Barthes put it) comes as a surprise to no one. One can also endorse, and apply to the *Canard,* the French critic's conclusion that "wine gives thus a foundation for a collective morality, within which everything is redeemed."[13] The *Canard* particularized this cult. The totem-drink of the weekly was Vouvray.

The *Canard's* cult of Vouvray began during the war. In June 1918, the paper insisted that the Socialist deputy Marcel Sembat pay for a mistake in an article by sending two bottles of the Loire white. Of course, he did no such thing, and the journalists continued the joke the following week by explaining that because of the delay the charge was now three bottles of Vouvray (none came).[14] In the early 1920s, references to Vouvray became regular topoi in the weekly, a stock reference to the *joie de vivre* of the paper's journalists. For example, in 1922 alone, Vouvray shows up as *Canard*-drink in February, in March, in June, and twice in September. Not surprisingly this association of the paper with bubbly was not lost on the *Canard*'s most loyal readers. A *Canard* fan club proudly reported imbibing the Loire white at its festivities.[15]

If wine was quintessentially French, why this wine? Light, gay, and sparkling, this Loire white certainly has similarities to the humorous weekly. Would red wine have had a more earthy association; would it have evoked the masculinity (and militarism) of blood? In either case, the *Canard*'s Vouvray functioned as a poor man's Champagne, embodying the festive gayness of the prestige beverage without its upper-class associations. For example, the *Canard* reported (in March 1922) that a drawing of lots in its office was lubricated with Champagne, for lack of Vouvray.[16] Literally, this signifies a preference for the Loire wine over that from farther east. Ironically, it mocks the tendency of some to substitute Vouvray for the more expensive Champagne. And the war must have exacerbated the price difference between the bubblies: the Vouvray district was well away from the fighting, while Champagne saw many battles. De la Fouchardière explained it in an article of July 14, 1926, entitled "Vouvray at Vouvray." The pretense of the article was the idea that the *Canard* editor, Maurice Maréchal, was sending de la Fouchardière to do investigative reporting in the Loire town to see whether the famous white really came from that location. After noting that the weekly referred to Vouvray so often that it seemed a running joke, de la Fouchardière reported that the wine really came from the cellars above the town. Few English or Americans ever stopped in Vouvray, and if they did, they ordered Champagne: "If one offers them Vouvray, they do not understand. The savages with a favorable exchange rate [we are in 1926] do not understand Vouvray; it is too refined for them. . . . Fortunately, because if they began to understand, they would not leave us any." De la Fouchardière continued: "Champagne is a wine of nightclubs, of wedding dinners, of political banquets. On the spot it provides an abundance of stupid ideas, and that is why one serves it at the moment of toasts and speeches; and the next day it provides a hangover."[17] Vouvray thus permitted the *Canard* staff to demarcate themselves not only from the world of oenologically ignorant foreigners (and hence, to reaffirm their Frenchness) but also from that of official celebrations with their pomposity and hypocrisy.

According to de la Fouchardière in this article, Vouvray made its drinkers "cheerful and gay." Drunkenness is not mentioned. But that does not mean that the *Canard* took a uniformly censorious attitude to that state. One of the paper's weekly *contes*, in September 1922, told the story of the Spartans and Helots in a new way. All educated French people knew that once a year the ruling Spartans allowed the slave population of Helots to become drunk so that the young Spartan men would see the disgusting aspects of this state and refrain from the abuse of alcohol. In the *Canard*'s version, however, a young man questions the inebriated slaves. Upon discovering that they are happy, he decides to imitate them.[18]

As with classical morality, so with Christian morality. In December 1922, the *Canard* author Jules Rivet contributed a story about Adam and Eve. In this version Eve brings apples to Adam, but instead of courting divine vengeance, Adam turns the apples into cider and Calvados. The suggestion that *Canard* contributors might also get drunk is also made (and its moral ambiguity manifested) in an article in which de la Fouchardière portrays the paper's lead cartoonist, Gassier, as drunk. Gassier replied the next week by sending in a cartoon of his dog attacking de la Fouchardière with the legend, "Bite him, Azor! Sic! Sic! He said that I was drunk."[19]

The incriminating story was an appropriate place to fight out the reality or legitimacy of drinking among *Canard* staff. Its author, de la Fouchardière, was the person who sang the praises of Vouvray, but the story was signed not by de la Fouchardière but by a fictional creation of that writer, Bicard. Alfred Bicard, also known as "le Bouif" (the cobbler), was the most regularly appearing character in the *Canard Enchaîné*—among fictional ones, the only one to repeat from issue to issue over many years. Bicard embodied a distinctive *Canard* discourse—one that used a drunk as the mouthpiece for hilarious but trenchant social and political commentary.

One of the *Canard*'s most frequent contributors, de la Fouchardière was also one of its most popular. In January 1917 the *Canard* asked its readers to vote for their favorite writers (the prize was a *paté de canard*). The winners were Anatole France followed by the leftist antimilitarist writers Romain Rolland and Henri Barbusse. But the next on line was de la Fouchardière, the only *Canard* writer to make his way onto the list.[20] Finding de la Fouchardière on a list headed by Anatole France was appropriate, and not just for their shared association with the satirical weekly. In many ways, de la Fouchardière was a lesser Anatole France, exploiting similar themes and similar politics in less sophisticated literary productions and in a less formal style.

Born Georges Delafouchardière in Châtellerault in 1874, Georges legally gave his pen name, the more aristocratic de la Fouchardière, to his son in 1922. The elder Delafouchardière had escaped service in the war but not the eyes of the police, who criticized his collaboration with left-wing and pacifist periodicals as well as his life-style, which was judged less than respectable.

Though married and a father, he kept a mistress (hardly an unusual situation for a Frenchman of any means during the Third Republic) and was accused of taking drugs. At the least, the carelessness of his appearance and his manners fit well with the cheerful amoralism of his fictional character. The police also noted that some accused him of having dissipated his inheritance in gambling and partying; even if only a nasty rumor, this accusation would also link him to Bicard.[21]

De la Fouchardière was important enough that the first number of the revived paper in 1916 advertised his appearance for the following week. Throughout the war de la Fouchardière appeared in about two out of every three issues. His were often the lead articles, and they dealt with such familiar *Canard* themes as the mendacity of the mass press, attacks on Barrès and Hervé, and, as we saw with "The Divine Tragedy" especially,[22] anticlericalism. Even on general political subjects, de la Fouchardière managed a tone that was just a wee bit more disrespectful than that of even the rest of the *Canard*.

On May 1917, in the same issue that carried the third "song" of de la Fouchardière's serial "The Divine Tragedy," a story with the byline "Bicard dit le Bouif" mocked the campaigns of the reactionary Action Française. This Bicard showed up again in the following weeks, but only in June was the pen name followed by that of de la Fouchardière. (De la Fouchardière had formally introduced his creation to Parisian readers the previous February in *L'Heure*.)[23]

Bicard graced the columns of the weekly a handful of times more for the balance of the war and clearly established himself as a drunk,[24] but he became a (journalistically if not physically) stable member of the *Canard* community only during the 1920s. With the armistice, Bicard took a two-year vacation from the pages of the weekly. His creator, who absented himself at about the same time, returned in June 1920, serving up a series of articles on general topics in politics, journalism, and society. In the last issue of 1920, however, de la Fouchardière brought back his colorful sidekick in a series entitled "La lanterne du Bouif" (The Bouif's lantern), renamed in mid-1922 as "Chronique de l'oeil-de-Bouif," which continued faithfully, and almost weekly, throughout the decade. The second, longer-lasting title contained a pun of sorts. It could be translated as the Bouif's (or cobbler's) eye—that is, his vision of things. But "l'oeil-de-bouif," especially with the hyphens, was also a reference to that distinctive classical French window design the *oeil-de-boeuf* (literally cow's or cattle's eye). Indeed, this is how the police agent who prepared the report on the *Canard* miswrote it.[25] After the first number, the series carried subtitles referring to the topics

CHRONIQUE DE L'ŒIL DE BOUIF

La torche sacrée

Figure 8. Bicard and de la Fouchardière, by Guilac (1922).

(mis)handled by Bicard and an unnamed interlocutor who was supposed to be de la Fouchardière. Drawings by Guilac that accompanied the articles represented either Bicard himself (usually with working-class cap and red nose) or Bicard and de la Fouchardière, recognizable as thinner and sporting a rakish, black, broad-brimmed hat (see figure 8).

The *Canard* stressed this fiction of a relationship between de la Fouchardière and his working-class alter ego. For example, on February 25, 1925, the paper explained that there would be no "Chronique de l'oeil-de-Bouif" column for that week since de la Fouchardière was traveling in the south of Tunisia. But in June 1926 the paper apologized for another absence by explaining that de la Fouchardière had been prevented "by a grave indisposition" from meeting his friend at the rue Bridaine bistro. In December 1927, however, the *Canard* lamented that this time it was Bicard who was sick—with the flu—and there would hence be no column for that week.[26] No other *Canard* series had ever had its fictional premise made into a narrative in this way.

Bicard and de la Fouchardière were a team, a couple. But de la Fouchardière did not formally label the speakers in his transcriptions of the dialogues. Sometimes we can tell who is talking by the fictional de la Fouchardière's use of the other's name in his answers. Bicard can most easily be distinguished from his partner in dialogue by his distinctive verbal style. The most obvious markers are shlurred shpeech and mishpronounshiations, on the one hand, and Archie Bunker-like malapropisms, on the other. De la Fouchardière used a number of devices to suggest charming semi-ignorance. Take the following example, in which Bicard is explaining why he wants to disrupt Christmas Eve and New Year's festivities at restaurants.

> Mon vieux; Y a deux plaisirs dans la vie: *primo*, de manger des truffes; *deuzio*, d'engueuler les types qui mangent des truffes. . . . Ah! j'aurais mieux aimé être de ceux qui mangent des truffes si on m'avait donné à choisir: mais on m'a pas donné à choisir.
>
> [Old boy, there are two pleasures in life: first, to eat truffles; second, to yell at those who eat truffles. . . . Now I would have preferred to be among those who eat truffles, if I had been given the choice, but I ain't been given the choice.]

Here it is the more subtle markers of lower-class speech that predominate: "Y a" for "Il y a" and the missing negative particle in "on m'a pas donné" are common forms of colloquial, though nonstandard, spoken French. And, of course, the passage also shows class war and class resentment unsullied by either idealism or hypocrisy.

Bicard is a cheerful ne'er-do-well who drinks and plays the horses and who apparently lacks regular employment; instead he makes a living from a series of scams—hardly a moral example, but then his family is not much better. Madame Bicard, Eugénie, is a towering figure who can intimidate her husband and who is a regular attender at mass. But she is also clearly having an affair with a policeman, Officer Balloche, who engages in a rivalry of tricks and beatings with Alfred Bicard. The rest of the family is equally colorful. Alfred's son, Ernest (pronounced, by his father, Ernesse), is a chip-off-the-old-block, as cynical and amoral as his father. But his schoolbooks are a regular source of historical and geographical information for the elder Bicard. The daughter, Charlotte, is a more attractive character, at least physically. She is making her way through the world with her charms in a series of adventures that regularly threaten to stray across the border of respectability into prostitution.[27]

As a man who loves his drink, Alfred Bicard makes his headquarters at the bistro of the rue Bridaine, a small street in the Batignolles district, near Clichy—then as now a working-class neighborhood.[28] The drink that Bicard abuses is not usually wine but the cocktails of his era, combinations like a picon-curaçao or an export-cassis (which came out as "esport-cassis"). If Vouvray was the totem drink of the *Canard* staff, the lower-class drunkard Bicard indulges in the stronger drinks that replaced the prewar absinthe. Unlike ordinary wine, such apéritifs were more directly associated with drinking for its own sake as opposed to drinking to accompany meals (or as a "coffee pusher," as was often said of brandies).

To be publicly drunk meant to tangle with the police; and the Bouif has his share of run-ins with the forces of order. No surprise, for example, when in the issue following May 1, 1926, Bicard explains that he was arrested and sentenced, for public drunkenness and insulting a policeman because he called Officer Balloche a "do-nothing." This remark was especially inappropriate, Bicard later recognizes, since he proffered his characterization on May 1, the only day on which the police actually worked—a sly reference to the heavy-handed actions of the police during the demonstrations of that day.[29]

Drunks and class-conscious workers equally at the mercy of the forces of order? This comparison was expressed even more clearly a year and a half later, in the column of October 26, 1927. Bicard opens by making the following suggestion to his interlocutor:

> You really ought to organize, from time to time, a demonstration Saturday nights, from nine until midnight.
>
> —And why, Bicard?
>
> —Because, while the police would be massed at the toll booths, and you would be sacrificing yourself in the general interest. . . .
>
> —And how!
>
> —Yes . . . You have to count on twelve cops to beat up an honest man *[honnête homme]*. Suppose then that twelve courageous citizens devoted themselves to the general interest; that makes twelve dozen cops who would be neutralized, and circulation would be possible in central Paris. . . . Last Saturday, I was stopped five times from the rue Bridaine to Place Clichy [only a few blocks], by diverse rounds, patrols, and other *vachalcades*.[30]

Vachalcades is a wonderful example of how Bicard's linguistic mangling could cover political polemic. At first sight the word, which needless to say does not exist in French, is a mistake for *cavalcade*. Except that *vache* both means cow and is a well-known insulting term for the police, as injurious as the English "pig." (In fact one could be arrested and convicted for publicly uttering the term in the presence of an agent of the law.) We cannot even tell whether a *vachalcade* would be a troop of cows/police or a group of mounted police/*vaches* (that is, a cavalcade). Indeed, the linguistic substitution is semantically apt since it replaces one quadruped (*caval* signifies horse in the compound cavalcade) with another (the cow) and thus conjures up the image of a troop of police mounted on bovines. Bicard was not the only comic figure to get caught up in the French language and in foreign words. The heroine in a comic series for girls, the Breton peasant Bécassine, also hilariously misconstrued big words. But her mistakes were politically neutral and integrated into a generally conformist, patriotic vision.[31]

But Bicard's attack on the police goes further than being a cleverly disguised insult. An *honnête homme* in the above example means more than just an honest man since it has implications of solidity and normality. So Bicard is saying that the police spend their time beating up "honest" men as opposed to criminals or derelicts. His suggestion that his interlocutor organize a demonstration repeats the assumption, only implicit in the earlier column, that the police attack otherwise peaceful demonstrators—an assumption agreed to by the fictional de la Fouchardière.

As a drunk, Bicard could be considered biased by the relationship his social role dictates with the forces of order. But his animosity toward the police is only a colorful reflection of that of the *Canard* as a whole. This hostility to the police predated the armistice, though its expression was partly limited by censorship, which banned, for example, a cartoon deemed to mock that organization. Nevertheless, de la Fouchardière (here without Bicard)—among others—was able to suggest that the police were *embusqués.*[32]

With the end of the war and the censor, the *Canard*'s *vacheries* (nasty remarks) about the forces of order only increased. One comment, from 1927, expressed the paper's continuing view: "The police have vigorously repressed the intolerable provocations of demonstrators who had camouflaged themselves as peaceful café customers."[33] Over three years earlier, the *Canard* had suggested that the prefect of police was going to save money by moving tobacco sales into the police stations. *Passer au tabac,* to be systematically beaten by the police, was the phrase used by Bicard when he spoke of the police having to beat an honest man. In the *Canard*'s take-off, people who enter the station will have to pay for their cigarettes, but poor people will continue to get their *tabac* for free, as in the past.[34]

In this area, as in others, the *Canard* linked its critique of the police to a judgment of their behavior during the war. In 1919, Dorgelès mocked the aggressiveness shown by the forces of order against May Day demonstrators by relating it to their avoidance of combat during the war.[35] When criticizing the gendarmes (militarized police forces under the Ministry of War) the *Canard* remembered to point out how unpopular these forces had been with the *poilus* during the war, echoing the opinions of the fighting soldiers.[36]

Just as Bicard was in sync with the rest of the paper in his attitude to the police, so was he in line with the paper's attitude toward those primitive enough to want to substitute some other fluid for booze. Discussing the French mythology of wine, Barthes agreed with Gaston Bachelard that its opposite had long been water, only to add that in his day (the late 1950s) it had become milk. We could argue that today it has become Coca-Cola, but in Bicard's era it was still water, or, as he often disrespectfully called it in *poilu*-slang, *la flotte*.[37] But placing wine (or other alcoholic beverages) in opposition to other liquids also distinguished the French from other peoples.[38] Bicard argues, for example, that tea is more dangerous than alcohol—his explanation for the difficulties being experienced by the Chinese, the Japanese, and the English. And the United States provided a more shocking example of what happens to a people who drink "mineral water, tea, and other garbage unfit for the consumption of a civilized people." His explanation also covered what he had heard about the law of "lunch," which de la Fouchardière had to correct to "lynch." Bicard spoke of a "lunch that consists of soaking with gasoline a black negro who had caressed the behind of a white woman in the Metro of the Far-Veste, and of setting the gasoline on fire while dancing around the negro and shouting like a carnibal [sic] until the cooking was complete." The reference to cannibalism turns this racist caricature of Africans on its head, and, combined with the transformation of "lynch" to "lunch" (not to speak of the reference to cooking and the *carne* in "carnibal"), it adds a rather unsavory subtext to the whole ceremony. The *Canard*'s ambivalent treatment of racist stereotypes will be explored in greater detail in chapter 10. Here, Bicard argues that what the Yankees had done to Sacco and Vanzetti was worse: they had refused to offer the condemned men a glass of rum at the ultimate moment, "a politeness that a properly brought-up executioner never fails to show to his customers in a civilized country."[39] Certainly, this was a drunk's perspective, but it hid a deeper argument to which the paper as a whole could subscribe: from a people who banned alcohol one could expect anything.

But even the alternative fluids of Bicard's discussions carry their own significations. If water is the opposite of alcoholic drink, it is still domestic; it is drunk by Frenchmen, for example, at Vichy. Tea, in the above examples, stands for foreignness—whether that of the Japanese and Chinese or of the English and Americans. But why tea and not coffee? Coffee's place in French drinking rituals (as sacralized in the *Canard*) was well expressed in a "Petite correspondance" in July 1927: "The *pousse-café* can go *in principle* until 3:30, and the apéritif does not begin normally until around 5:00. Between the two one has scarcely any other recourse than to have some beer."[40]

An expert in all things alcoholic, Bicard was also an authority on their integration into the other rituals of French life. In April 1925, at the time of Paris municipal elections, he sought to attach himself to a political rally in order to benefit from the free drinks that would be provided at a local bistro by the candidate. The column, bearing the subtitle "L'amélioration de la race électorale" (The improvement of the electoral race), combined a discussion of the lubrication of the political process with a reference to Bicard's other major hobby, horse racing. The expression *l'amélioration de la race chevaline* (the improvement of the stock of horses) was regularly used as a justification for race-track gambling.[41]

Bicard noted, in the summer of 1924, that both voters and conscripts who had just passed their physicals intoxicated themselves as a form of congratulation. "Ask the owners of the bistros," challenged Bicard, "whether they are advocates of the suppression of mandatory military service, and they will tell you that patriotism and universal suffrage are the two sources of nourishment of the café business."[42] In the Bicardian original: "le patriotisme et le suffrage universel sont les deux mamelles de la limonade." *Mamelles* are breasts/udders, and the expression "le labourage [plowing] et le pâturage [grazing] sont les deux mamelles de la France" was almost proverbial. As such it was richly mocked by the *Canard*—for example, by adding a third item and speaking of the three *mamelles* of France.[43] Bicard, here, however, has replaced France with *limonade* (literally, lemonade, but a *limonadier* was the respectable euphemism for a café or bistro owner).

In November 1921, about eleven months after reviving his Bouif series in late 1920, de la Fouchardière gave a public lecture on his creation. The large excerpt reprinted in the *Canard* was rare in its absence of irony. Modestly enough, de la Fouchardière insisted that he had not invented the Bouif. This character, "so Parisian," was based on Samuel Weller in Dickens's *Pickwick Papers.* Certainly the English Sam Weller and the French Alfred Bicard have some characteristics in common—they are both working class, and they both massacre their native tongues in amusing ways. But there the resemblance ends. Weller's mispronunciations (rarely based on ignorance) suggest no intoxication, and Sam was no more fond of drink than any of his fellow characters. Mr. Pickwick's faithful and hardworking servant contrasts sharply with the dissipated and amoral Bouif; and Bicard, who is always getting into scrapes, is far from the resourceful Weller. But de la Fouchardière further defined his literary genealogy. The Bouif character was essentially that of the cynic, explained his creator, and as such went back to Diogenes. Here, as with the reference to Dickens, one has the impression that de la Fouchardière's modesty is really about providing a distinguished literary pedigree for Bicard, for one has trouble imagining the Bouif searching, lantern or anything else in hand, for an honest man.[44]

In this same talk, de la Fouchardière argued that France suffered from a surfeit of respect, for people and for institutions that were anything but respectable. The finest quality of Bicard, in this line of thinking, was his absence of respect for prestige and authority. Certainly, Bicard failed to show respect to constituted authorities, to the police and other officers of the law first and foremost. But the systematic attack on respect as an idea better describes de la Fouchardière's work as a whole than it does Bicard's cheerful amoralism.

As a lower-class drunk, the Bicard character evokes another discourse. This one, in partial contradiction to the image of the French as sophisticated imbibers, blamed alcoholism for the misery of the French lower classes and stigmatized an unholy alliance of republican politicians and bar owners. In Barbusse's *Clarté,* defenders of the upper classes mock and exploit the inebriation of their inferiors. Hervé's *La Victoire* ran campaigns against working-class drunkenness and its effects on the population crisis.[45] Bicard can be seen as the *Canard*'s shameless counter to Hervé's moralizing. But, by exploiting the lower-class drunk, de la Fouchardière ran the risk of reinforcing the stereotype, especially in the absence of a worker positive hero. The resulting ideological ambivalence was, however, typical of the *Canard*'s politics of stereotypes.[46]

As a type, Bicard combined the cheerful ne'er-do-well with the wise fool, the individual who through a childlike simplicity and naiveté arrives at profound, and profoundly corrosive, truths. Nowhere did this truth-within-folly come out more clearly than on the subjects of war and militarism. In a 1918 column, later celebrated as a courageous outmaneuvering of the censor, Bicard criticized the recent proposal by the Socialist deputy Marcel Sembat that the belligerents mutually agree to cease bombing each other's open cities. There would be no more Gothas over Paris, and no more French planes attacking German cities. The problem, the Bouif insisted, was that once the belligerents began talking to each other, soldiers might mutually agree not to fire their artillery at each other, to use their bayonets only to slice sausages, and so forth. "Just go and ask a Russian maximalist or a Bochewhyski," he challenged. "That would lead us to peace," answered de la Fouchardière. "Worse still," rejoined the Bouif, "that would lead us to the end of the war."[47] The pacifist truth from a reductio ad absurdum is couched here in Bicard's critique of Sembat's position. For a patriotic French person during the war to have called for a cessation of combat would have been defeatism. Even the term *Bochewhyski* combines silly ignorance with sly politics. Besides being an error for Bolshevik (*Bolcheviki* in French spelling), it evokes Bicard's penchant for drink through *whyski,* whose spelling is dictated by its English original. But *Boche* refers to Germans. Its presence in this location, though linguistically incorrect, works as political semantics since these Russian revolutionaries were regularly dismissed in the French press as German agents.

After the war, Bicard, like the rest of the paper, could be blunter. In a 1924 column, he opined: suppose that Marshal Joffre or "Marshal" de Castelnau[48] were accused of having eliminated one and a half million young Frenchmen whose bones were found spread over the countryside.[49] One and a half million soldiers was the figure that the *Canard* regularly gave for French losses in the war (the actual number hovered around one and a third million).

A funnier comparison was provoked from Bicard by a weapons test carried out in that same year. French authorities wanted to test a new form of the explosive melanite and used a group of dogs (to considerable popular indignation) as guinea pigs. In his naiveté, Bicard assumes that the officers in charge tried to blow up the dogs as a form of amusement in hope of creating a sort of dog paté; and he mocks their lack of success when the explosion fails to harm the dogs themselves. But Bicard then goes after the journalists who "expressed pity for the fate of these twenty doggies without reflecting that during the war, when the melanite was of good quality, one put *poilus* by the thousands at the site of the explosion, and that made something like a *poilu* paté; and the tear-producing journalists found that perfectly normal and natural. A *poilu* is interesting only if he has four legs."[50]

Bicard's solutions to the problem of war also have a charming simplicity. To prevent war one simply has to put "in front" those who traditionally were "behind," namely, "Lord Baldwin, Monsieur Poincaré, Monsieur Millerand, Monsieur Mussolini, and delegations selected from the official bodies—as you would say, the Academy, the Annual of Longitudes, the Citroën Company, and the Fraternal Association of Guardians of the Peace."[51] Bicard's idea, whose departure from normal practice is underlined by his interlocutor, was echoed in other places in the *Canard*—the idea that wars are facilitated by the gap between those who declare them and those who fight them.[52] For this reason, too, our lower-class philosopher rejects the idea, presented by his fictional companion, that giving women the vote would put an end to war: "You think so? The principal cause of wars is that they are decided on by those who do not fight them. Just think of all the chicks who would be happy to dress up as nurses."[53]

As these examples show, the fictional de la Fouchardière was more than a neutral observer in his discussions with the Bouif. Often he was the voice of shocked respectability or that of prudent counsel. Sometimes he even added to Bicard's arguments with others that strengthened the case. As often as not, de la Fouchardière countered the wisdom of folly with the sad wisdom of experience. Bicard explains that one could end wars by writing in smoke in the sky above all countries "that in all the countries of the world there are pretty little church steeples, pretty streams, and pretty little villages . . . and also very honorable nice flags . . . and also sweet young ladies, and kindly old ladies that one should not bring to tears." But de la Fouchardière bursts Bicard's bubble: "Unfortunately, all that you can do is to write that in the sky, with smoke, Bicard, with smoke"—the symbol of impermanence.[54]

If the "Chronique de l'oeil-de-Bouif" wrapped serious political and ideological messages in a covering of humor, so, it could be said, did the *Canard Enchaîné* as a whole. And in another, related sense, de la Fouchardière's column functioned as a condensation (or a mirror) of the weekly. Subjects could shift with great suddenness. For example, Bicard's ideas for antimilitarist skywriting were prompted by a discussion of the skywriting advertisement campaigns for Citroën cars. In the same or different columns Bicard might discuss his own unsavory adventures, those of members of his family, or his opinions on matters from horses and drinks to the police, war, and politics. And the alcoholic's arguments could vary from the ludicrous (as when he suggests that President Millerand open a bistro called "Au Rendez-Vous des Anciens Présidents")[55] to the soberly serious.

Three examples will show the potential variety of materials. The first, from June 20, 1923, begins with inquiries about recent happenings in Paris municipal politics, which Bicard interprets with reference to the execution of Robespierre. He then continues with the exchange of insults between the Communist Vaillant-Couturier and one of his rightist opponents. Bicard prefers their brevity (they called each other shits) to the hour-long speeches of most deputies. When de la Fouchardière objects that deputies certainly could not speak this way to their constituents, Bicard agrees. They only think it, he says, as when a soldier thinks an insult but maintains "the exterior marks of respect" when speaking to an officer. Bicard and his companion then turn to horse racing. Bicard expresses surprise that the presence of Henri Chéron at the track did not raise the prices there since every action of this Minister of Agriculture seems to increase the cost of foodstuffs. From here Bicard goes to the campaign to save French laboratories and the patent medicines advertised in *L'Intransigeant.* He focuses on one prepared by Sister Aimée, which is supposed to restore virility to the old. It has been so successful, he claims, that the editors of *L'Intran* have ceased to shed tears.[56]

The second example comes from January 1921. Bicard insists that what has just transpired at Tours is a scandal. (During the Socialist Congress there, a schism had developed in the party, and the French Communist Party had been created.) De la Fouchardière declares that he does not want to hear anymore about it. He insists that Bicard understands nothing of politics, but Bicard protests. For proof of his qualifications, he notes that the owner of the rue Bridaine bistro always listens carefully to his political explanations. De la Fouchardière suggests that the owner does so only because while Bicard is talking, he is consuming drinks. It then turns out that Bicard had explained the Third International to a group of drunken actors while they were all held by the police. But Bicard protests that it was not the Congress at Tours that he was referring to but the "Saint Hubert Affair." The association for the protection of animals has moved to Tours, he says, and has chosen Saint Hubert, often considered the patron saint of hunters, as its patron. As Bicard and de la Fouchardière recount the story, Hubert abused the privilege of hunting (hunting even on the Sabbath) until one day he saw Christ between the antlers of a deer. For Bicard, the Saint Hubert story disproves the proverb "Qui va à la chasse, perd sa place" (he who goes hunting loses his place) since the saint had gone hunting but had received an excellent place on the calendar. This discussion of places soon leads the two to the position that the best places go to those who change their minds, to turncoats like Millerand (former socialist and now a conservative and president of the Republic).[57]

A more domestic view of Bicard's life emerges in our third example. This time Bicard begins by considering the elaborate funeral held in Chicago for a gangster and then a similar ceremony in Manchester, England. He's then reminded of the story of an Indian prince who paid a French lady and her husband thirteen million francs because of an adulterous affair: "Thirteen million for a chick when one can get a deputy for ten thousand francs." As the conversation evolves, Bicard notes that he does not believe the story that a bookmaker murdered a client for the money. Ordinarily, Bicard explained, a bookmaker does not have to do anything to get money from his customers. They surrender it to him of their own will. Bicard insists that he does not believe the story about the rajah because of his own experiences in the matter. Replying to de la Fouchardière's shocked questions about Mme. Bicard, the Bouif says that she had succeeded in attracting only a policeman and on one occasion a chestnut seller. Bicard's case concerned his daughter, Charlotte. Proudly she had informed him, since he was always telling her to stop wasting her time with two-bit gigolos, that she had attracted a rich Indian, her own rajah. This story brings many congratulations and, when Bicard needs money for the track, a request for a loan. It turns out, however, that Charlotte's boyfriend is just a poor salesman in a department store. A case of jaundice had given him an Oriental complexion, so the store set him to selling carpets. De la Fouchardière asks Bicard whether he kicked his rajah in the behind. "No," answered Bicard, "I am stupid. I was, again, enough of a sucker to buy him a drink and to lend him five francs."[58]

If Bicard's conversations reflected the *Canard* in their mixtures of politics and sexual adventures, they mirrored the paper in another important way as well. In his public lecture on the Bouif, de la Fouchardière labeled Bicard a cynic but said that he was neither an anarchist nor a rebel: "The Bouif accepts all regimes, except the dry one."[59] Bicard did share with anarchism the proposition that power was power, that all systems of government were equally repressive; changing the political color would not change the reality. No one understood politics better than the police, Bicard argued, for they adapted themselves easily to whoever gave the orders, and they would be as cheerfully repressive under a communist government as under a fascist one.[60] One could also say that Bicard greeted all forms of authority with an equal absence of respect.

If we think of Bicard and de la Fouchardière as a team, of one as the alter ego of the other, then what this team did not share with anarchism was faith in a better future, faith in the revolution. Like the Anatole France of *La révolte des anges,* de la Fouchardière (that is, the author of both fictional conversationalists) did not think that revolution would change the fundamentals of power in society. When Bicard spoke of the revolution as a party (and dreamt of sleeping in the bed of the president of the Republic), his wiser interlocutor brought him back to earth. Bicard's companion was happy to be thought a revolutionary under a bourgeois government but would cease to be one in the revolution itself. For a revolution would simply bring another Napoleon into the bed of the president of the Republic. Revolutions were religions (and we know what de la Fouchardière thought of them); they both lived in the future: "What one promises you that is wonderful is the future life; the future is wonderful and paradise is the pluperfect of the conditional."[61] Behind Bicard's cynical sensuality and wise folly, de la Fouchardière effectively encapsulated the philosophy of life and politics of the *Canard: carpe diem.*

7 Peace or Postwar
The Next Last War

At the end of Jean Renoir's 1937 film, *Grande Illusion,* two escaped French officers exchange a few last words before they cross into Switzerland. One says they "must get this goddamned war over with, in the hope that it will be the last." "You are kidding yourself [Tu te fais des illusions]," his comrade replies.[1]

One can understand why, by 1937, the officer's hope might seem an illusion. But the *Canard* dealt with this problem years before, with the suggestion that the recent war might not be the last one. The weekly, of course, treated this essentially tragic idea in a humorous way, through the leitmotif of "the next last war." We are used to the idea of the France of the 1930s living under the shadow of the coming war. But the 1920s are supposed to have been more insouciant, *les années folles.* Yet, in the 1920s, the prospect of another war was clearly visible in the pages of the *Canard.*

THE WAR TO END ALL WARS?

Not long after H. G. Wells had talked of "the war that will end war," French writers whose nonmilitarist patriotism was similar to that of the *Canard* adopted the basic idea. As one of the soldiers in Barbusse's 1916 *Le feu* put it, "One must kill militarism in the belly of Germany."[2] And yet this comforting idea, that the awful sacrifices would be redeemed by a lasting peace, was not immune to the *Canard*'s satire.

A cartoon by R. Guérin in the fall of 1918 bore the title "The Great Regret of the Class of 1930." A kindly-looking gentleman addresses two sobbing little boys: "Why are you crying, my little friends?" Their answer: "Boo hoo! That man said, just like that, there would be no more wars!"[3] When this cartoon appeared, on October 23, negotiations were already underway for a victorious armistice. Thus, with the end of the war approaching, one could start to joke about the next one. Yet this combination of drawing and text goes further. It would certainly have been absurd, for those who knew the miseries of war, that these children lament not having the opportunity to share in the experience. But the attitude of these little boys reflects the ways in which the cult of war was engrained in the masculine values imparted to future Frenchmen (and not only them). The message becomes, there will always be wars because boys play at them. The tears of the little tykes are as militarist as those of *L'Intran.*

In some ways, the most pessimistic aspect of this cartoon is its timing—before the armistice, the peace treaties, and all the postwar problems. The causes of war, it argues, are lodged in the human breast (we today would say in culture or in the construction of masculinity). Writing later, Dorgelès made a similar point. As battle-weary soldiers are transformed in their own minds into heroes by the sound of the regimental band, the narrator concludes, "Come on, there will always be wars, always, always."[4] What was true during the war, for the *Canard,* was still true during the peace. A 1922 cartoon by Mat reversed the relationship. This time it is the adult, a woman, who threatens the unruly youngsters: "If you do not behave, there won't be a war."[5]

If the first cartoon was occasioned by the prospect of peace, the second was suggested by new talk of war. The issue in which it appeared was full of suggestions that Poincaré's saber rattling would bring war—but redux. Making a pastiche from the famous patriotic song *Madelon de la Victoire,* the *Canard* offered a "Re-Madelon de la Re-Victoire":

> R'madelon, refill my glass
> Because we are going to redo that!
> The *poilus* will return to war.

A similar set of re-callings had already graced the *Canard*'s pages in March 1921.[6]

But a new war was not a new idea in 1921 for readers of the weekly. The most perspicacious might have noticed a reference buried in the "Petite correspondance" section in 1916: "*Bloc*—for the next war, certainly. It will be necessary to think about it."[7] Censorship may have had something to do with the fact that the idea was not followed up at the time. After the war, however, was another matter. In December 1918, the *Canard* noted a discussion in *Le Figaro* on the army of tomorrow. "So there will be an army after the war?" the paper asked disingenuously; "we who thought that this was the last and that we had gone to the end with the sole purpose of not repeating the offense."[8]

NEXT/LAST

It was late in January 1919, after the armistice yet well before the signing of the peace treaty, that the *Canard* came up with the formula that would encapsulate its position on the future of world peace, for then the weekly began talking about "the next last war" *(la prochaine dernière guerre).*[9] The phrase the last war/*dernière guerre* can carry the same ambiguity in French that it does in English. *Dernière*/last can be the last in the series of wars that have taken place and hence mean the most recent. Or it can signify the last in the series of all wars, hence the last war that will ever take place. (This meaning could be expressed without ambiguity through the phrase *la dernière des guerres*). But this ambiguity, which the *Canard* was also willing to exploit on occasion,[10] was almost too optimistic—since it could be read as the end of war.

The phrase "the next last war" is darker. There will be a "next" war. Linking it with "last" creates two possibilities. The first, based on the last of all wars, yields an oxymoron. There cannot be a next in a series that has come to an end. To make sense of the words, the reader is obliged to understand "last" as the most recent, thereby redefining pessimistically the phrase "the last war"/*la dernière guerre,* which had become so common. The least it does is to provoke one into examining just how one understands the idea of "the last war." And yet the meaning of the war to end all wars remains as a virtuality in the syntagm and thereby opens another perspective. This vision recognizes that the idea of the war to end all wars functioned as a way of sustaining the immense sacrifices of the conflict. As such it could serve again, in the next war to end all wars.

The sheer bulkiness of the verbal syntagm, its cheerful violation of normal usage, forces the reader's attention. Thus these fours words, *la prochaine dernière guerre* (or its shorter version, *la prochaine dernière*/the next last one), become a topos for the *Canard.* Like the tears of *L'Intran* or *bourrage de crâne* (the only one of the three not created in-house), the next last war could then function as a brief signifier of both the probability of future conflict and the hollowness of the idea of the war to end all wars.

The weekly snuck this highly charged phrase in through the back door, on page 3 of the January 29, 1919, issue. On the bottom right-hand column sat a small notice under the heading "Convocations: Association des Futurs Combattants de la Prochaine Dernière Guerre [Association of Future

Combatants of the Next Last War]."[11] As with so many *Canard* quips, this pastiche did double duty. While introducing the next-last-war topos, it also mocked the veterans' organizations by replacing their ubiquitous *anciens combattants* (former combatants) with *futurs combattants* (future combatants). Even this point is not innocent. Besides pointing to a future war, it opens the possibility that these veterans' leagues were effectively preparing the ground for future combats.[12]

The pessimism reflected in the next-last-war topos also informed the lead article of that same issue, antiphrastically entitled "A War Conference." This piece hinted that the good work of the founders of the League of Nations would be undone by the economic interests that benefited from war.[13] The *Canard* referred again, in June, to "the next last war," and then justified its terms in July 1919. After quoting Marshal Ferdinand Foch to the effect that "the next war will be a war of materiel," the *Canard* quacked triumphantly. Well-intentioned people had called the weekly defeatist (from a pacifist point of view) since it had spoken of the "next last war." Foch was proving the paper right. And the point was hammered in during the following week, when the lead article began "The last war—which one must not too naively confuse with the 'last of wars *[dernière des guerres]*.' "[14]

WILSON

The weekly's disillusionment was palpable, and it replaced the higher hopes the paper had expressed at the time of the armistice. The editorial that had saluted the end of combat eschewed all irony. "Honor," it proclaimed, was due to the common soldiers for their heroic abnegation. But honor was also due to U.S. President Woodrow Wilson:

> This brave man has promised the world a peace of honor and dignity—a peace that will not contain within it the seed of a new and immense infamy.
>
> Let us salute, therefore.
>
> Let us salute the one who has saved our country—and who will dictate the terms of the new charter of free peoples.

This was uncharacteristic praise from such an irony-filled newspaper. But perhaps the greatest honor bestowed by the French weekly on the U.S. statesman was visual. Illustrating the editorial were two ducks (see figure 9), which were unusual for both their size and their detail. In the middle of the column stood a *poilu*-duck, looking the mature citizen soldier with a pipe in his mouth, a helmet on his head, and a bottle (of Vouvray, one presumes) under his wing. At the bottom, underneath the signature ("Canard"), was a

Figure 9. Wilson and the *poilu* (1918).

Duck-President Wilson, marked not only by the stars and stripes that circled his figure and the olive branch under his wing but even more so by the distinctive Wilsonian wire-rimmed glasses.[15] Visually pairing the U.S. president with the aviary symbol of French heroism was already impressive. But representing a personality in the form of the *Canard*'s living logo was a tribute reserved for the author of the Fourteen Points. While ducks were used to represent a variety of social types, from French deputies to German soldiers, no other individual was so honored. The distinctiveness of the tribute reflected the optimism of the conclusion: here was the man who would guarantee a lasting peace.

Wilson received a consistency of support and an absence of ridicule offered to no other figure in the wartime or postwar *Canard*. In the issues that followed, the *Canard* continued to honor the U.S. statesman. An enchained duck presents flowers to a starred and striped duck above a "Vive Wilson" headline; another duck, whose torso is wrapped in the U.S. flag, sports a Western-style hat and Wilsonian glasses. But other symbols could also be called into play: a human Marianne coquettishly offers her hands to a handsome Wilson.[16] After the treaties were signed, in July 1919, the *Canard* said goodbye to its American hero with one more duck: a reprint of the flag-draped bird with hat and Wilson glasses. Above it stood the headline "Wilson has gone." Below it ran the legend "Good-bye and . . . thanks all the same." This "all the same" combined the *Canard*'s pessimism with its totally uncharacteristic support for the U.S. president.[17]

VARIATIONS ON A THEME: FUTURE WARS

Given this view of the peace conference, it is unsurprising that the *Canard*'s verbal topos of the next last war continued to serve—for example, in February 1920 and March 1922. In both these cases, the phrase was tossed off casually, in the middle of discussions of other issues.[18] The mere mention of the four words was enough to make the point. References to the next last war continued to figure, throughout the decade, in the *Canard*'s journalistic menu. Twice in 1923, the weekly responded to talk of a future war with the claim that its prediction of a next last war was thereby confirmed. Twice in the same issue in 1924, the *Canard* attached its four-word topos to discussions of military preparations. In 1927 the phrase found its way into the colorful chatter of Bicard himself.[19]

Next and last, taken together, constitute an oxymoron. But so do definitive and provisional. On February 18, 1920, the *Canard* reported Lord Curzon's suggestion that it would be necessary to revise the Treaty of Versailles. The paper went on to explain that, according to diplomatic tradition, one would need a new war in order to have a new treaty, "definitive this time, at least provisionally." In its next issue the *Canard* argued that a trip by Poincaré and President of the Republic Paul Deschanel to Bordeaux should not cause panic. They were just practicing in case the war should "re-break out." The concierge of the Elysée called the trip a "dress rehearsal." But the French for this phrase, *répétition générale,* clearly has other implications.[20]

The next last war suggests an open series. In December 1922, the *Canard* humorist whose pen name was Whip let his imagination take off from the announcement that the pilotless airplane would soon be a reality:

> It was in the night of the 11th of November 2034 that at 10:14 the telephonic receiver of the Eiffel Hole (the tower of the same name had been demolished in 1986 and replaced by a hole three hundred meters deep) recorded the following message sent by the Alsace balloon station:
>
> "Squadron G.K.W. of about 2,000 super-airplanes has just passed over us, headed towards Paris at 600 kilometers per hour."

The article went on to explain that "the seventeen wars between 1918 and 2034" had been carried on with increasing scientific precision and that now everyone lived underground.[21]

Such dystopian predictions of future wars, characterized by horrific aerial bombardments of civilian targets, were common between the wars. But for the *Canard* such ghoulish humor took on its meaning in its series of warnings of coming conflict. Poison-gas attacks on cities were the subject of humor in February 1925. An imagined *Intran* echo tells of a soldier (the soldiers were now in the capital, the civilians in the safety of the front) who responds to the situation with tears, but under the circumstances one cannot tell whether they are the product of patriotic emotion or of tear gas. This imagined war was referred to by the shorter version, *la prochaine dernière* (the next last).[22]

But maybe the series would not be unlimited. What if the last war were just the next-to-last war? In February 1921, the paper referred to the causes of "la dernière avant-dernière guerre [the last next-to-last war]."[23] On November 21, 1923, Roger Brindolphe entitled his article "To Fix the Date of the Next Armistice." He wrote that "it is not, in effect, a secret to anyone that within a reasonable time we are going to have, and this time definitively, a last war."[24] At this time, with French troops in the Ruhr, talk of war might not have been so fanciful. But it would be a mistake to see the *Canard*'s regular insistence on coming war(s) as merely a reflection of international crises. If such comments, with or without the topos of the next last war, showed up in the period of Franco-German confrontation that lasted from 1919 to 1924, they were also present in the period of relative international harmony from 1925 to 1928. If the *Canard* could speak of a "new last war" in 1923, it could also wonder in 1925 how much higher the defense budget would be if the 1914–1918 experience had not been "the last war *[la dernière des guerres]*." In 1927 the paper spoke of the coming war: "and then also this will be the 'last of the last.' " Except that "this time, that will not fool anyone."[25]

"LONG LIVE FRENCH MILITARISM"

Such consistency was fueled by more than the technique of the repeating gag. Behind it lay an analysis of the relationship of war to contemporary society. Among the reasons for a next last war was militarism, not excluding the French variety. The great military parade of July 14, 1919, represented the first Bastille Day festivities since the victorious armistice, and, as a result, it was a celebration of that even more than of the Revolution. The *Canard* covered the patriotic day with a full-page satirical cartoon by Laforge. Above the cartoon, a banner headline underlined the incongruity of celebrating peace through a military display: "Down with German militarism! Long live French militarism!" Frenchmen had spent four years fighting against what they considered German militarism. But this evil, the *Canard* was hinting, had changed sides.[26]

The page 2 article that reported on the victory parade took its title from a popular prewar song, "En r'venant d'la revue"—an ambiguous reference. The ditty in question took a lighthearted view of a family's enthusiastic presence at a military parade since all its members end up in the arms of new acquaintances. But it was also associated with the cult of the prewar nationalist general and politician Georges Boulanger.[27] The anonymous *Canard* journalist, after satirical evocations of the dead and wounded, added, "It is with regret that we went away saying au revoir and *'til next time [à la prochaine].*" The French could mean " 'til the next parade" or " 'til the next war." A story in the same issue told of a Mr. Tarte, a great verbal patriot during the war, who rented a window in Paris to see the victory parade. When it turned out that the window provided a view only of a dirty courtyard, Mr. Tarte consoled his wife with the thought that they would do better at "the next victory."[28]

The *Canard* returned to the idea of the militarism implicit in military parades in a 1923 Guilac cartoon. Below the drawing of troops with flags and bands, one reads: "It is not in Germany that one would see such a beautiful demonstration in favor of peace and disarmament." This case of antiphrastic irony (labeling militaristic activities with terms like *peace* and *disarmament*) is one the *Canard* used often in the 1920s, but here Guilac added another topos. One of the flags in the parade bears the inscription "Pour la prochaine dernière! [For the next last one!]"[29] The point was repeated in another article in the same issue: "France militarist? What a joke," the paper editorialized. "The truth is that, in authorizing the deployment of such a warlike display, our government wanted, on the contrary, to give the people an excellent object lesson and disgust them with militarism. We can only feel sorry for those who have not understood."[30]

French militarism meant more than parades. It led to an aggressive foreign policy, as in the following weather bulletin (from May 1921): "In France, [there is] a rather nasty wind of imperialism, and the temperature of certain chauvinist spirits has a tendency to rise." An imperialist France? As early as 1919 the *Canard* wrote the following mock message in its "Petite correspondance": "Contact the Committee for the Left Bank of the Elbe," a parodic extension of French claims to the left bank of the Rhine and the network of committees of that name. But it was Bicard, in that same May 1921 issue, who explained the issue most clearly. After a discussion of the life of Joan of Arc, the Bouif turns to the fictional de la Fouchardière:

—What disgusts me a bit, it's that all this is starting over.

—All what?

—All the Hundred Years' War, except that now it's us who are the English.

—Huh?

—We have settled ourselves in Germany, until the Krauts dig us up a Joan of Arc or a Napoleon to throw us out, which is always annoying.

The countries are interchangeable; only the process continues.[31]

And the idea of a continuing process could also be used to update old topics. In a non-Bicard article in June 1920, de la Fouchardière spoke of the League of Patriots, the prewar organization that, under the patronage of Maurice Barrès, had demonstrated in front of the statue of Strasbourg in the Place de la Concorde. In order to be able to continue their work, the author suggests, the League of Patriots should transport the statue of Strasbourg to Berlin and naturalize themselves as "krauts."

> [They could then] demand Alsace and Lorraine (which is the raison d'être of the League of Patriots) until they had obtained a new war (which is the raison d'être of all leagues of patriots).
>
> When Germany will have annexed Alsace and Lorraine again, the members of the League of Patriots will take the train back to Paris with their statue of Strasbourg, which they will put back on the Place de la Concorde, and they will be able once again to demand the return of Alsace and Lorraine to France.
>
> It's a wonderful system that will permit us to have, permanently, the League of Patriots and war.[32]

An unsigned article, a few months later, linked the same fiction to the suggestion that the Germans were preparing a revanchist war: a "Dr. Moritz Parrhès" was shown speaking in front of the "Strasburdenkmal" [sic, for the missing *g*] on the "Konkordiaplatz" in Berlin.[33]

The *Canard* turned Barrès into a symbol of Franco-German interchangeability. Implicit also in the traveling monument is the idea that with the return of Alsace and Lorraine nationalists like Barrès lacked a territorial issue. The writers of the *Canard* knew full well that the nationalist statesman had been a leading campaigner for French absorption of the territories on the left bank of the Rhine. But dealing with that issue separately and imagining Barrès as a German patriot helped to emphasize the idea of reciprocal revanche, so necessary to the idea of the next last war.[34]

ARMS RACE IN PEACE

Some things could be seen as both causes of a new war and evidence that one was planned—for example, the continuing arms race. On January 15, 1919, the *Canard* placed an article over the satirical name of Senator Dr. Simon Hégésippe. This worthy addresses the concerns of those who are surprised that factories continue to turn out enormous numbers of artillery shells. These people, whom the senator describes as "simple but pusillanimous," worry what the use would be for all these projectiles. It is unlikely that the *Canard*'s readers were reassured by the good senator's explanation that they would be remanufactured into nonthreatening objects.[35]

The *Canard*'s references to the French defense industry combined both a sense of the international context of French armaments and a characteristic rhetorical device. In October 1921, the *Canard* noted how the recent fire in the fort of Aubervilliers exposed the manufacture of poison-gas shells at that location. The weekly noted that this manufacture took place in the context of French demands for German disarmament. The title of the piece, "Les travaux de la paix," could be understood directly as war preparation in peacetime and antiphrastically as a comment on the bellicosity of the munitions factory.[36] The antiphrastic usage predominated in the pages of the weekly. Under the title "Against German Militarism," a September 1923 article reported an explosion in an arms depot near Metz, in reconquered Lorraine, of fifty-two thousand "humanitarian and pacific grenades destined to symbolize peace founded on justice *[la paix du droit]*." Evidently France was resolved to present "an unshakable pacifism against the imperialist designs of Germany."[37]

These points clearly made, the *Canard* could echo them in briefer texts. A series of short articles graced the front pages of three successive issues: November 14, 21, and 28, 1923. All were entitled "La paix par le droit," and all dealt with accidental explosions that caused fatalities. The first piece described explosions in Italy and Rumania. The next two referred to accidents in France. The *Canard* added here that that these shells were "destined to assure to the last war its definitive character."[38] In 1924 the *Canard* reported munitions explosions in France under titles like "La paix par le droit" and "For World Peace." The year 1927 saw a similar explosion in Kiel in Germany.[39] Clearly the problem was international.

Certain weapons systems were easily associated with future wars. For example, the *Canard* quoted *Excelsior* on a new biplane destined for aerial bombardment; the paper added only the comment: "When we said that *that* was going to start again."[40] Similarly, a new French warship was "pacific and humanitarian," while a U.S. one was designed to ensure "world peace."[41]

As in most matters military, the *Canard* drew on the experience of the recent world war. German airships and submarines had come in for special condemnation during that conflict: the Gothas and zeppelins because they were used to bomb Paris and other population centers, and the submarines because they were judged cowardly weapons and were frequently directed against unarmed shipping—attacks that also led to civilian casualties. (Unrestricted submarine war was the official cause of U.S. entry into the war.)

When, after the war, these weapons passed to the French and their allies, the invitation to irony was irresistible. The weekly celebrated the delivery of the German zeppelin *Nordstern* to France:

> It took all the barbarism of the Teutons and their stupid admiration of the kolossal [sic] to conceive and build war machines like the zeppelins.[. . .]
>
> It is quite clear, however, that in the service of Civilization and Justice the nature and appearance of the zeppelin changes completely.

The *Canard* applied the same argument to submarines, noting, in 1923, the launch of three such French "pacific submarines," with "humanitarian torpedoes," "in execution of the new program of naval disarmament." The linking of naval construction and disarmament (repeated, for example, in July 1924) could be read, with an ambiguity typical of the *Canard*, as a critique of military spending during a period when disarmament was under discussion or as a cynical comment on the meaninglessness of talk of disarmament.[42]

THE (L)IMITATION OF ARMAMENTS

But this last interpretation would have meant abandoning the hopes of many peace-loving Europeans. After all, Wilson's legacy was greater than just the Treaties of Paris, which ended the war. It included the League of Nations and an ideological and political current that favored disarmament, international cooperation, and peace. If from 1919 to 1924 this current, politically personified in France by Aristide Briand, seemed on the defensive, the later years of the decade, marked by the London Conference, the Dawes plan, the meeting at Thoiry, and the Locarno Pact, marked its apparent triumph under the patronage of the Franco-German diplomatic couple of Briand and Gustav Stresemann.

Nevertheless, the failure of disarmament was a *Canard* leitmotif throughout the postwar decade. And why did it fail? Commenting on the fact that the disarmament commission included Marshal Foch and a collection of generals, the *Canard* stated, "It is as if one allowed the question of the suppression of alcohol to be studied by a commission of barkeeps."[43] This was in July 1921. A similar point was made in January 1926.[44]

Not surprisingly, the weekly felt able to reassure its readers, in October 1921, even before the opening of the Washington disarmament conference, that "the menace of a general disarmament that was dangling for some time over public affairs seems fortunately to have attenuated." This being so, the *Canard* could go on a few weeks later to report on the conference activities in search of a peace "that will no longer be disturbed until the renewal of hostilities."[45] And, of course, the *Canard* continued to cast doubt on disarmament by linking it, rhetorically, to references to the arms race.[46] The *Canard* loved to underline the irony of the involvement of socialists (like the English Ramsay MacDonald) or other leftists (like the French Herriot) with displays of military prowess.[47] But its fundamental point was one of continuity: when it came to disarmament policy, it did not matter which group of politicians was in office.[48]

By 1927, the satirical weekly had come up with its own explanation of the disarmament policies of the powers negotiating at Geneva:

> —Let the Europeans eliminate their cannons! . . . says Mr. Coolidge.
>
> —What is necessary, especially, says France, is that my neighbors not be authorized to have an army.
>
> —England, alone, should have a navy! says Mr. Chamberlain.
>
> In sum, disarmament consists especially in disarming others.[49]

Or as the *Canard* put it in April of that year, each country wanted to be as well armed as its neighbors: *l'imitation des armements* (the imitation of armaments). Originally, however, the paper argued disingenuously, this phrase had been spelled differently. The *Canard* writers did not have to provide the solution to the puzzle: spelled differently *l'imitation des armements* could be *limitation des armements* (arms limitation).[50]

FROM THE LEAGUE TO LOCARNO

With this view of disarmament conferences, one can imagine how much respect the *Canard* displayed toward the League of Nations. Of course, respect was not the weekly's strong suit, but it had treated the League's creator, Wilson, with special regard. The U.S. statesman's institutional offspring did not fare as well. In French, the League of Nations is the Société des Nations (S.D.N.). The weekly referred to it that way in the title of an article on September 24, 1924, but inside the article the S.D.N. became the Société de Navigation. The *Canard* imagined that after the naval exercises at Spithead and Toulon, the S.D.N. organized their own on Lake Geneva with ships named "Peoples United," "Justice First," "Arbitration," and "Fraternity." But there were problems. "The *Disarmament* and the *Arbitration* hit an obstacle not present on the charts" (a reference to recent French naval accidents), but "one hopes to be able to refloat them before the end of maneuvers."[51] Behind the allegory and the jokes about a Swiss fleet (which the *Canard* evoked by pretending to disdain them) lay the basic point that in a world of arms the League lacked any of its own. Repeating this last point a month later, the weekly mocked a recent League of Nations decision against Great Britain by reporting that, in consequence, the international organization sent the British fleet to bombard England.[52]

Using its characteristic device of ironic antiphrasis, the *Canard* argued, in February 1927, that, thanks to the League of Nations, peace reigned "across the vast world." The claim was backed up by dispatches celebrating the peace and harmony in places like China, Nicaragua, and Syria—places where armed conflicts were in progress. The conclusion?: The members of the League of Nations "have nothing further to do. Besides, they are not doing anything anymore."[53] Later that same year, in March, Pierre Scize wrote a long article, in which sadness struggled with bitterness, saying goodbye to his earlier hopes for the League. The international body reflected no more than the usual maneuvers and combinations of nations and economic interests, draped in hypocritical oratory.[54] The *Canard* may have waited until 1927 to give such an unambiguous funeral for the League of Nations, but its readers had been invited to shed their illusions years earlier.

A similar skepticism also manifested itself in the *Canard*'s attitudes toward the Franco-German agreements of Locarno in 1925 and the less important results at Thoiry in 1926. In these cases, however, the weekly's approach was more subtle. One of the *Canard*'s favorite techniques for taking a position in the debates of the day without staking out a position of univocal support was to say nothing, or little, about a given political position but to mercilessly mock its opponents. For example, in the years after the armistice, as French intervention or support for Russian Whites was frequently in the news, the *Canard* gave hardly any space to life in Bolshevik Russia or to Bolshevism itself. A careful reading of the *Canard*, either in those years or later, would show little real sympathy with Marxism-Leninism as either ideology or political system. And though there was ample room for irony and parody in Russian communism, the satirical weekly avoided mocking Lenin or his lieutenants. Instead, the *Canard* relentlessly satirized, critiqued, and parodied the anti-Bolshevik campaigns then current in the mainstream French press.[55]

The coverage of Locarno was similar. The *Canard* did not come out and praise it; it mocked its critics instead. On October 14, 1925, the *Canard* replied to a right-wing journalist who had expressed his lack of interest in developments at Locarno: "Certainly! It is only a question of peace in Europe. And, then, when one is no longer of draft age, well, one does not give a damn."[56] But the weekly came back more strongly in the next issue with a phony article by Gustave Hervé and an equally imagined interview with Poincaré. Both figures railed against Locarno as "treason." Associating a position with the *Canard*'s wartime bête noire, Hervé, or with the postwar politician the *Canard* hated most, Poincaré, was hardly a way of recommending it. But objection to the anti-Locarno forces was not the same thing as subscribing to this new international agreement or to the diplomatic processes that had seen its birth.[57] Nevertheless, the weekly used the same technique again (parodying Poincaré) a year later with reference to Briand and Stresemann's meeting at Thoiry.[58]

The culpable opposition to Locarno and Thoiry was not only French:

> Our nationalists display toward the Thoiry propositions as much hostility on their side as the German nationalists do on theirs.
>
> This is completely idiotic.
>
> Because, finally, what displeases one group should for *that very reason* delight the other group.
>
> The truth is that both groups are in agreement.
>
> Agreement to fight.
>
> Or rather to make those fight who would wish to be left alone.[59]

The French of "to be left alone" was "f . . . [outre] la paix." If the enemies of Locarno and Thoiry were against peace, did that mean that these milestones of Briand's foreign policy would bring about that result? The careful reader of the *Canard Enchaîné* would not be comfortable with such a judgment.

The *Canard* was certainly willing to have fun with the two diplomatic names. Since much had been made of the fact that Briand and Stresemann shared a friendly drink at Thoiry, the *Canard* inserted phony advertisements urging one to order a "Thoiry," as if it were an apéritif. But then, the weekly had already dreamed up mock apéritif ads for a "Locarno."[60] Liquor was hardly a negative marker for the *Canard*, but the parodic ads lent little dignity to the politics of diplomatic cooperation.

Yet even when the *Canard* was mocking critics of Locarno, in October 1925, Bicard and de la Fouchardière had already formulated a more pessimistic view. De la Fouchardière quotes to his alcoholic companion the phrase of a French delegate, "Let us set up a barrier to the devastating torrent," to which the fictional journalist adds, "Just try a bit, Bicard, to stop a torrent with a barrier. . . . That is exactly the naive and conscientious work to which the Conference of Locarno devotes itself, as well as all the other conferences." Bicard's only suggestion is that since the problem is a larger German population, the French should send them condoms.[61]

In the last issue of 1925, the *Canard* noted the mutual-aid provisions in the Locarno accords: who would come to whose assistance in case of an attack by a third party. "In short, one has the impression that what has been foreseen by the Peace of Locarno are eventualities of war"—a prescient critique of the spirit of the agreements.[62] The article in which this appeared was called "The Spirit of Locarno." By the spring of 1926, that expression was being used as "peace through justice" had been before, as an antiphrastic commentary on warlike activities or preparations.[63]

OUTLAWING WAR?

When negotiations developed that led to the Kellogg-Briand Pact (which outlawed war and was signed by over sixty countries), the *Canard* began by repeating its Locarno strategy—that is, by parodying critics of the treaty.[64] Slightly later, in September 1927, the *Canard* with characteristic irony mocked the idea of eliminating war: "It is confirmed that the vote of the Disarmament Commission outlawing war is *as serious as can be.* The disappearance of standing armies can only be henceforth a matter of days."[65] Bicard in his infinite wisdom had dealt with this idea over two years earlier. Outlawing wars would be of no use since in every war there is never an aggressor—that is, the other side always starts it.[66]

Like so many of the *Canard*'s positions, its cynical pacifism could be read two ways. Its concern for a next last war could be read as a desperate, though humorous, attempt to derail French militarism before it was too late. But the weekly's lack of faith in disarmament or diplomacy could just as easily be used to justify the opposite policy—preparedness for the inevitable war, the need for military strength in a world where force still ruled. Readers with different world-views could find support for their positions.

Such ambiguities survived even in the largely nonironic, militantly pacifist articles of Pierre Scize. Scize took the occasion in January 1927 to reply to many readers who had expressed their dismay at the prospect of a new war and who had asked whether something should not be done before it was too late, perhaps a new newspaper or a new league should be founded. The pacifist journalist rejected all such solutions; the "naive appetite for organization" only underlined these readers' "weakness" and "solitude." The essential work against war had to be done inside each individual. Scize approvingly quoted another writer: "I have abandoned utopia long ago. I know completely that there will be new wars." But this writer had determined to refuse to collaborate in war making in any way, a better approach, according to the *Canard* journalist, than discharging one's responsibility onto an organization.[67]

How easy would it be to change thousands of souls? At the end of that same year, as the holiday gift-giving season approached, some women, conscientious pacifists, wrote to Scize asking what presents they could give their male children. War toys would encourage militarism, but if they did not give them, their little boys would cry. The disillusioned writer, however, was not even sure that banning war toys would help because aggression seemed to be bred into males. Scize ended by invoking Cain and Abel, the same kind of reference that would be used by a conservative to justify vigilance. Though Scize's insistence on individual transformation certainly echoed the approach of the pacifist philosopher who used the pen name Alain (whom he did not cite), his blunt formulations appeared less optimistic about achieving their common goal.[68]

Such a bleak view of the future certainly justified the expression *the next last war.* Yet other elements were part of the *Canard*'s treatment of the idea of the coming war. There was the weekly's characteristic mix of seriousness with the spirit of fun. There was still life to be lived, and perhaps that was the best answer to militarism. The right-wing veterans' organizer, Binet-Valmer, had explained that his motto was "*Commander pour servir* [command in order to serve]." The *Canard* answered that its motto was "*Commander pour se faire servir* [command, or order, in order to be served]." Thus the *Canard* would order *(commander)* "a Picon, a Pernod, a little rum."[69] Perhaps, then, while waiting for the next last war, one could order a "Thoiry" or a "Locarno."

8 Web of Memory

The fact that the Great War was over was no reason for the *Canard* to stop talking about it. Between the last war and the next last one stretched the ways French society digested the war, the way it understood it, the way it recounted it to itself—that is, its memory of the war.

In his introductory material for *Les lieux de mémoire,* Pierre Nora showed how memory could act as a locus of contest, but most especially so in its transition to history, in the processes through which the unconscious becomes conscious and the informal becomes the official.[1] The years following the armistice were crucial in this respect. The process of making memory of the war was not consensual; it was contested, and such contests were the natural territory of this war-born duck. Peace also allowed the *Canard* to take sharper positions. If during the war the periodical had frequently skirted antimilitarism, after the fighting the weekly enveloped both war and militarism in a web of memory.

In Henri Barbusse's 1919 antiwar novel, *Clarté,* the ideologically aware hero-narrator attributes the following program to the organizers of patriotic ceremonies for the dead: "Remember the evil not in order to avoid it, but in order to do it again, by heedlessly stirring up the causes of hatred. Make of memory a contagious malady."[2] Barbusse linked memory to commemoration and both to the danger of a new war. The *Canard*'s participation in the political battles over commemoration reflected similar concerns, but it also transcended them. A pacifist periodical, the *Canard* was also a veterans' one. As such it was concerned to defend the honor of the veterans, but especially the *poilus,* the front-line soldiers. These potentially discordant impulses informed the *Canard*'s interventions in the politics of memory. During the war, the weekly had taken pride in its role of deflator of *bourrage de crâne.* The process continued after the war, except that now the *Canard* could act more openly, challenging the emerging official memory with its own version of events.

ANNIVERSARIES

As a satirical weekly, the *Canard Enchaîné* needed occasions to construct its own duck's-eye-view memory of the Great War. Perhaps the most obvious occasions were anniversaries; except that here the *Canard* chose its own events to underline through mock celebration. The *Canard*'s anniversaries marked the antithesis of official heroism—for example, its commemoration of the flights of the government to the safety of Bordeaux in September 1914 and June 1918. In June 1919, one of the weekly's headlines, "A Great Sports Anniversary, the Second Paris-Bordeaux," turned the retreat into a rally. In October, it was time for the "fifth anniversary" of the Paris-Bordeaux, this time referring to the events of 1914. The Bordeaux departure was hung like an albatross around the neck of Raymond Poincaré (president of the Republic throughout the war).[3] The year 1919 provided other such occasions. When Parisians celebrated the Feast of Assumption on August 15 of that year, the *Canard* explained that they were commemorating an event of the previous year, when, under attack by Big Bertha and the Gotha bombers, Parisians had left their city to show their disdain for German weapons.[4]

The war was also *bourrage de crâne.* On August 24, 1921, the *Canard* noted that on this day in 1914, a *Le Matin* headline read, "The Cossacks at Five Stages from Berlin." The weekly reminded its readers that "one has, thank God, well-stuffed skulls since, but one has never surpassed this." The Cossacks-at-five-stages motif served in the postwar as a comical marker of wartime *bourrage de crâne.* In later years the *Canard* combined this evocation with the idea that now this was true, the first time because of the Russian advances in the Russo-Polish fighting of 1920, the second time because of the Russian-German agreement at Rapallo in 1922. Playing on the fact that the former Russian ally was now the Soviet enemy, the *Canard* explained that the Russian steamroller had all the virtues earlier attributed to it by conformist journalists, except that it had taken over seventy months to get it into operation. The satirical weekly neglected to note that it too had accepted, if only briefly, the Russian-steamroller myth.[5] But the *Canard* was not deterred from proposing its own war museum dedicated to the *bourreurs de crâne.* Its exhibits? A sandwich (used to make German soldiers surrender), General Winter, and a steamroller. Throughout the following decades, other wars, whether with France as a belligerent or not, provided the occasion for replays of the Cossacks-at-five-stages-from-Berlin motif.[6]

The *Canard* also recalled some of the more tragically absurd reporting of 1914. On August 22 of that year, the *Canard* reminded its readers, the newspaper *Excelsior* had reported, "Everyone is unanimous in recognizing that German bullets *are not painful.*" Often soldiers did not even notice that a bullet had struck through them until the next day. Two issues later, the weekly recounted stories from August 1914 on the limited nocivity of German shells and bullets.[7] After fifty-one months of bloodletting, such stories carried their own ridicule.

The rhythms of the seasons also carried messages. In 1922, a *Canard* writer warned the young men who were parading with their girlfriends, or just girl watching, to remember the lessons of the war. Then, spring had meant offensives, an evocation that contrasted with the life-affirming couplings of peacetime. The other side of the war experience was picked up later in the same issue. In a cartoon one man (obviously a civilian) says to another in a café, "Spring? What is that to us now that there are no longer any offensives?"[8]

Offensives meant battles, and the *Canard* also exploited their anniversaries—but in its own ways. One was noting the anniversaries of spectacular defeats, like the Battle of Morhange. As the *Canard* put it in 1926, "At the end of August 1914 five thousand French soldiers were massacred in execution of the glorious Plan 17." Plan 17 was put into effect in the beginning of the war; it called for an offensive into Alsace-Lorraine and was a bloody failure. The deadly costs of some military blunders were so well known that they did not need detailing—only commemoration. In an attack on Pierre-Paul Painlevé, the *Canard* argued that the sixteenth of April was a fatal date for the leftist politician. It was the date, among other occasions, of the Chemin des Dames offensive in 1917, when Painlevé was premier, and that offensive "has remained painfully famous."[9]

HONOR TO THE *POILUS*

The *Canard*'s construction of memory meant providing an accurate picture of the war as fought by France's front-line soldiers. And painting this picture involved, first of all, seeing that it was they who received credit for the victory, as the weekly had proclaimed in its lead column of November 13, 1918.[10] Support for the common soldier did double duty with anticlericalism in the *Canard*'s attacks on those who attributed the salvation of France to some form of divine—in this context, Catholic—intervention.

The weekly had already addressed this issue during the fighting.[11] But the blood was barely dry on the battlefields of the Western Front when the *Canard* felt obliged to reply to the linking of the victory and the cult of the Sacred Heart, a link forged by the right-wing Catholic paper *La Croix.* The cult of the Sacred Heart had long been a focus of reactionary anti-Republican sentiment. But the key to the *Canard*'s outrage lay in the way it introduced *La Croix*'s claim: "*Poilus,* listen well. When you are told that it is you who have saved France, when Marshal Joffre affirms it at the Academy, you are being fooled. The savior of France is the Sacred Heart."[12]

The *Canard* humorist Rodolphe Bringer evoked similar arguments in January 1925. "Decidedly, it was certainly Saint Genevieve who won the Battle of the Marne." The priest of St. Etienne du Mont had just affirmed it. "So do not speak to me any more about Marshal Joffre, his general staff, or even the courage of the *poilus.*" The problem, Bringer went on, was that, "to speak frankly, Saint Genevieve was not very, very nice to us." After winning the Battle of the Marne and saving Paris, she left the French to struggle on "for close to five years."[13]

As a good anticlerical, Bringer zeroed in on the tendency of such religious arguments to attribute positive outcomes to divine intervention while leaving negative events unexplained. For the *Canard,* the tragedy of combat deaths was the other side of the *poilus'* claim to the laurels of victory. When a priest was quoted in the *Echo de Paris* as saying that "Germany was broken against the rock of God," the *Canard* answered that "it was a shame that between Germany and the rock of God there were fifteen hundred thousand Frenchmen." What the *Canard* would not credit to God and his saints, it surely would not attribute to mere mortals, especially if they had not fought. When another journalist wrote that Barrès had served "much more usefully than an Army corps," the *Canard* translated: "Which is as good as saying that if France had had the good fortune to possess thirty-odd heroes of this caliber, the *poilus* could have been left tranquilly at home."[14]

A correct memory of the war also included destruction of the myth that combat was some sort of heroic sport. The *Canard* began its campaign shortly after the armistice by stigmatizing an example of wartime skull stuffing. A journalist had written that he imagined himself bounding from his trench and skewering a "Kraut." "And to say that you have this treat everyday, in addition to your rations. Ah, my good fellows, you are not to be pitied!"[15] But, with the fighting over, writers continued to hold that the war had been fun, and the *Canard* continued to mock them for it. In May 1921, a French journalist opined that it was harder to tear oneself from civilian occupations to "go without peril or glory to occupy" German territory than it had been in wartime. The *Canard*'s reply made the point explicit: "What is amusing in war is to shoot with a rifle and to be shot at!"[16] When a journalist wrote, in 1922, that an air show reminded him of "the good old days when French birds streaked across the skies above the battlefields," the *Canard* agreed: "How happy one was, feet warm, seated before a meal, while Guynemer [a French ace] and the others got themselves killed!"[17]

Not sport, the war was not a vacation either. A cartoon of February 1919 showed a prosperous bourgeois explaining to a recently demobilized and more modestly dressed man: "It's going to seem hard for you, to get back to work . . . after four years in which you have not been doing anything." An exaggeration? A year later, the *Canard* quoted from a business periodical, the *Journée Industrielle:* "During the entire war all the soldiers were spoiled"; they experienced "several years of a carefree and glorious life." This wartime lifestyle explained, according to the *Journée,* their lassitude when they had to get back to work. The *Canard* pretended to agree: "In the next last one we will be sure to spoil the soldiers less; they will return with less bitterness."[18] In 1920 the *Canard* quoted a comment made by the minister of commerce (to *L'Intran*) that one of the causes of the postwar price rise known as *la vie chère* was that "the mobilized soldiers in the trenches had gotten used to eating too much meat, drinking too much wine, and smoking too much tobacco." The statement reflected both a limited reality (many soldiers of rural origin had not been used to such a rich diet) and earlier anxieties (that after the relative excitement of peacetime military service draftees would not return to their villages). But the *Canard* treated all these explanations as blatant examples of civilian ingratitude and incomprehension.[19]

The *Canard* summed up its critique of the war-as-summer-camp motif with the following piece of nostalgia for the "carefree" time at the front: "and the smiling and paternal superior officers, and those nights under the stars, on a bed of fresh grass, lulled to sleep by the glorious voice of the cannon." The pointed satire in the last phrase was necessary because many looked back on the war in almost these terms. Only a few years later, the rightist Georges Valois wrote, "Do you remember comrades [. . .] the exaltation, the fear overcome, [. . .] and the ambushes on summer nights in the fields of wildflowers; and the long waits in the rain; and the exhaustion, and the delicious rest on the straw of the stables?"[20]

Stigmatizing those who looked back with longing on the war was also a way to attack figures who lived off the war mystique. Bicard gave this idea its clearest formulation when he attacked the rightist veteran organizer Binet-Valmer, who had said of the war experience, "THOSE WERE THE GOOD TIMES." Binet-Valmer was courageous, the wise fool argued: "All the guys who have died are dead, certainly, but there are some who have come back with one arm, and on the end of this arm they still have a hand which is good for socking Mr. Binet-Valmer one on the kisser." "It is curious," Bicard continued, "that this citizen has still not managed to understand that the war was not fun for everybody. All the better for those who had fun, but maybe that is not a reason to brag about it. And if they are not having fun during the peace, that is certainly not a reason to turn others against it." *Canard* journalists also socked it to politicians like Poincaré and writers like Henri de Montherlant for positive remarks about the war.[21]

The *Canard* would have no truck with the kind of nostalgia that could be found in the works of otherwise sympathetic writers like Dorgelès. The narrator of *Les croix de bois* insists to his incredulous buddies that after the war they will look back and say, " 'Those were the good days,' " a phrase he offers again at the end of the book.[22] Bicard's position is closer, though harsher, to the more philosophical conclusion of Cendrars, reminiscing with an old army buddy: "I lacked an arm. He lacked a leg.[. . .] No, those were not the good times. But the good times is to have survived."[23] For Bicard, the military contribution to civilization was murder and mutilation: "a magnificent esstension [sic] of cemeteries" and "the prosperity of manufacturers of artificial limbs."[24] By the time de la Fouchardière wrote these words of wisdom, in 1927, every French person knew that war was deadly. The *Canard*'s task was to remove the tragic glamour from the war experience without casting doubt on the essential heroism of France's *poilus.*

The *Canard*'s Pierre Scize, in many ways Bicard's serious alter ego, deglamorized the war with the account of the visit of an elegant young lady to an exhibition of military art. As she leaves, she is horrified by a poster for the Gueules Cassées. This was the popular name for the Union des Blessés de la Face, the association for the support of soldiers with disfiguring facial wounds. Her reaction: "What horror, one should not show such things." Scize asks what this woman imagined: "Did the idea strike her, suddenly, that *this* was war." These wounds had a message: "For nothing can stand up to the spectacle of your wounds. For I will close the mouth of the most enraged warmonger by showing him the holes that are your eyes, the ravines that are your nose, the crevices that are your lips. And the day will come when your Dantesque masks, having become an obsession for humanity, will be engraved in the memory of humanity." On that day perhaps people everywhere will abandon war, Scize hoped, using an argument that would be echoed a decade later in Abel Gance's antiwar film, *J'accuse.*[25]

Beyond the gendered discourse of the beautiful young woman who turns in horror from the disfigured male, Scize shows how a correct memory of the war relied on reading this tragic corporal language engraved on the bodies of the wounded, their faces texts imprinted by the violence of battle. Scize developed the language of disfiguration in an article that responded to a circular from the Quai d'Orsay announcing positions in the Foreign Service. Wounded veterans could participate in the competition only "on the express condition that facial lesions were superficial and have not left any apparent deformities." The combination of ingratitude and indelicacy made an easy target. And the idea of men permanently deprived of female companionship surfaced in his explanation of the masculine sex appeal required for the niceties of diplomatic socializing. But the *Canard* author also stressed the counter-lesson of the corporally inscribed memory. Their "ravaged faces [. . .] would attest that war is something other than the withdrawal of passports, speeches in front of marble monuments, [. . .] border adjustments, and conferences in resort locations."[26] Though Scize did not say so, he presumably knew that his technique had been tried. At the signing of the Versailles Treaty in 1919, a number of particularly gruesome facially wounded soldiers were purposefully presented before the German signatories.[27]

For the *Canard,* deglamorizing the war could be as simple as noting some of the less edifying exploits of the conflict, as when five hundred French soldiers on leave were killed "gloriously" in 1918 in a train accident.[28] Accidents, even mortal ones, combat deaths, horrible wounds—all had their place in the heroic discourse of war. But bleating? "Did not the soldiers who left for the front tend to compare themselves to sheep being led to the slaughter?" the weekly asked. "And who has not heard, during the departure of military trains, the baa baa baa which filled the train stations?"[29]

EXECUTIONS AND OFFICERS

The *Canard* further demythified memory by separating the violence of war from the ennobling context of action against the national enemy. In a take-off on recent reporting of the discovery of a mysterious human skeleton, the *Canard* reported a similar find in the department of the Aisne. The bones are found in a place called the "Chemin des Dames," and a physician determines that the individual in question died nine years ago (we are in 1926). Witnesses admit that nine years ago they heard, coming from the direction of the Chemin des Dames, "a veritable fusillade" while great flashes "lit up the horizon." Thus far, the account is a wonderful piece of satirical bisociation, describing the Chemin des Dames offensive of spring 1917 as if it were a crime scene. Death in battle becomes murder, and, in a swipe at the forces of law and order, the witnesses explain that they would have gone to the gendarmes but there were none in the area.[30] An old peasant woman sees more however. Peeking through some leaves, she spies a group of ten men lined up with rifles. On a signal from a man with a pistol, they shoot a man tied to a tree. The investigating magistrate concludes that this was a band of criminals punishing one of their number who had tried to quit the group.[31] The parody is no longer that of an offensive but of an execution for desertion. In this way, the weekly moved from the murderous offensives to the widespread mutinies that followed and to the executions that were part of their repression;[32] in the process, it shifted the focus on mortality from enemy action to the firing squads of the French army.

The wartime execution of French soldiers was a continuing topic in the peacetime *Canard.* The weekly held such actions up to opprobrium whether the killings were of actual deserters and mutineers or the result of judicial error or abuse of authority. In his list of the victimizations of soldiers by the war, Scize added to the obligatory references to Verdun and Craonne the "executed men of Vingré, mutineers of Coeuvres, cattle cut down by French bullets." At Vingré six soldiers had been shot as the result of a judicial error, officially recognized later. The execution got repeated attention from the *Canard,* along with other cases of soldiers shot in error or for trivial mistakes.[33]

In April 1928, the *Canard* reprinted an anecdote from Barbusse. After a unit had mutinied, 250 men were taken away and led to a field. Meanwhile French artillerists were instructed to shell that exact spot. The order was given unofficially, with "cowardice" and "hypocrisy." Executing mutineers, more or less openly, or shooting soldiers by error—it made little difference to the writers of the *Canard.* All showed war as "criminal, hideous, and shameful," whoever fought it.[34] When John Dos Passos's war narrative, *One Man's Initiation: 1917,* was published in French, the *Canard* obligingly replaced a passage deleted by the French censor. It told of a British soldier who placed a live grenade under the head of a wounded German prisoner, blowing him to kingdom come. The *Canard* concluded, "Because war, isn't it so, is the school of chivalry, of nobility, of generosity—for Americans as for others."[35]

If an Allied soldier was the criminal in Dos Passos's story, in the cases of the execution of French soldiers, their own officers were to blame. In his account, Barbusse spoke of "the monsters who commanded us." While the *Canard* was rarely this blunt, in its memory a distinction was clearly made between long-suffering, if not heroic, front-line soldiers, on the one hand, and officers, on the other. And, of the officers, the greatest derision was reserved for France's generals.

A brief note of 1924 read, "Seven generals, more or less famous, more or less victorious, have died in the space of six weeks. This many did not die during the war!"[36] It was only a step to imply that the common soldiers died in their place. In 1922, the *Canard* commented on an echo from *L'Intran* in which a general gives up his place on a bus for a private: "Three words are missing: *comme au front* [as at the front]."[37] Presenting in a facetious mode an argument that a recent military historian endorses in its essentials, Bicard explained that "during the war the generals were very badly placed to see what was happening, and those who were in the best position to see what was happening were not able 'to draw the appropriate conclusions' given that they were dead."[38] And it was the generals, not the Germans, whom the *Canard* blamed for French combat deaths. In 1922, as the General Staff counted up deaths by region and battle, the *Canard* reported that "the Aisne offensive cost us a mere hundred odd thousand men! This is absolutely ridiculous, and we wonder what our generals could possibly have been doing: perhaps they were all on furlough."[39]

The number-one name on the weekly's hit parade of murderous generals was Charles Mangin. The *Canard* stretched its rhetorical wings to multiply references to the fact that this general was known as "the butcher of Verdun." (He was responsible for some of the costly offensives to retake the forts around that threatened city.) When a deputation of butchers from Alsace visited the Tomb of the Unknown Soldier, the *Canard* asked why not, since Mangin had already been there? The weekly also mocked a French author who said that "the Butcher of Verdun" was "the *kronprinz*, and not at all the general that our *poilus* had baptized with this name." Mangin's transit through the port of Brest brought "a moment of panic" (or so said the *Canard*) to the local population, but "there were no losses to report." The *Canard* linked Mangin's reputation with the judgments of combat soldiers, as in its account of Mangin's reception in Avignon. As soon as he began to speak, "Flowers and fruits . . . and diverse products of the vegetable garden described gracious trajectories and landed around the general, whose well-known modesty had trouble accepting all this southern enthusiasm." Outside the hall, some young people, "among whom we recognized some glorious disabled veterans," were so enthusiastic that they wanted to make the general cross the Rhone River "without using the bridge." The *Canard* then reacted with feigned shock to the news that Mangin had been greeted by hostile demonstrations, which would have been "contrary to all the feelings that the *poilus* unanimously hold with regard to this beloved and respected leader."[40]

In a 1919 article, the war-veteran journalist Henri Béraud distinguished between lieutenants like himself, "reserve officers and republicans," and reactionary career officers. Béraud ended his diatribe with a reference to the Ligue des Chefs de Section, the organization of Binet-Valmer that sought " 'to maintain in peace the cadres of the war.' " Demobilized soldiers would want to continue this association, Béraud explained ironically in another article, since they had such a wonderful memory of military discipline.[41]

VETERANS

The *Canard* saw itself as both a veterans' paper and a pacifist one. Veterans' leagues with clear right-wing agendas, like that of Binet-Valmer, were obvious targets (the newspaper had regular fun with Binet-Valmer's Swiss origins).[42] But when it came to ostensibly apolitical organizations, the weekly hesitated between support and sympathy for combat veterans, on the one hand, and concern for the reactionary and militarist implications of such associations, on the other.

The weekly commented on a prospectus from the Union Nationale des Combattants (National Union of Fighters). The association's motto was "united as at the front," the *Canard* noted, but the first three signatures on the prospectus were those of a cardinal, the chief rabbi, and Maurice Barrès. The implication was clear: these people were not combatants and had nothing to do with the front. Bringer expressed misgivings about the whole tendency to divide the French between those who had fought and those who had not—a way of preserving the war. Yet his own suggestion mockingly brought back the *poilu/embusqué* distinction so dear to the wartime *Canard.* The French should found one final group: a "league of former noncombatants," to include individuals like Léon Daudet.[43]

Scize's sympathy for the disabled veterans of the Gueules Cassées was clear. Yet two of their defenders earned his ire for their condemnation of the sale of Joffre's battle orders for the Marne to benefit the disfigured former soldiers—because the seller had not fought. Scize correctly saw that this reason, by glorifying combat, promoted militarism; and he unflatteringly compared such anticivilian squeamishness with the willingness of these same veterans' leaders to trade the sacrifices of the dead for political gain. Scize's idea of a scandal was the fact that, at a charity ball for the Gueules Cassées, none of these faceless soldiers were permitted to dampen the festivities by their presence.[44]

Scize's attitude to veterans' organizations turned on whether they followed his pacifist politics. The Estates-General of Wounded France, organized in 1927 to represent disabled veterans, excited a mixture of compassion and discouragement. These men should have acted after the armistice, Scize wrote, echoing a *Canard* hope from that time.[45] Now it was too late. Sacred anger had been converted into patriotic ritual. All the veterans were showing, the journalist claimed, was their inability to think for themselves, their rush for the security of groups. When, at the meeting itself, the veterans booed the former sergeant, disabled veteran, and minister of war, André Maginot, Scize's sense of comradeship returned, and he saluted his former fellows-in-arms. Even their need to congregate had changed its meaning. Now it was their holy and ordinary humanity, their weakness in a corrupt society dominated by the aggressive and the unscrupulous, that "necessitated" their banding together.[46]

YOUNG VERSUS OLD, SOLDIER VERSUS CIVILIAN

As the *Canard* looked back on the war, it redefined its old division between *poilus* and *embusqués* as a gulf between young and old. Generational thinking was rife in France (as in much of Europe) in the years before and after the war.[47] The *Canard* used age to reflect its image of the war.

The young were those who had won the war. When a senator, a veteran of 1870, wanted a seat at the signing of the peace treaty, the *Canard* objected. The old were going too far; they had taken the lead everywhere but at the front. In the same year (1919), Maurice Maréchal suggested removing older voters from the lists "because we are fed up with the old, more than fed up. And we refuse them henceforth the right to cast ballots on which will perhaps depend the existence of millions of young people."[48] War depended on those who did not fight sending those who did, Bicard had argued.[49] For the postwar *Canard,* those who sent others to fight were the old, the "patriots in the flower of their senility," as Dorgelès put it. An article of 1921 explained that by the old the paper did not mean just those of advanced age but all dry, miserly people who rejoiced in the war because they did not have to fight it.[50]

By the middle years of the decade the juxtaposition of old and young was sharpened into one of fathers and sons, war being the sacrifice of the latter to the former. At a trial involving Léon Daudet, the Action Française lawyer Marie de Roux exclaimed that he would not hesitate to place his own son in front of Daudet to protect him. The *Canard* replied, "Well then? Like the war? The daddies continue to sacrifice their sons to defend Mr. Léon Daudet and his ilk?"[51]

In June 1926, Scize reacted with his usual indignant pacifism to a new painting at the Gare de l'Est. The painting, still in the lobby of the station today, represents the departure of the troops for the front in 1914. Beyond the cheerful colors, the signs of bravery, the iconography stresses the generational and domestic separations as fathers, mothers, and wives send their young men off to war. The artist was an American, and Americans were unpopular in France at this time because of their insistence on the repayment of war debts.[52] What bothered Scize most, however, was the painter's sincerity—his own son had died fighting in France:

> If I had a son, I would take him to the Gare de l'Est. I would show him the painting in question. And I would say to him:
>
> —Look at that well. It is the proof that the war has taught nothing to those who did not fight it. It is the testimony that a father can give the flesh of his flesh without feeling anything more than an affected and declamatory suffering.[. . .] *And do not go again!* Never! Even if, having become old in turn, and stupid, as is quite natural, I beg you with tears in my voice. Even if I promise to save your memory with a pen, with a paintbrush, with a chisel. . . . *Because it is for the sons to disobey their fathers* since even death could not open their eyes!

An accompanying drawing by Guilac linked memory with repetition. It was a project for another painting, "The Gare de l'Est in 192 . . ."[53]

If Scize relied on the soldiers-versus-civilians distinction, he also recognized that the way it was articulated in memory contributed to future conflagrations. In early 1928, another evocation of the war stirred his angry pen: a film about an English nurse shot by the Germans for helping prisoners to escape. Scize sympathized with the heroic Miss Cavell, "who died for having wanted to save men." But, he said, the powerful image of the sacrificed woman would only stir up the patriotic anger that pacifists like himself had been trying to calm. Most of all, Scize criticized the stigmatization of German "atrocities," as in this case the execution of a woman. The notion of atrocities implied the existence of another war, a clean or "fair" war. To "take a son from his mother, a husband from his wife," and send them into combat was "fair." It was fine to "skin, tear apart, saw, boil, scalp, break, twist, flatten, lacerate poor bodies, as long as they wear the badge of a combat unit." "It used to be said, speaking of civilian deaths, 'the innocent victims,' " which enraged the soldiers. Their response: " 'Innocent? So, us, *we are guilty?' "* When speaking of the horrors of war, the combatant/civilian distinction, like that between traditional and newer, "barbarous" arms, served only to hide the fundamental atrocity of all war.[54]

LANDSCAPES OF MEMORY

The *Canard* constructed its memory in a dialectic with the other memories being formed in French society. Partly this dialectic stemmed from the *Canard's* satirical, and therefore frequently parasitic, modus operandi. But it was also a testimony to the density of the imbrication of World War I memory in France. Ever on the lookout for the confluence of the political and the ridiculous, the *Canard* was not above sticking its beak into the frequent trivialization and commercialization of the memory of the conflict.

The addition of religion only made the target more tempting. The sale of Joan of Arc victory medals elicited the comment that it was interesting "to see religion and patriotism reduced to articles of commerce and invoked in order to sell little objects." The *Canard* sharpened its mockery by adopting its version of German or Yiddish pronunciation of French with "gommerce," "bedits opchets," and so forth. In a manner that was not devoid of anti-Semitism, the weekly used such spellings as a sign of crass commercialism. "Groceries and chauvinism. One must never never separate them. They are united by the logic of things." That was the *Canard's* response to the use of pictures of war heroes by the Félix Potin grocery chain.[55]

Some commercializations of memory were almost comical on their own. For example, a "patriotic" camembert sold with an appropriate poem and tricolor wrapper. Its readers knew, the *Canard* smirked, that cheese came in patriotic and treasonous varieties. And then there were the candies sold with a picture of *poilus* parading under the Arc de Triomphe. The bonbons themselves were labeled "Dessert of Heroes" and "Fours Extra-Fins [little cakes]." The weekly went after this latter phrase, noting how "the dessert of the heroes, after the Great War for Justice and Civilization, was in effect a *four*" (a fiasco).[56]

Even when such evocations were not commercial, the *Canard* chastised the trivialization of war memory, as when a journalist compared a bowling match to the Chemin des Dames.[57] Some expressions of memory could not have been resisted by any self-respecting satirist. In Algiers, a banquet for the benefit of war orphans had a thematic menu that featured such tasties as "Cartridges of foie gras Chemin-des-Dames" and "Asparagus à la Verdun." In its commentary, the *Canard* taught a double lesson by making a cleverer pun and by invoking a famous defeat. The diners had been spared a "Camembert à la Charleroi" (*camembert* was a slang term for a machine-gun magazine).[58]

The memory of the Great War not only was imprinted on candy wrappers and on the faces of the wounded but was also inscribed in the landscapes of the battlefields, through gravesites and markers, formal and improvised, and through topography, scars on the earth itself. Not long after the echoes of artillery fire had died out, these same battlefields became sites to visit. But were such trips pious pilgrimages or thrill-seeking—and hence impious—tourism? While recognizing the occasional presence of the first motive, the *Canard* tended to see visits to the battlefields as inappropriate and as an ideal way to evoke yet again the opposition between those who fought and those who stayed comfortably at home.

The *Canard* had already latched onto this subject during the war itself. In fall 1917, when the issue of the fighting was still in doubt, the weekly published a story of "anticipation." The war is over and the Germans, with the help of the High Command, have put their own versions of events in travel guides. As the fighters leave the front, groups of civilians arrive, and the tourists with Michelin guides get into fights with their opposite numbers sporting Baedekers.[59]

In May 1919, the paper noted that tourist agencies were organizing visits to the battlefields, but the clients were not getting their money's worth, the weekly averred, since the area had been "much more interesting between 1915 and 1918." The next issue featured a fat bourgeois on his way to the former front asking the driver of the tourist bus whether he is sure that the war is over.[60] The implication behind the question, that there might still be some danger, turned into fantasy in an article by Dorgelès published in October of that same year. The leftist writer started by suggesting that the government tax those who visited the battlefields. "With the exception of those poor folks who go to look for the body of a missing individual, kneel on a tomb, see the tragic surroundings where a loved one died, the tourists who are drawn by an ignoble curiosity to the immense cemetery from the Artois to Verdun deserve to be fleeced of their last nickel." Would it not be fitting if one of them picked up a grenade and it blew up in his face? Then he would be "dead on the field of honor." These tourists could have come earlier, Dorgelès continued; the transportation would have been free, only the return trip was not guaranteed. This fantasy of civilian deaths had already been expressed during the war.[61] And Dorgelès's anger enunciated the same idea: the incommensurability of the front experience and the turpitude of those who sought their thrills in a pale (and safe) evocation of it.

Yet even Dorgelès made an exception for those who came to the front for legitimate mourning. This excuse appears in unexpected places. Mr. Bonin-Lagron is a fictional war profiteer; and his plan to visit the battlefields (and do a little business on the side) is the epitome of cynicism and selfishness. But when outlining the projected itinerary to his wife, the greedy businessman adds that, after lunching at the Chemin des Dames, they will go by Verdun, "where your nephew died, because it is so important to you." But the tale of Mr. Bonin-Lagron also evoked a larger issue, the disintegration of the physical "memory" of the battlefields. He tells his wife that they must visit the front now while it is still fresh: "In September the front will be less 'pretty'; [. . .] the corpses are disappearing from day to day and even the isolated crosses are coming together bit by bit."[62] This explanation states the issue somewhat colorfully, but the dilemma was genuine—how much of the reality of the front should be preserved? In mid-1922, the ever-cynical Bringer argued that, despite some reconstruction, the ruins were being left in place because "the cultivation of the visitor is more productive than that of other *betteraves*"—a term meaning both beets and fools.[63]

The *Canard* addressed the issue in 1927, in response to *L'Intran* (as was its wont). The film critic of that paper complained that "around Verdun, nine years after the massacre, hell has become paradise" because of the regrowth of vegetation. He concluded, "It is up to Man to show periodically that he does not want to forget. We must seek, despite nature, to keep alive the vision that is disappearing." The *Canard* pretended to agree: "Would you believe it? The ruins caused by the war are being repaired too quickly. The shell holes are filling up with desperate haste. In place of ruins, new houses—O scandal—are rising. In short, if we are not careful, the memory of the victorious war will disappear from the devastated regions." Then came the suggestions. For the vision to remain as lively as *L'Intran* wanted, "it would have been better not to have buried the corpses. But one would still have forgotten. What we really should have done, you see, would have been to continue the war. In this way everyone would have been obliged to think about it still, and we would not need the cinema to bring back the good old days of the trenches." Here was a view of memory even harsher than that of Barbusse. Was not the desperate attempt to keep memory alive, the call to never forget, yet another way of maintaining the spirit of war? In that same article, the weekly even hinted that prohibiting films about the war would be a good thing. The antimemory implications of the *Canard*'s position are even clearer when one notes that the film reviewed by *L'Intran* presented itself as an antiwar work.[64] Of course, this case also evoked another of the *Canard*'s favorite themes, the contrast between the forces of life, here both natural and human creation, and those of death. In 1924, the paper complained about a tribute to Marie Curie: "Where they should have produced a work of art that evoked the struggle against the ills that plague humanity, the young students had the singular idea of giving [. . .] a statuette of 'Victory'—a symbol glorifying the worst of the ills of the world: war."[65]

Any war monument risked being militarism cast in stone. Early talk of a monument to the *poilu* earned the weekly's skepticism: it would probably be ugly. When someone suggested replacing the Obelisk of the Place de la Concorde with a victory monument, the paper interviewed the column from Luxor. The obelisk disapproved. Were not the two triumphal arches on either side of it enough?[66] The cult of the railroad car in which the armistice was signed was also the occasion for mockery. Bicard said it was only logical to commemorate the railroad car along with other murderous objects (a reference to the frequent rail accidents in the years after the war).[67]

And any of these commemorative objects could be integrated into the next-last-war theme.[68] The paper noted, in September 1923, that, after the 1870 war, the city of Chartres had put up a monument to the dead at one end of its main boulevard. After 1918, a similar monument appeared in the middle of the same boulevard; but geometry had its requirements, and the poor boulevard awaited its third monument at the other end. "It is true that the next last one is coming quickly," the *Canard* concluded. A cartoon of December 1922 showed a one-legged former soldier with a crutch examining the "taxi of the Marne" in the Invalides. "Vacant," he notes, "does that mean that it is ready for new passengers?"[69] As for the Invalides, the combination museum and old soldiers' home where the taxi was parked, de la Fouchardière called it a "museum of comparative criminology," in which one could "see both the cause and the effect, the instrument and the product, the saber and the handless man, the rifle and the one-legged person."[70]

The salute to Mme. Marie Harel, in the spring of 1927, gave the *Canard* an opportunity to contrast the commemoration of the objects of war with memorials to articles of peace. "Mme. Marie Harel did not, like Joan of Arc, save France or even, like Saint Genevieve, save Paris. She did not invent gunpowder either. But she invented camembert, which is much better. And, for once, the dedication of a monument will be a pacific, bucolic, and alimentary ceremony."[71]

HONORING THE DEAD

One might think from these criticisms that the *Canard* opposed all forms of war commemoration. But the weekly did respect one cult: that of the war dead, as represented by the monuments to them springing up in virtually every French village and town. Such practices fit the *Canard*'s desire to honor the self-sacrificing heroism of the *poilus*. The cult of the war dead was also so genuinely popular (in both senses of the term), so clearly founded in public sentiment, that it would have been impossible to challenge its legitimacy.[72] Instead, the weekly set itself up as judge of the proper way to honor the fallen.

The *Canard* wanted memorial ceremonies to keep their black cloaks of mourning. Respect for the dead mixed with the necessity of reminding people of the tragic nature of the war. Hence, the sadness of the deaths of so many comrades should not be diluted by adding other, more joyful, forms of social activity to the ceremonies. Commenting on a story about a mass and two days of dancing organized in honor of the war dead, the *Canard* showed its disgust: "Certainly, certainly . . . our dead are glorious! Gay, gay, let's dance!" The use of confetti in Algiers earned this comment: "The dead, the dead . . . are certainly much at fault! But we will cry over them, bem, bem, bem . . . while drinking a glass, tra la la lass, . . . while throwing confetti, tra la la iti!" One commune was pilloried for having a dance with a jazz band, another for ending its ceremonies with a ball.[73]

On most subjects, the *Canard* limited itself to mockery or criticism. The cult of the war dead was different. In September 1922, the paper paired commentaries on two ceremonies. In the first a commune held a *vin d'honneur* (a reception where wine is served) and a ball; in the second, of which the weekly approved, the owners closed their bars so that the dead could be remembered in calm and dignity.[74] In March 1925, the newspaper complained of the frequent and "useless" speeches at monuments to the war dead. But "the city of Moulins has just provided a salutary example: it has put up a monument to these dead—which is, by my faith, quite beautiful—but the day of the inauguration no speeches will be given. Bravo!" Here, the antiwar weekly essentially echoed the position of Barbusse, who wrote that the only appropriate attitude to bring to the commemorations was silence.[75]

The *Canard* condemned other forms of disrespect for the dead, from a mayor who was pushing to get the bronze sculpture produced by his own company to the minister of transportation, Le Trocquer, who received a copious (even by French standards) meal before his dedication speech.[76] But here, as with drinking and dancing, the *Canard* was merely guarding the purity of the ceremony, not its politics. The *Canard* also defended (though it did not require) antimilitarist versions of the cult of the dead. The weekly bestowed its "gilded nut of honor" on the mayor of Joinville who ripped the pages from a speaker who had tried to "read a speech to honor the dead without exalting war."[77]

The Parisian suburb of Levallois-Peret witnessed a battle over its monument for the dead. In November 1927, Scize noted the incongruity of the fact that the leading veterans' associations were opposing the creation of a monument to the dead because the projected *poilu,* instead of dying with "one hand on his heart, while embracing the flag [. . .], showed by eloquent gestural language that he was fed up with that business."[78] The *Canard* had noted in April, "A monument to the dead which shows a worker grateful for the armistice, a soldier sad at having been gassed, and a Negro unhappy with being a volunteer in our armies—we repeat that this is a scandal." The *Canard* then mockingly recommended preferable subjects, suitably drawn by Guilac. These included a French infantryman with two German soldiers and an officer impaled on his bayonet.[79]

Dignified treatment of the war dead meant respect for all, without special treatment for some. In 1925 the *Canard* answered a passage by Dorgelès that argued that soldier-writers sacrificed not only their lives but also their "future" and their *"oeuvre."* For the satirical weekly its occasional contributor had gone "a bit far." Who could say that there was not "as much 'future' locked in the brains of the other soldiers, were they workers or bourgeois or other professions"?[80] Though they too lived by the pen, the journalists and writers of the *Canard* rejected the prestige French society granted to their profession because of the devaluing of the common sacrifice it implied. The creation of a "Fighting Writers Dead for France Square" in 1928 provoked the *Canard* to ask about a "Fighting Teachers Dead on the Field of Honor Street." In the next issue Bicard went one better, suggesting a *"Fighting-Lead-and-Zinc-Workers-Dead-in-the War-Square, a Bus-Ticket-Collectors-Dead-in-the-War-Square, a Collectors-of-Direct,-Indirect-and-Assimilated-Taxes-Dead-in-the-War-Square."*[81]

Appropriately honoring those who made the ultimate sacrifice also meant, in the *Canard*'s visions, honoring them alone. When the Senate voted that Clemenceau "had earned the gratitude of the Fatherland," the *Canard* explained that obviously that body intended to honor all such persons but that they were doing so in alphabetical order and had decided to begin with the letter "c." In 1920, French lawyers put up a plaque similarly honoring Poincaré, who was a lawyer as well as president of the Republic during the war. The weekly then announced that the "Association of Bazaar Employees" had created its own plaque: "Constantin Mouillebéc, stock boy, has earned the gratitude of the fatherland; but him, he got himself killed for it."[82]

The problem of honoring those who had not fought was tied into the larger issue of the Legion of Honor. The Legion of Honor was an originally military order that was extended to encompass civilian forms of distinction. Hence one could be appointed to the Legion for military bravery or for success in virtually any area of national life. The *Canard* stigmatized those who had received a military ribbon without having actually fought. For example, the paper went after a banker with important government connections, Raymond Philippe, calling him "the Zouave Philippe" because of the claim that he had fought in that infantry unit.[83]

Even where the *Canard* saw no outright fraud, it distrusted a system where a civilian could get a decoration that looked mightily like the one earned on the battlefield. The journalistic bird objected to the hypocrisy of the Council of the Order of the Legion of Honor when it refused the nominations of three poets for "lack of military qualifications," in a country in which so many who had not fought were decorated. The *Canard*'s sense of propriety was also offended when decorations were withdrawn from authentic combat veterans, either because they expressed pacifist opinions or because they wrote novels judged too risqué.[84]

But the *Canard* also saw the Legion as the best example of the French mania for decorations. After noting the dramatic expansion of the order, the *Canard* mocked it in a variety of ways, claiming on one occasion that there were no French left to decorate and on another that the Museum of the Legion of Honor should contain, as a rare treasure, the only French person not a member.[85] In such a context, the highest dignity could be refusing the Legion. Accordingly, the *Canard* saluted one individual who repeatedly refused to be decorated and expressed its regrets that another, otherwise a fine fellow, had accepted the honor.[86]

But the best jab at the Legion of Honor came through the *Canard*'s suggestions that it was made up essentially of crooks. The Legion of Honor went to businessmen as well as artists or journalists. Also, since it was given by ministers—hence politicians—it was often given for political reasons or to reward favors. A *Canard* cartoon showed a man looking up angrily from his newspaper as he says to his wife, "Not decorated! Wretch, you did not sleep with the minister!" Over and over the *Canard* reported stories of recipients charged with fraud, tax evasion, and similar white-collar crimes. The weekly eventually created a regular column, called "the Legion of Honor," which detailed the judicial adventures of members of that order.[87]

REMEMBERING THE ARMISTICE

If the monuments to the war dead evoked some respect from the *Canard* and the Legion of Honor just contempt and derision, the commemoration of the armistice was the occasion for the weekly to pass from concern for appropriate commemoration to frank mockery of the whole business. And, as always, these games reflected both the politics of memory and that of the war.

The armistice of November 1918 could represent many things: the end of the war, the victory. But for the *Canard,* first and foremost, it represented dissension among the French. When the Germans first requested an end to the fighting in the fall of 1918, opinions in France were mixed. Some, like President of the Republic Raymond Poincaré, were hostile to the idea of granting the enemy a cessation of combat. Opponents of the armistice felt that it would be better to await, if not the encirclement or destruction of the German army, at least the planned Allied offensives that would surely drive it from the national territory. After the armistice and the emergence of the first difficulties of the peace, many more both on the right and in the center argued that the armistice should have been signed in Berlin—in a word, that the armistice of November 11 was premature.[88]

The *Canard* had already criticized those who wanted to continue fighting at the time of the armistice itself.[89] But the weekly returned to the subject year after year on the anniversary of the armistice (e.g., in 1921, 1922, 1923, 1924). Rather than discussing the alleged utility of continuing the combat, from the point of view of France's national interest, the weekly simply accused the opponents of the armistice of preferring war and bloodshed to peace. Its strongest argument was based on human lives: "When one thinks that six months would have sufficed to win another armistice [. . .] without a doubt there would have been extra victims, but we are not, thank God, down to our last monument." That was in 1923. A year later, the *Canard* switched from irony to direct attack: "They wanted to go to Berlin, and so what if that had killed two or three thousand more Frenchmen."[90]

Should this premature armistice be a subject for celebration? In fact, armistice commemorations were torn in France between happy celebrations of victory (and an end to the bloodshed) and sad commemorations of the atrocious human cost of the war.[91] The *Canard* played with this ambiguity and reinterpreted it. It affected to hesitate between sadness and gaiety over the armistice almost as often as it evoked its alleged prematureness. Bringer asked in 1926 whether he "should, *to remain a good Frenchman,* weep or on the contrary party like a teenager."[92]

But for the *Canard* mourning could also be construed as an expression of unhappiness with the armistice itself, either its prematureness or the fact that termination of the conflict put an end to war profiteering. The *Canard* saw the moment of silence at 11:00 A.M. (Poincaré's contribution to the commemoration of the end of hostilities) as "ridiculous because it is shabby *[mesquin]*. But it is also hypocritical" since its sponsors never forgave the armistice for ending the war. We saw how the *Canard* linked the minute of silence to the tears of *L'Intran* ("la larme . . . istice"). In this context one does not know whether it is the war or its ending that is the occasion for tears.[93]

In 1922, the newspaper *Le Matin* helped to defray the expenses of an armistice commemoration at Rethondes (site of the final negotiations and signature). The *Canard* responded with a cartoon picturing the site filled with tombstones with texts like "Frenchmen, salute the triumph of right and justice and the revue of the Folies Bergères." The same issue recounted Bicard's efforts to sneak into the commemoration by donning the uniform of a funeral director: "It is an honorable uniform and one that ought to be in the first row in all the celebrations of the victory given the central role of undertakers during the war."[94]

But how should the event have been commemorated? The *Canard*'s suggestions, like the ambivalent emotions of the event, ran from the mournful to the gay. On the sad side, the paper recommended, instead of reading out the names of the dead of each commune, trying to read out everywhere the names of all one and a half million French dead.[95] But the *Canard* also had fun with the minute of silence. On November 10, 1926, the *Canard* published a story of a woman who awakes to find a burglar stealing her pearls. Before she can cry out, he silently points out that the minute of silence is beginning and profits from the situation to escape.[96] All in good fun, but reading the story as a (probably unconscious) allegory obliges one to ask what other crimes are covered by the minute of silence.

By November 1927, eight years after the event, the *Canard* was ready for a truly joyous version of commemoration. In a clever dialogue, one speaker gradually coaxes from the other a description of how he spent the national holiday of November 11. No, he was not at the Arc de Triomphe. He commemorated the armistice at home, but, no, he does not have a view of the Place de l'Etoile. "Then you marched in your own home, individually, by going around the room three hundred fifty times and by blowing on a little trumpet?" No, the neighbors would object, and he has not even paid his rent. It turns out that this person observed many moments of silence, before and after—that is, he invited his young female neighbor from across the way.

—And she came?

—Why yes. She even brought over some croissants. I made some coffee. And when we were fully refreshed, well . . . we celebrated the armistice, as I told you, for at least an hour and twenty minutes.

—Of silence?

—Well, of relative silence. In any case, it was a silence that was as patriotic as can be because we observed it while concerning ourselves, in principle, with the draft class of 1947.[97]

It is hard to imagine a better mockery of military ceremonies than marching around a room while blowing a trumpet. But the *Canard*'s 1927 armistice day festivities replace the evocation of death (either heroically or mournfully) with the creation of life. It is time to stop mourning, to stop cultivating sacred hatred, and to start living—a time not to remember but to forget. That was the *Canard*'s dialectic and its ambivalence about the memory of the war: was it better to correct it or to escape it?

The *Canard*'s romantic breakfast was the ultimate vision of life replacing death. But what if the dead were not left alone, or, more darkly, what if the dead would not leave the living alone? That is the story of the cult of the unknown soldier, another chapter in the *Canard*'s politics of memory.

9 Between Cannibalism and Resurrection

The Body of the Unknown Soldier

In *Tristes Tropiques,* Claude Lévi-Strauss describes two different types of attitudes toward the dead. "Some societies let their dead rest," and, in return, "the departed refrain from troubling the living." Other societies "allow them [the dead] no rest, but press them into service.[. . .] These societies, more than others, are worried by the dead, whom they exploit. They believe that the dead pay them back in kind, and are all the more demanding and importunate towards the living, since the latter are making use of them."[1]

Was the distinguished anthropologist thinking of France when he wrote this passage? Nothing in his discussion (which touches on European practices) suggests such an association, but as a student in interwar Paris, Lévi-Strauss could not have missed the cult of the fallen soldiers. More significantly, the *Canard Enchaîné* would have recognized, in Lévi-Strauss's second, guilty society, its own characterization of the cult of the unknown soldier. Further, for the satirical weekly, the two poles of the Lévi-Straussian system, exploitation of the dead and revenge by them, were concretized in two extreme images, that of cannibalism and that of resurrection or return.[2]

Whether or not one wished to accept Benedict Anderson's judgment that "no more arresting emblems of the modern culture of nationalism exist than cenotaphs and tombs of Unknown Soldiers," there is probably no more visibly original symbol of the cultic practices created by the Great War than these monuments.[3] The *Canard*'s brutal reconceptualization of the unknown soldier stands as a powerful commentary on the marriage of nation and mass war.

THE CULT

The *Canard* took a more negative view of the cult of the unknown soldier than it did of the practices that developed around the many local monuments to the war dead. If the latter deserved respect, the cult of the unknown soldier earned only mockery. The weekly's most persistent rhetorical desacralization consisted of breaking up the syntagm "unknown soldier" by replacing the second element with some other social type. The results were various: unknown civilian, unknown murderer, unknown taxpayer.[4] Not only did the multiplication of "unknowns" remove the sense of specialness associated with the sacred, but the intrusion of noncombatants underlined again the *Canard*'s division between heroic soldiers and *embusqués.* Special topics also generated their own "unknowns." The *Canard*'s campaign around rail accidents led it to suggest that the victims of a recent mishap be buried as "unknown travelers," "under the triumphal vault of a tunnel." The *Canard* regularly targeted André Citroën as *embusqué* and war profiteer, so Bicard suggested he gather the remains of the victims of Citroën car accidents into an "unknown customer."[5] There was an "unknown deputy" and an "unknown bondholder" in an article that explained that the unknown soldier gave his life for capital.[6]

But what better way to desacralize the cult than to define the unknown soldier? In an article attributed (with obvious falsehood) to Marshal Pétain, the *Canard* defined the soldier: in times of war he "automatically becomes a '*poilu.*' If he is killed, he becomes a hero. Any *poilu* who is lucky enough to be able to get rid of his identity papers before becoming a hero can apply for the title of 'unknown soldier.' "[7] People in this situation were not lacking, the *Canard* averred. Accordingly, it mocked the request of Marseilles for its own soldier by suggesting one for every village. Or as de la Fouchardière put it, in response to the requests of a number of provincial cities, "Thank God, there are corpses for everybody."[8]

The unknown soldier was the focus of a cult, as the *Canard* saw it, virtually of a religion. For the anticlerical weekly such an association carried no respect. In March 1921, the *Canard* reported on a "new cult" that involved putting a flower on the slab over the *"poilu inconnu,"* and the article noted that even beauty queens were doing it. By raising (and ironically refuting) the idea that this was a "profanation," the *Canard* might seem to imply that there was a correct, nonprofanatory way of honoring the unknown soldier.[9] But this was really just another example of the paper's having it both ways, for the weekly was unsparing in its mockery of the official, orthodox cult of the unknown soldier.

Central to the ceremonies of this new creed were the guarding and relighting of the eternal flame that burned above the mortal remains of the dead soldier. As the fictional de la Fouchardière explained it to Bicard, "In all the other religions, there are always burning lamps perpetually guarded in front of other sanctuaries by other sacristans. That is why Mr. Binet-Valmer had the idea of maintaining a lamp in the sanctuary of the unknown *poilu,* like the perpetual adoration of the Sacred Heart and of the Goddess Vesta." But here de la Fouchardière serves as straight man for the less respectful Bicard, who adds, "But I have heard that there are sacred crocodiles maintained by the yellow sacristans in the sanctuaries of Boudin [sic] and Vichenou."[10] The bisociations (crocodiles under the Arc de Triomphe?) could not be sillier; and *boudin* is both a mispronunciation of Buddha and a kind of sausage. If we remember that a *boudin* is frequently a *boudin noir,* or blood sausage, then still other associations are possible.

Even de la Fouchardière's comparison with the cult of Vesta was not without spice since it made Vestal Virgins of the guardians of the flame (a comparison exploited in other articles). And the reference to the Sacred Heart was both political, since this cult had a strong reactionary coloring in nineteenth- and twentieth-century France, and displeasing to Catholics in its link to non-Western religions. Nor were the cultic actions themselves immune. *Allumer,* to light, had other meanings, opening the way for disrespectful puns. One other sense for the verb, as a past participle, is drunk. Hence the headline announcing that André Maginot, a politician with a reputation for liking his champagne, would light the flame "if he was not too lit himself." But *allumer* also means to stimulate sexually. Hence the *Canard* warned its readers not to confuse "Mlle. Gaby Boissy, whose role it is to light in our hearts the flames of concupiscence, and Mr. Gabriel Boissy, who has only lit the flame of the Arc de Triomphe."[11] What was lit under the triumphal arch? According to the *Canard,* it was a "heroic punch," one that was *flambé* (standard treatment for a "punch" in France).[12]

The only respectable attitude toward this cult, the *Canard* implied, was to refuse to participate. Accordingly, the paper reported positively the decision by the Association of Fighting Writers to refuse "to pretend to light the flame of Maginot."[13] For the *Canard,* this new religion added odium to ridicule. But the noxiousness of the cult of the unknown soldier did not essentially stem, for the weekly, from its links to militarism (though that issue was never completely absent). The worst thing about the cult of the hero under the Place de l'Etoile was that it represented the clearest example of the exploitation of the war dead by the living.

NECROPHAGY

The *Canard* commented on a book, *The Ceremonial of the Great War,* under the subtitle "A Patriotic Work Teaches Us the Rational and Intensive Exploitation of the *Poilu.*" The war had taken everything possible from the combat soldier. "It had mobilized him, clothed him in sky blue, dragged him through mud and glory, covered him with lice and medals, given him a deplorable war godmother, and killed him at low or high heat."[14] This posthumous exploitation could be seen most clearly in the ceremonies that evolved around the unknown soldier. The daily newspaper *Le Journal* proposed a race:

> On the fourteenth of July, before daybreak, a *blind* veteran will light a torch at Verdun and will give it to a runner. This veteran-runner will run [. . .] toward Paris, and when he has covered a kilometer, he will pass his torch, still lit, to another runner, and so on and so forth.[. . .] That evening the torch will be given to *a double amputee of the legs* who will use it to light, under the Arc de Triomphe, the eternal flame.

The *Canard*'s advice to war veterans who were serving as advertising for the newspaper was that they should "break their crutches on the haunches, left bank and right bank, of the organizers of this sinister pleasantry."[15]

In November 1920, Maurice Barrès was again "honored" by the *Canard,* and for these lines: "From the Arc de Triomphe to the Pantheon! A path without equal! Who would not give his life to travel it as a corpse?"[16] The old rightist's salute plowed familiar ground: the exploitation of sacrifice by those who did not fight. But when it came to encapsulating the exploitation of the man the weekly most frequently called the *poilu inconnu, Canard* writers preferred the idea of cannibalism.

Cannibals did other duty in the weekly however. We have already seen how Bicard characterized racists in the United States as cannibals. Anthropophagy was also associated, by the *Canard,* with sub-Saharan Africans in a racist topos.[17] But when the weekly associated cannibalism with black Africa it was speaking literally. Its linkage of cannibalism with the cult of the unknown solider was essentially—though sometimes only barely—metaphorical.

De la Fouchardière was quite open in calling the patriots who served as high priests of the religion cannibals, both through his character, Bicard, and under his unmediated byline. Such a charge was far from unknown. Four banned verses of the *Internationale* (sung during these same years) proclaimed, "If they insist—these cannibals—on making heroes of us, they will soon know that our first bullets are for our own generals."[18] Patriots were cannibals, or perhaps they were worse. In a discussion of cannibalism in Russia, which was associated with famine in that country, Bicard argued that there were others, those "who wish to kill their fellow men and who do not even have the esscuse [sic] of eating their victims." His interlocutor implies that Barrès and Poincaré fit Bicard's description.[19]

The term *cannibal* had also been used by anticlericalists to stigmatize the kidnapping of mortal remains by ecclesiastics determined to give them a religious burial. In linking the idea to the unknown soldier, the *Canard* combined the pacifist with the anticlerical tradition.[20] In an antimilitarist context, cannibalism is a metaphor for extreme exploitation—or ultimate social parasitism. Further, as a form of short circuiting—man eating man instead of man eating animal—it adds the image of collective self-destruction, of a species turning inward on itself, an image appropriate to war.

For the *Canard,* still other elements adhered to the image. As Bicard put it, "Have you noticed how the ministers of the government have a taste for exhuming and burying people. It's the unknown *poilu,* it's [Léon] Gambetta's heart, it's now Voltaire's heart.[. . .] I call this the proceedings of cannibals." By combining the commemorations of idols of the Republican left with that of the unknown soldier through the image of a kind of musical body parts, the wise fool makes the image of cannibalism physical. Beyond being mere exploiters, the ministers become virtual butchers and hawkers of human flesh, their hands metaphorically dirty with body parts. The interchangeability of body parts also showed up in a poem published after the installation of the tomb of the unknown soldier in November 1920. In it a young woman sneaks out of the Panthéon and goes to the Arc de Triomphe "because she could have put, by raising the ribs, Gambetta's heart in the body of the *poilu.*" The young woman is easily recognizable as Marianne, personification of the Republic (the poem also satirizes the political deals that created the multiple ceremonies). The piece was entitled "Taking the Symbol to the Limit," and its author was "the Unknown Poet."[21]

Taken literally, cannibalism is eating, and the *Canard* did not shy away from even this extreme use of the metaphor. De la Fouchardière's piece on the availability of other potential unknown soldiers bore the title "L'art d'utiliser les restes." *Restes* means remains, so it is the art of using remains, here mortal remains. But *restes* are also leftovers, as from a meal, and the title could just as easily (and more commonly) be translated as the art of using leftovers. After mentioning the availability of corpses, the author adds, "There are also patriots who are just as gloriously cannibalistic and to whom it is appropriate to throw a couple of bones to gnaw on."[22]

Gnawing on the bones of the unknown soldier? Treating the unknown soldier as a meal? The image becomes more palatable with a change of species. In a story published in September 1921, an old rabbit tells a group of young bunnies that one of their number has recently died, *au feu*. The phrase means under fire, but also on the fire, as in cooking. Though the older rabbit insists that this end—on a bed of onions—is worthy of envy, the younger animals keep insisting that they would prefer to grow old without glory. They also keep asking the senior rabbit why he avoided such an honor. The older rabbit presents various excuses: he had health problems, he is too old. He winds up his peroration by explaining the honor that awaits them:

> On the plate on which you will be served, surrounded by fragrant herbs and enhanced by a glass of old Médoc, you will be, my children! . . . you will be . . .
>
> —Oh! say it, say it, Grandpa, say it. . . .
>
> —You will be THE GLORIOUS UNKNOWN RABBIT.

And the title of this story in dialogue form pulled together honor and cuisine: "The Laurel."[23]

The comparison of shooting game with shooting soldiers had already been used by the *Canard* during and shortly after the war, but essentially to mock the cowardice of civilians who were aggressive and healthy enough to track and shoot animals yet not strong enough to serve in combat. But that comparison tended to examine the question from the point of view of civilians. For soldiers like Cendrars, hunting men the way one hunted game was almost a disloyal form of combat. Seen in this light, the unknown-soldier-as-rabbit comparison adds the ignominy of treating men like dumb beasts.[24]

But such culinary imagery also gives a special flavor to comparisons like Bicard's between the sanctuary of "Boudin" and that of the unknown soldier (a paradigmatic replacement of a person with an item of food). A sausage (especially if it is a blood sausage) makes a good stand-in for a corpse. But even the "heroic punch" could serve. Speaking of the unknown *"poilu,"* "M. Boissy first flambéed him like a punch." The fallen hero becomes then both a punch and an object set ablaze.[25] Even de la Fouchardière's transference of Anatole France's image of blood-drinking gods from the French Revolution to the Great War strengthened this idea.[26]

But cannibalism is also a "metaphor of incorporation," to use Maggie Kilgour's term.[27] The cannibal seeks to absorb whatever virtues or powers inhere in the victim. Certainly, this metaphor also applies to the cult of the unknown soldier. The professional patriot is trying to take over the heroism that the fallen soldier earned through his sacrifice. But another form of incorporation through ingestion is well established in Western, and hence French, culture: holy communion.

RESURRECTION

From the Eucharist to Christ is a small step—and one taken by Bicard. The alcoholic philosopher spoke of Louis IX and the other crusaders going "to the tomb of the other unknown *poilu,* down there," to which his interlocutor adds, "at Jerusalem."[28] In all Christian cultures Christ is a potent symbol of sacrifice, and as such he was of course available to symbolize the sufferings of soldiers.[29] But this was not a *Canard* motif (though the weekly was willing to crucify other symbols). Indeed, Bicard's comparison evokes the tendency of both unknown soldier and Jesus to serve as places of pilgrimage and of collective hostility, the wise fool adding that the crusaders undertook their military actions because "in their minds that p . . . d off the Turks." After Christ crucified comes Christ risen. For Easter 1925 the fascist veterans' newspaper, *Le Nouveau Siècle,* ran a front-page cartoon of a group of veterans giving the Roman salute over the tomb of the unknown soldier, as his spirit, only partially corporalized but in uniform, rises from the memorial slab. If the title, "Easter 1925," did not make the evocation explicit, the legend did: "He is risen!"[30] The identification of the fallen hero with the incarnated deity could not have been closer in such a conservative and Catholic newspaper.

And this connection has continued in the France of our own time. Staying within the same archetype—while shifting the register to antichauvinistic mockery—the comic-strip artists Lob, Gotlieb, and Alexis imagined a comical French super-hero, Superdupont. This Gallic reply to Superman gets his powers from the unknown soldier, who transmits them to his progeny in a crypt under the Arc de Triomphe. And the future Superdupont is guided to the sacred spot by a star, "like the Three Magi."[31]

The resurrection is a positive image, the promise of eternal life. But as the awakening of the dead, it can have a negative, obverse side, well captured by the French term *revenants*—the dead who rise to walk among the living. Such a vision of horror obviously better fits the dead of the Great War. In Abel Gance's 1938 antiwar film, *J'accuse,* the pacifist hero, unable to stop preparations for a new bloodbath, calls on the war dead to rise again. In a classic horror scene, the corpses emerge from the cemeteries near the front by the thousands and spread throughout the country. Gance had also filmed such a return of the dead in his, otherwise quite distinct, 1919 film of the same title. But it is the later work that is more relevant here because it speaks of the dead rising after years of peace and in order to prevent a new war.[32]

The angry corpse, the resurrection as horror, speaks to the second half of Lévi-Strauss's equation: societies that exploit their dead should fear their unhappy return. The *Canard* certainly portrayed the unknown soldier in this way. Roger Brindolphe expressed it clearly. If he were the unknown soldier he would not appreciate "a bunch of creeps advertising themselves at my expense." Further evidence of the feelings of the anonymous hero come from the testimony of one of his colleagues in death. From his sarcophagus, the recently disinterred Pharaoh Tutankhamon exclaims, "I am like the unknown *poilu*. They won't leave me alone."[33]

The war dead rising again was not an idea that the *Canard* needed to create. "Debout les morts! [Arise ye dead!]" was such a stock motif of Great War propaganda that the *Canard* could mock it during the war in Morocco: "Debout les Maures! [Arise ye Moors!]"[34] But the *Canard* went further, giving the phrase a suggestion of horror. Reporting with disgust the presence of Maginot at a commemoration at Mount Kemmel, the weekly expressed its disappointment that no one had interrupted the minister's speech with "Debout les morts!" The implication had to be that they would have given the politician a bad reception. Maginot was also quoted in the satirical paper to the effect that if France did not receive a share of the first reparations payments from Germany (we are in 1921), "our fifteen hundred thousand dead will rise from their tombs to protest." The *Canard* suggested that after having done so they might go on to the Ministry of Pensions to demand prompt payment of the sums due their families. The title of the article, "Eventuality of a Promenade," well expressed the notion of the remobilization of the dead soldiers (in the sense of making them again mobile).[35]

Such resurrections were left in the domain of wishful thinking. Only the unknown soldier was a powerful enough figure actually to speak in the pages of the *Canard*.[36] During the ceremony of the relighting of the flame, as "presidents, ministers, marshals bow at this tomb, a voice distinctly pierces the slab and laments, 'Ah! [. . .] When are you going to leave me in peace!' And among the 'officials' there is a wave of panic: the terrified flight of people who do not have a clear conscience." "Just a Dream" was the subtitle of the article.[37]

In the real world, Bicard discussed the reasons for the passivity of the unknown soldier. If one is a keeper of the cult, one can yell, "Debout les morts" without

> the unknown *poilu* escaping from beneath his slab to give you a solid set of kicks in the behind with his boots: first of all because he is definitively unfit and further because the precaution has been taken to take off his boots before laying him down beneath the Arcque de Triomphe [sic]. . . . Without these two difficulties, have no fear, there would be more than one high-ranking patriot who would have the soles of the unknown *poilu* photographed on the bottom of his ass.[38]

The *poilu* does emerge from beneath his slab in a cartoon by Pedro in September 1927. This image, softened neither by the suggestion of a dream nor by that of a conditional action, fully displays resurrection as horror. A tragic reply to the fascist resurrection of 1925, Pedro's cartoon showed the unknown soldier emerging from his tomb. But unlike the resurrected dead depicted on the tympanum of the cathedral of Bourges, he is neither naked nor corporally intact. Instead, he is a skeleton wearing combat dress. This vision of terror pushes aside a slab covered with flowers, ribbons, and the top hat of a visiting dignitary. The resurrected figure also speaks. "La classe!" translates as the draft contingent and is the cry of solidarity of common soldiers.[39] As we shall see shortly, this phrase is also a repeating, even authenticating utterance of the unknown soldier. For the prewar French, resurrection could be a symbol of hope and national renewal in a barely secularized version of the Christian doctrine. That resurrection for the postwar *Canard* was a symbol of horror testifies to the pessimistic current in which the weekly participated.[40]

The idea that others might speak for the anonymous hero was enough to provoke de la Fouchardière and his sidekick into giving speech to the dead soldier. The fictional de la Fouchardière criticized the plans for a courier to carry the greetings of the Belgian unknown soldier to his French equivalent. "You will see that one day they will install a radio apparatus, so that the unknown *poilu* can profit from the speeches that Mr. Poincaré gives in other cemeteries, and a telephone so that he can communicate with his pal in Brussels." Bicard likes the idea. "The unknown *poilu* will finally be able to say what he thinks, quietly, without being overheard by the higher-ups who are trampling the begonias on his slab.[41] He will telephone the other fellow in Brussels: 'Hey, old boy! What a bunch of turkeys.' And the guy in Brussels will answer, 'Come on! Come on! Don't take it personally. It comes with the job.' "[42]

But the unknown soldier had better opportunities to express himself in the pages of the *Canard*. That weekly provided two long soliloquies in which the unidentified *poilu* summed up the complaints of the living and the dead—the miseries of life as a soldier combined with the indignities of serving as an exploited corpse. The 1923 armistice day celebrations brought out a "Soliloquy of the Unknown *Poilu.*" The soldier under the arch awaits a comrade who will come "to join him in his solitude." "Is it you, my comrades? No. Who are these people who step forward? I have never seen them. What company are they in? I have never met them. In the long nights of Hartmannwillerskopf, in the cold mornings of Champagne, at Verdun, on the Yser, they were not next to me." The soldier in the grave spots Millerand, president of the Republic, and Poincaré, the prime minister and former president, along with Minister of Agriculture Chéron, whom he accuses of "starving my children." "And there are the generals, about whom I never heard anything except to learn that I have fifteen days in the stockade."

> No, today for my anniversary, I would have wanted others to come and warm me up. On my nameless tomb, why all these unknown visitors?
>
> What I would have wanted to see is you, Sulphart, whose jokes kept me warm during the nights of guard duty, and you, Vieublé, and you, Volpatte.

The unknown soldier spots his comrades in the last row, "though, back then, no one contested your place in the first one." He would like to join them but "you see, comrades, today again I am on fatigue duty."[43] The author of the article was given as Jacques Leclerc, not a familiar byline in the *Canard.* But the soldiers' names, Sulphart and Vieublé, belonged to characters in Dorgelès's *Les croix de bois,* while Volpatte was from Barbusse's *Le feu.*[44] Since this was the *Canard,* such a reuse of names could be a coded signal of authorship or, more likely, the tribute of another writer.

When the unknown soldier spoke at length for the second time in the *Canard,* in 1927, the byline lacked ambiguity: Pierre Scize. "La classe!" it began, and this phrase was repeated after each angry paragraph.

> Because I set off without wanting to and fell without knowing it, I certainly deserved the humble and tragic spot where the hatred of men struck me down.[. . .]
>
> Because I do not deserve to feel my skeleton rattle each time one of your buses shakes the wooden pavement of the Place de l'Etoile.
>
> La classe!
>
> Your eternal flame stinks of gas, your piety stinks of lies, and your homage stinks of rotten flowers. A poor corpse from the last one has a right to his ration of trees in the wild and of sunsets and of bird songs and of butterflies making love on the wildflowers that spring up in the filled-in trenches.
>
> La classe!

> The others are free. They have left this state of attention in which you have confined me. They are not obliged to listen, as formerly to military instruction, to these grandiloquent speeches that you rain on me in little drops. Lucky guys! They do not have to put up with your silences, worse than your words, these "moments of silence" during which you think about your oil stocks, about the neck of a girlfriend, about the time of your date, or about the difficulties of your digestion.
>
> La classe!
>
> I am sick of seeing the kings—yellow, black, or white—the war leaders, the mercenaries, the members of Parliament bow their caiman snouts over my slab.
>
> [. . .]
>
> Too many tourist buses around me, too many Kodaks pointed at my floral crowns, and too many too expensive flowers pridefully brought by persons who show that they have "enough to do things right."
>
> La classe!
>
> Because you do not know me! Because, as the Unknown, I am the very image of your remorse, the blindly chosen exemplar of your crime, the ambassador of all the murdered of the world.

Do you know what I looked like, the unknown soldier went on.

> And if on waking up I would recognize you as my peers, or if I would not chase you away with great kicks in the caboose? You dare to palaver over this question mark that you know is buried in your ground? And you do not ask yourselves whether the soul that haunts this body will not come and slap you across the face for your attentions.
>
> [. . .]
>
> Old that you are! It was not enough for you to lay down in the earth the youth of the world by millions! You do not tremble when collecting the bones of one of those who went off to defend your pride and your big bucks.[. . .] And the tears provoked by my death, unwitnessed tears, lost tears, are you not afraid that one night I will come to call you to account for them?
>
> La classe! La classe![45]

Taken together, these twin laments repeat familiar *Canard* themes, like the contrast between combat soldiers and those, politicians or others, who stayed home. Scize's unknown soldier adds pacifism and the suggestion that the dead hero will take vengeance. As the allusion to such a resurrection is repeated, it shifts from the more comical idea, shared by Bicard, of kicks in the rear to the register of horror created by the angry corpse returning at night. Similarly, the reference to the rattling of bones under the enormous traffic circle that is the Place de l'Etoile echoes Pedro's skeletal resurrection. Indeed, both spirit and mortal remains threaten since this version also speaks of a haunting soul slapping the official mourners.

Both passages also link the miseries of life with those of death. The 1923 speech speaks of the unknown soldier being warmed by his comrades both as an action during the war and as a pious wish from the corpse under the Paris pavement. The warming, clearly both physical and emotional, links the cold of the trenches with that of death and that of the urban entombment. And the idea from the earlier plaint, that the soldier is still on fatigue duty, is developed in 1927 into the notion that the anonymous hero is still at attention, and the speeches he cannot avoid hearing are like the lectures he received as a trooper. The exploitation of the dead continues and matches that of the living. The point is important because it distinguishes the *Canard*'s revived soldier from the resurrected warriors of Dorgelès, of Gance's 1919 *J'accuse,* or of the artists discussed by Winter. They rise to protest the war; the *Canard*'s corpse avenges both the war and the peace.[46]

But by linking these two situations (that of living soldier and that of consecrated corpse), the words attributed to the unknown soldier mix the worlds of reality and fantasy. The sufferings of soldiers, whether cold or danger or the thousand stupidities of military life, were part of reality. The miseries of a corpse, from insincere speakers to pavement-rattling buses, are fantasy or metaphor. More important, when one shifts from the speech, even the supposed speech, of live soldiers to that of dead combatants, one has crossed from the natural to the supernatural.

In the pages of the *Canard,* the unknown soldier becomes the vehicle for the association of two themes: the distinction between self-sacrificing combatants and *embusqués,* on the one hand, and the exploitation of the war dead, on the other. War service becomes the first stage in a two-part exploitation. The dead could be vengeful for two separate reasons: because of their wartime suffering and death and because of their post-mortem exploitation. But this opening of the floodgates of the supernatural also links the horror associated with risen dead (as zombies, as living dead, or as *revenants*) to the real horrors of war.

At once real soldier and symbol, the hero under the Arc de Triomphe can function, as visually in Pedro's cartoon, as an allegory of war. The rising of the real soldier would be the vengeance of the dead, the symbol pushing aside the slab would be the reemergence of war. We already saw how the *Canard* predicted this eventuality with the motif of the next last war.[47] Through the militarist and chauvinist exploitation of his memory, the unknown soldier unwillingly links the last war with the next one.

PROFANATION

The sharp tone and the clear horror in Scize's article and Pedro's cartoon reflect more than the pacifism of both figures. They were also a response to a new level of intensity, one of virtual hysteria, in the cult of the unknown soldier. On August 23, 1927, a small group of men, apparently motivated by revolutionary sentiments, allegedly profaned the emplacement of the unknown soldier by urinating on the site. The guardians of the cult organized a giant ceremony of reparation, to which the pieces by Scize and Pedro were a reaction.

The *Canard* had treated the cult of the unknown soldier with rich disrespect. But defending such profanation would be impossible. Instead the *Canard* took two tacks: casting doubt on the reality of the acts in question and mocking the reparation ceremonies. The *Canard* summed up its understanding of the facts by calling this "one of the finest examples of *bourrage de crâne* since the war." The guardian of the flame had seen nothing, nor had the conservator of the Arc de Triomphe. The two policemen who reported the incident were not in agreement, the "more affirmative said 'he thinks that.' " "The most curious thing, in this whole business, is that no one knows what happened . . . and even if anything happened."[48]

Scize's article bore the subtitle "Words Heard under the Arc de Triomphe," but its title was "After the Reparation." A more typically Canardesque response, however, came in an article on a ceremony of reparation at the Casino at Deauville, where "a minute of silence was observed at the roulette wheel." Another ceremony took place in Paris, where a gas lamp had been broken in the course of leftist demonstrations: "A delegation of employees of the gas company, lighters and revivers of the streetlights, proceeded yesterday to the boulevard de Sébastopol. No speeches were delivered. The delegation limited itself to observing a moment of silence in front of the gas lamp damaged by the troublemakers."[49]

Such parodies of public events were almost routine *Canard* coverage. When it came to redirecting the meaning of the cycle of profanation and reparation, none could do better than the couple de la Fouchardière and Bicard. Bicard explains to his amanuensis that someone profaned the tree of remembrance in the Fontainebleau forest. Was it a dog, a bird? the other asks. No, surely German agents, explains Bicard, since they wrote something "insulting and pejoratic [sic]" on the bark of the tree. De la Fouchardière wonders whether this was "Long live peace" or "Down with war." No, Bicard answers, " 'Julot loves Titine.' " It comes out that, after a ceremony of reparation with a moment of silence, the patriots prevented further profanation by planting another tree three kilometers away to replace the original one, which Bicard assumes must have been a begonia. As Bicard explains, "Julot and Titine can come and do their dirty stuff under the begonia; the begonia doesn't give a damn. It is no longer the Tree of Remembrance; it's the other one. . . . And if Julot and Titine dishonor the other tree, there is no lack of spare trees in Fontainebleau forest."[50]

Celebrate life and not death (make love, not war): that is the *Canard*'s recipe for escape from the horrific cycle of cannibalism and resurrection. Julot and Titine making love under the begonia echo the young couple (in the same issue) who celebrated the armistice during eighty minutes of "relative silence."[51] And the reference in that story to the "class of 1947" stands as a reminder that when the *Canard* invokes such coupling, it is honoring not merely sensual pleasure but also the creation of life. And is this not the dream of Scize's unknown soldier, symbolized by the butterflies mating on flowers sprung from the former trenches of death?

10 Anti-Imperialism and Its Stereotypes

War in the Colonies

Even more daring for the time than the *Canard*'s antimilitarism was its principled condemnation of imperialism; in this regard, France's wars of colonial repression in Morocco and Syria in the mid-1920s earned the weekly's ridicule and opposition. An anti-imperialism of the left went with antiracism—at least in theory. We have already seen how the weekly exploited prejudices and stereotypes—from greedy Auvergnats to drunken revelers. In no area was the tension between stereotype and politics greater, however, than in those colonial wars. Here the weekly's combination of antimilitarism, anti-imperialism, and antiracism came up against its regular exploitation of racial stereotypes for humorous effect.

Nonconformist politics and conformist humor? This was only one of the complications in the *Canard*'s discourse on the Moroccan and Syrian wars. The debates around "Orientalism" (in which Edward Said's books have played such a central role)[1] have sensitized us to the roles that barely spoken prejudices play in political and cultural judgments regarding the Middle East and the Islamic world. The *Canard Enchaîné*'s mixture of the comical and the political worked within these tensions as it sought to both exploit French racism and redirect it toward a politically conscious anti-imperialism. The problem of "Orientalism," or of epistemic assumptions about the nature of Arab and Islamic societies, is only a part of a larger question of cultural geography, the ways in which different parts of the world are represented, the spatialization of stereotypes. The *Canard* had its own cultural geography, though it was more often implied by its jokes and stories than explicitly formulated in its articles.

The *Canard*'s world was effectively composed of three zones. The first included not just France, as one would suppose, but also similarly advanced or powerful states like Britain, Germany, and the United States. Such countries, their governments, and their citizens were subject to mockery, but a mockery based on strength. They were pilloried for their militarism, and often for their hypocrisy (especially, as we saw in chapter 7, in the cases of France, Britain, and the United States). But these were the vices of Great Powers (or, for Germany, Great Powers in eclipse). The *Canard* also joyfully caricatured regions within France, like Auvergne—or even Provence. A proud son of the south had objected to a story in *L'Oeuvre* in which de la Fouchardière suggested that the inhabitants of Provence spent all their time playing boules. The weekly replied that in fact the same two people played boules all the time and the other Provençaux spent their time watching.[2]

Non–Great Powers, smaller European states, made up the second zone: these countries were chiefly Spain and Italy, but also Greece. None of these enjoyed a reputation for military prowess or national strength in the pages of the *Canard.* Size played a role here, but so too did a certain contempt for more southern, Mediterranean countries. These prejudices were reinforced by the *Canard*'s principled dislike for the dictators of Spain and Italy. Miguel Primo de Rivera and Benito Mussolini became odious clowns; they were ridiculed on the basis of traditional prejudices while being excoriated for their antidemocratic policies. Rivet, for example, claimed that Mussolini had destroyed communism in order to replace it with "mandolinism."[3]

The third, and last, zone was one of frank exoticism: what we today call the third world, a land outside European civilization. The *Canard*'s view of these territories, whether in or outside the French empire, was not exempt from racism. The point is important, as are the other distinctions, because the larger of France's two colonial conflicts of the 1920s, the Rif war in Morocco, involved a zone-one country (France) in alliance with a zone-two country (Spain) against the Berbers of the zone-three Moroccan Rif.[4]

RACISM AND ANTIRACISM

Colonial troops had played a major role in the Great War, and correcting the paternalistic image of the devoted colonial troops was part of the *Canard*'s battle of memory. In July 1924, the grateful city of Reims erected a monument to "the black army"—that is, to the colonial troops who had successfully defended the city against the German invasion. The *Canard* journalist noted the painstaking accuracy of the details, from helmets to specific weapons. This journalist's only regret was that the sculptor had failed to represent the double cords placed at either end of the village to recruit the troops. The satirical weekly had already explained on more than one occasion how the Senegalese "volunteers" were recruited. Ropes were stretched across the two ends of a village and all those in between were considered volunteers "and presumptive heroes." The *Canard*'s combination of antiracism and antimilitarism was bold. This same statue, which the weekly ridiculed for its hypocrisy, enraged the Germans for its glorification of African soldiers. Today's visitor to Reims will not see that memorial. Destroyed by the Nazis during the Second World War, it was replaced by a photograph, a plaque, and a marker memorializing the conflict between French paternalism and German hostility.[5]

As a *Canard* topos, the cord-as-recruitment-tool evoked with economy the wartime lie of colonial volunteers, and it was thus available for other uses. In April 1923, the weekly reported that the rope trick was still in use in Senegal, with those collected offered prison or the barracks. As the French writer put it, "They receive investiture as eventual heroes for the next last one"—a reference to another of the weekly's topoi.[6] Or, the Senegalese recruitment trick could be used to interpret other forms of exploitation of non-European populations. "Well, since we must not lack domestic servants and colonies are not made only for the English, we have but to stretch out ropes in a number of villages in Guadeloupe."[7]

References to African soldiery often led to evocations of the commander of the colonial troops, General Charles Mangin, and especially the remark attributed to him that these were troops "to be consumed before the winter." The alleged remark itself became a minor *Canard* topos, subject to repetition, allusion, or even explanation (he was trying to spare his men head colds).[8] The *Canard*'s defense of African soldiery skillfully combined anti-imperialism with antimilitarism. It also deliberately avoided (if one excepts a comment about the "patriotic gentleness" of these troops) references to the reputation that the Senegalese and other African soldiers had as particularly aggressive and savage assault troops.[9]

U.S. racism, whether at home or among tourists in Paris, was held up to ridicule and censure. After an incident in which a group of Americans started a ruckus over the presence of blacks in a Parisian bar, the weekly reacted with critical articles and a cartoon by Guilac. Entitled "The Drowning American, or One Cannot Do Anything with the Negroes," it showed a white fisherman drowning in a lake while a black man watches and comments, "A shame dat me jus a poor colored man." While clearly antiracist in its vengeful schadenfreude, the cartoon also indulges in the *Canard*'s version of black speech, with the *r*'s dropped as in the dialects of the French Caribbean. Such pronunciations have remained standard among French humorists. The African pirate in René Goscinny and Albert Uderzo's *Astérix* comic-strip series, for example, speaks this way. We have already seen in chapter 6 Bicard's condemnation of lynching; and U.S. antiblack racism tended to reappear when the *Canard* had a serious gripe with the republic across the Atlantic. Apparently this combination of antiracism and anti-Americanism appealed to the weekly's readers. The "Caneton" club of *Canard* fans announced:

> With a delicate consideration for which those concerned will be grateful, and in order to repair an injustice that America tolerates but that the morality of our investigating magistrates condemns, our young friends have decided to reserve this soirée exclusively to men of color. Obviously, by men of color we mean all men and by exception all women whose epidermis is covered by any pretty tint at all, going from black to the most perfect white, passing through light green and bright vermilion, without forgetting pearly yellow.[10]

But as the use of dialect by the African American in the Guilac cartoon testified, the *Canard* still felt free to exploit stereotypes of black Africans in remarks that ran from the marginally insensitive to the classically racist.

The weekly also regularly returned to a series of puns on black and white, exploiting the racial and nonracial meanings of these two words in common French. These word games could adorn an otherwise antiracist article, as in a notice in a phony women's column of the arrival of a boatload of "Negro" servant women from the Antilles in March 1923. But such humor could also be used to ridicule civil-rights activities. In August 1921, René Buzelin reported on a demonstration in New York that brought out 150,000 African Americans. What did they want? After the yellow peril, "the black race" wanted to play a role in the League of Nations. "Incontestably, the success achieved by their frenetic jazz bands is inciting the Negroes to demand a more important place in what we have come to call the Concert of Europe." The coverage of this international conference then descended further: the delegates had to wear white gloves in order to be seen at night, one had to eat one's white bread first, the streets were black with people, and so forth. A month later, Rivet treated similarly a meeting in Paris in an article entitled "The Black Peril." In it, for example, the usual puns accompanied suggestions that the delegates criticized the deputy Alexandre Blanc (white). In neither of these cases would the reader have had any idea of the suffering of blacks in either country or of the nature of their political goals.[11]

Another pun that the *Canard* was unable to resist played on the words *Nègres* (Negroes) and *nègres* (ghost writers). The *Canard* accused the writer Pierre Mac-Orlan of setting up a factory for the "denegritisation of

Negroes"; accompanying the article was a drawing of newly whitened "Negroes" hung out to dry. And then there was the claim that U.S. visitors were horrified to discover that the journalist Pierre Decourcelles (a frequent *Canard* target) used "Negroes" in his work.[12]

Surely the most racist of the *Canard*'s black African topoi was the idea that black Africans were cannibals. A cartoon from January 1924 by Mat showed a black savage hawking parts of human bodies to two potential customers under the heading "Great White Sale." Stories and cartoons presented Africans serving up whites to European and African diners, sometimes with a jazz band in the background; these pieces linked the fantasized blacks of darkest Africa with those of Paris. During the war, the censor had blocked one *Canard* attempt to link African troops and cannibalism. Indeed, the racist character of the weekly's exploitation of this theme stands out more clearly when compared with its evocation in the wartime *Bécassine.* There the alleged cannibalism of Africans was mocked through a story that exploited the Breton heroine's credulity in this regard.[13]

It was characteristic of the *Canard* that it could combine such mindless exploitation of popular stereotypes with the occasional subversion of the same clichés, as when Bicard turned the idea of cannibalism against lynch-happy Americans.[14] Yet when *Canard* writers got angry with individual African Americans, racist images came swiftly to their pens. The Parisian success of the African-American entertainer Josephine Baker elicited images of Baker as a savage in the jungle and verbal references to Central Africa. The apparent romantic suicide of a Frenchman at the feet of the star in 1928 was too much for Rodolphe Bringer. "Oh, how far we are from *Uncle Tom's Cabin,* which caused so many tears to be shed. But you will see that this Negress will make herself so unbearable that it will be necessary to reestablish slavery!"[15]

France's colonial wars of the 1920s took place not in sub-Saharan Africa but in Arab Syria and Arabo-Berber Morocco—countries in the Middle Eastern–North African–Islamic cultural sphere. One of France's enemies in the Great War was the Ottoman Empire, the premier Islamic power of the day. And the *Canard* had mocked Ottoman institutions in its early issues just as it had attacked Germany and Austria-Hungary. An example was a crack about the patriotic support of the palace eunuchs: "the members, if we may speak this way, of this impotent corporation."[16] But the wartime *Canard* declined to exploit well-established stereotypes of Islam. One reason was the weekly's decision to concentrate its satirical fire on French journalists. But even if the *Canard* had wanted to target Islam, the censor would not have allowed it any more than it had allowed the troops-as-cannibals association. The guardians of the press insisted on the scrupulous avoidance of any targeting of Islamic customs or symbols in anti-Ottoman propaganda for fear of offending France's Muslim troops and subjects.[17] The end of the war eliminated this concern; and the *Canard* occasionally evoked popular stereotypes. A Bicard discussion of 1922 went from the Ninth Crusade to the claim that every Turk had twelve wives (Islam allows only four). A story about a new governor for Algeria consisted essentially of jokes about the desert and houris.[18] Such stereotypes of Islam, relatively rare, became more frequent in discussions of the Rif war.

The *Canard*'s exploitation of racist stereotypes did not keep the weekly from touting a consistently anti-imperialist line. For example, the paper reported an Italian victory in Libya by noting that the rebels, who lost three hundred men, "will have learned what the right of self-determination really means and the rights of Tripolitanians to Tripolitania."[19] The refusal of the British to allow self-determination to countries like Egypt was even more regularly pilloried—in effect, each time Egyptian pro-independence activities showed up on the wire services.[20]

Attacks on British imperialism were not new in France. More important was the *Canard*'s willingness to link all European imperialism under the rubric of denied self-determination. A 1922 article, for example, was entitled "Peoples Have The Right to Self-Determination, but within Certain Limits." It juxtaposed three incidents. In the first an Egyptian was arrested for shouting, "Long live Free Egypt." In the second, Kemalists were repelled by Allied forces, and the *Canard* observed that "the persistence of the Turks in wanting to occupy Turkey has become worrisome so the Allies, including France, have decided to oppose them with the force of Right, supported by that of bayonets." Lest French colonialism be forgotten, the article concluded with the story of six Moroccans shot for yelling, "Morocco for the Moroccans."[21]

The weekly did not spare French activities in Morocco even before the Rif war. In late June 1923, the *Canard* reacted with mock indignation to English reports of losses in a French battle with Moroccan soldiers. First, the *Canard* insisted, there could be no "Moroccan troops" on the enemy side, only "Moroccan bands." And there could be no battle, only "pacification," and if this pacification was going full steam, the French public had every right not to be informed of it.[22]

Speaking of that same June 1923 fighting in the North African protectorate, Bicard opined that the "dissident fractions" against which France was at war were "Negro patriots; . . . they have planted a flag on a mountain, they sing songs around their flag, and they refuse to make coal deliveries." (The last point was a reference to France's attempts to force German coal deliveries.)[23] The collapsing of largely Berber Moroccans into "Negroes" reflects a general tendency that we will see again, but the use of the lower-class Bicard permits de la Fouchardière to evoke popular racist attitudes while maintaining a certain distance from them. The image of these people of color singing around their flag exploits contempt for "uncivilized" peoples, but it also mocks French nationalists whose behavior becomes like that of a band of savages. These Africans are patriots; or French patriots are little better than the colonials they look down on. Such ambiguities are typical of the *Canard Enchaîné*'s discursive strategies.

THE RIF WAR

But the war in the Moroccan Rif, which was France's largest colonial engagement of the decade, began not as a war between the French and Moroccans but as one between Spaniards and North Africans. Only after Spanish troops were effectively driven from the Rif area and an independent government was set up under the leadership of Abd al-Krim did France become involved. This fact colored (if we may use such a term) the *Canard*'s coverage of the conflict.

The first, Hispano-Moroccan, phase of the war allowed the Gallic weekly to stand somewhat outside the fray. At the same time the thorough thrashing administered to the Spanish troops, considerably more humiliating between the wars than a similar defeat would be today, made an ideal subject for humor. The *Canard*'s pronounced distaste for the reactionary regime of Alphonse XIII and Primo de Rivera only made the target more appealing. Two brief articles in the August 20, 1924, issue were typical. One explains that the Rifians are ingrates. The Spaniards had sent "an entire army to maintain peace," yet they are making war on them. "It was a crime, even an Abd al-Crime" (the pun works better in French). The second zeroes in on Spanish reverses, while also mocking the hypocrisy of French World War I communiqués: "It has been announced in Mélilla that the advance of the Spanish troops in the rear of positions prepared in advance continues to take place with the greatest success. The rebels are obliged to pursue them while multiplying their attacks."[24] And, in another article, the mockery went on: "The Spanish armies continue, north of Chechouan, their irresistible flight toward the sea." When, in an official communiqué, the Spanish government explained that the people owed a debt of gratitude to Primo de Rivera for the way his troops evacuated besieged positions, despite vigorous opposition, the *Canard*'s writers wished aloud that Primo would write for them. Never could they have conceived such a fantastic report.[25]

Such humor is not exactly imperialist. But by focusing on the military incompetence of the Spanish authorities, the *Canard* almost made it seem as if this were their principal crime. The paper's writers could in addition have celebrated the victories of the African liberators. The weekly also reprinted sections from a pamphlet by a Spanish opponent of the regime that blamed it for leading so many soldiers to their death or capture at the hands of cruel North Africans.[26] Both European leftist politics and contempt for a zone-two nation muddled the *Canard*'s anti-imperialist message.

While some of these themes continued into the second phase of the war, France's entry as a major belligerent in May 1925 (in alliance with Spain) directed the weekly back to more traditionally antimilitarist and anti-imperialist positions. Nevertheless, if Spanish weakness was mocked, French strength was underlined. The *Canard* noted that large numbers of French troops had been sent "to pacify without pity" the Rifians, who had the effrontery to act as if they were in their own country. But the weekly added, with an irony that respected the reputation of the country of Napoleon and Foch, this was also an excellent occasion to show the superiority of the French military (then the largest army in the world) over the Spanish.[27]

Soon, however, *L'Intransigeant* gave the *Canard* the ideal tool to tie together its antimilitarism and anti-imperialism with yet another of its causes, its attack on the mass press.[28] *L'Intran* earned the weekly's ire on this occasion by explaining that the French military demonstration being prepared, replete with combat aviation, would show the Rifians how far they were from the French level of civilization. Certainly, the leftist periodical replied (echoing the argument of George Duhamel's *Civilisation* and of some front-line soldiers[29]), the recent world war had brought twentieth-century civilization to a very high level. It went further, however, and began an *enquête* (inquiry) into the meaning of "civilization." The question was posed with relative seriousness, and the replies, printed in subsequent numbers, were unusually direct. The resulting lower levels of irony, and hence of ambiguity, were typical of the *Canard*'s approach when it felt that a crucial issue was under discussion. A variety of leftist politicians and writers answered, saying that the notion of civilization was perfectly hypocritical or that it was used relatively, and inconsistently, according to whether one was on good terms with the other country in question.[30] Cartoons rang changes on the theme of a civilized Europe. A Pedro strip provided "a few undebatable signs . . . of a superior civilization": a barracks, a street urinal, a movie house, police, soldiers, taxes.[31] Once it had established its point, the nonconformist weekly went on to use the idea of civilization-as-high-tech-warfare as a leitmotif whenever it wished to condemn the war and its hypocrisy. When the Spanish entered Abd al-Krim's capital of Ajdir in October 1925, as the *Canard* explained, they "immediately applied the latest methods of civilization: they set fire to the principal houses."[32] The civilization motif, which we shall see again, did double duty. It emphasized the insanity of Europe's technologically advanced warfare capabilities and the hypocrisy of its claims to moral superiority over less civilized peoples.

Not surprisingly, the anti-imperialist paper also attacked the argument made by the left-of-center French government that France had right on its side. The official position was that Rifian troops had invaded French Morocco, and thus the French were required, according to international law and the terms of the protectorate, to defend that territory. The *Canard* could have, but did not (unless one counts a single highly ambiguous allusion), repeat the argument circulated in some communist circles that the French deliberately provoked the Rifian attack.[33]

The *Canard* eschewed this essentially correct argument in favor of a more general line that had the advantage of discrediting the entire French colonial enterprise. Who were the invaders? The French!—since the Moroccans were in their own country. The point was served up with many different sauces. The prime minister was made to explain that all the French were doing was expelling foreigners who had penetrated into "our place," that is, Morocco, and that these foreigners were Moroccans. Bicard put it in broader historical perspective. After his interviewer declared that "these Moroccan pigs, imbued with imperialism and conquest, speak of invading the country that we have taken from them and of throwing us out of their place," Bicard opined that the Moroccans were in the same situation as the French had been vis-à-vis the English at the time of Joan of Arc.[34]

The *Canard,* which arranged so much of its coverage of the 1920s through the lens of the First World War, often used the Rif war to evoke the earlier conflict. The comparisons, like good metaphors, redefined both conflicts. The Rif war became thus a reminder that the era of war had not ended, while its smaller scale made the comparison at the same time potentially humorous. But evoking the Great War through the colonial one became another exercise in memory—forcing the *Canard* readers to reexperience the world war through the lens of *bourrage de crâne.*

A page 1 article of September 16, 1925, was a masterpiece of First World War memorabilia. Its title, "The War in Morocco, the Spaniards at Five Stages from Ajdir, the Steamroller Is in Action," derided the famously overly optimistic *Le Temps* headline that put the Cossacks at five stages from Berlin in 1914, and it evoked as well the equally famous Russian steamroller. The text went on to mock Poincaré's reference to a divine minute: "It is almost a second divine minute. Here we find again the feverish enthusiasms of 1914. In a magnificent outburst the Nation has understood that once again it is a question of the last of all wars." After this allusion to the next last war, the paper went on to evoke the nonenlistment of Maurice Barrès, the questionable veracity of military communiqués, and other features of the earlier war.[35]

Pedro drew his own Moroccanized World War I anthology, taking some of the more outlandish Great War claims and redrawing them with Moroccan figures. The claim that German bullets did little damage became the assertion that Moroccan rifles did not fire; the notion of capturing a battalion of the enemy with a sandwich became capturing a battalion of Rifians with a sandwich or a banana. The transplantation of the earlier absurdities to the exotic locale of North Africa added further ridicule to the patriotic falsehoods.[36]

The *Canard* had played the war-as-redux game before. In 1920, during the Greco-Turkish War, the paper had claimed that the Greeks were at "five stages from Athens," and it described the Hellenic patriot Marikos Barressos.[37] But the Rif war was France's battle, and the writers of the leftist weekly updated their old themes in ways that spoke to the specific realities of imperialism. In a savage attack on the upper-class origins of nationalist youth, the paper imagined these young people joining up to protect the interests of their families. And the bankers declare, "People say that we sent soldiers down there to conquer mines, land, businesses for us. But we want, henceforth, to make our own conquests ourselves. Give us rifles!"[38]

When it came to the course of the war, the *Canard* hammered away at old themes, mocking the resolutely optimistic communiqués and suggesting that military reports were misleading at best.[39] All this was almost reflex antimilitarism in a French context. Far more distinctive was the idea that this war was being fought not just alongside the Spanish ally but in a sense also for it. The *Canard* effectively built on its earlier anti-Spanish campaign to remind French readers of this fact. Two points were made repeatedly: Frenchmen are fighting (and by implication dying) for Spanish interests, and they are doing so, at least partly, because the Spanish are incapable of fighting their own battles. Proof that the French are not imperialists? As soon as France has pushed Abd al-Krim north of the Ouergha River, it will conquer territories that will be immediately occupied by the Spanish. The French make the assault, and the Spanish occupy the positions as they are taken.[40] Another formula was even clearer. Frenchmen would not fight for the king of Prussia. They were not so stupid. They fight instead for the king of Spain.[41] The implications of such arguments are essentially nationalist; the paper sought to turn anti-Spanish sentiment against the war in Morocco and in its own way play up to French pride.

The Spanish alliance also came up when Abd al-Krim repeatedly indicated his interest in a negotiated peace. The *Canard* mercilessly mocked the left-of-center French government, which seemed either to be dragging its feet in its negotiations with the Rif leader or, worse, to be giving the Spanish veto power over any eventual agreement. Since French nationalists had already claimed that the armistice that had brought an end to four years of carnage in November 1918 was premature, the *Canard* felt free to borrow such arguments and protest against a too-early cessation of hostilities in the current war.[42] By the summer of 1926, however, Abd al-Krim was defeated, and the antimilitarist weekly was reduced to noting that while the war was officially over, "pacification" (which looked a lot like war) was continuing. As the *Canard* put it, "The surrender of Abd al-Krim has fortunately not put an end to the work of pacification that we have undertaken in the Rif and surrounding areas." Or as the weekly noted in a "Petite correspondance," "If it were not for the Taza pocket our generals would have to search desperately in their own pockets" for the continuation of the war. As a post-Abd al-Krim locus of hostilities, the "Taza pocket" served the *Canard* as a symbol of the open-ended, continuing character of imperial repression.[43]

STEREOTYPES

Part of the *Canard*'s task of opposing the militarism of France's mass press involved antiracism. When another paper spoke of the concerns of French mothers, the *Canard* answered with those of Moroccan mothers, "for nothing so much resembles one mother as another one."[44] The weekly also mocked a competing periodical, *L'Illustration*, which had attempted a little comparative ethnography. That magazine compared the loyal Moroccans, "rude and magnificent warriors with noble and energetic features," with the rebels from the Rif, "stout little blackish men with round heads and common features." Since *L'Illustration* provided pictures only of landscapes (and not populations), the *Canard*'s Pedro provided his own: a handsome, noble-looking Moroccan wearing French decorations, on the one hand, and a warped little fellow with a bloody knife and a German-style pointed helmet over his jellaba, on the other.[45]

Yet some of the weekly's other cartoonists were not as careful with their characterizations. The artist who signed Prouvost drew his Moroccans with stereotyped sub-Saharan features. In fact, the tendency to visually merge North African Berbers (in either army) and sub-Saharan Africans was one Prouvost shared with Henri Monier, author of many of the *Canard*'s Moroccan political cartoons. More significantly, both Prouvost and Monier were more than willing to draw on racist stereotypes when putting words into the mouths of their Moroccans. The Moroccans of the *Canard*'s cartoons speak a language the French sometimes call *petit nègre.* One of Prouvost's Rifian soldiers, looking at a field kitchen, declares, "Moi y en avoir trouvé canon contre avion! [Me find cannon against airplane!]" Both Monier's Moroccans and those of another cartoonist, William Napoleon Grove, spoke a similarly fractured French. This was essentially the same language put in the mouths of African (Malagasian or Senegalese) troops by the same artists. Its only suggestion of linguistic specificity came in the not-too-common use of Arabic expressions like "Roumi" or the Moroccan "beseff" (which had already passed into French slang).[46]

Yet even these racist stereotypes could serve anti-imperialist purposes. The collapsing of sub-Saharan African and Berber categories may have been sloppy ethnography (and even that could be excused given that the sultan of Morocco had his own black African troops). But it served a political point. A Monier cartoon showed two soldiers with identically stereotyped black African features. One, however, wore a vaguely Islamic outfit and the other a French colonial uniform. The text read, "Do not confuse the barbarian with the champion of civilization."[47]

Some stereotypes were more specific to the North African/Islamic cultural sphere, chief among these the harem. As a long-standing focus of erotic fantasy in the West, the veiled-women-harem complex not surprisingly tempted a periodical like the *Canard,* which rarely missed the chance to make an off-color allusion. The *Canard* reproduced the classic erotic juxtaposition of veiling and nudity in the mock recruitment poster it proposed for the Rif war. A French soldier contemplates an exotic female with veiled face, harem pants, and bare breasts. A caricature and an exploitation of stereotypes at the same time, the drawing burlesques tourist posters and compares the military campaign to a pleasure trip to exotic locales.[48]

But veiled women also stood in as humorous visual markers of Moroccanness. The weekly's anticlericalism combined with its exploitation of stereotypes in the article from July 1926 entitled "Paris Finally Has a Mosque, Which We Really Needed." The picture of the mosque, with Moroccan and French officials sitting on its steps, contains a medallion inset of alluring veiled women. The text explains that an interior court is used for belly dancing. And when the *Canard* reported the surrender conditions of Abd al-Krim, it noted that the vanquished rebel "was surrounded by a severe discipline and also a certain number of houris." In this Rif war dialogue of stereotype and anti-imperialism, popular images vied with the politics of having the loyal sultan of Morocco thank his French and Spanish mother-countries while assuring them of his "faithful treason."[49]

DESERT OF STEREOTYPES: SYRIA

Syria, France's other major zone of colonial conflict during these years, was far less well known to the paper and its readers. North African, more particularly Moroccan, realities were far more familiar to both French soldiers and civilians (not least because of the role troops from this region had played in the recent world war) than were the lands of the eastern Mediterranean. If stereotypes feed on ignorance, total unfamiliarity has a paradoxically opposite effect. The *Canard*'s coverage of Syrian events virtually completely avoided any appeal to stereotypes. Not only was Syria not Africa, but the Druse, major players in France's Syrian troubles, were even harder to categorize in popular terms. Historically associated with Islam, but a distinct religious community, the Druse could not easily be invoked through the harem or the veil. In this desert of stereotypes, the weekly tried to make of absence a presence.

As the fighting in Syria warmed up, the *Canard* exploited the relative novelty of France's involvement by offering "a live rabbit and a pipe of red sugar" to the first person who could explain "what the hell we are doing in Syria" and at the same time "indicate the exact source of our rights to Syria."[50] If Syria was relatively unfamiliar, the Druse, who were in open revolt against the French occupation, were even less known. Again the *Canard* exploited this ignorance: "We still do not know what the Druse have done to us, or even where Drusia [sic] is located." But for some reason many of them had apparently developed the idea of wanting to be their own masters. Hence the Druse could be divided into two groups: "those who are sincerely French and who have all the virtues of our race . . . and the others who, under barbarous pretexts, emit the pretension of remaining Druse: the latter are recognizable by the knife they have between their teeth and the ring they arrogantly refuse to have placed through their noses."[51] The crack about knives between teeth is a reference to a famous postwar electoral-campaign poster picturing the red menace as a grinning head with a knife clamped in its jaws.[52] The ring-in-the-nose was used by the *Canard* as a humiliating reference to the powerlessness of France's loyal colonial monarchs, as for example for the king of Cambodia on the occasion of his accession.[53]

Syrian affairs were treated under generic anti-imperialist categories. As early as 1919, the *Canard* said that Franco-British differences over Syria "had caused the populations to conceive the ridiculous idea that they had the right to govern themselves." How to put this situation into visual form? A cartoon showed Clemenceau and Lloyd George studying a map of Syria.[54] Six years later, in 1925, a cartoon by Grove sought to stand French racist images on their heads. A black soldier reading a newspaper in front of a tent in the desert exclaims, "Zut! Y en a falloir à prisent civiliser li Druses! [Damn! We gon' have ta civilize da Druses now!]"[55] That it was an African soldier in Morocco who was represented, and not a Druse, was not a coincidence either. No Druse show up in *Canard* drawings, which is perhaps the best index of their unfamiliarity. To caricature Syrian developments, the cartoonist was obliged to link Syria to Morocco and define both under the category of anti-imperialism.

Clearly, linking the "civilization" argument to events in Syria was too good to pass up. And the *Canard* took every opportunity in the second half of 1925 and the opening months of 1926 to link the Druse revolt with the Rif one under the sign of imperialism. The combination also helped to cement the image of France as an imperialist, militarist country. Was France "drunk" with military glory? Actions in the Ruhr, Syria, and the Rif proved it. Speaking of plans to eventually reduce the duration of military service, the *Canard* explained that "this period of transition will last, in principle, until 1946, on the condition, of course, that the pacification of Syria, of the Rif, and of Brazil will be by then an accomplished fact." Truth imitates fiction. In 1946 the Syrians were still fighting the French for their independence, and the Moroccan struggle went on still longer.[56]

The fact that France was fighting, at the same time, at both ends of the Mediterranean, facilitated the association of the two conflicts. What was peace, the weekly asked, but "the interval between two wars"? Since Morocco was one war and Syria another, peace was the space between them. The weekly also imagined the minister of war, Painlevé, known for his absent-mindedness, confusing the two zones of conflict and putting the Syrian al-Atrash in the Rif. But the *Canard* had also touched on a tendency to amalgamate the colonial conflicts, a conflation produced both by their simultaneity and by the relative absence of popular knowledge of Syrian affairs. In his pro-imperialist paean to the port of Marseilles, the journalist and author Albert Londres described French soldiers boarding ships for "Morocco or some other Syria."[57]

The fighting with the Druse, in which French troops also did poorly at first, allowed the *Canard* to refresh its attacks on the questionable veracity of official accounts; it mocked the triumphal tone in which defeats were recorded and the tendency of communiqués to announce when a territory was captured but not when that same topography was lost to the enemy.[58]

But the Syrian campaigns were not exclusively against the Druse or in the mountains. Arab nationalist disturbances in Damascus were met with bloody bombardments of residential neighborhoods in that city, a fact that lent itself to especially caustic irony, as in the headline "Peace in Syria, Mr. Henry de Jouvenel Has Brilliantly Succeeded in the Bombardment of Damascus." And the article claimed that the families of the three hundred victims ran through the streets yelling, "Vive la France."[59] By the same token, the *Canard* was particularly harsh on those who thought that aerial bombardment of cities was somehow uplifting or exciting. A major Parisian daily, *Le Journal,* published an account by the novelist and journalist J. Kessel (who served in aviation during the war), of how he dropped bombs on the Syrian city of Soueida.[60] When Kessel gets to the part where he is instructed to drop the "packet," the *Canard* interrupts his colorful narrative: "The packet, that is, of course, that of bombs, which are democratic, laic, social, and civilizing, the one of grenades and incendiary shells. M. Kessel drops it. He drops it with nobility, tranquillity, and indifference. You know, when one is in an airplane, one has the right to see things from on high, to float, to dream. . . . Ah, these poets." And the text returns to Kessel's graceful account of columns of smoke rising from the city.[61]

The *Canard's* genuine disgust could not be clearer.[62] But the criticism of military activities occasionally intersected in unexpected ways with French political rivalries. That same Henry de Jouvenel whose bombardment of Damascus in 1926 earned the weekly's scorn had provoked the paper's ire earlier, in 1925, by scheming to replace General Maurice Sarrail, an officer well known for his left-of-center political connections,[63] as high commissioner in Syria. In an uncharacteristic move, the satirical periodical reported a journalistic investigation that appeared to exonerate Sarrail of some of the charges levied against him by the right-wing press. Sarrail had been right to bombard a neighborhood of Damascus in 1925, this new report argued, for that had been necessary to protect the lives of Syrian Christians and foreigners in the city.[64] Hence, Sarrail was here excused for the very same crime held against his political enemy, de Jouvenel, only months later. The *Canard Enchaîné* defending the bombardment of a residential neighborhood? And by a French general? The article in question does not admit an ironic interpretation. It is uncharacteristic, and General Sarrail usually got the same contemptuous treatment meted out to other military men,[65] but the *Canard* was led to this position by its involvement in domestic French politics.

The *Canard*'s coverage of the Rif war had to navigate among the shoals of popular stereotypes and across a geography of Great Powers, second-rate ones, and third-world countries. By contrast, its treatment of Syria evolved in a referentially less crowded environment. Into this space considerations of antimilitarism and domestic French politics flowed all the more easily. The tensions and complexities inherent in the *Canard*'s discourses on France's colonial wars of the 1920s, its willingness to use these events as sites of memory to comment on the world war or as sites of humor to exploit established stereotypes, certainly affected its anti-imperialism and antiracism. Yet the *Canard Enchaîné* took positions on the colonial wars of the 1920s that were so far outside the spectrum of respectable political discussion that even many in the Communist Party, then in a radical, class-war mode, could not accept them.[66] The *Canard*'s ideological meanderings were part of its formula, its mixture of humor and seriousness, and its uncanny ability to play both sides of an issue at the same time, to exploit stereotypes while undermining them.

11 Politics as Usual

An Antiparliamentarism of the Left?

The ideological flexibility of so much of the *Canard's* discourse allowed it to vacillate among its roles as leftist, satirical, and veterans' periodical. The result was often a kind of leftist antiparliamentarism or even a veterans' antiparliamentarism. The *Canard's* antiparliamentarism was not the antidemocratic one of the radical right or even that of prewar anarchists and syndicalists or followers of the Jacobin tradition, who wished to replace representative institutions with other forms of popular expression. The antiparliamentarism of the *Canard* was a critique of the parliament as a working body; and it was, thus, the centerpiece of an analysis of the political system of the French Third Republic. As the postwar decade advanced, disillusionment increased, and the *Canard's* relatively optimistic electoral activism yielded to a condemnation of the whole system.

DERIDING CLEMENCEAU

Peace did not signal the immediate return of normal political life. During the interregnum between the armistice of November 1918 and the signing of the peace treaties in the summer of 1919, the Clemenceau government maintained tight censorship of the French press and backed it up with repression of leftist activity.[1] But the end of the fighting did permit a far broader debate in France than had been possible during the war. The *Canard* criticized the continuation of censorship, contrasting it with the greater press freedom in Britain and the United States, and called for amnesty for political prisoners and an end to the state of siege.[2] The weekly also gave a pro-veteran twist to the secrecy of the peace negotiations. A Gassier cartoon showed soldiers discussing the fact that they were not invited to the peace conference. A satirical article invoked the wartime division between soldiers and *embusqués.* Had one seen the diplomats involved

Figure 10. Clemenceau ridiculed, by Gassier (1918).

in the fighting? No, they had left that to the soldiers. Hence the soldiers should now leave the peace discussions to the diplomats.[3]

More courageously, the paper resolutely went after Prime Minister Georges Clemenceau. In the same issues in which the weekly treated Wilson to a visual cult of personality, it mercilessly mocked the one then surrounding Clemenceau—but also visually. A series of sketches showed Clemenceau as a variety of pompous and ridiculous statues (for an example, see figure 10).[4]

The *Canard* had effectively supported "the Tiger" (as Clemenceau was called) during the war but refused to make of this an argument for the peace. In January 1919, the weekly published a little story entitled "The

Lady Who Was Sick and the Doctor." A thinly disguised allegory of the war, it told of a lady, gravely ill for four years, who brings in a new doctor. He puts her on a severe regimen, and it (along with some American "infusions") cures her. But the physician insists that she continue her treatment despite the cure and posts a policeman at her door to make sure she does not leave. Puns on *santé* (health, but also the prison where the government incarcerated its political prisoners) and *chambre* (room, but also the Chamber of Deputies) completed the transparent critique of the prime minister.[5] Other pieces reminded the *Canard*'s readers of Clemenceau's prewar record of sending the army to shoot strikers.[6] Clemenceau's henchman, Georges Mandel, made an easier target, and the *Canard* was not above exploiting anti-Semitic stereotypes (and false rumors) to criticize Mandel, whom the paper opposed for essentially political reasons.[7]

VETERANS VERSUS DEPUTIES

Contrasting Clemenceau with Wilson was typical for pacifist and other leftist papers during early 1919.[8] And the *Canard* showed its leftist bona fides through its support of the May Day general strike.[9] But the preferred symbolic clientele of the weekly was not organized workers, it was returning soldiers. In a rare direct appeal, the *Canard* admonished the *poilus:*

> Remember this modest "Canard," which was often your joy in the darkest hours and which always came to your defense.
>
> Remember that we were your friend and that, in spite of the censor and the imbeciles, we found a way, in our four little weekly pages, while laughing, to tell more truths than were told even in the big dailies.[10]

But the weekly expected more from the former soldiers than gratitude. On Christmas 1918, the lead article of the *Canard* repeatedly evoked "the sound of boots, of boots, of boots." The boots were those of the returning troops, who worried the government, the profiteers, and the professional patriots, for theirs were the "derrières" that the soldiers were preparing to boot, the weekly intimated with undisguised glee.[11] In case the allusion was too fine, the *Canard* made another direct appeal to the demobilized soldiers in March 1919. "Are you fed up with the deputies who, for five years, have behaved like cowards and lackeys?" the weekly asked. If so, then do as we will, we who have never voted before, and register to vote. Veterans against deputies—the *Canard* was recycling its binarism of soldiers versus *embusqués* while making an appeal to the unpoliticized. The title of the front-page appeal was "Hey you! The Demobilized!" The paper avoided the term *anciens combattants* (veterans), which, as we saw in chapter 7,

Figure 11. The veteran prepares to vote, by Gassier (1919).

was already associated with militarism in the eyes of the web-footed weekly. The paper spoke as if it and the former soldiers were one group: "Soon, comrades, we will be able to wield the broom."[12]

From the verbal metaphor to the visual: a Gassier cartoon of April 1919 bore the title "The Demobilized Soldier at Drill" (see figure 11). It showed a man, whose costume partook of both the military and the civilian, holding a broom as one would a rifle with bayonet. The brush of the broom is pointing toward the portrait on the wall of a Mr. Duconault, deputy. The man explains to his wife, who is looking on with surprise, "But, as you can see, my dear, I am preparing for electoral reform!"[13] While others in France were debating electoral systems or adjusting districts, the *Canard* considered the essential remedy a clean sweep of the existing deputies, a point made again in July and September. As the weekly put it in a headline (with the last sentence in the language of Shakespeare), "Will the outgoing deputies be defeated through electoral-list voting *[scrutin de liste]* or through single-member voting *[scrutin d'arrondissment]?* That is the question."[14]

As the above suggested, the *Canard* did not limit its attacks to the Clemenciste majority. Many Socialist deputies (like those in the reformist wing of the party) should also feel the wrath of the voters, the weekly opined.[15] But it did not allow criticism of the politicians to lure it into the right-wing trap of an attack on all electoral politics. It mocked the rightist, patriotic claim to be above political divisions: "No politics, citizens," it had a candidate declare; "all Frenchmen should unite in a single party: ours!"[16] The *Canard* found a way to mock both the deputies in general and the right in particular. For five days we have had neither deputies nor a Chamber, the paper noted on October 22, but was the country any worse off? The same column, however, included an attack on the right-wing electoral alliance, the National Bloc, already soundly thrashed in a page 1 article two weeks before.[17] The *Canard* continued its formula of demobilized soldiers and a clean sweep as the elections approached. In August, the weekly reminded recently demobilized soldiers (via a Laforge duck with a broom in his bill) that they had only twenty days after their release to register to vote. The October 29 headline described the first round of the elections, to be held on November 16, as the "Début du corps de balai," a pun on ballet and *balai* (broom).[18]

Maréchal appears to have assumed that most veterans, and many others, were so disgusted with the corruption and sufferings of the war and armistice period that they would vote against the government. But, instead, the patriotically charged atmosphere of the war and victory, combined with superior electoral alliances on the right, produced one of the most conservative Chambers in the history of the Third Republic.[19]

THE-MAN-WITH-THE-KNIFE-BETWEEN-HIS-TEETH

The weekly also underestimated the effect of the red-scare campaign, which was fed by the real threat of a spread of Bolshevism westward across Europe. A major feature of the campaign was the now classic anti-Communist poster of a dangerous-looking revolutionary with a knife between his teeth.[20] Immediately after the elections, the *Canard* took up the challenge of this propaganda masterpiece. Since the danger of Bolshevism was still imminent, the paper argued, one needed more such images, and it instituted a mock contest for a new anti-Bolshevik poster, with contributions attributed to leading conservative journalists. Two of the three examples brought out the implied cannibalism created by the placement of the murderer's knife between his teeth. One showed a Bolshevik grasping a Russian victim who, reduced in size to that of a turkey leg, finds himself between the monster's teeth. The second represented Bolshevism as a horrific devil with a bloody fork between his teeth. The third shifted from cannibalism to sex, showing a pregnant woman and a dog. Its text: "The Bolshevik not only wants your money, he will rape your girlfriend and give your dog the mange."[21]

The next issue made the connection of poster and election results clearer. Entitled "At the National Bloc Banquet," it showed a scruffy man with a knife between his teeth and blood on his hands entering a fancy room in front of a group of distinguished politicians. The legend: "Photograph taken by Mr. Adolphe Carnot at the moment of the sensational entrance of the great victor: the man with the knife between his teeth"[22] (Carnot was the creator of the poster campaign). A few months later, in March 1920, the *Canard* indignantly reported that National Bloc politicians were now thinking of normalizing relations with the Russian communists. So soon after the electoral campaign this was a fraud: "Today they want us, without further ado, to swallow the knife that Mr. Adophe Carnot had so ingeniously placed between the jaws of his Bolshevik character."[23]

But the famous poster was also linked to the question of attitudes toward the new Soviet government in Russia. The *Canard* had welcomed the Russian revolution of February/March 1917, and it had countered indignation over the murder of the tsar with an illustrated (by Gassier) little history of the assassinations and domestic murders that had marked Russia's ruling families.[24] After the war the weekly joined the general campaign on the French left against French intervention in Russia.[25] When it came to Lenin's government itself, however, the satirical weekly eschewed commentary on events in Russia in favor of mockery of the coverage of Russian developments in the conservative French press.[26] Here, the man-with-the-knife-between-his-teeth became a convenient symbol of the excesses of French propaganda and of the relation of anti-Bolshevik coverage of events in Russia to domestic political concerns. In February and March 1920, the *Canard* ran a feuilleton entitled "The Fiancée of the Bolshevik or the Bloody Knife." A sendup of clichés about Russia and the reds, it ends as the distraught father realizes that one of his daughters has been impregnated by a Bolshevik. The otherwise adorable newborn has a knife between his teeth.[27] But the absurdity of misplaced literalness could be exploited verbally as well, as in the following sentence, allegedly taken from a future book: "To sharpen his pencil, the Bolshevik removed the knife that he was holding in his teeth."[28]

The *Canard* appropriated the image by transferring the knife from the mouths of Bolsheviks into those of their opponents. After the May Day strikes of 1920, the *Canard* published sketches of the police in a variety of savage attitudes, including two officers of the law with knives between their teeth. The image did double duty, ridiculing the rightist cliché while supporting the claim of the accompanying article that, when it came to disturbing order and making trouble, no one could equal the French police.[29] Three years later, the *Canard* illustrated a long attack on the then president of the Republic, Alexandre Millerand, with a picture of the conservative politician with a knife between his teeth.[30] Indeed, the image, verbal or visual, of the-man-with-the-knife-between-his-teeth became a *Canard* topos, a mobile element that could be combined with other materials, as in the coverage of the Rif war.[31] The topos economically evoked the absurdity of red-scare campaigns. And, through its association with the National Bloc poster of 1919, the anti-Communist image also reminded readers of the collusion of red scares with electoral tactics.

The *Canard*'s opposition to anticommunism as a political ploy, like its principled opposition to the repression of the Communist Party, in no way signaled sympathy for this new political movement. We saw the skeptical attitude of Bicard/de la Fouchardière. In 1928, while defending the Communist deputy and sometime *Canard* contributor Vaillant-Couturier against government harassment, the weekly's passionate pacifist Pierre Scize added, "He spoke to me of the red army, of red discipline, of the red order. Through our conversation, I saw Communism rise up like a vast cage in reinforced concrete." Scize's 1928 appreciation, with its unconscious evocation of the worst of Stalinist architecture, encapsulated the *Canard*'s position on the legacy of Lenin. As much as the *Canard* could not tolerate the Soviet system's authoritarianism (if not totalitarianism), it could not digest its joylessness.[32] The exploitation of the red scare by the French right, added to the weakness of the proletarian party throughout the decade, invited the periodical to give the Communists virtual immunity from satire.

AGAINST PARLIAMENT

Since the National Bloc majority took over so soon after the peace treaties, the criticism of this majority blended with that of the parliament itself. The *Canard* noted that the Chamber contained a high number of millionaires. And, more than being rich, members of parliament were corrupt. When a scandal broke out over payments from a bank to a number of lawmakers, the *Canard* headline read: "But That Is Completely Natural." And the *Canard*'s regular attacks on the deputies for raising their own salaries, during a time of general budget tightening, painted them as more greedy than self-sacrificing.[33]

The Senate received special treatment. Senators were generally older than deputies, and throughout most of the Third Republic this body, with its higher rural representation, tended to be more conservative than the Chamber of Deputies. In addition, in its role as a high court, the Senate had earned the special ire of the *Canard* when, at the behest of Clemenceau, it had convicted the Radical politicians Louis Malvy and Joseph Caillaux of treasonous activities, despite very weak cases.[34] For the *Canard,* the senators were senile old men—in French, *gaga.* The weekly exploited this association by having the senators pushed around in wheelchairs (which resembled baby carriages with nurses) while saying "gagaga" or the like. Added to this mix was the claim that these senior lawmakers regularly visited the houses of prostitution on the rue des Martyres. Imagining the wheelchairs in the houses of ill-repute exploited the traditional comic trinity of old men, sex, and impotence. These associations became yet another set of topoi and another reduction of politics to bodies.[35]

The *Canard* brought all of these criticisms together in response to Millerand's proposal for reform of the Constitution. The satirical weekly made its own suggestions. "The Republic is installed," the document would declare, and deputies would be obliged to renounce both bribes and the subventions of private corporations; they would easily be able to meet this obligation since they were all honest men. To be a senator, the document would continue, one must not have fallen into second childhood and one must avoid the rue des Martyres. Finally, the sons of the president of the Republic must perform their military service. This last point was a slap at the fact that Millerand's son, Jean, had avoided his.[36]

But the weekly also focused on the leftist antecedents of many of the leading conservatives. In February 1923, the *Canard* opened another contest, for the cleanest man in France. As explanation, the weekly invoked "our master" Anatole France. France had said that there was a moral hygiene like the physical one and that one should change one's ideas as one would his shirts. The cleanest man in France was, thus, the man who had most often changed his political ideas.[37] Movement from left, even the radical left, to the center and right was almost routine in French life, so the *Canard* had plenty of contestants. In succeeding weeks, the weekly presented, one at a time, its political quick-change artists, with savage précis of their careers.

On May 23, the *Canard* announced that its readers had chosen Millerand as the cleanest (hence politically the dirtiest) man in France.

Now president of the Republic and a leader of the right, Millerand had started his career as a fire-eating Socialist. To celebrate his coronation, the weekly quoted one of his articles of 1894, now so ironically appropriate: " 'The president of the Republic is the living incarnation, the proud descendant, of the great legal bandits who plundered our ancestors through usury, through monopolies, by the clever application of all the procedures that the legal system, made by them and for them, put into their hands.' "[38]

POINCARÉ

To find the greatest villain of the postwar years the *Canard* had no need for a contest. The greatest misfortune in France's recent history was clearly the war, and for the *Canard* this catastrophe was associated with Raymond Poincaré, who was then president of the Republic. Attacking him was one of the few things the censor effectively blocked the wartime periodical from doing. The 1920s gave the satirical weekly ample opportunity to make up for any earlier—and involuntary—restraint.[39]

But the *Canard*'s focus on Poincaré also reflected his role as probably the most influential French political figure of the 1920s and a symbol of republican probity and patriotism. President from 1913 through 1919, Poincaré returned to parliament and became prime minister in January 1922 as the champion of a more resolutely anti-German policy. The Lorraine statesman served until the left victory of May 1924, but he returned to power in July 1926, as the monetary crisis led to the collapse of the Cartel des Gauches. Winning a parliamentary majority in the elections of 1928, he resigned only for reasons of health and age in July 1929.

The *Canard* summed up its general attitude to Poincaré in January 1926 by quoting another periodical's comments on the former president of the Republic: " 'From the beginning of 1912 to the month of May 1914, one can say that the history of our country is linked to the personality of Mr. Raymond Poincaré.' " To that the *Canard* added:

> Up to May 1914. Yes,
> *And even further,* alas!
> Alas! alas!
> Alas! alas! alas!
> In the name of God, alas!

The black humor of this passage functions only because a regular reader of the *Canard* would know what was behind every "alas!" When word came that Poincaré was elected president of the Republic in 1913, someone is supposed to have exclaimed, "Poincaré, c'est la guerre! [Poincaré, that means war!]" When the Great War broke out the following year, the prediction seemed to many to have been borne out. Certainly, the *Canard* did not hesitate to make of the sobriquet *Poincaré-la-guerre* a rhetorical albatross that it hung around the neck of the politician from the Meuse. In this case, as in much of its polemic against Poincaré, the *Canard* was a fellow-traveler since the Communists used the same phrase in their propaganda.[40]

The charge was based on Poincaré's identification with a tougher policy of national preparedness against Germany before the war and especially on his involvement (with Prime Minister René Viviani) in state visits to France's Russian and British allies as the international crisis was developing in the summer of 1914. Did he use his influence to push his country's partners toward more intransigent positions? Poincaré's response was to argue not only that blame for the war lay essentially with Germany (a position held by most French of the right and center and a large share of those of the left) but also that, as the largely ornamental president of the Republic, he was not involved in the diplomatic and military decisions that preceded the conflict. A lawyer and public speaker with a taste for amassing arguments, Poincaré defended himself in public lectures and articles. But his self-defense only further exposed his flank to the *Canard*'s rhetorical assault.

One tactic was to link Poincaré with Henri-Désiré Landru, the alleged serial killer who never confessed to his crimes. The *Canard*'s Landru requests that, like Poincaré, he be allowed to give a series of lectures in his defense, noting that he is accused of killing only a dozen or so women while the war had liquidated a far greater number of Frenchmen.[41] A year later, the weekly announced that it would publish the memoirs of William II, in which the former monarch would prove that, like Poincaré, he was not responsible for the war. Though this link to the last Hohenzollern might be seen as mitigating Poincaré's responsibility for the conflict, it was scarcely more flattering in a French context than the association with Landru. Throughout the early 1920s, the *Canard* ran the Poincaré/responsibility motif through all the rhetorical variations. The weekly put into Poincaré's mouth the following revelations: While in the Elysée he was kept in the dark about everything. He did not know there was a war on. Being uninformed, he was not responsible for either the war or the peace that followed.[42]

The *Canard,* in its pursuit of Poincaré on responsibility for the war, made no attempt to be fair; the newspaper's understanding of the causes of the war was not that simplistic.[43] But the weekly's unfairness can be seen even more clearly in its exploitation of the notion of Poincaré as the-man-who-laughs-in-cemeteries. In the spring of 1922, a photo appeared in which the

Lorraine patriot appeared to be smiling in a cemetery. His defenders said that he was really grimacing because the sun was in his eyes. Another explanation eventually surfaced to the effect that Poincaré was laughing nervously as photographers who, walking backward while taking his picture, caught their feet in some wire and almost tripped. The Communist daily, *L'Humanité,* seized on this photograph and started a campaign on the theme of Poincaré as the man who laughs in cemeteries. Picking up the story, the *Canard* made no mention of either explanation for this apparently unseemly conduct, instead stating, "Everyone shows respect in his own way. Mr. Poincaré laughs." A few weeks later, the *Canard* switched registers, concluding that Poincaré had not laughed since merriment was not in his character.[44]

Despite this denial, the *Canard* continued to pursue the nationalist politician with the cemetery/laughing topos. A trip in the east of France ended, the weekly reported, "in the gaiety of the cemetery." In August 1922, the *Canard* responded to a prediction of the end of the world with a cartoon signed "Varé." Under a series of images of men and women knocked off their feet, the cartoonist wrote the following doggerel verse.

> Chaos! nothingness! the entire earth
> is no more than a vast cemetery
> Over which looks down
> the sweetened smile of Poincaré.

Between the verses, a half moon encloses a Poincaré, his mouth wide open in laughter, surrounded by crosses. Here, the *Canard* takes the apocalyptic idea and again reads it as a coming war, this time by tying it to Poincaré, the man who can link the last war to the next last one.[45]

What was the former president doing in a cemetery? Probably giving a speech. Poincaré gave numerous speeches in cemeteries, in front of monuments to the war dead. The frequency and length of these talks made them easy subjects for satire. Under the words "Silence Is Golden," the *Canard* commiserated with the poor province of Lorraine, which had just heard three such speeches.[46]

That Poincaré was personally unpopular among the French, indeed was hated by many, especially former soldiers, was assumed by the satirical weekly. The *Canard* noted that Poincaré was being whistled at (that is, his image was being whistled at) at the cinema, as he had been during his visits to the front. A cartoon that appeared shortly after Mardi Gras 1922 showed a man covered with bandages. When his wife asks what happened, he answers that he had disguised himself as Poincaré.[47]

Of course, many politicians were mocked in the *Canard* (and other papers as well), but the weekly nourished a hostility to Poincaré that led it to go directly after his character. In November 1922, a deputy created a tumult in the Chamber by speaking of "the good faith probably" of the minister from the Meuse. The *Canard* argued, "That he is lacking in good faith has been seen on twenty occasions." But, the weekly added, it was intolerable that, as prime minister, Poincaré should be publicly called "probably."[48] A headline put it more pithily: "Poincaré Had Given His Word of Honor to Pardon [the Communist André] Marty: Why Are You Surprised That He Has Not Done It?"[49] Worse for the pacifist weekly was that it affected to believe (and probably did believe) that the mere presence of Poincaré in a position of executive authority risked war. Under the byline of René Buzelin, the weekly greeted the return to power (as president of the Council, that is, as prime minister) of the nationalist politician: "The new presidency brings us as many hopes as did the former one. Besides, they are the same"—that is, war.[50]

"POINCARUHR"

The *Canard*'s linking of Poincaré to the risk of war seemed borne out when the prime minister sent French troops into Germany's Ruhr district in January 1923. This decision also earned him a new nickname in the *Canard* (one also used by the Communists), "Poincaruhr."[51] Germany was a foreign country, and the *Canard* was perfectly willing to exploit stereotypes. But it did so in a way that allowed no ambiguity in its positions. The Ruhr venture was stupid and criminal. The only contrasts in the weekly's coverage lay between antiphrastic and direct condemnation.

The occupation of the Ruhr brought together many of the obsessions of the postwar *Canard:* the reference to the last war and fear of a new one, the attack on Poincaré and French bellicosity generally, the criticism and ridicule of the military, and, last but not least, the mockery of French attitudes toward Germany. But these issues could be found throughout the *Canard* and in relation to other topics. The Ruhr occupation allowed the weekly to broach a topic that received little other treatment in its pages: the relationship between military and sexual conquest. We have already seen how the presence of Allied soldiers on the national soil generated sexual anxieties, but during the war itself French soldiers had few opportunities to camp in foreign lands, even less in enemy ones.[52]

The *Canard* greeted Poincaré's decision to send troops into the Ruhr with a series of references to German women. Even before the actual entry, the weekly presented the region as a land of riches, open to French appetites: "for us, women with perfumes rare and the glasses of beer." Two weeks later, the *Canard* justified the occupation, first of all because of the *petites femmes* there. After all, they were too good for the Senegalese, but just right for the French boys. The reference to the colonial troops who performed so much of the occupation duty in Germany echoed the linkage of racism and sexual politics.[53] It took Bicard, however, to put the matter into more general perspective. The net result of the occupation, he explained, would be that in twenty years there would be one hundred thousand extra Germans. The French youth there would impregnate German women, while their absence from France would reduce the birthrate at home. The population imbalance between a victorious France and a defeated Germany was a subject of national concern, with the right pushing for pronatalist policies.[54]

The exit from the Ruhr two and a half years later was treated as sexually by the *Canard* as the entry had been. The departure of the French troops left the local women in tears, begging the soldiers to write to them. Here the *Canard* used a Franco-German mishmash: " 'You vill zend me postcards. Especially vit ze Eiffel Tower, nicht wahr, mein Schatz?' " The mayor sends the men off with a speech in which he notes that the women conceived a real affection for them "and also little children, with whom we will have the honor of forming a Reichswehr that will surely impress you. . . . And the mayor spoke these admirable words, which say a lot about the memories that we are leaving behind: 'See you soon, right? Until the next one . . . ' "[55]

The *Canard*'s treatment of the motif of sex with the enemy women did more than pull prurient fun from a political situation. It mocked the sense of French superiority. French male desire for German women is expressed before the invasion, hence is distinct from the satisfaction of the needs of lonely soldiers. The superior elegance of French women was as much a part of the national mythology as the superiority of French wine, and the contrast between such Gallic charms and the alleged disgraces of Teutonic womanhood had amply excited wartime French cartoonists. In this context, the *Canard*'s sexualization of the lust for the Ruhr called attention to another, older lust. Newly mobilized French soldiers apparently also dreamed of German women as a prize of war in 1914. In 1928, Scize went back to his own memories of conversations in the barracks on July 31, 1914. The intellectuals talked of collecting paintings by Cranach and Dürer, the less educated of making it with German women. Similar fantasies are put into the mouths of the newly war-drunk French soldiers in Dorgelès's novel *Le Cabaret de la Belle Femme.*[56]

Thus, the *Canard Enchaîné,* which had belittled German rape of French women,[57] publicized the other side of the coin, French lust for the women of the enemy, though it softened this desire by treating these encounters as consensual sex. The sexist bonhomie of the weekly's treatment of the theme contrasts clearly with the positions of German nationalists, for whom the violation of their women, especially by colonial troops, was a source of patriotic outrage. Certainly, the transformation of wartime rape into voluntary coupling softens, and in the moral system of the *Canard* virtually legitimizes, such encounters. And the *Canard*'s sexualization of the Ruhr reinforced its tendency, seen in the *Intran* anecdotes, to highlight foreign "conquests" rather than intra-French adultery. Yet the *Canard*'s underlining of the preexisting desire for the women of the other suggests that the causes for wartime rape go further than the specific conditions of an invading army.[58]

Sex was also a metaphor for other desires. The *Canard* never accepted the Poincaré government's position that it invaded the Ruhr only as a sanction for German nonpayment of reparations and as an inducement for Germany to fulfill the treaty. Instead, German nonpayment was an excuse for those who had always wanted to annex the Rhineland or at least to detach it from Germany. "A single reply to this docility of the Krauts, which resembles recalcitrance: enter the Ruhr *and only come out on the other side,*" wrote the *Canard* when Germany agreed to the terms of the Reparations Commission. Unsurprisingly, the weekly was unimpressed by Poincaré's finding in January 1923 that Germany was remiss in the delivery of telegraph poles.[59]

Like the Rif, the Ruhr gave the *Canard* another chance to replay (the first time as tragedy, the second time as farce?) its World War I themes. And this time at least the cast of characters was the same. The third day of the French action, the *Canard* published the official communiqué (like those during the war).

> 11 P.M. Situation unchanged on the boulevards. The presence of Mr. Maurice Barrès has not yet been signaled on the Place de la Concorde. Toward the Quai d'Orsay, preparation of poisonous gases and tear-producing newspapers.[60]

Poincaré argued that French troops went into the Ruhr to get coal, both to use and as a form of pressure on Germany. So another Varé cartoon showed a group of freezing French soldiers in the Ruhr writing back to headquarters, "We are freezing, send coal." But the changing seasons did not spare the French forces ridicule. In August 1923, the cartoonist Mat drew a fat, contented German burgher sipping a cool beer under the awning of a sidewalk café. Covered in sweat, the French soldiers march by, singing in chorus (from the *Madelon de la Victoire*): "We have won the war. Hey! would you believe it that we got them?"[61]

Since, ultimately, the Ruhr occupation was set in motion to gain money, the *Canard* hammered away at the occupation's nonproductivity. In January, it wrote:

> [As soon as French soldiers set foot in the Ruhr,] heavy trucks began to move toward the Gare de l'Est full to the brim with the thousand things that the Germans were only awaiting a little shove to give us.
>
> Here, first of all, are the billions of gold marks with which we are filling the wagons of the Bank of France; here is enough coke and coal to burst all the radiators of the Republic; here are the tons and tons of sauerkraut, of beer, of sausages, of mashed peas, of delikatessen [sic] of all sorts.[62]

In August of 1923, the *Canard* published the following report: "The interallied technical committee has discovered new veins, carefully hidden, of *podzébi.* It immediately took possession of them by virtue of article 445 *ter* of the Treaty of Versailles and will commence their exploitation." These gains, added to others taken in cash, made "a total of ninety centimes in gold francs." *Podzébi,* a reference to *peau de zébie,* or zebie skin, equaled nothing since the zebie was a nonexistent beast. When the Germans ceased passive resistance in the fall of 1923, the *Canard* declared that France had no more than when it started—that is, *pohdezebi* [sic] and *nibdenib,* which also meant nothing. Trying to make the occupation pay was contradictory. French troops seized eight billion marks in Essen, but these would have to be applied toward the costs of occupation, "The more soldiers we put into the Ruhr, the more the Krauts will have to pay; and the longer we stay there, the more Germany will be prevented from paying reparations, and the more we will have a reason to stay there," the *Canard* concluded.[63]

It was not just that, with German hyperinflation, a billion marks was not what it used to be but that seizing such funds put the French military in an unflattering position: "Our troops have gloriously confiscated a sum of one billion destined for the foundries of Geisenkirchen. They have also heroically sequestered two billion marks, which were to serve as payment for the workers of the Rhein-Elbe mines." What would happen to these workers? They would starve. The *Canard* reported coverage in the *Petit*

Parisien of the situation in three Ruhr cities. There was great misery, famine, and over 250,000 unemployed workers. It would be "piquant," this other correspondent noted, if the French ended up feeding the workers of the Ruhr. "Piquant," the *Canard* replied, "completely piquant, in effect, the situation of these 250,000 guys who are starving to death and whom we are going to have to feed if we do not want them to revolt."[64] And the weekly was quick to alert its readers when a number of these unemployed were shot by occupation troops. "It is unpleasant for their families, but that, in fact, makes for three fewer of them."[65]

Starvation and unemployment in Germany formed an excellent platform from which to mock French attitudes toward the former foe. When the finance minister, Charles de Lasteyrie, expressed his fear that a rapid German recovery would endanger French industry, the *Canard* responded, "These words, spoken at the moment when the Reich, bankrupt, is collapsing into civil war, are particularly opportune. In effect, the famine raging in Germany has permitted it, up until now, to make important economies of foodstuffs."[66]

Nor did the *Canard* evince any sympathy for French attempts to detach the Rhineland from Germany. Already in 1920, the weekly expressed its attitudes toward any potential German collaborators with French designs: "These Germans who form a committee to effect a dismemberment of their country seem to us to be rather comfortable bastards." During the Ruhr occupation, the *Canard* spoke of the proponents of a Rhenish Republic: "And it is as if by magic that Mr. Deckers and his friends, Krauts though they had been, have become almost French." The weekly then compared Deckers and his associates to "a von Kahr, a Hitler, and even a Ludendorff." Referring to the now-famous Beer-Hall Putsch of 1923 linked the pro-French troublemakers of the Rhineland with the anti-French ones of Munich.[67]

FROM THE BLOC TO THE CARTEL

In January 1924, the *Canard* drew the political conclusions of the Ruhr episode with unusual directness: "High prices = international exchange/international exchange = Ruhr/Ruhr = Millerand-Poincaré/Millerand-Poincaré = National Bloc."[68] This demonstration of consequences was directed to the upcoming elections. The exchange crisis generated by the Ruhr intervention, with its accompanying high prices and taxes, made the National Bloc a tempting target. Whatever its reservations about the French parliamentary system in general, the *Canard* approached the legislative elections of 1924 with anticipatory glee. Even back in November 1923, the weekly interpreted by-election results as showing that "the entire country is certainly, in effect, behind the National Bloc. But it is in order better to give it kicks in the _____!" As in 1919, the *Canard* wanted to throw the bums out, and it reintroduced the broom motif, though this time without any reference to the veterans' vote. In April 1924, the weekly spoke of disinfecting the Chamber with universal suffrage.[69]

Yet hostility to the right did not mean an unqualified endorsement of the left. In 1924, the *Canard* congratulated itself on beginning its ninth year of publication. The weekly was "independent as the devil" and "passed joyously through life pecking at the right and at the left—at the right especially."[70] In reality, the *Canard* balanced opposition to the National Bloc with a more general critique of politics and politicians. In April 1924 the weekly ran, on its last page, a series of phony electoral newspapers. All these take-offs mocked politicians of the right: the first was for François Arago, the second for Georges Mandel, and the third for unnamed Catholic candidates. But the *Canard* followed these right-wing and candidate-oriented sheets with a guide for the voters entitled "The Little Illustrated Voter, Organ for the Defense of French Citizens over Twenty-One." It included advice like the following for electoral cuisine (again making food of people): "Seasonal Salad—You take an ordinary fellow, preferably without a criminal record, but with money," and serve him up in a public meeting. And then there was this definition of electoral results: "The results of the elections consist in new taxes, laws in spades, parliamentary scandals, increases in the prices of public transportation, and other 20 percent surtaxes."[71]

And this same issue (the last before the first round of voting on May 11) was filled with cynical comments:

> But provided that we have not had our skulls stuffed again and that our good deputies, once elected, do not do exactly what their predecessors did: that is to say nothing.
>
> But no, but no, that is not possible. Things are going to change, damnation!
>
> We have, in any case, five more days to believe it.[72]

The *Canard*'s unflattering coverage of the petty maneuverings around the creation of the electoral lists of virtually all parties shed as much unflattering light on the Cartel as on the Bloc. Nor did the paper hesitate to accuse the Cartel's leader, the reconstructor of the Radical party, Edouard Herriot, of having taken right-wing money in 1919. Herriot had already earned the

Canard's scorn months earlier when, like other Radicals, he had failed to take a clear position against the Ruhr occupation.[73]

Whatever distances the weekly had traveled from the Cartel, its victory on May 11, 1924, was treated as the *Canard*'s. It was told-you-so time. The *Canard* claimed that its three mock electoral newspapers had hit the bull's-eye since Arago, Mandel and the Catholic deputy Leret d'Aubigny had not been elected.[74] The weekly also claimed to have helped, along with five other papers; turn public opinion against the conservative coalition; they had "won a victory all the more striking since they were grossly outnumbered."[75] Public opinion certainly played a part, but so did the unpopularity of Poincaré's new taxes and the fact that this time it was the left, through its Cartel, that had the superior electoral alliance system.

But this *Canard* rarely put all its eggs in the same nest. In the same May 14 issue in which the weekly quacked in victory, Rodolphe Bringer had some advice for the newly elected deputies. Fold up your platform carefully, he suggested, and keep it in your pocket; you may even want to pass it some day because anything can happen—more likely you will sit on it. And be nice to your opponents across the aisle, the worldly journalist continued. Your interests and theirs are often the same.[76] Even the victory claim noted above was colored by the *Canard*'s turn to irony in the same article, in which it pretended to be shaking down the victors for political favors.

The *Canard* had been born under the invigorating chill of censorship and had grown under the stimulating hostility of conservative governments. The new Cartel government under Herriot (with Socialist support) posed challenges to a periodical that lived on the mockery of the powerful. One response was to take on the job of keeping the victors honest. "Won't it be necessary to remind the victors of May 11 of their electoral promises?" the *Canard* headline read on May 21. "More than ever, read the '*Canard Enchaîné*.' "[77] Another possibility was to adopt the strategy used against the Communists: instead of attacking Herriot, attack those who attack Herriot. The *Canard* used this technique in June and July and came to Herriot's defense against his right-wing critics during the London Conference, which negotiated France's withdrawal from the Ruhr.[78]

By summer, however, the weekly was showing signs of genuine impatience with the Cartel government. So it created a new column entitled "Hey Mr. Herriot" (or "Hey Edouard"), with the logo of a man speaking through a megaphone into the head of a recumbent Herriot placidly smoking his pipe. The texts were reminders of electoral promises not kept or other actions not taken.[79] But these were gentle nudges. The *Canard* opened up on the leader of the Radical party in an article that appeared on

July 30. Labeled "A Madman," it told of an individual who insisted that, despite appearances, Herriot was not prime minister. His argument: "Have we evacuated the Ruhr? Has the embassy at the Vatican been eliminated? Has the 20 percent surtax been eliminated? Has Alsace been brought under French law? No, isn't that so? So, *you can easily see that Herriot is not minister.*"[80]

After this point, the notion that Herriot and the Cartel were not carrying out their electoral program became a recurring topic served up in a variety of sauces. "Let's be fair," the *Canard* pleaded. Voters were beginning to say that the National Bloc and the Cartel were *kif-kif*—that is, tweedledee and tweedle-dum. But this view was not correct, the weekly asserted. Voters felt this way because the Chamber had gone on vacation without having acted on any of the reforms in its platform (except the amnesty). But voters should bear in mind that the deputies had, in compensation, passed a law that was not in their platform—free postage for deputies.[81] A few months later, in October, the *Canard* affected to teach a lesson to the French right: none of what the opponents of the Cartel had so feared had been carried out. After the familiar list of nonactions, the weekly concluded that "honest citizens were wrong to have been alarmed."[82]

The following year, in March 1925, Maurice Maréchal took the rare step of signing an article. This article was also unusual in that it began with a direct critique. Herriot was "made to be prime minister about as much as we are to be pope." He was too easy-going, not tough enough on his opponents, too afraid of unpopularity—hence his compromises on important issues. After an ironic passage calling on Herriot to be more daring in the defense of corruption, Maréchal ended delicately balanced between irony and direct discourse. If Herriot did not act, the people "would have the right to think that nothing had changed in France since May 11."[83]

PARLIAMENTARY CRISIS

As the French financial and monetary situation deteriorated, the Herriot government was forced to resign in April 1925. It was followed by a dizzying series of cabinets as the crisis of the franc deepened and the Cartel majority gradually decomposed. The impotence of the recently elected Cartel majority did not cast French parliamentary institutions in a flattering light, and it led, in the *Canard*, to a strengthening of the antiparliamentary side of its political message. For example, in September 1925, the weekly imagined a tourist guide explaining to his foreign clients in front of the Palais Bourbon (Chamber of Deputies), "The deputies spend half of their time making laws and the other half of it going from one ministry to another to ask that these laws not be applied to their more influential constituents."[84]

But the sharpest pecks of the *Canard*'s beak were provoked by the decision of the deputies to raise their salaries (again) in early 1926: "The Chamber has just decided, in effect, to raise from twenty-seven to forty-two thousand francs the level of the parliamentary 'indemnity' of our deputies and senators." But this increase would not take effect until corresponding taxes were voted on: "This ingenious distribution of the increases of salary for the legislators and of taxes for the taxpayers constitutes a brilliant victory of the democratic and social spirit."[85] The *Canard* returned to the attack in succeeding issues, waxing ironic over the deputies' alleged need to respond to inflation and suggesting that the voters would get their revenge at election time.[86]

Disappointment with the deputies was also disappointment with the Cartel. In June 1925 the *Canard* argued that "never was the politics of the National Bloc better carried out than by the Cartel."[87] In fact, the shifting parliamentary majorities were evolving rightward. One of the agents of this shift was Pierre-Paul Painlevé, whom the *Canard* attacked, among other things, for his vigorous prosecution of the Rif war.[88] The *Canard* dealt with Painlevé in two, mildly contradictory, ways. It affected surprise that this leftist militant was carrying out such reactionary policies. Everyone assumed, the paper said, that the prime minister they were listening to was Painlevé, "but it is not Mr. Painlevé, who died a few months ago, while he was president of the Chamber. He was a gentle man, of peaceful habits, living willingly in the realm of the abstract.[. . .] In politics he displayed advanced ideas, sitting in parliament on the edges of the far left." Then one night in the middle of a ministerial crisis, "he lost his head. It is claimed that, in order not to worry the country, this tragic death was kept secret. An individual who had governed formerly under the name of Poincaré agreed to replace the deceased."[89] The other technique was to suggest that Painlevé had always been a militarist by alluding to his association, as minister of war in 1917, with the disastrous Chemin des Dames offensive.[90]

The parliamentary crisis of 1925 and 1926, as cabinets succeeded one another with a speed surpassed only by that with which ministers of finance were renewed, led many in France to wonder whether they were witnessing not the collapse of the Cartel but that of the French parliamentary system, or even of the Republic. These months saw the dramatic growth of right-wing antiparliamentary leagues. The *Canard*'s attitudes toward this crisis of the French political system showed the limits of its antiparliamentarism.

The *Canard* had never taken purely parliamentary events too seriously. On April 15, 1925, Guilac drew a cartoon over the text "Easter 1925, France anxiously awaits the solution to the ministerial crisis." The picture accompanying this text was its bucolic and ironic counterpart and a virtual *Canard* idyll. Couples of various ages are spread out in the countryside, picnicking (with wine, of course), kissing passionately, playing cards; one man is sprawled out on the grass reading the *Canard Enchaîné—joie de vivre* trumps politics.[91]

But by the end of 1925 the situation was harder to ignore. So the *Canard* ridiculed a sort of worst-case political scenario. It imagined a series of letters, dated 1927 and 1928, from a "Miss Kate G." to "Miss W." in Boston. The letters are written in franglais with occasional English words, infelicitous expressions, and renditions of American mispronunciations of French words like "dépioutés" and "pioublic." Paris is in an uproar because the "blue boys" (in English in the text) are rioting with the Communists, and the government had to send tanks to the Place de l'Opéra to clear away the demonstrators. "The Parisians are quite angry at the Dépouités who are always voting taxes. They have taxed gloves and socks. Thus people walk barefoot in their shoes." On December 1, 1927, Miss Kate reports:

> Politics are quite funny now. The Chamber is open all day and all night. At the door they sell sandwiches to eat while listening to the speeches and cooked potatoes to throw at the deputies. It is strictly forbidden because potatoes are scarce, but people do it anyway. . . . The blue boys invaded the Chamber at midnight calling out, "Deputies out. Dictator! Dictator!" The deputies ran out the other side. Then the boys seized the location and continued the session, but the firemen soaked them with the fire hoses prepared in advance by the government, and the boys ran out all sopping wet.

By 1928, the American in Paris reports, the situation has been straightened out.[92] The *Canard* had no way of knowing that the crisis would be resolved in July 1926. Though the weekly was clearly having fun, this scenario was one projected, for example, by the French fascist leader Georges Valois, whose Blue Shirts were probably the inspiration for Miss Kate's blue boys.[93]

But the *Canard* was also prepared to be perfectly serious when it came to calls for dictatorship. It characterized one newspaper inquiry on a possible future dictator as "scandalous"; and it gave a proper thrashing to a former anarchist, Jean Goldsky, who had become an advocate for some sort of dictatorial solution for France.[94] The *Canard*'s beef had never been with the parliamentary idea as such. The weekly had focused on the actual French system with its corruption and had remained hostile to any scheme for strengthening the executive. Its reaction to the next phase of France's political and parliamentary evolution would remove any ambiguities on that score.

POINCARÉ AGAIN

Though the return to power of Poincaré in July 1926 did not take the *Canard* by surprise, its initial response was almost pure reflex. The return would mean war, or at least the reoccupation of the Ruhr.[95] Poincaré organized a cabinet of national union, with political celebrities in the various ministries; their political origins spread from the right (André Tardieu and Louis Marin) through the center-left (Herriot and Painlevé). A Pedro cartoon in the July 28 issue mocked these unnatural alliances. A fox, on the ground, addresses a cock on a branch, "Come on down, we will make national union." (The Gallic cock here replaces Jean de La Fontaine's crow.) The weekly went further, drawing frankly antiparliamentary, antipolitician conclusions from the new cabinet:

> During the entire electoral season Mr. Herriot and Mr. Painlevé crisscrossed France, repeating: Poincaré, that means war, Poincaré, that means catastrophe.
>
> On his side, not to be left out, Poincaré repeated: Herriot and Painlevé, that means revolution.
>
> Tardieu said: Poincaré sabotaged the Treaty of Versailles.
>
> Barthou shouted: Tardieu did not know how to make the peace. Meanwhile Marin raced across the country, screaming: Stop, thief! Herriot is a counterfeiter.
>
> And finally Herriot had Albert Sarraut excluded from the Radical party for treason.
>
> Today Poincaré, Painlevé, Barthou, Tardieu, Herriot, Marin, [and] Sarraut serve in the same cabinet and are as chummy as pigs.
>
> If after this, there is still someone who believes in the declarations of politicians, we ask that he be framed and exhibited at the Neuilly Fair.[96]

Cartel-Bloc, Bloc-Cartel, the *Canard* reversed its earlier quip about the Cartel carrying out National Bloc policies; now it was evident that none could better carry out the Cartel policies than the members of the National Bloc.[97] Such reversals of majority could not take place, however, without the flexibility of the Radical party, many of whose members were as comfortable working with the center-right as with the left (if not more comfortable). The *Canard* went after the turncoat party on the occasion of its national congress in October 1926. A leading Radical politician is made to explain that "only yesterday the allies and associates of the fanatics of the far left, we were able to repudiate, once it became necessary, the fallacious and deadly doctrines that purely electoral considerations oblige us to profess to the country every four years."[98] Such policies demanded special "dispositions" on the part of the deputies. A cartoon showed a mother and another woman speaking of a little boy. "What docility," exclaims the woman. "You will make a soldier of him?" "No," the mother answers, "a Radical deputy."[99]

The chief traitor, for the *Canard*, was Herriot. The paper treated him as an obedient student who did as Poincaré told him. It also wondered aloud whether Herriot was still a supporter of "peace"—that is, of Foreign Minister Briand's policy of Franco-German rapprochement as opposed to Poincaré's anti-German policy. Questioning Herriot on this score removed the one area where the *Canard* had always supported him against his opponents.[100]

By joining the Poincaré cabinet, Herriot also lent his political caution to Poincaré's style of government. Virtually until the 1928 elections, Poincaré ran the Chamber by a kind of blackmail of confidence (much as Charles de Gaulle did in a later crisis). If he did not get his way, he would consider it a lack of confidence and resign; and no one was eager to take that political responsibility and risk a return to the franc crisis. In this way, also, Poincaré persuaded the Chamber to accept a "procedure of extreme urgency," which, among other things, eliminated the right to propose amendments to bills. Not only did such a curtailment of the traditional powers of parliament go against the republican tradition, of which the Radicals were among the proudest champions, but it was Herriot's refusal to Caillaux of these kinds of increased executive powers that had contributed greatly to the parliamentary crisis. The *Canard* was careful to remind its readers of precisely this point.[101]

Naturally, also, the weekly mocked so much pusillanimity. As Bringer put it in November 1926, "Mr. Poincaré has agreed to call the houses of parliament into session, but on the condition that no one either speak to him or ask him what he is planning to do"[102] After eliminating the right of amendment, why not eliminate that of speech, or even the right to meet, the paper asked. A cartoon in the same issue made an even nastier comparison. Labeled "The Bad Example," it showed a bandit holding up a peaceful citizen at gunpoint: "Excuse me, but the circumstances force me into this procedure of extreme urgency!"[103]

DÉJÀ VU

And through all these crises, the deputies still found it possible to raise their own pay, not to 42,000 francs but to 45,000; thus, the *Canard* saw in the deputies' support for Poincaré the opposite of patriotic abnegation.[104] Its expectations for the next set of legislative elections, scheduled for the spring of 1928, were all the lower. Gone were the avenging brooms. Whom should the weekly support? Not the right and Poincaré surely, for the *Canard* remained anxious about the Lorrainer's anti-German predilections.[105] Nor the Cartelists (Radicals and Socialists) who had shown themselves no better.

The former Cartelists had the advantage of not needing new electoral platforms. Throughout 1927, the *Canard* re-served the basic idea that the Radicals had been smart to do nothing:

> One reproaches the good deputies with not having carried out their platform.
>
> That's a good one!
>
> For, finally, if they had carried it out, what would be left for the next elections?[106]

Reusable platforms were only part of the general *Canard* theme of here-we-go-again. In its end-of-year and New Year's messages for 1927–1928, the *Canard* explained that nothing had changed.[107]

For the New Year, the *Canard* provided a set of predictions. They came down to a repetition of the events of 1924–1926 squeezed into one year with the rising Radical politician Edouard Daladier replacing Herriot. A slightly abridged selection:

> January 9—The Communist deputies are arrested.
> January 22—Mr. Poincaré obtains a large majority.
> March 14—All the candidates promise one-year military service, the abolition of the laws of political repression, and lower taxes.
> April 29—Great Republican victory.
> June 2—Constitution of a great Daladier-Renaudel cabinet.
> June 9—The pound reaches 180.
> July 13—The Communist deputies are arrested.
> September 10—The Renaudel-Daladier government appoints its eighteenth minister of finance.
> October 2—Mr. Doumergue calls on Mr. Poincaré.

October 15—The new national union government reestablishes three-year military service and raises the tax on salaries.
November 4—Those Communist deputies who are left are arrested.[108]

Redux applied to electoral propaganda too. When the official electoral notice boards went up in March 1928, Bringer wondered why the officials in charge had cleared away the posters from the previous elections: "At the moment when our elected officials ask of us the renewal of their mandates, would it not be interesting to see what they promised us at that time?" The weekly also noted sarcastically the sudden rise in anti-Communist hysteria that accompanied the electoral season.[109]

The *Canard* also updated its mockery of elections, candidates, and voters, describing, for example, the candidate as a charming fellow determined to take his voters for supremely intelligent people.[110] After telling the story of a broken promise, Barbusse concluded in the pages of the *Canard* that "deputies have nothing in common with candidates." On a lighter note, in January 1928, Jules Rivet celebrated the news of the creation of a new political party because "the more parties there are, the more candidates there will be, and the more candidates there are, the more free rounds there will be at the local bar. If our ancestors, as Pierre Bénard put it, had known the vermouth-cassis and the picon-curaçao, they probably would have given us universal suffrage several centuries earlier."[111]

In the last weeks before the elections, the *Canard* hammered away at both sides, mocking the electoral corruption (through fund raising) of the right and the duplicity of the democratic left.[112] The right's victory in the parliamentary elections of April 1928 hardly came as a surprise; the *Canard* had been predicting four more years of Poincarism.[113]

After the conservative victory, the weekly ran a story that expressed its disillusionment with electoral politics. An unlucky rival accused the agent for the leading National Bloc politician, Charles de Lasteyrie, of having offered to buy his withdrawal from the second round of voting. The *Canard* wanted its readers to know that it was not shocked. Such offers were common. What was shocking was the price, which worked out to 32 francs 50 centimes per voter. In the future, the duck-journalist suggested, why not eliminate the middleman and pay each voter?[114] For the postelection *Canard,* the French voter was a sucker. The weekly even called him "Mr. Ubu, voter," adding:

> Oh! The good fellow, how he seems satisfied with the role that he has been allowed to play for twenty-four hours!

> His smile, full of discretion, is a pleasure to see. And, in a typically French gesture, he already has his hand in his pocket.
>
> For he is well aware that, in a very short time, he will receive, on a tax form, the little bill to pay.[115]

This was harsher language than any the *Canard* had ever used before to characterize French voters. Its tone reflected the abandonment of one of the weekly's tactical options. The *Canard* would continue to be a leftist paper—that is, it would continue to attack left and right, but more the right than the left. But the newspaper no longer believed that electoral brooms could sweep out the Augean stables of French politics. In the weekly's balance between partisanship and a global satirical vision, the *Canard* would now adopt only that degree of partisan engagement that would not interfere with its dominant vocation as critic of the entire French political and social system. This was now the basis of its antiparliamentarism, one informed by democratic values but highly skeptical of their realization.

12 *Canard* Economics, or the Costs of the War

Like the French state and people, the *Canard* had to come to terms with the economic, budgetary, and monetary problems that beset the country in the first postwar decade. But the weekly brought to this challenge a characteristic ideological flexibility. The most obvious of France's economic problems was the dramatic rise in prices known as *la vie chère*, or the high cost of living. Associated with rising prices were the crises of the French franc, which came to a head in the spring of 1924 and the summer of 1926. Most citizens of the Gallic republic also understood the relationship between the trials of their currency and international payments—reparations due from Germany and debts due to Britain and the United States.

The *Canard* could choose between two types of explanation: the search for scapegoats and the exploitation of stereotypes, on the one hand, and insistence on fundamental, structural causes, on the other. Each approach had advantages. The first, the exploitation of stereotypes, lent itself most easily to humor. The second, structural approach fit better with the *Canard*'s reasoned antimilitarism, its conception of the war and its effects on French society. Faced with this alternative—between the demagogic and the structural, the facile and the analytical—the newspaper chose both. These approaches not only constituted the warp and woof of the *Canard*'s economic discourse but also reached back into the war because they had their origins in *Canard* themes of that time. As they developed across the first decade of peace, they articulated a certain perception of the war, an understanding created by reasoning backward from effects to causes. Thus, *Canard* economics too was part of the construction of the memory of the Great War.

STIGMATIZING COMMERCE: THE *MERCANTI*

The economic scapegoat/stereotype of the war was the profiteer/*mercanti,* an individual whose unpatriotic greed contrasted with the self-sacrificing heroism of the front-line soldiers. The two weekly issues that followed the armistice were packed with associations of war and profit. A Laforge cartoon dominated the first page of the November 20, 1918, issue (see figure 12). "Mr. and Mrs. Mercanti go into retirement" showed a couple standing before a multiturreted chateau and bore the legend "The little place that they have just bought." Another cartoon in the previous issue addressed "the scruples of the nouveau riche": Now that the war was over, had they profited as much as possible from it?[1] Such scruples, like the retirement evoked by Laforge, suggested that the career of the war profiteer had come to an end. As the pacifist writer Henri Béraud put it, "When the armistice is signed, the *mercanti* cries in his camembert." Béraud predicts that the merchants will form a "Fraternal Society of Former War Contractors" that will bring flowers each year to the monument to their brothers who died of "seizures on the field of honor the morning of the armistice." A similar point about war profiteers had been made in the previous issue.[2] These images of suffering war profiteers can be read not only as a revenge fantasy but also in contrast to the sacrifice of the front-line soldiers. That the war profiteers would keep their money is assumed in all these examples, as it was in a joke that one cartoon duck told to another. He had frightened a *mercanti* acquaintance by telling him that the government was going to redistribute the war profits to the returning soldiers. Making this idea a joke was a *Canard* way of saying it would never happen.[3]

By linking the enrichment to the war itself, the *Canard* implied that the profiteering was over. Why else would the *mercanti* cry in his camembert? Thus, though the weekly maintained the pessimistic assumption that the mercantis/profiteers would keep their ill-gotten wealth, it indirectly promoted the optimistic presumption that such mercantile abuses, born with the war, would end with it. Within a few months, however, the paper abandoned its more positive corollary. The closest that the weekly came to recognizing that it had shifted its analysis from the *mercanti* as war profiteer to the *mercanti* as peacetime exploiter was in an article of February 1919. The *Canard* argued that the *mercantis,* like a flock of locusts, had just moved from the soldiers, now dispersed, to the civilians.[4]

What had really happened was that French consumers were getting their first taste of *la vie chère,* the price rises of the 1920s. It was natural for the *Canard* to blame the same unscrupulous merchants it had pilloried

Figure 12. The war profiteer and his castle, by Laforge (1918).

during the war. But who was at fault—the dealers (the middlemen and wholesalers) or the neighborhood merchants and artisans? When it came to scapegoats, the satirical weekly did not discriminate—it went after both groups throughout the first decade of peace.

In November 1922, in a column entitled "What You Will Never See," the *Canard* asked about trials for sugar dealers accused of fraud.[5] Early in 1926, the paper waxed ironic on the suspension of dealers at Paris's main wholesale market for foodstuffs, Les Halles, and later in that same year linked high prices to grain hoarding.[6] But the *Canard* did not let retailers off the hook. Department stores (like the Samaritaine) were frequently accused of illegal activities; and the paper explained in 1919 how the government persuaded another store to rehire fired workers by agreeing to close an investigation into price gouging by the department stores.[7]

In the August 20 issue, André Dahl told the story of a war profiteer who is still making money and whose wife fears that they might be the target of the population, which was becoming fed up with high prices. But the crowd only attacks a vegetable cart kept by a poor old woman, while the successful dealer even joins a consumers' defense league. The moral of the tale was obvious: those who attacked the small shopkeepers and retailers were misguided; they distracted the public from the real culprits, the middlemen and wholesalers.[8]

Yet this was a moral the weekly chose not to act on. It did present arguments. In June 1920, the paper observed that the fall in wholesale prices had been met with rises in retail ones. In a more ambivalent line of argument, the paper agreed in 1922 with the recent amnesty of small shopkeepers for illicit speculation. After all, since the big dealers were going scot-free, equality before the law dictated that the small ones be spared as well.[9]

But the hunt for the *mercanti* (or *merkhanti* as the *Canard* spelled it in one reference) could get specific. The *mercanti* in a cartoon of August 20, 1919, was a grocer selling dry goods, while his neighbor had produce for sale.[10] In comparison with its wartime coverage, the postarmistice *Canard* gave little attention to sellers of wine or coal, and it dropped the Auvergnat merchant stereotype almost completely. (A lone reference in December 1918 pointed to the results of wartime commerce rather than to contemporary activities.)[11] Coal was less of an issue than in wartime, though it was still in short supply and still an occasional subject for humor. Wine, as we shall see later, was the subject of other criticisms. And while the Auvergne was still a subject for humor—for example, in connection with Maurice Barrès—it was no longer linked to petty commerce.[12] The abandonment of some of the narrower stereotypes of the war represented a broadening of the *Canard*'s attack on shopkeepers.

An article in 1924 on mendacious advertising singled out neighborhood dairy stores called creameries for their "pure milk" signs; everyone knew, the paper declared, that no one had ever bought pure milk, least of all at a creamery. An article of 1922 implied that dairymen watered down their milk.[13] As with dairy so with meat: just after Bastille Day 1921, the *Canard* noted an enormous difference between the prices in Les Halles and those at the butcher shops during the holiday. The *Canard* strengthened its charges about price-gouging butchers by ironically noting the few tradespeople or municipal officials who sold meat at lower prices.[14]

More important than dairy stores and butcher shops were purveyors of the staff of life, bakeries. The *Canard* evinced no sympathy when the bakers went on a twenty-four-hour strike to protest government price regulations.[15] In August 1923, the *Canard* mocked the "poor bakers." One could see that the profession was in difficulty from the high advertised price for a bakery. Two weeks later the *Canard* reported that an indignant baker had written back. Such letters were rare—either rarely written or rarely acknowledged by the newspaper. The baker explained that the price was almost certainly not for a simple bakery but for a bakery, pastry store, and candy shop. The baker added that in the eighteen months since he had opened his store he had already lost twelve thousand francs, which he had laboriously saved up over thirteen years of backbreaking work. This former worker was not a stereotype *mercanti,* and the *Canard* beat a semiretreat. It was not the bakery workers, whose difficult labor it appreciated, or the little owner-operators that it was attacking, the weekly claimed. It had in mind instead "the powerful and the big businessmen of baking." "You are right but we are not wrong." As with the other shopkeepers, the *Canard's* campaigns never really excluded the mom-and-pop businesses that supplied most Paris neighborhoods. And the campaign against bakers continued after the letter as before it.[16]

FARMERS AND POLITICIANS

The *Canard* saw an unholy alliance of bakers, millers, grain dealers, and farmers with the governmental authorities regulating them. When the government created a permanent office for bread prices, the *Canard* called it the "National Office for the Augmentation of the Price of Bread." As for the Flour Commission of the Department of the Seine, the *Canard* wrote as if its chief function were to manipulate flour prices so as to justify continual increases in bread prices.[17] In 1925 and the first half of 1926, the franc was generally falling. But in 1927, when the franc crisis was over, the *Canard* congratulated the Commission for heroically managing to raise bread prices again despite the strong franc.[18] The government could hold down bread prices when it wanted to, argued the weekly in April 1928. It did not anticipate rises in flour prices to be translated into higher bread prices at least until the elections were over.[19]

In the *Canard's* view, the ultimate supporters of high prices were the ministers of agriculture, especially Henri Chéron for the National Bloc and Henri Queuille for the Cartel. The paper blamed Chéron, minister of agriculture from January 1922 to March 1924, for high food prices (calling him "Père-la-Vichère," or Father-High-Prices), spoke of him as divine punishment and as a national plague, and virtually accused him of starving the French people.[20] Queuille was accused of following in Chéron's footsteps, and the paper imagined the earlier minister of agriculture sending a telegram of encouragement when the Cartel minister acted to raise prices.[21] The *Canard* saw the holders of the agricultural portfolio as servants of France's food producers—at the expense of the rest of the population. Speaking of the actions of the minister in 1925, the paper wrote, "Bread goes up, everything goes up naturally, and all the producers—that is to say the true France—make their expected profit."[22] Queuille went on to serve in Poincaré's cabinet of national union, and the *Canard* was quick to stigmatize his act of raising tariffs on imported grain.[23]

The *Canard* was no more supportive of the policy, followed under both Chéron and Queuille, of exporting Breton potatoes to England. In 1926, the *Canard* associated these sales with the famous "word" of General Cambronne to the British *(merde)*. A Ferjac cartoon of June 1927 showed a group of Breton peasants dancing around a sack of potatoes while singing, "The potatoes for the English, the peels for the French!" The export of foodstuffs, like the taxing of imports, was, to the *Canard*, essentially a policy of subsidies to the French agricultural sector.[24] If the weekly understood the relationship of such policies to the defense of the franc, it gave no such indication—largely because the *Canard* considered French farmers, peasants for the most part, a privileged class.

As the paper put it in 1925, "the peasants do not pay any taxes," leaving that burden "to the bastards in the cities."[25] Indeed, French farmers were a relatively protected group in terms of both taxes and trade policy during most of the Third Republic.[26] To echo this point, the *Canard*'s Ferjac drew a take-off of Jean Millet's famous painting *L'angélus*, with its sentimentalization of peasant piety. Under the title "Fiscal Inequality," Ferjac's version showed the peasant couple praying in front of a basket of vegetables with a price on it.[27] That was in December 1925, and during the coming weeks the *Canard* returned to the theme of farmers' tax breaks, mocking, in particular, any suggestion that the farmers were willing to pay higher taxes.[28]

The weekly, which spared wine sellers after the war (bistro owners were almost mascots of the newspaper),[29] went after the producers of the French national beverage. A continuing theme was that successful harvests did not necessarily bring lower prices. In September 1922, the *Canard* noted that despite an abundant harvest, wine would be more expensive. In the autumn of 1927, the *Canard* mocked those who wanted the government to take steps so that the harvest, which promised to be abundant, would not lower wine prices. Just a few months earlier, the weekly attacked the then high prices for wine, ending with the ironic argument that it was surely the fault of consumers for drinking the stuff. Two cartoons in that same issue illustrated the range of the *Canard*'s ironies. One, by Ferjac, shows a drunk complaining that if the price of wine goes up any more his family will go hungry. In the other, by Henri Monier, one peasant complains to another that the harvest "threatens to be excellent."[30] If the drunken Frenchman was a well-established humor device, the greedy grower was a far less sympathetic stereotype in the *Canard*'s social catalogue.

The *Canard*'s hostility to peasants and even to neighborhood shopkeepers reflected its predilection for the urban salaried classes. True, the *Canard* cut great ironic swaths through French society, but in this case as in others it is instructive to see what groups were spared. A working-class individual like Bicard could be satirized for his personal habits, but workers as a class were never ridiculed. Generally, either they were defended against bourgeois prejudices or they were presented with a dignity uncharacteristic of the newspaper. Professors and teachers, a salaried group whose professional characteristics have long made them an easy subject for humor, also escaped essentially unscathed. Instead the weekly made a joke out of their stingy treatment by the government. The hostility to shopkeepers and farmers reflected a fit between the *Canard*'s apparent readership and the continuation of the hostility developed by soldiers during the war against the shopkeepers and peasants who charged them high prices for the petty luxuries of the front.[31]

STRING 'EM UP

The weekly was not afraid to point the webbed foot of opprobrium at those—from peasants and dealers to local merchants—it held responsible for high prices. But the satirical paper went a great deal further in recommending violent direct action, from pillaging to hanging, against the *mercantis*.

In July 1919, the weekly called news that people had pillaged food stores in Florence "an example to follow." Any sympathy for the victims of such mob justice would have been removed by a cartoon that appeared the following month. As a crowd is pillaging a vegetable store next door, the wife exclaims to her shopkeeper husband, who is hastily closing their shutters, "It had to happen . . . with all this riff-raff that has come back from the war." The attack on the heroic *poilus* turns these *mercantis* from potential victims to the successors of those who had exploited the self-sacrificing soldiers.[32] Eight years later, in 1927, a *Canard* writer lamented that in Paris the *mercantis* ruled. "There was formerly, at Montmartre, a grocery that was pillaged as a public reprisal. But that was during the war, the good times."[33] True, the last line contained just enough irony to blunt the literal message, but taken together the weekly's sympathy for pillage was certainly more direct than ironic.

This viewpoint becomes even clearer when we examine the *Canard*'s other, more frequent recommendation: that the *mercantis* be hanged, an idea expressed through a combined visual and verbal topos. Most often some reference appeared in both systems, the iconic and the alphabetic, but the elements could appear separately; the visual icon, for example, could evoke the theme when the textual reference was absent or merely allusive. These combinations of visual and verbal dominated the *Canard*'s discussions of the *mercantis* from 1919 through 1927.

The *Canard* both visually and verbally evoked hanging for the first time in July 1919. The full-page victory parade imagined by Laforge on July 16 showed, among other things, the *mercantis* carrying the gallows "on which they will perhaps figure one day." A cartoon the following week was more graphic. Its legend, above and below the frame, read, "To lower the cost of living . . . let's raise the *mercantis.*" Any ambiguity hidden behind the play on words was eliminated by the picture—three prosperous-looking men hanging from the limbs of a tree, the one facing the viewer with his tongue hanging out in death.[34] Laforge's victory parade was a summary of the war, as such it looked backward. The cartoon of hanging businessmen looked forward. The crude imagery of a lynching redefined, in advance, every reference to hanging, raising, or suspending those accused of economic crimes, and there would be many such.

But was this not incitement to murder? Of course, the *Canard* frequently said that it did not mean what it said, except when it did. In the very next number, that of July 30, Victor Snell wrote of "reflection and moderation." After gently reproving various acts of violence against shopkeepers, the article concluded:

> We disapprove [of] all acts of unjustified violence. Thus when one has pillaged a grocery, it is perfectly useless to open up the grocer in order to stuff him with his own prunes. It would be better to eat them, leaving one free, if one wishes, to carry the *mercanti* to the nearest mast or street lamp. However, it is appropriate to act properly and only after assuring oneself that one is not acting contrary to the wishes of the government.[35]

A masterpiece of irony, certainly, but the piece hardly counsels patience. And here again the *Canard* introduces a potent corporality (not exempt from cannibalism). Prunes that one buys from the grocer in order to eat are used to turn that merchant into a stuffed bird or roast. And hanging (further discussed below) works by raising bodies.

The year 1923 saw the crystallization of the visual campaign in a Guilac drawing of a gallows. These gallows became a topos used for years to signify the weekly's call to hang the *mercantis.* The drawing commented on the recommendation to raise the speculators instead of raising the price of flour;

"just a few centimeters above the ground would suffice."[36] The gallows could also appear with Guilac's duck. On February 13, 1924, a *Canard* headline read, "The Rope Will Save the Franc," a take-off on the various optimistic prognostications about the resolution of the franc crisis; in these formulations, this or that national treasure, wheat, savings, or whatever, would "save the franc." Guilac's duck and gallows under the text defined the choice of the rope.[37] Over a year and half later, when the *Canard* evoked "the rope" again, it explained verbally the need to hang the speculators. Here the visual message, because technically redundant, could be omitted.[38]

But the converse was also true. As the icon of the *Canard*'s campaign, Guilac's duck and gallows could suffice to specify the remedy when the verbal text only indicated the problem. A January 1925 article congratulating Queuille and the Flour Commission on the rise in the price of bread was bordered on the bottom by a set of gallows. A Guilac cartoon on maneuvers against the franc later that same year limited its visual message to that artist's familiar duck peeking around the gallows. In 1927, Guilac drawings continued to add their hanging motifs to articles where the theme was not otherwise present.[39]

Once visually established, the gallows was available for variation—empty or full, depending on whether the artist wanted to stress the absence of punishment or the wish for it. A multiframe Guilac cartoon of October 1924 used a cobwebbed gallows to signify the nonaction of the government against the *mercantis.* In February 1925, yet another short article explaining the need to raise hoarders instead of flour prices was illustrated by a Guilac drawing of three bourgeois-looking types hanging from gallows.[40] Of course, the verbal notion, the pun on physical raising, was also subject to playful variation. Also in February 1925, an article reported that a currency trader had been "suspended for a month," though it was quick to add that it was not clear what he had been suspended from.[41]

In these February 1925 examples, as in many others, the paper appeared to be calling on the government to hang the culprits—hence to be asking for legal action. But hanging was not the form of capital punishment in France—that was the guillotine (plus the firing squad for soldiers). The *Canard*'s Guilac even replaced Dr. J. I. Guillotin's machine with hanging (profiteers) in a portrayal of the French Revolution. It was the only image of the revolution in this little illustrated history of France.[42] Drawings of hangings could be read as a relatively playful evocation of execution since people were not being hanged. They were a way of getting around the *Canard*'s general hostility to capital punishment.[43] The paper never called for the guillotining, which would have meant the legal execution, of anyone. Hanging was a typical *Canard* solution, sadistic enough to amuse but still playful, real but not real, evocative of legal punishment but also of lynching.

Many stories described action by amateurs. Borrowing a trick from Montesquieu's satirical *Persian Letters*, the *Canard* imagined the travel diary of a Polynesian visitor to Paris. The islander reports that since they do not know how to obtain their own food, the French are at the mercy of *mercantis*. "They do not know that a well-made slip knot attached to a tree or a nice little well-made fire are arguments that the most stubborn of merchants resists with difficulty." The humor is heightened by the fact that, until one gets to the last clause, the advice could apply equally well to trapping and preparing animals.[44]

Popular justice could also mean hanging the politicians. In the small print of the "Petite correspondance" section of June 21, 1922, the *Canard* replied to concerns about the high cost of living: "Why has Chéron not been hanged? One would think that there was a lack of lampposts." Three years later, in the same column, the weekly wrote, "We always told you: it was necessary to attach Chéron to a lamppost. Now that won't do any good anymore." Other forms of execution made briefer appearances.[45] Though hanging was by far the most common remedy for high prices, the *Canard* vacillated between hanging and less violent (and more legal) modes of punishment. On several occasions it argued that prices were high because prison cells were empty or, in one case, that meat prices were up because Chéron was still a free man.[46]

THE FRUITS OF VICTORY

Despite its waverings between official and popular action, the *Canard*'s campaigns against the *mercantis* and their politician supporters relied on an economics of criminality. France's problems were caused by individuals and could be remedied by punishments. As such they fit in well with a journalism of stereotypes. But an attentive reader could also have found a deeper level of analysis. It relied on the structural proposition that, whatever the errors of France's leaders (and the weekly did not ignore these), the fundamental cause of the economic difficulties of the victorious republic was the war itself—that victory had brought poverty.

As it did with other themes (for example, the next last war), the *Canard* introduced the idea of the costs of the war before it was over. In March 1918, as the French awaited the German offensive, the *Canard* imagined the future through a phony newspaper, *The Postwar*, whose *millésime* was left open (19__). The biggest problem at this future time is financial. It is time to pay the bill since "this little fantasy [the war] cost us 1,897,533,429,689 francs and 64 centimes. And we are not counting, of course, the victory loans; [the interest on] the last of these, 38½ percent, repayable in eleven hundred years, is a heavy charge."[47]

In February 1919, in the middle of discussions about the peace treaty, Clemenceau gave an interview to the Associated Press warning that a treaty without sufficient security guarantees would saddle France with "a Pyrrhic victory."[48] The *Canard* turned Clemenceau's comments into an attack on war by calling back from the dead the mercenary general famous for having taken such losses against the ancient Romans that his victories added up to a defeat. Pyrrhus is cross with his modern colleague. He would never have said anything so stupid. "Peoples are grown up enough to recognize for themselves, without it being necessary for their leader to have the imprudence to tell them, that after a war the victors are in as bad a shape as the vanquished."[49] Pyrrhus was also famous for his elephants, and once Clemenceau had let escape the phrase *Pyrrhic victory,* it was available as a code that was in turn evocable through the giant pachyderm. Opening Laforge's victory parade was Georges Mandel, naked save for an ancient Greek helmet, leading an elephant that bore Clemenceau and Poincaré. Alternatively, the *Canard* could simply toss Pyrrhus's name into a discussion of the war to recall its opinion of the victory.[50]

One of the easiest ways to show that the war had impoverished France was to compare the country before and after the conflict. A subtle way of doing this was to compare the news before and after. The *Canard* writer Whip reports his joy on finding the newspaper full of good news. Herriot, the mayor of Lyons, is going to replace the slums with nice little houses, jobs are being offered to the unemployed, the government's 3 percent treasury obligations are doing well at the exchange, and so forth. Then the fictional reader notices that someone has substituted the *Journal* of almost nine years earlier (21 February 1912) for his daily paper.[51]

This was a topic well suited for visual comparisons. In August 1924, to commemorate the entry of France into the war, Guilac drew a cartoon he called "Anniversary Dialogue." An older man is speaking to a younger one (old enough to have fought). Next to the older man is an inset frame of the familiar 1914 scene of newly mobilized soldiers marching off while being cheered by the crowd. The younger man's frame shows a woman in front of a food store and a tax office. The dialogue draws the conclusion:

> —August 1914! *Belle époque*, sir, *belle époque!*
>
> —Yes. We were not yet victorious. . . .[52]

Another cartoon, this time from 1926 and by Pedro, extended the historical series forward in time. A triptych represented the average Frenchman of 1913, of 1920, and of 1926. The first, corpulent and merry, is labeled "heavyweight." The second, of middling girth but a bit scruffy, is a "middleweight," while the last, emaciated man bears the title "featherweight."[53] Even without an explicit chronological reference, weight loss made a convenient metaphor for impoverishment. In October of that same year a satisfied customer gives a testimonial in a phony advertisement on the last page of the newspaper. He had been too fat and suffered physically and emotionally from this condition. But after taking "Victory Pills" for eight years he has become thin. Here, the *Canard* took the fashion shift away from a comfortable solidity and toward the modern, youthful cult of thinness and exploited it as a commentary on involuntary loss of substance.[54]

To extend the topos of the shrinking waist, the *Canard* made liberal references to the belt (for belt tightening) as a symbol of the victory and the postwar epoch.[55] Victory as belt tightening was also victory with food shortages and high prices. As the *Canard* commented in regard to the celebration of Bastille Day 1919, butter costs eighteen francs, "and if we do not have a nickel, we are rich in memories and in laurels, which are not for the soup." Or it could be a victory with high taxes. Commenting on the imposition of a 20 percent surtax, the *Canard* assured its readers that "this vigorous decision will be appreciated by all good citizens, for whom victory is not a vain word."[56]

The *Canard* also arranged all these individual losses into a formula: the fruits of victory. If "Victory Pills" were one remedy against obesity, "Victory Fruits" were another.[57] Speaking of the fruits of victory in 1922, Rivet argued that "it is sufficient to toss a simple glance around you to see that everything here exudes abundance, order, and respect." He continued, "In the street handicapped veterans pass, laughing at life, proud of their decorations and of being so richly pensioned by a benevolent and paternalistic state." After such an ironic catalogue of existent fruits, it was easy to construct a cartoon around absent ones. A drawing by Mat was called "A Minute of Silence." In it, two men are talking in a café, one of them with a crutch replacing a missing leg. One remarks, "One minute . . . That will be more than sufficient to harvest the fruits of the victory." Later that year an anonymous *Canard* writer approved of the symbolic botany of victory trees. People never plant plums or apricots, which bear fruit, the writer stated; instead they plant other species, like poplar or elm, which are as "sterile" and "hollow" as the victory.[58] And lest its readers forget, the *Canard* of July 1926, in the middle of the combined franc and ministerial crisis, brought together all the problems of the postwar as "fruits of the victory."[59]

Perhaps the harshest attack on the idea that victory in war was profitable was to reverse it and argue that defeat would have been better. That claim, though it rang false, by a twist of irony did not end up signifying its opposite. Semiotically, the reader is left in the center, with the notion that victory is little better than defeat. In 1922, the *Canard* mocked those who said that Germany was flourishing: since it was doing so well, the important thing was to make sure that next time France was not victorious. Five years later, Ernest Reynaud argued that if people had known what victory would bring, they would still be fighting because no one would have wanted to be victorious.[60] In effect, new victories threatened France. When the Gallic Republic defeated its enemies in the Rif, the *Canard* affected to fear that this victory would be as expensive as the last one, with a rise in the price of rugs and peanuts, local "fruits of victory."[61] In 1927, Rodolphe Bringer worried about a recent prediction from a fortune teller: there would be a war from 1928 to 1936. This he could live with; after all, "we supposed that there would be a new last war!" The problem was that France would be victorious again! "And I ask you," he added, "after this last victory, how much are we going to have to pay for an apéritif?"[62]

WILL GERMANY PAY?

France's monetary difficulties were also, in the *Canard*'s thinking, fruits of the war. But here again, the weekly balanced criticisms of individuals with general explanations. Though there were plenty of suggestions for hanging those involved, when it came to explanatory generalizations the *Canard* correctly focused on a specific policy, accompanied by a specific prediction: that Germany would pay. In early 1919, Clemenceau's finance minister, Louis-Lucien Klotz, proposed a capital levy. This proposal was rejected by the parliament, backed up by the press, which insisted that the costs of reconstruction and the war should be borne by defeated Germany. Klotz, and his successors, then shifted war and reconstruction costs to a budget of "recoverable expenses" and paid for these noncovered costs through loans. For the public, this postponement of financial sacrifice was justified with the slogan "the Krauts [les Boches] will pay"—a phrase that became associated with the finance minister himself.[63]

These decisions were the basic cause of France's later financial and then monetary problems. The *Canard* said as much in 1922. While the government was threatening to prosecute those who spread false financial news, should it not go after Klotz? "Is it not him? Why yes, it's him! . . . Who first and for months spread this claim—inaccurate, tendentious, full of subsequent perils, pregnant with ensuing catastrophes—'Germany will pay'?" The weekly maintained this explanation through the monetary troubles of early 1926. For an "exhibition of fiscal art" it imagined a "portrait of Mr. Klotz pronouncing the magical formula 'Germany will pay,' which contained the seed of all the financial prosperity whose full blossoming we will not fail to experience soon."[64] This fiscal portrait illustrates both sides of the *Canard*'s analysis: the argument that it is the costs of the war the French are paying and the blaming of specific politicians (especially Klotz, symbol of the hollow promise).[65]

But the weekly did not wait until the 1920s to discover this hard truth. It went after the illusion of German payments as early as December 1918, well before the crucial financial decisions, let alone the emergence of problems collecting reparations. In the patriotic euphoria then dominant, the *Canard* turned to quiet derision. The "Petite correspondance" of December 4 and 11 contained the following advice: "Go right ahead and have your suit made and a pretty little lady's outfit for Anita. What difference does that make since the Boches will pay?" "Have the car delivered and the piece of Louis XV furniture; the Boches will pay."[66] The weekly became more specific two weeks later. "If Germany starts to pay not only its debts but ours too, all is well. It would be well to add the bill of 32 francs 60 that we owe at the corner bistro and the 125 francs for the suit that Laforge just had delivered."[67]

Part of the humor of such examples is the way they relate international financial dealings to concrete, everyday expenses. The *Canard* used a similar technique in May 1919 to show the primitiveness of reparations claims. The delegates at Versailles have finally realized, the weekly reported, that the point of war is the division of the spoils among the victors. Of course, those who had lived at the public expense (soldiers) would get less than those who had stayed home and supported themselves. Thus, for each soldier a jar of jam and four marks, and for war suppliers ten tons of copper, a plow or two sewing machines, a Munich furniture set, a German shepherd dog, a barrel of kirsch, and so forth.[68]

"Germany will pay" took on a particularly antiphrastic sense when it was used to stigmatize expenses the *Canard* considered excessive, like those for official voyages by Millerand and Mangin.[69] But tax bills provided a good occasion to reveal the phoniness of the promise. The *Canard* stated its agreement with a poster campaign of the right-center Alliance Démocrate political party: Germany should pay before the French should be taxed. The weekly's advice: when the tax collector comes around, explain that you are not going to pay, and if he objects, refer him to the Alliance. That was in March 1919. Sixteen months later, the *Canard* counseled citizens who had just received their tax bills. An official explained that the bills were "only a matter of form. Making the victorious French pay for the costs of the war, or even those of the peace, has never been contemplated; as all the successive finance ministers have promised us, it is the Krauts who will pay." All the taxpayer had to do, then, was to mail his tax bill "to Berlin, to the Director of Individual Repayments, 148 Hindenburgstrasse, who will take care of it."[70]

The *Canard* did note in passing some of the economic arguments against major German reparations—for example, explaining the difficulties of accepting large-scale payments in kind or mocking those who saw Germany as prosperous.[71] But its dominant approach was to avoid technical arguments and to continue to deride the obviously (for the *Canard*) unrealistic expectation. When King Tut emerged from his sarcophagus in 1923, he asked "whether the Hyksos, who were the Boches of his time, had ended up paying."[72]

Maintaining the centrality of the Germany-will-pay explanation meant continually coming up with new ways to ridicule it. For the *Canard*, there were two ways to establish a fact: assert it or assert its opposite. In February 1925, Guilac published a cartoon of seven little unrealistic scenes, one of which showed a heavy Germania, without armor but with a chain around her waist, handing over a bag of money to a more fashionable looking Marianne.[73] With more compassion for the average French citizen (and more satiric bite), a year earlier, Pedro had depicted "the dream"(see figure 13). The sleeper sees a pig-faced Germania with pointed helmet showering him with money and goods from a cornucopia. He awakens to find a man on a ladder holding an enormous list of taxes. The first scene carried the title "The Dream Passes *[Le rêve passe]*." But this phrase was also the title of a French song of military glory, hence the title for the diptych: "The Patriotic Song."[74] Commenting on a charity banquet for war orphans, the *Canard* said that the bill was very " 'Treaty of Versailles,' in the sense especially that it was not the Germans who paid it."[75]

But how about the *Canard*'s opposite assertion, that Germany had paid (or was paying)? France did receive some reparations, and the *Canard* mocked these,[76] but when it said that the Germans had paid, it meant paid all that was expected. At the beginning of 1922, Rodolphe Bringer mused about what the previous year could have brought. He imagined Poincaré not having pushed out Briand, and Germany having paid. A utopian situation results: wagon-loads of gold arrive, prices fall, military service is re-

Figure 13. The dream of repayment, by Pedro (1924).

duced to three and a half months, and England gives up its colonies.[77] The last point was sufficient, in a French context, to signify radical impossibility.

Pierre Bénard carried the satire on German fulfillment to its greatest length in a futuristic feuilleton, "If the Boches Paid." The five-part series veered cleverly from a utopian to a dystopian vision. Germany pays in full, and the sudden availability of money brings the franc up too fast, in turn generating unemployment, economic dislocation, and civil war. Perhaps most interesting about this spoof is that the arguments (without the fictional exaggerations) were essentially those against any revalorization of the franc. And it was precisely such arguments that persuaded Poincaré to halt the rise of the franc in 1926 and 1927.[78] At that time, however, the *Canard* had no use for such arguments against revalorization.

FORTUNES OF THE FRANC

The *Canard* was unsympathetic to blaming the franc's problems on speculators, still less on foreign ones. The weekly did not want to support the notion that problems with the franc were the result of anti-French campaigns led by German or other foreign interests. In Canardesque antiphrasis: "There are also the speculators. . . . But it is known that the French never speculate, never, never. It is the foreigners. Frenchmen do not wager on the franc, and when they do, it is to make it go up." Or, from an article two months later in 1926: "The government is increasingly determined to pursue the struggle against the speculators—all foreigners—whose maneuvers lower the franc."[79] But the *Canard* had introduced this argument in 1922, explaining that "never, never would French bankers dare to make any profit whatsoever by speculating on the decline of our national franc."[80]

In her retro-predictions for the year that had passed (1923), the *Canard*'s fortune teller explained that the franc had declined because "our capitalists [. . .] bought English pounds and American dollars."[81] The year 1923 had seen both the occupation of the Ruhr and a sharp decline in the franc (while the mark died in hyperinflation). The *Canard* was happy not only to underline the lack of financial benefit from the Ruhr venture but also to show that it led to a decline in confidence in the French currency. But it was careful not to construct this loss of confidence in such a way as to credit the idea of a conspiracy of Anglo-Saxon and German financiers designed to force France out of the Ruhr. Instead, the weekly mocked this argument.[82]

Two "reflections" from a 1924 article summed up the *Canard*'s positions on the role of international speculation. "When the franc is down, that is evidently the doing of foreign speculators.[. . .] But when the pound sterling is down, that is incontestably to the credit of Poincaré and de Lasteyrie, who are extremely clever." And the second stated, "The recovery of the franc made the speculators lose millions of pounds. That is well done, for those millions of pounds were gained by people who, themselves, were *evidently not speculators.*" This point was made more succinctly in a March 1923 "Petite correspondance": "When the franc falls, it is the underhanded maneuvers of foreign finance. When it rises, it is the entirety of honest finance which pays homage to our policies."[83]

The *Canard* recognized that speculators often made money on the fluctuations of the French monetary unit, especially if they knew in advance about government actions that would affect the franc.[84] But if it refused to give center stage to speculators, it did so only partly to avoid scapegoating "international finance," the bogy of the French right. Far more guilty were the politicians, and not just Klotz and Clemenceau, for their Germany-will-pay policy. Unlike the situation with high prices, when it came to the franc, the *Canard* did its best to blame the man others considered the savior of France's currency: Poincaré.

Politicians and finance were fused in a new *Canard* column called "La Bourse" (the name for the French stock exchange). Begun in late 1921 under the title "La Bourse de Paris" and with the byline Louis Dor (for Louis d'or, the most common gold coin), it eventually settled into the shorter title and a format by Guilac, generally with a duck and either a safe or the neoclassical Paris exchange building. As such, "La Bourse," which appeared on and off for a few years and then steadily from early 1925 onward, was a journalistic marker of the importance that exchange levels had come to have in French politics. The typical notice contained two parts. On top was a listing of between five and ten alleged companies with their stock quotations. Underneath was a paragraph or two of commentary and predictions about the fortunes of such companies, whether listed in the top portion or not. The satire came in what were treated as businesses. Many were political figures with their names foreignized to make them look like international corporations. President of the Republic Alexandre Millerand became the Mill Rand; the longtime foreign minister Aristide Briand was the Briandsk; Mandel became Mandeling; Herriot, Herriota; and so on. The *Canard's* stock-exchange expert then discussed the shifting fortunes of these politicians as if they were businesses—competing, dodging bankruptcy, negotiating mergers. These few lines in small print on page 4 often contained more effective political reporting, and more insider's tips, than the entire rest of the paper.

But, from the beginning, these "Bourse" listings also included real businesses, like Standard Oil, or the politically influential Lazard Bank, which became the "Banque Le Hasard" (the hazard). Also available were currencies-as-businesses, like the "Lira italiana." The troubles of the French franc were covered under "Pepetta francese"—a name that combined purposely disparaging allusions to Italian and Spanish finances with the evocation of *pépettes,* slang for coins. Finally, company names could be built on abstractions and metaphors, like "Katastrophas" or "Trouzalalunas" (holes in the moon).[85] The obvious results of all this play were familiar ones, readers did not know when they began the column whether they would be learning about parliamentary maneuverings, business news, or the state of the economy or the world. The more refined message of the Bourse mélanges was the interconnection of the worlds of politics, business, and finance, with the stock market as the symbol of their speculative essence.

The *Canard* blamed the franc's lower exchange rate on Poincaré. The "Bourse" of May 31, 1922, explained that Poincaré "has done well to get emphatic with Germany. Thanks to the measures he has taken, gold is flooding onto the market: everyone can see it. The English pound of twenty-five francs cost us no more than forty-eight francs, which is a bargain." And such arguments continued in 1923, associating the Ruhr occupation with the franc's continuing slide. In the first months of 1924 Poincaré, still in power, faced a serious run on the franc. He won this battle of the franc by imposing new taxes and economy measures and carefully maneuvering on the exchanges. Once the Lorraine statesman defeated the run on the franc, the weekly was reduced to complaining about private groups that had cashed in.[86] More perceptively, the *Canard* showed how Poincaré's way of managing the parliament, threatening to resign if it did not go along, depended on the fragile financial situation since "it is not when the pound goes for 120 francs that some imprudent person is going to want to get his hands on a ministerial portfolio or the premiership."[87] In the *Canard,* Poincaré became a cynical and irresponsible politician who, having ruined the franc through his inconsiderate actions, then used the resulting crisis to maintain himself in power.

The corollary to blaming Poincaré was removing blame, at least in relative terms, from the politicians of the Cartel, who took over from Poincaré in May 1924 and on whose watch the franc ran into serious trouble again in 1925 and 1926. Rather than praising the Cartel's actions in the financial sphere (we have already seen that it was chastised for its handling of prices), the weekly mocked right-wing arguments that Herriot and the Cartel would bring about financial ruin. In June 1924, Victor Snell noted that under Herriot's new leadership the franc had gone up and not down. The explanation for this bullish franc? Poincaré had not given a speech. Later that year, the paper accused Millerand, who had just launched a political offensive against the government, of trying, with little success, to talk down the franc. In April 1925, when Caillaux, the bête noire of the patriotic right, came in, the *Canard* took pleasure in noting that both the franc and the government's bonds were doing better, not worse, on the exchanges.[88]

The *Canard* did, of course, mock the financial situation and the parliamentary game of musical finance ministers.[89] It also went after certain individuals, like Raymond Philippe, agent of the Lazard Bank and of the government.[90] More important, the weekly denied any real credit to Poincaré when, returning to power in July 1926, he halted the franc's decline and set it rising again. Basically, Poincaré benefited from executive authority and accommodations from the Bank of France that were refused to earlier, Cartel, governments. The *Canard* also insisted that Poincaré indulged, with impunity, in the same actions (like fiduciary inflation) that had been condemned by the right and center when they were engaged in by the Cartel governments.[91]

But Poincaré did not allow the franc to rise to its prewar level. He even acted to halt its rise, effecting a de facto stabilization (legalized only later) at about one-fifth of the prewar value. The Lorraine politician made this decision on the advice of financial technicians (for example at the Bank of France) and of business and labor leaders. A continuing revalorization of the franc threatened to increase unemployment (since it would make French prices too high on international markets) and to create the economic problems evoked humorously in the *Canard*'s own fantasy of German repayment. The choice between stabilization and revalorization pitted bond holders (a large part of the middle classes) against the business sector, both owners and workers.[92]

Ignoring its working-class and employee prejudices, the *Canard* effectively supported those who wanted to revalorize; at least it criticized Poincaré for stabilizing (while blaming Poincaré for the limited unemployment that resulted anyway). The *Canard* claimed, on several occasions, that the reason the government held the franc down was because so many "patriots" had bought pounds or dollars. The weekly treated those who wanted to stabilize as profiteers, greedy to make money on the backs of the poorer bondholders, or *rentiers.* But rather than presenting their arguments directly or openly defending the *rentiers,* the *Canard* mocked the concerns of industry (and ignored the positions of the labor unions), ironically reassuring business owners that the franc would not go up too quickly.[93]

Poincaré's achievement was easier to mock if one looked at it from the point of view of the prewar franc. And the *Canard* went further in this vein by linking the Lorrainer's recent actions with those of 1924, when it was he who had brought down the franc before saving it, while in 1926 he appeared only as a savior. In the duck-history of the franc, the Cartel was a colorful, but essentially irrelevant, interlude. Klotz and Clemenceau began the franc's demise through the Germany-will-pay myth. Poincaré then finished it off by trying to make Germany pay, coming back in 1926 to clean up the mess he had made the first time around. The *Canard* even argued that his solution was not permanent and would come apart after the 1928 elections.[94]

If the *Canard* was harsher with Poincaré (and more forgiving of Herriot and company) on the question of the franc than on the related one of retail prices, the reason was largely the tendency of the weekly to connect Poincaré with the aggressive, militaristic side of French politics. Behind any discussion of taxes or the franc lurked the basic *Canard* binarism of those who made money versus those who gave blood.

The closest the *Canard* came to defending the interests of *rentiers* came in an article of September 1926, which effectively summed up the results of the franc crisis. Commenting on the decision of the Bank of France to give 114 francs for each gold Louis, the *Canard* noted that this represented a 470 percent profit. The weekly explained that this was a just recompense for those who had had the moral firmness to resist the demands to buy government bonds and to keep their gold to themselves.[95] That same article argued that "the primary virtue of our race, let us not forget, is the spirit of saving." Saving can mean avarice. In 1920 the *Canard* gave an overarching interpretation of French economic behavior viewed in the context of the war: it compared the nation's resistance to parting with its money to the generosity with which it had sacrificed its soldiers. "As long as war is limited to the successive massacre of combat units, the evil is bearable" because one is not a soldier voluntarily, but it is quite another thing to ask people to freely bring their money.[96]

Ten issues later, Dorgelès tackled the topic with a characteristically lower level of irony. The French, he argued, were reluctant to subscribe to the new loans. "In 1914, we were more numerous at the recruitment offices. Blood shows itself, money hides." The veteran writer went on to note that those who refused to fight were shot and suggested that the *mercantis* be forced to give up their ill-gotten gains. The French, he said, were more careful with their wallets than with their progeny. "That is why people who gaily sent their child to get killed in Champagne or at Verdun hesitate today to subscribe to the loan with what would have been the inheritance of the dead man. They guard their money better than their sons."[97]

There is more here than the traditional *poilu*-versus-*mercanti* theme, and Dorgelès's point transcends the fact that the French did, in fact, sign up for the new loans. His argument is one of national psychology. The French were suckers—and the *Canard* represented the French taxpayer numerous times as a pear, or *poire,* which also meant sucker[98]—but they were also tightwads who resisted paying for the war. Five years after Dorgelès's article, when so many respectable French took offense at the phrase "we must take the money where it is," by the Socialist deputy Pierre Renaudel, the *Canard* explained their attitude. "As long as it was a matter of the defense of territory, our admirable population refused to count: parents 'gave' their sons to France with an admirable eagerness and generosity." "Or, to put it another way," the writer continued, "as long as it was a question of human lives, that was okay. But the minute one wants to get to money, halt! If tilling and pasturage are the two breasts of France, the piggy bank is incontestably the third.[. . .] Anything one wants, but not cold cash."[99]

Blood versus money: the war had cost both, and in this analysis the *Canard* suggested that the problem lodged not only with the *mercantis* or the politicians but with the population as a whole, which was not prepared for the financial costs of the four-year massacre. If this suggestion appealed to a stereotype, that of the traditionally economical French small farmer or business owner, it was a national stereotype. It opens, therefore, another level of analysis, that of the French versus foreigners.

13 The Wealth of Nations

Virtually all of France's postwar economic difficulties had international connections. But in two cases these relationships were particularly visible: the decline in the franc, which provoked a sharp increase in the number of tourists, and the problem of debts owed to Britain and the United States. This highly visible foreign involvement meant that the familiar *Canard* tension between stereotyped (or scapegoated) treatment and structural, ultimately antimilitarist, explanation came out as foreigner bashing versus a more balanced critique of France's role in the international capitalist system. The foreigners open for bashing were the Anglo-Saxons. Though both countries were targeted in both areas of controversy, the British played a privileged role in the discourses on tourism, the United States in those on debts.

ATTACKING TOURISTS

English tourists were a good subject for caricature. But anxieties could easily lie behind such humor. For Easter 1926, the first page of the *Canard* featured two tourist cartoons. The first, by Pruvost, depicted an aggressive tourist guide with bullhorn pointing out an intimidated Frenchman to a crowd of English-speaking tourists. The title of the cartoon was "The Invasion."[1] The second, and larger, image dominated the bottom of the page. By Guilac, it represented the Gare du Nord train station on Easter day. The arrival hall has a sign, "London to Paris," while that on departures reads, "Paris to all destinations." The departing crowd consists entirely of fashionable, attractive Parisiennes. Arriving are English tourists with their comically plain women. The legend draws the comparison: "Some come. . . . Others leave. . . . All the same one loses in the exchange!"[2] The double meaning of exchange adds the political twist to the self-serving confrontation of stereotypes.

A few months earlier, Pruvost visually represented an exchange-related anti-English claustrophobia. Three images: the first, "the pound at 100," with a single English tourist and a French policeman; the second, "the pound at 110," had three tourists from across the Channel; the last, "the pound at 120," was filled with a crowd of English men and women. Perhaps more threatening, the linguistic background behind the figures also evolved, from an initial street scene with only French signs to later scenes with signs doubly coded in English ("English tailor" in English and "Bistro's," a fashionable anglicization of a French word). The *Canard* had a running joke that Nice, with its boulevard des Anglais, was virtually an English colony.[3] But the loss of linguistic mastery in Paris (then as now) was obviously more dangerous.

Yet the *Canard* was quick to cast aspersions on those who seemed to be attacking the tourist trade. Back in 1923, René Buzelin, after noting the record number of visitors, exclaimed, "Now what happens but that a deputy, whom we would like to consider better advised, proposes putting a one-thousand-franc tax on every foreigner who will have committed the stupidity of coming to France to contribute, through his expenses, to raising the exchange rate of our franc." Buzelin concluded with a cynicism that cut both ways that it would be better to let the hotelkeepers strangle the foreigners gently; they were masters at it.[4]

In the summer of 1926, as the combined monetary and parliamentary crisis reached its height, French irritation with foreign tourists rose sharply. Some citizens harassed and insulted visitors—for example, by throwing vegetables at tours. The *Canard,* which had unequivocally encouraged mob violence against shopkeepers, took a neutral, even mildly reprobative, attitude to such expressions of popular anger. The July 26 *Canard* told two stories of attacks on tourists. At the Place de l'Opéra, the paper reported, "cries and whistling greeted several buses filled with tourists. The crowd threw at the passengers tomatoes, cabbage stumps, and other vegetables." The Americans collected the stumps to take home with them and expressed thanks before leaving. Hardly a tragic accounting, and one ridiculing both parties. The other story was an epistolary account of the adventures of an English secretary in Paris. At first, she is thrilled by the exchange rate, stays in a luxury hotel, and buys gifts for everyone. After Poincaré comes in, however, and the pound goes down, she is obliged to return her purchases and move to modest lodgings. She is particularly angry when she is pelted with rotten eggs and insulted by Parisians, and she returns to Britain, destitute, blaming Poincaré, who, she says, hates England.[5]

This second story almost makes Poincaré look good. But the schadenfreude at the expense of the obviously naive young Englishwoman could just as easily be turned against Frenchmen, in this case Bicard (in the following issue). Bicard's friend, Gradouille, has hired a bus for the guests at his daughter's wedding. To show off, he decides that they should all stop and have a drink at a café on the Place Clichy. There, because they came in a bus and because Gradouille decides to order whisky and cocktails (to impress the onlookers), Bicard and company are taken for English tourists. They are copiously insulted, blamed by angry shoppers for high prices, and, under a hail of fruits and vegetables, are obliged to seek refuge in the bus. But, at just this time a tour bus full of real English tourists arrives and unloads its passengers. Bicard and Gradouille lead their company into the wrong bus and, on arriving at the Panthéon, realize their error. Worse, they realize that the English tourists have gone in their bus to their wedding feast. They finally get to the dinner and find that the Britains have already reached the cheese course and have gone through the wine bottles. As Bicard and Gradouille toss the tourists out the restaurant windows, the police arrive and haul everyone to jail to cool off.[6] If the Bicard story did not make angry French men and women look silly enough, a Ferjac cartoon in the same issue made the point with admirable brevity. A working-class individual gestures angrily at a bus full of tourists, "Go home, hey! Xenophobes."[7]

Having mocked French xenophobia, the *Canard* reversed the valences. On September 15, a Pruvost cartoon was labeled "That's quite different." It showed a Chinese figure threatening a pith-helmeted European with his sword and saying, "Death to foreigners." The European answers, in French with an English accent, "Oh, I am not a foreigner. I am English."[8] The *Canard* had been consistent in its condemnation of English and other European imperialism in China.[9] Indeed, the weekly had refused to condemn as xenophobia the desires of the Chinese (or other non-European peoples) to run their own affairs. The anti-English stereotype helped to relate the Chinese sense of invasion to the French one. Mat expressed the French view in a relatively good-natured cartoon entitled "The Parisian returns." A Frenchman on the Metro says, "All the same, it's great to be home," but we see him surrounded by other passengers whose non-Gallic identities we can guess from their stereotyped dress: English (male and female), Chinese, German, North African, West Indian, and so on.[10]

Gently mocking all sides was one way the *Canard* de-dramatized French resentments. Another way was fantasy reversal. In May 1926, during the general strike in Britain, the *Canard* played with the idea that this economic disruption (coupled with the actions of the French government) might so completely reverse the situation that the franc would be worth 150 British pounds. "It will be our turn to visit London; ours will be the *girls* [in English], ours the whisky!" When they arrive in Victoria Station, everyone will rush to help them, ignoring the lone English traveler. "We will visit Trafalgar Square, which, thanks to the improvement in exchange rates, will have become a great success for our navy, and Waterloo Station, the station at which, the guide will reveal to us, Napoleon arrived in London after his famous victory."[11]

The *Canard* even removed the barbs from the Gallic stock of xenophobic insults. In January 1927, Bicard complained that the French language was poor in colorful insults, and the situation was even worse when one wanted to insult foreigners. "All you can come up with against foreigners are the names of edibles. And when you call an Englishman a rosbif [roast beef], a German a choucroute [sauerkraut], an Italian a macaroni, a Breton a potato, and a Norman an andouille frite [fried sausage], you instead make them happy because you are invoking the national and appetizing dishes of their territory."[12]

THE POLITICS OF STEREOTYPES

One reader, at least, felt that his favorite weekly was guilty of foreigner bashing. On August 25, 1926, the *Canard* printed large excerpts from the letter of a Mr. Jean Armand, who had been living in Argentina for twenty-two years.[13] Armand started by establishing his bona fides; a faithful reader of the *Canard Enchaîné,* he possessed the entire run of the paper. His complaint? "You also, *Canard,* by your continual attacks on foreigners (whose satirical character renders them perhaps more effective than the Prudhommesque asininities of the so-called serious press), contribute to the aggravation of one of the most regrettable defects of the French mentality: national presumptuousness, the ignorance of people and matters abroad, disdain for the foreigner."

Armand acknowledged that the *Canard*'s role was to joke and mock, and "you find it quite natural to profit from a number of very convenient conventions, which furnish you with as much as you want of this indispensable material." Quite aptly, the writer compared the weekly's style with the U.S. cinema's exploitation of a number of stereotypes:

> In the same way, you have adopted the mandolin, castanets, checkered suits, pronunciation with "ao" or "oa," the South American gigolo, the ignorant and vulgar Yankee millionaire, the Englishman who makes the pound go up [. . .] a collection of consecrated stupidities from which you pull jokes and pleasantries that make one laugh but that by their permanence reveal too much that state of mind at once troglodytic and self-satisfied that I noted above.

After this perceptive (if somewhat one-sided) critique of the *Canard*'s manipulation of stereotypes, the Frenchman from Buenos Aires addressed the issue of foreigners and exchange rates: exchange rates reflect the desires of buyers and sellers, and many who find themselves with francs in their hands do so for creditable reasons; "they are not all bastards." Why do many want to get rid of their francs? Because they have lost confidence in the French economy and government "when there is one." Yes, there are speculators, Armand admitted. They buy and sell francs "just as Messrs. Youtoo, Bibilolo, and Company would if they had the means to do so." Most important, speculators buy and sell francs to make money, not to drive the currency down. "Seen in its true light," the role of foreigners in exchange levels was "damnably attenuated." Yes, "the subject is a gold mine," he admitted in conclusion, but could not the writers of the *Canard* find other subjects and "be gay without being aggressive, clever without being unjust?"

Armand hit close to home, and the *Canard* received many letters in reply. In the three following issues, the weekly published excerpts from seven of them, edited to give about equal time to both sides. Armand's critics invoked two major arguments. The first was that, living in Argentina, he did not understand what the French of France were going through, their economic and emotional distress in the face of an "invasion" of foreigners with a favorable exchange rate. The second argument addressed the problem of stereotypes more directly. A reader who had traveled a lot wrote that the stereotypes were largely true. "The saloon keepers of the Far West really chewed big cigars; [. . .] the Yankee millionaires were usually ignorant and vulgar; [. . .] many young people of Buenos Aires (with Mr. Armand's permission) engaged in a charming sexual procurement; and [. . .] the English were often perfect bastards." Besides, the French should see the way they were treated in the U.S. press. The other side agreed with Armand and, with many expressions of affection, blamed their favorite newspaper. Such stereotypes were beneath the dignity of a sophisticated periodical like the *Canard* and ran counter to the weekly's overall goal of creating a more humane world and better international understanding. And who were the foreign tourists? People of modest means spending five days in Paris on a Cook's tour, employees, small shopkeepers and artisans, hardly the "sharks of international finance," who stayed better hidden. And would not most French do the same if they could? "Have you not forgotten so quickly the fall of the mark and the [Austrian] crown? How many French acquired furniture, machines, automobiles, etc., at bargain rates?" There were morally questionable individuals in foreign countries? What of it, since there were in France too. "The French, whatever one says, have too great a tendency to consider the Americans as imbeciles, although many things would justify the reverse." With this last, and pro-Armand, letter, the *Canard* decided to end its "courteous" debate. The weekly pleaded neither guilty nor innocent, saying instead that it would continue its activity of *débourrage* in its own way, "that is, with a smile."[14] Strikingly, it was the stereotyping of European peoples (or transplanted Europeans) that was controversial. None of the correspondents seemed concerned with the weekly's exploitation of racist stereotypes of Africans and others.[15]

DEBTS

Armand not only spoke of exchange rates but also referred to France's debts to Britain and the United States. The idea that the French, bled white by the war, should make major payments, for decades, to the United States was never popular in the Gallic republic. One of Armand's critics spoke bitterly of modestly paid employees and workers who had sacrificed their money and their skins, "obliged to tighten their belts patriotically in the name of Messrs. Mellon and Coolidge and for the greater good of our hereditary friends"—this last a reference to the English.[16] Armand himself gave the *Canard* relatively high marks for its coverage of the issue: "We reproach our creditors for demanding their money. Please. And us, what have we not done to recover what the Germans and the Russians owe us? You know, and you know the result. I congratulate you in passing for your fine campaign against these clumsy maneuvers."[17] Though the *Canard* presented arguments undercutting French claims, that did not stop the weekly from also attacking the United States mercilessly for its greed or from linking this critique to an unflattering analysis of American civilization.

The occupation of the Ruhr furnished the *Canard* with an ideal occasion for exposing the French double standard. In August 1923, the paper complained that the English kept requesting repayment. "Goodness, we know well enough that we owe them money. We even owe them what we borrowed from them." But, the satirical periodical went on, "we will pay England when our ability to pay permits it. That's all! While Germany, which owes us, well, it must pay us immediately. The proof is that we are in the Ruhr, justly proud of our being in the right and in order to coerce the debtor." Suppose, the *Canard* imagined, the English applied similar means with France and took Calais as security? But that was not the same thing. "Money owed to us is always more important than that which we owe."[18] There were ways to argue the French position—by noting, for example, that neither England nor Germany was damaged by the fighting—but the *Canard* contented itself here with ridiculing the French position on reparations and debts.

When it came to making a position look ridiculous, few could top Bicard. The general public knows little, he claimed, about French war debts to the United States, and Poincaré is like a fellow who always talks of what is owed him, never what he owes others. If the French have taken the Ruhr, Bicard suggested, the Americans might take Périgord as security since truffles are more valuable than coal.[19] In August 1925, when the English debt came up again, Bicard wonders whether the British will occupy the Somme. This was a grizzlier joke since that region was already occupied by a prodigious collection of English corpses because of the battle that was fought there. In the next issue, after further discussion, Bicard's interlocutor suggests the solution for the French: do not think about the debts, for that has worked well until now.[20]

That same year, the *Canard*'s Pierre Bénard created a fictional travel account of a Soviet official in Paris: "I was in Paris, in the heart of this France that says to us Russians, 'Pay me back. I am so poor!' and that repeats to the Americans, 'I cannot repay you. I have so little money.' Is France really so impoverished?" After a visit to the Longchamps racetrack and other Paris high spots, comrade "Popoff" concludes in the negative. Another French argument killed by ridicule. The weekly also mocked French avoidance of its debts, though, as elsewhere, its irony could cut two ways.[21]

Inherent in the *Canard*'s critique was, essentially, that the French had gotten themselves into a mess partly of their own devising. The retired Clemenceau protested in August 1926, "Must the lie of German reparations end with Americans receiving cash?" The *Canard* answered, "Pardon! Who told the lie of 'Germany will pay' if not Mr. Klotz, the Clemenciste minister of Clemenceau?" Two weeks later, the weekly invented President Calvin Coolidge's answer to Clemenceau's charge. It came to this, that at the Peace Conference, Clemenceau had accepted all the arrangements and taken no interest in economic matters since he assumed that Germany would pay for everything. As with the franc, "Germany will pay" was the original sin.[22]

Arguments used by Americans to justify repayment could be turned against both countries. One such argument was based on the size of France's military. As the *Canard* put it, the Americans argued that France kept a large army, therefore France must have money left over. "If we insist that it give us this money, France will disband its army, and the world will be a more peaceful place." The *Canard*'s reply contained, through its irony, at least an implicit acceptance of the pacifist argument for repayment: "If we no longer had our army, who would victoriously assure the peace in Morocco and Syria, and when necessary the state of war necessary to the consequent pacification of the natives?"[23]

The weekly came up with an effective reply to the U.S. charges in August 1926. U.S. Senator William Borah had said that he would not annul France's debt because France was an imperialist country. Citing an article on a new U.S. combat airplane, the *Canard* replied, "Pay America? No thank you. *In order for it to buy bombers or battleships?* We love peace too much to support such a vice!" In 1927, after France had started making payments to Britain and the United States, the paper noted how the money was being used. The British vessels "will cost the exact three billion francs that England was able to extract from the well-known imperialism of the French."[24] All the countries seemed to be using the disputed money for the same unhealthy purposes.

A large part of the debt owed to Uncle Sam came not from war materials used by the French to repulse the invader but from the extensive stocks built up by the U.S. army in expectation of a longer war and sold to the French after the armistice.[25] The usefulness of the stocks and the prices paid for them became issues in arguments over the reasonableness of the debt bill. In a cartoon—by Mat in 1927—a girl at a bar asks a visiting U.S. veteran, "What will you offer me, darling?" The Yank answers, in mangled French, "I offer you a nice stock of chewing-gum for a ridiculous price."[26]

If the United States had acted abusively in the last conflict, perhaps justice would dictate changing the roles played by the different parties the next time around.

> We do not know what Providence has in store for us in its inexhaustible bounty, but if it is in its plans to accord a new last war with Germany, we would be well advised to take a few precautions.
>
> We will fight the Germans, freshly, joyously, and as long as one wishes, but on the condition that this time it will be their turn to have the United States as allies.
>
> For them the delivery of overcoats at high prices, the arrival of the regiments of volunteers, the construction of swimming pools behind the trenches, the conquest of nightclubs by revolver, the annexation of Berlin, the fat of corned beef on the lace of their train cars, and the masculine usage of their sentimental Gretchens.
>
> They will lack only victory to know complete ruin.

This 1925 version of the noxiousness of victory received another variation later that year. One Frenchman says to another in a café, "The Americans?

Me, sir, I would declare war on them immediately, and I would let them have the victory. Then, they would see what it is."[27]

Despite the conceit (which, as we have seen, played other roles), losing a war was clearly not the ideal situation. A year earlier, in April 1924, the *Canard*'s Rodolphe Bringer had constructed the ideal fantasy of anti-American revenge. The prospects of a war between the United States and Japan brought renewed hope to French hearts.

> Then it will be necessary to make shells, cast cannons, and fit out tanks—cannons that we will not maneuver ourselves, shells that we will not fire ourselves, tanks that we will not get into ourselves, [. . .] and when we receive something it will only be nice, beautiful, golden dollars.
>
> And it will be our turn. . . .
>
> Then when matters will have reached a certain point, when we see that our friends have got things well under control, then, but only then, as is proper, we will come and give them a hand.

After the peace is signed in Cincinnati, Bringer explained, the French will leave old stocks and useless machines that they will have dragged back across the Atlantic for the purpose and that they will let go for a song. The French will then go back home, whistling the *Madelon* and saying, "Good-bye, brotherhood and . . . our best to your chicks!"[28]

Bringer's fantasy redefined the Great War, as the controversy over the U.S. contribution became part of the evolving memory of that conflict. It was thus not surprising that such memory could have its monumental aspects. In June 1926, the *Canard* reported on a monument for the port city of Saint-Nazaire, which was supposed to be of a U.S. soldier handing a sword to a French one. But the design was changed at the last minute to a column with a bill collector handing out a bill. Similarly, the weekly announced that in return for France's having sent a "taxi of the Marne" to tour the United States, the Americans were sending an automobile belonging to the Federal Reserve Bank.[29]

UNCLE SHYLOCK

The Mellon-Bérenger, Franco-American debt accords of April 1926 were not ratified by the French parliament for three years. Poincaré's decision, in 1927, to make provisional payments before ratification not only infuriated the *Canard*,[30] but also contributed to keeping the issue alive throughout 1927 and 1928. From the end of 1926 through the beginning of 1928, the *Canard* set the debts issue in the larger frame of the character of "Uncle

Shylock," as it labeled the United States.[31] In so doing, it linked Franco-American relations and the war debts to a number of issues whose relation to them was only indirect, from prohibition to Charlie Chaplin, from Charles Lindbergh to Sacco and Vanzetti.

Prohibition had long been a sore point for the patriotically wet *Canard*. By 1926 it had become a metaphor. The United States had never been so wet since it became dry. Rich Americans drove across the border to Canada to get sloshed in their hotel rooms. Bicard (an expert in such things) noted how visiting U.S. veterans headed straight for the bars—instead of the "dry" official functions.[32] Prohibition was not associated with specific dates; it was a permanent fixture of U.S. life in the 1920s. Other events gave a rhythm to the *Canard*'s coverage of the United States: Chaplin's divorce in February 1927, Lindbergh's trans-Atlantic flight in May, the execution of Sacco and Vanzetti in August, and the visit of the American Legion to Paris in September of that same year.

The writer who dominated the *Canard*'s coverage of these issues, whose dialectic of hope and despair never forgot the reality of French war debts, was the pacifist ideologue, the relatively nonironic Pierre Scize. Scize set the stage with the postulate that the inferior level of American civilization made extended payments unthinkable. Cities in the United States were soulless agglomerations, its people barbarians. "Go and you will understand the Yankee of the rue de Daunou who, drunk with our wine, belches at us, and the millionaire harpy from the state of Tennessee who brings tears of humiliation to the clothing models of the rue de la Paix." Visit a few villages of Burgundy, Champagne, or La Causse. "I am not worried that after this you will feel with an incredible violence that it is unjust, profoundly iniquitous, immoral, and, to put it all in a single word, monstrous to think that this people could accept to become the serfs of that tribe."[33]

American treatment of Charlie Chaplin only confirmed the postulate. Some *Canard* authors had fun with Chaplin's domestic difficulties. De la Fouchardière (and Bicard) played with the fact that Mrs. Chaplin included in her divorce case the charge that her husband had requested "the perversion" defined in article 288. De la Fouchardière had everyone hilariously, and fruitlessly, trying to find out what the act in question was (if anyone at the *Canard* knew, its readers were not told).[34]

For Scize, the Chaplin divorce was another example of American hypocrisy. "Because the virtuous America never mobilizes lightly, [. . .] behind the homilies that hastened the intervention of this lovely nation in the European war were all the calculations of the interest on the war debts, all the evaluation of the baby scales and the chewing gum of the stocks."

The United States was motivated by "vengeance and hatred," comparable to those that lit the flames under the pyres of heretics. And the author addressed Chaplin by his French nickname:

> Charlot, pitiable Charlot, what you are paying for today with your dollars, with your tears, with your broken love, with your paternal suffering, what you are paying for to the Methodist Tartuffes of Ohio and Connecticut, are the avenging pages in which you scourged their turpitudes.[. . .]
>
> You showed, in *The Kid,* the sanctimonious harpies of an unsmiling welfare administration, in the name of the Bible, trampling on the sacred rights of mothers and tearing babies out of their cradles. They have taken yours, imbecile! Now cry.

You thought, Scize went on, that in America you could magnify the poor man at the expense of the millionaire, "plead in favor of the gentle drunkard." American Puritanism contrasted with French *joie-de-vivre.*

> You should come to a country that I know, vaguely hexagonal in shape, located at the western edge of Europe. There, at the feet of the most beautiful vines in the world, flow the four most beautiful rivers that I know of. And on their banks, a crowd of regular fellows who love you and who celebrate your name drink long draughts of the wine of their hillsides while caressing their sweethearts.

For Scize, Chaplin's difficulties were emblematic of those of France. "The same people who took your child in the name of morality want to enslave our grandchildren." Let's make a film, Scize proposes, one that "will provoke laughter by showing the sordid gold eaters of Wisconsin and Colorado." For the conclusion, Scize leaves the geography of avarice for that of pleasure, "And we will drink the Vouvray of the last harvest, seated in the cool of the cellar, while thinking of our loves."[35]

The gross binarism, the clear stereotyping, of Scize's portraits are in the obvious service of his diatribe on debts. But the *Canard*'s moralist (for even his attack on moralists is moralizing) doubted his own country more than his black-and-white Chaplinizing would suggest. Just a short while later, he accused his fellow citizens of xenophobia and anti-Americanism. But for that the United States needed a new hero, and that hero was Lindbergh. Yet Scize also found a way, while criticizing the French and praising an American, to again invoke war debts. He began: "Mr. Myron T. Herrick is a fearless old gentleman who, having accepted the rude task of representing in France a country quite fully occupied in passing a rope around our neck, acquits himself of his mission with a maximum of decency and good humor." Ambassador Herrick had just warned U.S. flyers to consider postponing their trips to France since they risked receiving an unfriendly reception if they succeeded in crossing the Atlantic. Scize agreed with the diplomat that the French lacked "sportsmanship." Not only had they behaved badly against foreign teams at the 1924 Olympics, but they had a history of threatening teams and referees even in their own soccer matches. More recently, two French flyers, Charles Nungesser and François Coli, had tried unsuccessfully to cross the Atlantic. On the boulevards, emotional crowds cheering the false news put out by some papers of a successful arrival in New York (the flyers were lost somewhere over the Atlantic) booed and threatened all those who doubted the news, especially if they represented foreign organizations. The incident gave the *Canard* a splendid opportunity to repeat its theme of the mendacity of the mass press. For Scize it also signaled a danger that France would cover itself with "so much shame."[36]

When Lindbergh landed at Le Bourget field a few days later, there was no shame, only a Franco-American love feast, in which the *Canard* was fully active: poems, a fictional letter from Lindbergh to the staff thanking them for the Vouvray, the Spirit of St. Louis met in the air with a bouquet of flowers held by an enchained duck in flight, and so forth.[37] For Scize it was the occasion for a partial *mea culpa.* Relieved and delighted at Lindbergh's reception, he was ashamed to have feared worse. Scize was also, like everyone else, captivated by the flyer's boyish charm. None of which stopped him, of course, from suggesting that, in return for his generous reception, Lindbergh ask his government to be more forthcoming on debt relief.[38] Two weeks later, Scize found nourishment in the Lindbergh story for his anti-American campaign. After announcing his desire to visit the major cities of Europe, Lindbergh brusquely changed plans and took a boat back to the States. Scize offered the explanation that none of the other papers would: Lindbergh left on the instructions of his ambassador. Why? To keep him from visiting the Sweden of his birth—to preserve all his glory for the United States. Scize concluded: "The most comical thing is that this gesture comes from this harlequin of races, of peoples, of nations, of beliefs, this hodgepodge where men of every skin color and every soul live side by side, collected rather than united by the weakest of political bonds, and which is called the United States of America."[39]

The conviction and sentencing to death in Massachusetts of Sacco and Vanzetti, two Italian-born anarchists, on what many considered weak evidence, made them a cause célèbre for the international left and wide circles in France. For post-Dreyfus French intellectuals, this was an obvious injustice and a stain on the reputation of the United States. A *Canard* headline, in August 1927, read, "Lindbergh, Byrd . . . yes, but . . . Fuller, Borah, Thayer."[40] Richard Byrd was the polar explorer, and William Borah the Republican senator who insisted on debt repayment. Webster Thayer was the judge and Alvan Fuller was the governor who were responsible for the execution. The lead cartoon of the front page was a Guilac rendition of a skeletal Statue of Liberty. Subsequent issues featured electric chairs with the slogan "Injustice is done" and a pun on the situation calling Fuller "le Père La Chaise," which is both the famous Parisian cemetery and "father of the [electric] chair."[41]

So much for the tone. The weekly's case against the trans-Atlantic republic was left to Scize's prose. In the face of this crime, Scize barely alluded to the question of debts, though he did evoke the dashed hopes in the United States of 1918, showing the disillusion behind his bitterness. Scize returned to a favorite image, that of the melting pot as vice. What can we say, Scize argued, to those orators who "assure us that America is not that band of hypocritical pastors and greedy financiers who torment Charlie Chaplin and coin money with their dead?" What can we reply, he continued, to those who say that behind the skyscrapers "there is nothing but arid hearts, bodies without soul, a mess of painfully federated *Heimatloss*, an immense primitive herd, Negro lynching, Psalm singing, herbal tea drinking, and gum chewing?" The spark from the electric chair will "efface even your smile, Charles Lindbergh!"[42]

Such rhetorical flights were characteristic of Scize. Uncharacteristic of the *Canard* (at least up to this point) was the encouragement it provided to xenophobic violence. The weekly told its readers that Governor Fuller was also the chief stockholder in the Packard automobile company. "If Sacco and Vanzetti are [. . .] executed, Packard owners would do well, if they wish to avoid nuisances, to disguise their automobiles." If the connection with international issues was left vaguer, the threat was clearer in an anecdote that appeared in the same issue. A tramway conductor found a bag with six hundred thousand francs and delivered it to its owner, a Mr. Thomas W. Brown of Ohio. The foreign gentleman offered the (French) good Samaritan two hundred francs as a reward. This story, the weekly commented, should serve as a lesson to those who return bags they happen across. "Let us add," the *Canard* noted in conclusion, "that the windows of the honorable Thomas W. Brown are intact."[43]

More than just indignation at judicial murder was involved in the *Canard's* anger. The United States had become the collector for a range of frustrations. Many of the issues that created these frustrations—the war, the debts, prohibition, judicial hypocrisy—were brought together by the next act in the Franco-American drama—the visit of the American Legion to Paris in September 1927. The high point of the festivities was the parade, in historical costumes, of the state veterans' organizations. Both a war commemoration and a military exercise, the parade evoked familiar concerns: "a surprising cavalcade of colors, noisy, fresh, and joyous like a simple last war." Since this was the United States, Sacco and Vanzetti made their appearance: "When the musicians from Massachusetts appeared, dressed all in red, there was virtual delirium. The chairs . . . of the cafés were taken by force by the spectators . . . electrified and desirous of getting a better look at the fellow citizens of Governor Fuller." At the end of the parade came the French, "the debtors who closed the triumphal march of the creditors."[44]

The trio of war, debts, and judicial murder wound through the issues of the *Canard* that preceded and followed the visit. The headline on September 21 read, "The Lanterns Are Extinguished . . . the Debts Too?" In the same issue, Drégerin opined that it was foolish to throw such a luxurious party for one's creditors—especially when crying poor.[45] The weekly published an alleged letter, in English, from a visiting Legionnaire. Naturally he is having a great time with the Paris night life, but he has trouble understanding the locals: "But you say, 'And Sacco and Vanzetti'? Alas! Sacco and Vanzetti, what is it? And your little sister?"[46]

Guilac and Scize each summed up the event in his own way. Scize called it "a beautiful party, appropriate to the cruel times in which we live! The debtor welcomes on his devastated territory, in his mourning and his poverty, twenty thousand creditors, more or less sober." Referring to the Kellogg-Briand Pact, Scize wrote that "the people who wanted to 'declare peace to the world' can be proud of this bellicose parade in the worst image of the war as presented to the crowd: the one that offers it as a sport and as a game!"[47] Guilac drew his own parade floats: "Justice and Liberty," which carried an electric chair; "Stocks and Debts"; "Remembrance and Paternity," with a woman and a group of babies; and "Prohibition," with a carafe and a glass of water.[48]

LOST ILLUSIONS

Barely a few weeks after the American Legion left France, Scize summed up the results of almost a year of obsession with the United States in an article of October 12. Occasioned by tariff disputes, it made explicit the reasons why the United States provoked such anger in a democratic pacifist like Scize. America had stood in for all the generous illusions of the war and peace. It was the locus where stereotypes (generous and otherwise) became transmuted into memory. "It is sadly true that nothing under the sun offers a more bitter flavor than the falseness finally recognized of a generous illusion." What was this illusion? The miraculous possibility "of a world that would not be uniquely composed of wolves and lambs, of tigers and goats, of bastards and suckers." Who among us did not "greet the arrival in our country of the men in khaki from the United States with cries of enthusiasm and tears of joy?" asked Scize. He went on to compare the situation of the French with that of a "Negro" tribe welcoming the civilizing whites. Behind the hugs and handshakes, Americans were operating, drawing up debt papers, evaluating the artwork, carrying off the girls. Beyond the illusions of the war were those of the peace. "I remember the shouts which greeted Wilson one morning in the month of November 1918 on the Place de la Concorde. I remember the vast hopes that we received and the clamors that were like the flutterings of the wings of peace."[49]

Scize's embittered "goodbye to all that" closed a cycle of illusion and disillusion. It represented all the disillusions (and cynicisms) of the postwar *Canard,* from the next last war to the elections, from "Germany will pay" to the debts. The United States could play this role for Scize and for the paper as a whole because of the absence of that other dawn of hope that emerged from the First World War: the Bolshevik revolution. It is not just that the time of disillusion had not yet come for most communists. As we saw, neither Scize nor the *Canard* as a whole ever put their faith in Lenin. The first Russian revolution, that of February, had been welcomed with an enthusiasm that bordered on naiveté, but the weekly never saluted the communist one of October. True, the *Canard* observed that taboo on criticism of the Bolshevik system among broad sectors of the French left that is so clearly outlined by François Furet. But the weekly, its anti-anticommunism tempered by an allergy to totalitarian systems, kept its Voltairian distance.[50]

This had not been the case with Wilson. One has but to remember the unique honor he received in the *Canard.* If the *Canard* was never enthusiastic about the peace arrangements, it nevertheless maintained the idea of a pure and noble Wilson.[51] The illusion died hard. November 1918 to October 1927—the *Canard* had always been quick to mock the illusions of others, but it took the paper nine years finally to abandon this one.

14 Conclusion
Politics of Humor, Politics of Memory

Through the years of war and peace, the *Canard* served up its weekly combinations of humor and politics. Its most common humoristic techniques are by now familiar: antiphrastic irony, pastiche, repetition, and the exploitation of stereotypes. These techniques did more than generate humor; they gave the *Canard* its distinctive coloration. They were a rhetoric that created a politics—in turn linked to a world-view and a discourse of memory.

It would clearly be dangerous to argue that certain literary or humoristic techniques are compatible only with particular political positions, since the possibilities of language and the creative mind cannot be circumscribed in advance. Nevertheless, there are apparent affinities between given formal procedures and definable political attitudes, and there are equally general discordances between these same techniques and other ideological tendencies. This relationship between humoristic techniques and politics is clear in the pages of the *Canard,* whose discourse not only mixed the two but built formal and ideological bridges between them.

IRONY AND INDIGNATION

The most pervasive *Canard* technique, antiphrastic irony, was quasi-official for the weekly: it was suggested by its title and laid out in its two opening statements of principles. By now, it is obvious, however, that antiphrasis was not the only mode of discourse. Such a result would be impossible, as even the introduction in the first issue showed with its examples of both antiphrastic and direct discourse. Saying the opposite of what one meant stood side by side, in the columns of the *Canard,* with its opposite—that is, saying exactly what one meant. Constant unannounced shifting between ironic and direct discourse was the characteristic duck print.

The resulting games, the written winks, constituted a major element in the complicity between journalists and readers.

Such games carried risks. On November 12, 1924, the *Canard* ran the headline "'We Owe Them a Debt' / But Why Do They Want to Remind Us of It?" The reference was to disabled veterans and other victims of the war; and the headline mocked those who, while admitting the obligation, criticized the veterans for insisting on their rights.[1] One reader, at least, did not see it that way. He must have written quickly since his letter was excerpted in the next issue. A disabled veteran from Grenoble, he began by establishing his bona fides as a faithful reader of the weekly from its inception, expressing for the "newspaper all the esteem appropriate for an organ that had maintained its frankness and its independence during the war (and even since)." But he felt "surprise and sadness on seeing your organ diverge from its habitual line of conduct." The *Canard* responded without humor:

> On our part, will our correspondent permit us to express our surprise at seeing an assiduous reader of the *Canard* misunderstand to such a degree the meaning of a sentence whose irony seemed nevertheless to us so obvious?
>
> But this proves, one more time, that irony is a "double-edged sword" that should only be handled with extreme care. And it is, besides, in this spirit that we will make it a point, increasingly from week to week, to use the "direct mode," which cannot leave room for any equivocation.
>
> No hard feelings?[2]

Direct discourse, even extended exercises in it, preceded 1924, though, as the postwar decade advanced, it became more common in the pages of the *Canard*. The weekly used nonironic writing, for example, when discussing the fortunes of the paper, when appealing for subscribers or loans, or when asking readers to spread the good word to their friends and acquaintances.[3] But subscriptions could also be a subject for humor (and the subscription campaigns of other papers could be subject to mockery). "Rather Than Drinking Vichy Water, Going to Mass, or Voting for the National Bloc / Subscribe to the CANARD ENCHAINE." This headline uses opposites to define the weekly: imbibing, anticlerical, and politically leftist. Another headline appeared in 1922: "Mr. Millerand's Trip Cost a Total of Forty Million / But a Subscription to the *Canard Enchaîné* Is Only Ten Francs per Year." In 1919, the weekly mocked *L'Avenir,* which had offered sugar (a scarce item) to new subscribers; instead, it proposed giving subscriptions to *L'Avenir* to all those who promised not to buy their ration of sugar.[4]

Though this offer was not entirely serious, the *Canard* never dipped into antiphrasis on the matter of its own survival. Unlike *L'Oeuvre* and its "imbecilic" readers,[5] the weekly never suggested, even in jest, that anyone not read it. Nevertheless, in references to readership and support, not only was the *Canard* careful to keep the advertising messages within its jokes clear, it also doubled humorous treatments of the subject with unequivocally straight ones.

Doing politics straight was another matter. The *Canard* deliberately eschewed irony in two basic situations. The first involved direct recommendations, as when the paper greeted the Russian revolution of early 1917 with "Long Live Liberated Russia," and the following advice: "And this is no joke: Hey you! The Germans! It's your turn!"[6] In this instance, the putative audience almost certainly did not hear the suggestion. This was much less the case, however, in 1919, when the *Canard* reminded veterans to register to vote; and it certainly was not the case when the weekly explained, in a few direct words, the relationship between the National Bloc, the Ruhr occupation, and the country's monetary difficulties. Similarly lacking in any hint of irony were the weekly's armistice salutes to the heroic soldiers of the trenches and U.S. President Wilson.

This first type of direct discourse, born of optimism, became scarcer as the postwar decade advanced. Little of it was in evidence by 1928. More frequent by that time was the direct discourse of indignation. An early example was an article, in June 1920, by Roland Dorgelès stigmatizing the treatment of striking railroad workers.[7] The reliance on indignation over irony was a personal preference; Dorgelès, only an occasional contributor anyway, rarely chose to channel his anger into one of the *Canard*'s ironic modes. The same could be said of Pierre Scize, a regular voice in the later years of the decade. Scize made of indignation a specialty; he used it in reference to the horrors of war (past or threatened) but extended it to French xenophobia, American avarice, and the persecutions of movie stars and anarchists. It was largely Scize's prose that made the weekly increasingly indignant as the twenties advanced. The angry former soldier occasionally dipped into irony, but he was scarcely more attracted to it than Dorgelès had been. In its place, Scize used powerful language and dramatic imagery, piling up adjectives or verbs as the war had piled up corpses.[8]

But if Scize was echoed by de la Fouchardière in his radical, though pessimistic, antimilitarism, he was not in his righteous fury. De la Fouchardière and Scize, the two most distinctive voices of the postwar *Canard*, mimicked that other opposition, between antiphrasis and direct discourse. By using Bicard, de la Fouchardière created an equivalent to ironic antiphrasis.

Instead of stating the opposite, one stated the truth, but put it into the mouth of a ne'er-do-well—that is, in a context that suggested unreliability. The similarity of de la Fouchardière's political positions and Scize's meant that the direct discourse of indignation could carry much the same ideological freight as that of antiphrasis. Declamatory prose à la Scize and Dorgelès was used not so much to make new points as to underline positions already copiously displayed in the *Canard*'s more humorous columns. Only in the relative shift between two nonironic modes, enthusiastic activism and anger and ill-concealed frustration, can one see a gradual disillusionment with the shape of the postwar world. Though there is anger in de la Fouchardière and French *joie de vivre* in Scize's defense of Charlie Chaplin, the difference between the mocking and the indignant schools of criticism came out clearly with the profanation of the unknown soldier: an angry rattling skeleton versus a couple having sex beneath a tree.

The play of antiphrasis and direct discourse permitted the *Canard* to have it both ways: on the one hand to mock everything and on the other to hammer home key points, to appeal to its readers' anger as well as to their sense of humor. And yet, even in the later years of the 1920s, indignation and other forms of direct discourse were only counterpoints to the weekly's dominant antiphrasis. The messages of antiphrasis went further than the initial justification for it—that is, that the world of journalism was one of lying, as were virtually all things touched by the war. Speaking through opposites was a school of cynicism and of careful reading. How could one not, when reading one's regular newspaper or any other text, ask oneself if perhaps, this time too, the truth lay not closer to the opposite than to the normal sense of the words: that peace conferences were about war, that price-control boards were dedicated to raising prices, that the Legion of Honor honored the corrupt?

Instability of meaning could not help but create instability in ideas, even in some of the *Canard*'s favorite ideas, and, in general, a culture of doubt and a suspicion of all ideologies. The constant shifting back and forth between antiphrasis and directness, between humor and seriousness, gave the *Canard* considerable political flexibility. On most subjects, the *Canard* developed, when not full-blown contradictions, at least considerable tensions between different views of the same problems. Antimilitarism contended with patriotic support for the *poilus;* the front-soldiers-versus-civilians distinction, so dear to the right, rubbed shoulders with the rich-versus-poor contrast traditional on the left; colonial peoples were naked savages or victims of European imperialism; high prices were the result of the war or of the greed of unscrupulous merchants. The play of antiphrasis and its antithesis facilitated these political gymnastics and in a sense represented them on the level of discourse: two potential readings for every sentence, two potential approaches to any problem.

PARODY

Effects that were in many ways concordant were created by the *Canard's* next most common device: parody or pastiche. Parody could function as a form of irony, disqualifying an argument by restating it in terms that made it seem ridiculous, as in the idea that the benefits of a delayed armistice were worth a few thousand more French cadavers.[9] Such irony tended to spill over into antiphrasis; if the proposition was ridiculous as it stood, then its contrary was true.

But pastiche transcended irony to become a leading *Canard* game. The echoes-of-*L'Intran* contest made *pasticheurs* of the weekly's readers. What better way both to ridicule the originals and unmask their structure? Making counterfeiters of readers cannot have raised the reputation of most journalists in their eyes either. The *Canard* organized other such contests, like one in 1927 that asked readers to come up with anti-German jokes at least as stupid as those of the journalist Louis Forrest of *Le Matin*.[10] These pastiches, while they did not ignore style completely, were essentially of narrative structure. But the *Canard* also challenged its readers with closer comparisons between real and fake. In January 1919, the weekly started a contest that consisted of choosing—between two texts with the same byline—which was real and which the *Canard* pastiche. After analyzing the eight pairs of texts, none of the several thousand *Canard* entrants got a perfect score, and prizes went to those with the greatest number of correct answers.[11] Parody exposes and discredits ideological writing. In the pages of the *Canard* it also strengthened the instability of truth and falsehood since, in addition to real letters to the editor, the weekly felt free to include phony, parodic ones—just as it presented phony, parodic advertisements.[12]

Parody and pastiche were especially important when it came to countering journalistic opponents who were skilled polemicists, like those of the *Action Française*. The fourth page of the *Canard's* issue of July 11, 1923, contained a mock first page of the royalist daily, with parodies of the styles and lines of argument of its better-known journalists. The best of these was probably Léon Daudet, who made a specialty of colorful insults. A *Canard* journalist pretended to cover one of Daudet's speeches. His trick came in arguing that, because of the large crowd, many members of the audience could hear only snatches of the talk. The result consists of characteristic

Daudeticisms without the connecting arguments: ". . . Bastards! Traitors! Bandits! Caillaux! . . . residues of dirt buckets! . . . the sewers where the red-sashed pigs eat . . . overflows of impurities! disgusting personages . . . The Slut . . . stinking filth! . . . garbage . . . sellouts!" "The Slut" *(la gueuse)* referred to Marianne and the Republic, Caillaux to the Radical politician. After such treatment there was no need to underscore the nature of the royalist journalist's imagery.[13]

REPETITION AND STEREOTYPE

Parody is a form of repetition since the copy always evokes the model. "To repeat is pleasing" is an ancient rhetorical dictum;[14] and the *Canard* made extensive use of this traditional comic technique, filling its pages with repeating visual and verbal gags. But the *Canard* also exploited a kind of repetition/recollection that went beyond humor. Earlier events (whether actual happenings or merely journalistic, textual ones) were called up so that later ones became echoes of them. We saw this with the rewriting of later wars using the imagery of the Great War, with the treatments of Franco-German crises as replays of the war.

Besides reminding readers of earlier events, such presentations of current events as redux gave the sense that nothing really changed in the world, that history itself was a cycle of human follies, as Bicard expressed it in his comparison with the Hundred Years' War. The clearest exploitation came when the *Canard* predicted for the new year a repetition of the events of the past one, with just a few names changed. Here we go again, the *Canard* effectively argued when, for example, in 1927 Pedro drew a cartoon of the Radical politician Albert Sarraut putting up the old poster of the Bolshevik as the man-with-the-knife-between-his-teeth.[15] The fiction of the repeated action (the poster was not reused) underlined the repetition of political tactics since Sarraut was reusing the red scare for the elections of 1928. This sense of structural repetition under the seeming novelty of events went well with the weekly's skepticism about revolutionary change.

The *Canard* matched the repetitions of politicians with its own repeating motifs, like the duck with gallows. Not only was the weekly repeating its device to comic effect, it was also repeating its analysis of the situation over a span of years. The gallows and its related verbal references to hoisting the *mercantis* above the ground, taken together, were one of the *Canard*'s many topoi, those concentrations of verbal or visual signifiers (or both) characteristic of the weekly. When such topoi exploit preexisting caricatures of ethnic, national, or professional groups we call them stereotypes.

As with other forms of mockery, the primary question with stereotypes was who was being typed, for though the *Canard* stereotyped many it did not type-cast everyone. The *Canard* exploited conventional unflattering images (visual and otherwise) of Auvergnats and sub-Saharan Africans, of the English and Americans, of Italians and Spaniards, of Muslims and Jews. With the English and Americans the images were largely of tourists; with Spaniards and Italians, directed toward the leaders and policies of their reactionary political regimes. Anti-Semitic comments were directed largely at politicians whom the *Canard* disliked for other reasons, like Mandel and Maurice Bokanowski. Muslims were associated with traditional fantasies of veiled women and harems. Sub-Saharan Africans were painted as cannibals, but the racism of the association was countered by its conscious reversal to white racists, while both antiblack and anti-Muslim stereotypes were paired with conscious anti-imperialism and antiracism. Here, the *Canard*'s declared antiphrastic irony also came into play. The paper was often in a position, as with the mock recruiting poster and its veiled, seminude woman, where it could be seen as either exploiting or mocking the conventional image, or both.

Who was left out? The Germans—though the Teutonic people played a large role in French considerations, even after the war, as well as in the pages of the *Canard*. The kaiser and kronprinz were attacked early in the history of the weekly, but not for national traits.[16] And the wartime ducks of interior pages sported spiked helmets, but the national enemy, and occupier of much of France, was left remarkably free of ridicule both during the war and after. If, for the 1920s, the sparing of the neighbor to the east reflected a general tendency in the leftist press, wartime restraint was much more distinctive. Such restraint contrasted sharply with the war culture Stéphane Audoin-Rouzeau and Annette Becker have characterized as "pregnant with hatred of the enemy."[17] Not that the *Canard* could entirely pass up the humorous exploitation of stereotypical aspects of German culture. But it did so in ways that cast more ridicule on France than on the people across the Rhine. For example, French expectations of riches from Germany or fantasies of conquest were mocked through references to beer and sausages.

The same was largely true of language games. The *Canard* loved to play with foreign languages and accents. "Parizzi la Sortia" (*par ici la sortie,* this way to the exit) graced the wall in an anti-Fascist cartoon.[18] English versions of French (and French attempts to learn English) were also subjects for humor.[19] German-accented French was typically used not against citizens of the Empire or the Weimar Republic but to signify French people of either Alsatian or Jewish origin.[20] And aside from the cracks about "überkhranenburrer" and the similar "Deutschekranenburrergesellshaft" [sic, for the missing *c*], the *Canard* avoided using against the national enemy the humorous possibilities (for non-Germans) of the modes of word formation of the German language. Instead, it even mocked French critiques of German. More often, the satirical periodical used real German to mock French chauvinism. When the French press honored the visiting Albert Einstein by trying to obfuscate his German nationality, the *Canard* labeled a phony illustration "Grosse Begeisterung auf dem Estbahnhof" (Great enthusiasm at the Gare de l'Est).[21] When a Parisian theater coyly advertised an operetta as the *Chanson de l'Amour,* the weekly added, "Why not say that the operetta is called Das Dreimadelhaus, musik fabriket mit einigen Melodien von Fr. Schubert? Es ist nicht schlecht das dieses Theater eine deutsch Operette spielt [It is not bad that this theater is performing a German operetta]."[22]

Germans were spared in order not to encourage French xenophobia in this area, where it had been most stimulated both by the real actions of Germans and by the anti-German propaganda of the war. By the same token, the *Canard* largely spared the Soviets, despite its lack of sympathy with Bolshevism. One of the readers who supported Jean Armand's attack on *Canard* stereotypes accused his favorite paper of working against its general purpose of improving understanding between peoples. Yet the easy ride given the Germans would seem to have been motivated by precisely such scruples. Sparing the Germans was simply the strongest example of the *Canard*'s attempt to keep its exploitation of stereotypes from clashing with its political goals—here, the countering of wartime hysteria and its postwar sequels.

The one area where stereotypes openly clashed with politics was Africa. Residual racism was clearly one reason. But if we look at the *Canard*'s antiblack jokes in the context of its German policy, then attention shifts to a relative blindness to the role of racism in French society. The weekly simply did not see this racism as decisive, unlike, for example, hatred for the Germans. Where racism was considered to be a significant factor in society, in the United States, it was aggressively pilloried. In other words, the *Canard* did not see racism as crucial to French colonialism, which, for the weekly, was more a matter of greed for profits and hypocrisy in regard to self-determination.

Did the *Canard* succeed in creating a nonxenophobic world of stereotypes? If one assumes that any reinforcement of such conventions leads to cultural chauvinism, certainly not. But the weekly attacked French smugness regularly and devastatingly. The result is a clear sense of French difference and French identity. The *Canard*'s largely good-natured play with foreignness kept its hostility to aggressive nationalism from turning into either cosmopolitanism or a homogenizing internationalism. This bird loved France for all its special qualities, from its wines and cheeses to its literature and language, but it could still laugh as much about its own country as about foreigners.

Economic stereotypes told their own story, which, if it was not internationalist, was at least antinationalist. The weekly, which was happy to stigmatize French merchants on the subject of the high cost of living, refused to play the same game with speculators on the subject of France's monetary difficulties. The tension between scapegoating and structural approaches ran through the *Canard*'s economic discourses—except in regard to speculators. For the paper, speculators were French as often as foreign, and they acted simply on the economic realities produced by the politicians. True, speculators were not as concrete as mom-and-pop neighborhood grocers or coal sellers. But that had not stopped the *Canard* from going after the wholesalers at Les Halles.

The French right made a clear distinction between what a leftist could have conceived as merely two different types of exploiters. For the rightist and conformist press, shopkeepers and businessmen generally were worthy pillars of the community, while largely foreign speculators were at the root of France's postwar currency problems. By refusing to go after speculators, the *Canard* was refusing to blame foreigners. Partly, it did so in order to better vilify the National Bloc politicians. Partly too, it was responding to an analysis of the war and its effects. But these reasons alone would not have dictated the hands-off-the-speculators policy. This refusal to scapegoat told the French to accept responsibility for their own messes.

FROM TOPOS TO LANGUAGE

Stereotypes are like pretilled ground. A relatively small allusion can call up a preexisting set of images, associations, and prejudices. The stereotype sets off a conditioned response. The *Canard* created its own conditioned responses through its topoi. These could be exclusively verbal, like the next last war, or largely visual, like the ubiquitous ducks. The gallows-for-*mercantis* topos existed in a space between the verbal and the visual since it could be indicated by a variety of either verbal or visual elements or combinations of both. The *Canard* also took verbal phrases and made them visual in comically literal ways, as with *bourrage de crâne* and *cherrer dans les bégonias.*

In all these cases, by laying out the associations in its pages, the weekly created signifiers that were both complex and subject to formal variation yet possessed of great semiotic economy. Beyond the literal (or most obvious figurative) meaning of the topos/sign lay a potentially limitless set of signifieds. The topos—be it, for example, the next last war or *bourrage de crâne*—makes a specific point—that war will come again or that newspapers are full of lies. But these points become points of view, inviting the reader to examine large areas of French life—international relations or the world of written expression—in terms of the *Canard*'s conclusions. And through its association with the paper, every topos also signified Canardicity, reminding the reader that he or she was reading a special newspaper. It is this Canardicity that fans sought to re-create in their club meetings.

Besides being semiotically dense, these topoi are generally also funny. Part of their humor comes from their own internal games, but part also derives from the pleasure of recognition (itself dependent on repetition). The *Canard* topoi, and foremost of these the web-footed mascot, greet the reader like old friends—a role they still play today. Taken together the topoi form a lexicon of complex signs inviting complicity in decipherment and in the possession of a shared, specialized language.

Language, lexicon: these terms, which can be understood in either narrowly linguistic or broad semiotic terms, tell us that the *Canard* created a system (or a set of codes or a language). The topoi were a species of vocabulary whose verbal/visual ambidexterity was announced in the verbal/visual pun of the *canard* as duck/falsehood/newspaper. Antiphrasis, parody, repetition served as syntax and grammar, acting with the games of recognition involved in the topoi to give a ludic quality to the whole paper.

The weekly mixed preexisting (and hence to some degree conformist) elements with its own ideologically motivated creations in a way that linked humor with politics. Some of the *Canard*'s topoi, like the next last war, were essentially homegrown, but even this one depends on the preceding investment in the idea of the last war. *Bourrage de crâne*, by contrast, was not invented in-house, though the weekly carried it to new lengths through visualization and through its contests. Stereotypes came ready-made but could still be used economically, as in the insertion of references to mandolins in discussions of Italian politics.

A favorite trick of the *Canard*'s was to take its weapons from its adversaries in a combination of parody and semiotic hijacking. *L'Intransigeant* was the weekly's best source here, providing both the leitmotif of civilization as high-tech warfare and the tears of patriotic emotion. In the hands of the satirical weekly, "civilization" was turned from a signifier of French superiority to one of brutality and hypocrisy. Patriotic lacrimation was diverted from its primitive, mimetic role of emotional evocation to the more sophisticated one of symbol, both of the whole game of emotional transubstantiation that nourished civilian belligerence and of the exploitation of this process by the press. When the other side had developed a highly successful image—the Bolshevik as the-man-with-the-knife-between-his-teeth—the *Canard* first ridiculed it and then used it as a signifier of red baiting. The ring-in-the-nose forms part of the racist imagery of savagery, but the satirical periodical turned it into a negative marker of French imperialism. In almost all these cases, humor is not something added to politics; the two are consubstantial in the formation of the topos itself.

Whatever their origin, the *Canard* topoi possessed the common formal property of semiotic economy. A word or three, a few lines of a drawing, could call up a major line of argument—in an article devoted to another topic. It was thus easy for *Canard* writers not only to evoke humor with seriousness (or the reverse) but also to drop in allusions to an enormous variety of subjects or even to invoke the *Canard* point of view with great brevity while pretending to be merely recounting events. When added to the paper's mixture of materials, these devices tended to imbricate the paper's discussions of different topics with each other. The topoi, winking at the reader at any place from the headlines of page 1 to the "Petite correspondance" on page 4, provided a density and consistency of ideological reference that transcended the weekly's contradictions, tensions, and variations.

THE *CANARD*'S WORLD

In October 1924, Guilac contributed to the fourth page of the weekly a "modern alphabet for use by little ducks." With each letter came a word and picture: for example, Adultery, Curnonsky, *Double décime,* Elector, Gyraldose, Herriot, Joffre, *Mercanti,* Poincaré, Urodonal, Vouvray, Whip. The accompanying pictures added gentle humor or derision: Marshal Joffre was shown sleeping, the elector was a pear (for *poire,* sucker). The politicians need no introduction (nor does the *mercanti*); *double décime* was Poincaré's infamous 20 percent surtax; Urodonal and Gyraldose were patent medicines advertised heavily in the mass press (and satirized by the *Canard*). Whip was a *Canard* pen name used largely for silly articles. The name Curnonsky appeared only occasionally in the weekly, but this was the nickname of Maurice Edmond Sailland, a famous gourmet and wit.[23] The alphabet is a representative sampling of the themes and topics of the *Canard.* Adultery gets first place through spelling, but it has earned its spot through its ubiquity in the *Canard,* where it was the most frequent nonpolitical source of gags and humorous stories. Politicians and patent medicines speak to the weekly's chosen targets. Curnonsky and the more familiar Vouvray speak to another, and crucial, element in the *Canard*'s mix: *joie de vivre.*

Even adultery was not taken tragically in the weekly's pages. Bicard, for one, took his wife's affair with Officer Balloche in stride. Though marital jealousy was part of the standard adultery plot, the *Canard* was perfectly willing to celebrate its opposite. One story told, without any sign of disapproval, of a fellow who was pleased to discover his wife's adultery. Now, at last, he had something to reply to his mother-in-law's annoying speeches on the virtues of her daughter. The weekly reported the case of two Germans who swapped wives on a monthly basis. The journalist described it as an ideal arrangement, free of jealousy and hypocrisy, but the two burghers were convicted of immorality and sent to prison. After the trial, or so the *Canard* imagined, "the presiding magistrate snuck off for an assignation with the wife of the first assessor, while the assessor slipped into the boudoir of the wife of the presiding magistrate."[24]

Even during the war, this pleasure-loving periodical never celebrated the "austerity" that Jean-Louis Robert identified as the opposite of profiteering in his survey of wartime caricatures. One has but to remember the *Canard* cartoon of the "bad Frenchman" who had eaten an éclair. It is difficult to tell who is more ridiculous, the gluttonous victim or the hateful crowd that is pursuing him. Not only did the *Canard* feel it had a right to its Vouvray, but the weekly protested (without irony) against the suppression of brandies. The profiteer was, for the weekly, but a subgroup of the *embusqué,* and his opposite was the soldier or (as in the story of the "good landlord") the manual worker. The *Canard*'s Rabelaisian treatment of alcohol during and after the war contrasts sharply not only with the moralism of the French right but also with that of prewar satirical anarchist periodicals like *L'Assiette au Beurre.*[25]

Joie de vivre also linked up to another of the *Canard*'s predilections: its corporality. From its cheerful sensualism and sexual humor through its evocations of cannibalism to the use of weight and thinness as metaphors for wealth and poverty, the *Canard* reduced many social issues to the measure of the human body. Corporality was highlighted by the war, from the bodies of the dead and wounded to the alimentary restrictions on civilians (though these were milder in France than among its enemies).[26] But the *Canard* tended either to downplay such manifestations or, as with the tears of *L'Intran,* to hijack them for its own antimilitarist purposes.

Joie de vivre as a characteristic element of the *Canard* ideology sheds a new light on the weekly's humor and makes it more than sugar coating on a political pill. The enjoyment of humor is a right, the laugh a political act. Without humor and *joie de vivre* the *Canard*'s ideological universe would be grim indeed. The war had been horrible; the armed peace that followed it was no picnic; worse still, a next last conflict was only a matter of time. Newspapers were dishonest, politicians were more or less corrupt, and the rich got the Legion of Honor.

The decision of the *Canard* to also function as a humor periodical for adults had political effects. The exploitation of sex seems to have been a requirement for any adult humor periodical in the France of these years. But when compared with the sexual innuendo and soft-core pornography of many of its competitors *(La Baïonnette, Fantasio, Le Sourire, Le Rire, Le Ruy Blas)*, the *Canard* was relatively chaste. The *Canard*'s use of sexual material was supported by ideological messages on a variety of levels that gave political meaning to the pursuit of pleasure.

The *Canard* was a leftist paper; and for most leftists social injustice was a normal part of the landscape. Leftism projects a better future world, if not through revolution then at least through major reforms and a transformation of society. While the *Canard* was not unsympathetic to attempts to bring more justice into the world, it was highly skeptical of any project that promised more than the most gradual improvements in French society—a skepticism linked to its profound distrust of authority.

In the world-view of the *Canard*, the combination of humor and *joie de vivre*, never overshadowed by the anger of a Dorgelès or a Scize, replaced the eschatological hope in the revolution, socialism, or the new society. Where others (for example, communists) balanced a bleak view of society with utopian politics, the satirical weekly countered it with an appeal to a life outside politics. But was not such apoliticism, such escapism, then essentially reactionary, distracting its readers from the need for social change? The answer is a bit more complicated. The *Canard*'s humor and celebration of life stand in a complex relationship to both the war and the traditions of French politics.

Léon Daudet, reactionary and *Canard* target, was also a well-known gourmet and bon vivant. But in the hands of Daudet and other royalists the pleasures of French life became arguments for xenophobic nationalism in an essentially defensive conception.[27] For the *Canard* it was otherwise—a limitation on the power of government and a counterweight to war.

As a celebration of life and a French sensuality, the weekly's *joie de vivre* also supported (and was supported by) its anticlericalism. Unconvinced by revolutionary eschatologies, the *Canard* had no sympathy for more traditional ones. *Carpe diem* replaced evangelical as much as utopian hope. But the weekly's consistent anticlericalism seemed to run against the currents of French history. Jacqueline Lalouette, Jay Winter, and René Rémond have all stressed the fact that the war produced both a revival of religious activity and a decline in the Third Republic's traditional anticlericalism. The *Canard* not only opposed this result of the war but maintained its antireligious stance after the conflict, in a society in which anticlericalism was becoming increasingly marginalized. In fact, the aggressive mockery of the Abrahamic religions remains today one of the weekly's most visible archaisms (or fidelities, depending on one's point of view).[28]

But echoes in the paper of the pre-World War I French ideological environment did not mean that the war had not also colored the *Canard*'s anticlericalism. Missing in the weekly's attacks on the Church was the alternate faith that had been so important to anti-Catholics before the war, the faith in science and progress. Despite an occasional comment in favor of a Madame Curie, the *Canard* more often saw in science the perfection of humans' ability to massacre each other, whether this was in the topos of civilization-as-high-tech-warfare, developed for the Rif war, or the dystopian visions of the next last war. Better to celebrate the invention of Camembert![29] The weekly's postwar disillusionment with Wilsonism only reinforced its skepticism, just as U.S. prohibition led it to emphasize the celebration of alcohol. *Joie de vivre* also distinguished the *Canard*'s view from that of Georges Duhamel in his prize-winning *Civilisation.* While the weekly agreed with the physician-author's linkage of civilization and modern warfare, its never echoed Duhamel's conclusion: "I hate the twentieth century, as I hate this rotten Europe, and the whole world over which this wretched Europe has spread out like a grease stain."[30] Satirist that it was, the *Canard* was never that pessimistic. Politically, the difference is important since one cannot, for example, defend democracy without at least some sense of hope.

This anticlericalism also related to the weekly's implicit antitotalitarianism. The *Canard*'s attack on the absolute as a category and a basis for politics (evidenced as much in its raillery as in its specific political or ideological allergies) fundamentally undercut communism (which as François Furet has shown based much of its appeal on this thirst for the absolute)[31] as much as it undercut fascism, and in this way too the *Canard* contributed to the survival of democratic values. The weekly's anticlericalism was more than just a position in French politics; it was nourished by a fundamental antireligiousness, a hostility to ideological absolutism, that made it incompatible with the generally anticlerical but ideologically absolutist Communist movement.

Serge Berstein has defined the "republican tradition" after the Dreyfus Affair in the following way: henceforth a "republican" was not just a defender of elective government but "a convinced believer in the preponderance of parliament in [political] institutions, a defender of the rights of the individual against *raison d'état,* a determined secularist hostile to any Church influence in society or the state, a man particularly suspicious of established authorities, especially of the judiciary and the army."[32]

The *Canard* certainly followed this "republican" tradition. But it effectively updated it for postwar France, helping to give it a new lease on life. The *Canard* showed a "republican" hostility to a strengthened executive in its attacks on Poincaré and his decree-laws. In this sense the weekly stood for parliamentary preponderance. But distinguishing the *Canard* from the prewar republican tradition was the satirical newspaper's tendency to include the parliament (both Senate and Chamber of Deputies) in its global condemnation of French political institutions.

Such antiparliamentarism appeared to borrow from the French right, large segments of which targeted the elected assemblies from prewar Boulangism to the antiparliamentary riots of February 6, 1934. The *Canard's* antiparliamentarism drew on a humor and skepticism that spared no political institutions. It can be said to have fortified the lack of respect for the Chamber and Senate, which grew in France as postwar governments struggled with the nation's problems. But, unlike the right's attack on parliament, which sought to substitute other authorities—whether Church, army, or newly empowered executive—the *Canard*'s was directed against all authority, including political authority. The weekly's ideological ambidexterity helped to bring together the earlier republican tradition with its newer version.

The *Canard*'s celebrations of sensuality countered the discourses of French conservatives, just as its linking of lust and aggression exposed the sexist underside of militarism. Yet the *Canard* was mockingly ambivalent on the subject of woman's suffrage; and the sexism of the weekly's *joie de vivre* (which extended to belittling rape) reinforced that part of the republican tradition that denied women the vote in interwar France. The *Canard* contributed in its own way to what Margaret and Patrice Higonnet call "the double helix," that system for leaving power relations between men and women intact while modifying so much else.[33]

We saw that the *Canard,* directed by a man who never fought, acted as a combatants' and then a veterans' paper, exploiting the contrast between *poilus* and *embusqués.* This was one of its most important additions to the prewar republican tradition. The *Canard* distinguished its pro-veterans pitch by tracing its boundaries differently from the way they were drawn by the right. Within the military, the *Canard* separated combat soldiers not just from civilians and support troops but also from the generals and most higher officers. These officers bore much of the blame for the deaths of the *poilus,* whether in combat or by firing squad.

Pro-veteran and antiparliamentary: that would almost be a classic definition of the fascism, and particularly the French fascism, of the 1920s. Yet despite the distinguished French intellectual pedigree in modern authoritarianism and the existence of protofascist movements before the war, fascism just did not "take" in France. Though larger questions of social stability were clearly important, it is also true that French fascism kept butting its head against well-engrained republican prejudices: against authority and against dictatorship. Certainly, Vichy's antecedents were largely homegrown. But reading the interwar years through the lens of 1940 obscures the fact that it took military collapse, foreign conquest, and considerable political deception for Vichy to come to pass. Interwar France was (and twentieth-century France remained) a fundamentally democratic society (in a way that neither Germany nor Italy nor Spain—not to mention Eastern Europe—was). How did this democracy survive (intellectually, that is) the war and its devastation? The *Canard* gave one answer: by taking antiauthoritarian and democratic elements from its traditions and updating and refurbishing them for war and postwar conditions while serving them in a distinctively French sauce. And this last point is crucial too since the *Canard*'s discourses left little room for its opponents to turn national pride against its arguments.

By taking the potentially rightist currents of antiparliamentarism (or hostility to politicians) and of appeal to the fighting men and integrating them into a new antiauthoritarian version of the republican tradition, the *Canard* stole thunder from the new radical right. And if we argue, as I think we must, that fascism, despite its antecedents, was essentially a product of the Great War, then the *Canard* was acting here too against the pernicious consequences of the conflict.

Humor and *joie de vivre* represented a reserved space outside of politics. The Guilac cartoon that appeared in the middle of the parliamentary crisis of Easter 1925 showed French men and women ignoring politics and indulging in the pleasures of springtime, from kissing and drinking wine to reading their favorite newspaper. This was neither a leftist nor a rightist response to the combined parliamentary and monetary crisis. By reminding its readers that there was more to life than politics, the *Canard* argued against letting politics become a religion and against its invasion of all of life—that is, against totalitarianism.

Totalitarianism was not a consciously debated idea in the weekly of the twenties; it preferred to remain conceptually in the more familiar terrain of authority and dictatorship. But the *Canard* was quick to stigmatize some of the impulses of Mussolini's Italy that in hindsight portend later horrors. The 1923 cartoon that featured the playful "Parizzi la Sortia" bore the title "In the Paradise of Fascism." It showed a group of experts, accompanied by a *carabiniere,* measuring two groups of naked adults, men on the right and women on the left. To our eyes, the scene might conjure up images of inmates of an extermination camp—except that the two groups are discreetly ogling each other. Guilac is having fun with sex, but he is also commenting on current events. A long text in the cartoon explains that a Fascist deputy has just sponsored a law requiring couples intending to marry to prove that they have furnished each other with medical certificates of health: "The future married are thus obliged to submit themselves to a veritable draft physical," and the legend of the cartoon reads, "Matrimonial Draft Physical."[34] This clever idea allowed the mixing of the nudity of such physicals with the erotic potential of putting men and women together. Guilac's matrimonial draft physical linked the totalitarian idea of regulating marriages (for the good of the race, as one used to put it) to its origin and ultimate justification: total war. That the resulting vision, never intended as a literal representation of reality, looked like later forms of totalitarianism only testifies to the premonitory power of satire.

WAR AND MEMORY

A potentially universalizing derisive humor thus works against totalitarianism. What is its relationship to war? For the philosopher Alain, whose suspicions of authority resembled those of the *Canard,* the counter to the spirit of war and heroism was that of the fable, especially those of La Fontaine, with their disrespect for authority. "The person who has understood that will estimate more highly that old troublemaking spirit that the fable has always resurrected against the epic. And the Great War could not fail to bring forth a work worthy of Rabelais, of La Fontaine, and of Voltaire in its insolent raillery."[35] Was the philosopher of radicalism referring to the *Canard*? No other referents come to mind; and our weekly, clearly in the spirit of Rabelais and Voltaire, also used an animal character, though it did so far differently than animal fables did. If the *Canard*'s derisive humor and its Rabelaisian love of life emerged like Hegelian antitheses from the heroic seriousness and death of the war, their incorporation into the politics of peacetime served as antidotes to the continuation of the spirit of Mars. The praise of alcohol also set the *Canard* against the moralizing natalist master narratives that, as Mary Louise Roberts has shown, were crucial to French moral rearmament after the war.[36]

Humor and pleasure were also an antidote to the continuation of the militarist spirit through memory. Memory elicited complex responses from the *Canard.* Appropriate mourning, but also truth telling and a continuation of wartime battles against *bourrage,* memory was also understanding the war through is effects, financial and otherwise. Most radical was the weekly's attack on memory and the cult of commemoration. Much of what the *Canard* wrote after the war could be seen as countercommemoration, even anticommemoration. Memory, this bird seemed to argue, far from being a duty, was a danger. Whether on battlefields or movie screens it was better to cultivate life than the memory of death. The themes of cannibalism and resurrection even set memory against respect for the dead. The paper presented *joie de vivre* as an alternative to participation in patriotic rituals, from the armistice celebration to the cult of the unknown soldier. About such rituals Alain's advice was do not go, do not participate.[37] The *Canard* added suggestions of what else French men and women could do with their free time. *Joie de vivre* worked, in this way, not just against the spirit of war but also against that emphasis on politics as spectacle that is a major characteristic of fascism and other forms of totalitarianism.

Is not remembering the horrors of war key to preventing the next last one? Samuel Hynes quotes a young Briton nourished on pacifism: "Even in our Anti-War campaigns of the early thirties we were half in love with the horrors which we cried out against, and, as a boy, I can remember murmuring the name 'Passchendaele' in an ecstasy of excitement and regret." It may well be that Hynes is right, that "every new generation will respond anew to war's great seduction, [. . .] to the chance to be where the danger is."[38] But at least the *Canard's joie de vivre* attempted to replace this seduction with an alternate model of masculinity.

Remember/forget is a fundamental duality when confronting the horrors of the past century. The weekly's strong (though not consistent) call for forgetting was not the abandonment of a moral imperative in favor of a kind of laziness. It was part of a larger attempt to escape from a cycle of madness. One need not endorse this position to see that it represents a radical critique—even more radical, for example, than that developed by Tzvetan

Todorov in his *Les abus de la mémoire* or that of Walter Benjamin (as interpreted by Martin Jay)—of an increasingly dominant cultural politics of commemoration and memory.[39] It also seems inescapable that this politics of commemorative museums (which the *Canard* also pilloried) had its origins in the reaction to the First World War. Our first modern mass slaughter brought out our first modern mass commemorations and set the conditions for our politics of memory. Here again, the *Canard* penetrated to the essence of the war's effects on society and sought to counter them.

The *Canard*'s name underlined its justification of its position as a response to the climate of patriotic mendacity that surrounded the war. But lack of honesty was also a problem of representation—how does one describe the horrors of modern industrial war? The *Canard*'s solution of using satire and humor exploited this gap between representation and reality. On one level, the weekly's strategies were truth telling. But on another, they, too, avoided conveying the unvarnished reality of war. If humor as a reaction to unprecedented tragedy may seem a contradiction, it is also a form of nonrepresentation or of deflected representation of this tragedy. The *Canard* was modern in its focus on the modalities of representation. But it was also modern in its suspicion of those representations that concretize memory. Against the prevailing discourses, which were soaked in the blood of past and future wars, the *Canard* offered humor and *joie de vivre* as antidotes.

Jay Winter's point is well taken: even the modernists of the war and postwar often readapted traditional forms.[40] Certainly, the *Canard* continued a long tradition of French political satire. But it did so not by facing backward as in mourning. This journalistic bird faced forward to the challenges of the future, even and especially when it was indulging in the politics of memory. Its future was not the technomodernism of Modris Eksteins or even the aesthetic modernism of Paul Fussell.[41] It was a modernization of French democratic, antiauthoritarian traditions themselves, revivified through new forms of wit and satire and a highly practical journalistic formula.

Did the *Canard*'s general skepticism, its absence of a positive program, contribute to the collapse of the Third Republic? Did its militant pacifism disarm France in front of the threat of Nazi Germany? Without getting into the weekly's reactions to the crises of the thirties (which need systematic study), one can at least say that the issue comes down to whether one thinks that the causes of the Second World War lie in the inability of the French and British to face down Hitler early on (or to choose between Hitler and Stalin) or, instead, in the failure of all concerned to achieve an effective reconstruction and reconciliation during the 1920s. If one chooses the second explanation, the *Canard*'s positions on reparations, debts, and the League of Nations seem both prescient and ultimately constructive. At the very least the *Canard* sought to preserve its view of humanity in a century whose inhumanity it predicted but feared it could not stop. There is a sense in which the *Canard*'s potentially universalizing skepticism may have reinforced political passivity, just as its characteristic ambivalence could be said to reflect some of the vacillations of French democrats. Judging such positions, however, comes down to deciding whether the century that has just ended suffered from insufficient commitment, or overcommitment, to great political ideologies.[42]

Born of the First World War, the *Canard Enchaîné* survived to become a journalistic institution. Its success was due to its creative formulae but also to its ability to find in the First World War those trends that would shape the twentieth century. It is not a coincidence that the *Canard* has survived a century of wars and totalitarianisms—for it was, from its inception, splendidly adapted to it.

Notes

ABBREVIATIONS

ACE:	Archives du *Canard Enchaîné* (Paris)
AN:	Archives Nationales (Paris)
BDIC:	Bibliothèque de Documentation Internationale Contemporaine (Nanterre)
CE:	*Le Canard Enchaîné*
SHAT:	Service Historique de l'Armée de Terre (Vincennes)

INTRODUCTION: WAR, LIES, AND NEWSPRINT

1. A. des Enganas, "Vive le conseil de guerre!" *CE,* No. 427, 3 September 1924, p. 1.

2. Paul Fussell, *The Great War and Modern Memory* (London: Oxford University Press, 1975).

3. See, for example, Jay Winter, *Sites of Memory, Sites of Mourning: The Great War in European Cultural History* (Cambridge: Cambridge University Press, 1995); Stéphane Audoin-Rouzeau, *L'enfant de l'ennemi 1914–1918* (Paris: Aubier, 1995); Stéphane Audoin-Rouzeau, *La guerre des enfants: Essai d'histoire culturelle* (Paris: Armand Colin, 1993); Stéphane Audoin-Rouzeau and Annette Becker, *14–18 Retrouver la guerre* (Paris: Gallimard, 2000).

4. Pierre Nora, ed., *Les lieux de mémoire,* 3 vols. (Paris: Gallimard, 1984–1997).

5. Patrick H. Hutton, *History as an Art of Memory* (Hanover, N.H.: University Press of New England, 1993); Matt K. Matsuda, *The Memory of the Modern* (New York: Oxford University Press, 1996); Winter, *Sites;* Daniel J. Sherman, "Art, Commerce and the Production of Memory in France after World War I," in John R. Gillis, ed., *Commemorations: The Politics of National Identity* (Princeton, N.J.: Princeton University Press, 1994), pp. 186–211;

Daniel J. Sherman, "Bodies and Names: The Emergence of Commemoration in Interwar France," *American Historical Review* 103 (1998), pp. 443–466; Daniel J. Sherman, *The Construction of Memory in Interwar France* (Chicago: University of Chicago Press, 1999); Jay Winter and Emmanuel Sivan, eds., *War and Remembrance in the Twentieth Century* (Cambridge: Cambridge University Press, 1999); and see Michael Sherry, "Probing the Memory of War," *Chronicle of Higher Education* 46/18 (2000), pp. B4–B6.

6. Michael B. Miller, *Shanghai on the Metro: Spies, Intrigue, and the French between the Wars* (Berkeley: University of California Press, 1994); Charles Rearick, *The French in Love and War: Popular Culture in the Era of the World Wars* (New Haven, Conn.: Yale University Press, 1977).

7. Fussell, *The Great War;* Modris Eksteins, *Rites of Spring: The Great War and the Birth of the Modern Age* (New York: Anchor Books, 1990); Winter, *Sites.*

8. See, for example, Robert Soucy, *French Fascism: The First Wave 1924–1933* (New Haven, Conn.: Yale University Press, 1986); Robert Soucy, *French Fascism: The Second Wave 1933–1939* (New Haven, Conn.: Yale University Press, 1997).

9. See, for example, Jean-François Sirinelli, *Génération intellectuelle: Khâgneux et Normaliens dans l'entre-deux-guerres* (Paris: Fayard, 1988); Jean-François Sirinelli, *Intellectuels et passions françaises: Manifestes et pétitions au XXe siècle* (Paris: Fayard, 1990); Christophe Prochasson, *Les intellectuels, le socialisme et la guerre 1900–1938* (Paris: Editions du Seuil, 1993); Christophe Prochasson and Anne Rasmussen, *Au nom de la patrie, les intellectuels et la première guerre mondiale (1910–1919)* (Paris: Editions la Découverte, 1996).

10. Here I am talking about more than the interplay between image and text that exists in most political cartoons. This study of the *Canard* looks at all kinds of images (both those within and those without traditional editorial cartoons or caricatures) in their interaction with the noniconographic elements in the paper generally. It posits, thus, three semiotic domains: the verbal, the visual, and the one created when both are read together. Its methodology thus differs, for example, from that of Jean-Louis Robert, "The Image of the Profiteer," in Jay Winter and Jean-Louis Robert, eds., *Capital Cities at War: Paris, London, Berlin 1914–1919* (Cambridge, England: Cambridge University Press, 1997), pp. 104–132, which covers some of the same topics. Compare also, for example, the discussion by William H. Sewell Jr., "Language and Practice in Cultural History: Backing Away from the Edge of the Cliff," *French Historical Studies* 21/2 (1998), p. 248.

11. Jonathan Dewald, "Roger Chartier and the Fate of Cultural History," *French Historical Studies* 21/2 (1998), pp. 224–225; William H. Sewell Jr., "The Concept(s) of Culture," in Victoria Bonnell and Lynn Hunt, eds., *Beyond the Cultural Turn* (Berkeley: University of California Press, 1999), pp. 44–58.

12. No attempt is being made to naturalize discourse. Instead discourse is understood heuristically, not as an irreducible level of meaning, still less of

causation. Compare Richard Biernacki, "Method and Metaphor after the New Cultural History," in Bonnell and Hunt, *Beyond*, pp. 62–63.

13. Compare Sewell, "Language and Practice," p. 250.

14. The use of verbal (as opposed to semantic) syntagms, which characterizes much semiotic study of political discourses, is methodologically much more limiting and would be seriously inadequate for the study of an object like the *Canard*.

15. Laurent Martin, *Le Canard Enchaîné ou les fortunes de la vertu: Histoire d'un journal satirique 1915–2000* (Paris: Flammarion, 2001). The tasks Martin assigned to himself in his work did not permit him to undertake the kinds of cultural analysis that are the focus of *War, Memory, and the Politics of Humor.* Aside from differences in scope and topic, there are also differences in point of view. For example, Martin seeks to trace a *Canard* political line, while I emphasize ambiguities, tensions, and contradictions. On the early history of the *Canard*, see also Jean-Jacques Becker, "Les débuts du *Canard Enchaîné*," *L'Histoire*, No. 28 (1980), pp. 81–82. For other bibliography, see Martin, above.

16. Arthur Koestler, *The Act of Creation* (New York: Dell, 1975), pp. 33–42, 95–96.

17. AN F7 13981, " 'Le Canard Enchaîné' (Rapport 1929 complété à 1932)," pp. 9–10; "Sur Maurice Maréchal," in *Documentation*, prepared and provided by the *Canard Enchaîné*, p. 1; ACE, Correspondance, Messageries Hachette to Parmentier, 5 July 1916.

18. Roland Dorgelès, *Au beau temps de la butte* (Paris: Albin Michel, 1963), pp. 23–24; SHAT, 16N 1561, Paris, 10 May 1918; AN F7 13981, " 'Le Canard Enchaîné' (Rapport 1929 complété à 1932)," p. 11; Christian Delporte, *Les crayons de la propagande, dessinateurs et dessin politique sous l'occupation* (Paris: CNRS Editions, 1993), pp. 199–200; Jean Defrasne, *Le pacifisme en France* (Paris: Presses Universitaires de France, 1994), p. 70; H. P. Gassier, "Monsieur Balanant vu par Gassier," *Le Journal*, 18 March 1925, p. 1; H. P. Gassier, "Il neige," *L'Heure*, 6 February 1917, p. 1.

19. AN F7 13981, " 'Le Canard Enchaîné' (Rapport 1929 complété à 1932)," p. 7; Henri Monier, *A baton rompu* (Paris: Editions Pierre Horay, 1953), pp. 23–24, 53–55, 102; Marcel Berger and Paul Allard, *Les secrets de la censure pendant la guerre* (Paris: Editions des Portiques, 1932), p. 86; *CE*, No. 252, 27 April 1921.

20. Claude Bellanger, Jacques Godechot, Pierre Guiral, and Fernand Terrou, *Histoire générale de la presse française*, vol. 3, *De 1871 à 1940* (Paris: Presses Universitaires de France, 1972), pp. 438–439; Berger and Allard, *Les secrets*, pp. 86–94; SHAT, 16N 10, Grand Quartier Général, 2 July 1919, No. 3302, Ordre de Saisie.

21. AN F7 13981, " 'Le Canard Enchaîné' (Rapport 1929 complété à 1932)," pp. 8–9, 29; and see, for example, Bellanger et al., *Histoire*, pp. 3:438–439, and chapter 6 in this book. For mockery of *L'Oeuvre*, see, for example, Rodolphe Bringer, "Curieux effet du cinéma," *CE*, No. 27, 3 January 1917, p. 1.

22. AN F7 13981, " 'Le Canard Enchaîné' (Rapport 1929 complété à 1932)," pp. 16–17, 22; Monier, *A baton*, p. 55; Rodolphe Bringer, "Mes joies," *L'Heure*, 10 February 1917, p. 1.

23. Monier, *A baton*, pp. 55, 100–101; AN F7 13981, " 'Le Canard Enchaîné' (Rapport 1929 complété à 1932)," pp. 15–16, 20–21.

24. Victor Snell, "Les livres," *CE*, No. 114, 25 September 1918, p. 4; Monier, *A baton*, pp. 54–55, 63; AN F7 13981, " 'Le Canard Enchaîné' (Rapport 1929 complété à 1932)," pp. 13–14, 18–20; Jean Norton Cru, *Témoins, essai d'analyse et de critique des souvenirs de combattants édités en français de 1915 à 1928* (1929; reprint, Nancy: Presses Universitaires de Nancy, 1993), p. 456.

25. Monier, *A baton*, p. 54; Dorgelès, *Au beau*, pp. 23–24. See also Micheline Dupray, *Roland Dorgelès, un siècle de vie littéraire* (Paris: Presses de la Renaissance, 1986).

26. Monier, *A baton*, p. 54; Roland Dorgelès, *Portraits sans retouches* (Paris: Albin Michel, 1952), pp. 159–196.

27. See, for example, "Les Journaux et les journalistes," *CE*, No. 7, 15 August 1916, p. 3. On Barbusse, see Philippe Baudorre, *Barbusse, le pourfendeur de la Grande Guerre* (Paris: Flammarion, 1995), and for Vaillant-Couturier, for example, Baudorre, *Barbusse*, pp. 148–150, and Cru, *Témoins*, pp. 625–626.

28. *CE*, No. 302, 12 April 1922, p. 1; *CE*, No. 303, 19 April 1922, p. 1.

29. Monier, *A baton*, pp. 54–55, 92–93; Delporte, *Les crayons*, pp. 198, 202–204; Pedro, "Décoration," *L'Intransigeant*, 8 May 1925, p. 1.

30. AN F7 13981, " 'Le Canard Enchaîné' (Rapport 1929 complété à 1932)," p. 29; "Le Canard Enchaîné," in *Documentation*, prepared and provided by the *Canard Enchaîné*.

31. "Le 'Canard' de nouveau enchaîné," *CE*, No. 201, 5 May 1920, p. 1. The case, if there was one, remains obscure. The *Canard* claimed that its summons was relative to an article it threatened to print (and in effect did print) defending strikes and written by the then-president of the Republic and former socialist Alexandre Millerand. Mme. Marie-Andrée Corcuff of the Direction des Services d'Archives de Paris found no judicial instructions directed against Maréchal for 1920 (personal letter of December 8, 1997). Most likely, the *Canard* was having fun with the government's actions against *L'Humanité* and other leftist periodicals (and a *Canard* journalist, Raymond Lefebvre). See, for example, "Poursuites contre le journal 'L'Humanité,' " *L'Oeuvre*, 30 April 1920, p. 2, and "L'agitation ouvrière, les grèves prennent de l'extension," *L'Oeuvre*, 4 May 1920, p. 1. The author of the police report of 1929 spoke of the *Canard*'s having received a warning on May 25, 1921, about its criticisms of members of the government like André Maginot and Yves Le Trocquer. Certainly the weekly did not relax its attacks on either of these men; AN F7 13981, " 'Le Canard Enchaîné' (Rapport 1929 complété à 1932)," pp. 7–8.

32. *CE*, No. 435, 29 October 1924, p. 1; "Les journaux à 4 sous," *CE*, No. 436, 5 November 1924, p. 2; "A nos lecteurs, Le 'Canard' à 40 centimes," *CE*, No. 448, 26 January 1925, p. 1.

33. Jean Galtier-Boissière, *Mon journal dans la grande pagaïe* (Paris: La Jeune Parque, 1950), p. 48; Jean Galtier-Boissière, "Le panier de crabes: Souvenirs d'un polémiste," *Le Crapouillot,* November 1938, pp. 56–62. See also, for example, ACE, Annual salary summary for 1934; Cru, *Témoins,* pp. 138–139.

34. Monier, *A baton,* p. 56; and see, for example, "Les Canetons," *CE,* No. 318, 2 August 1922, p. 4; "Canetons," *CE,* No. 396, 30 January 1924, p. 4; "Canetons," *CE,* No. 398, 13 February 1924, p. 4.

35. Monier, *A baton,* p. 53.

36. Jean-Galtier Boissière, "Ce qu'on dit du Canard Enchaîné," *CE,* No. 284, 7 December 1921, p. 3.

37. AN F7 13981, " 'Le Canard Enchaîné' (Rapport 1929 complété à 1932)," p. 7; R. Manévy, *Histoire de presse 1914–1939* (Paris: Editions Corréa, 1945), p. 48. On *bourrage de crâne,* see also Stéphane Audoin-Rouzeau, " 'Bourrage de crâne' et information en France en 1914–1918," in Jean-Jacques Becker and Stéphane Audoin-Rouzeau, eds., *Les sociétés européennes et la guerre de 1914–1918* (Nanterre: Publications de l'Université de Nanterre, 1990), pp. 163–174; and Jean-Jacques Becker, *The Great War and the French People,* trans. Arnold Pomerans (New York: St. Martin's Press, 1986), pp. 29–44, which includes a mini-anthology.

38. Dorgelès, *Au beau,* pp. 154–155.

39. See, for example, ibid., p. 261; SHAT, 19N 868, No. 26,204, Pétain to Min. de la Guerre, 23 August 1917; Henri Barbusse, *Le feu, journal d'un escouade* (1916; reprint, Paris: Flammarion, 1965), pp. 64–65; Henri Barbusse, *Clarté* (1919; reprint, Paris: Flammarion, 1978), pp. 204–205; and the texts cited in Jean Norton Cru, *Du témoignage* (Paris: Gallimard, 1930), pp. 159–164.

40. Barbusse, *Le feu,* pp. 327, 374–379. The point is not whether the incidents recounted in these or similar novelistic works are realistic or actually took place but that they form part of a collective representation of the war, especially by former soldiers. The sense that noncombatants will never understand is also expressed by Cru, *Témoins,* p. 226.

41. Dorgelès, *Au beau,* pp. 276–278. Compare Cru, *Témoins,* pp. 41, 108, 128.

42. See, for example, Erich Maria Remarque, *All Quiet on the Western Front,* trans. A. H. Wheen (1929; New York: Fawcett, 1982), pp. 180–181; Helen Zenna Smith, *Not So Quiet* (1930; reprint, New York: Feminist Press, 1989), pp. 30–32; and the nonfiction account in Joanna Bourke, *Dismembering the Male: Men's Bodies, Britain, and the Great War* (Chicago: University of Chicago Press, 1996), p. 21. For a Belgian example, see Cru, *Témoins,* p. 121. For France, see, for example, Pierre Drieu La Rochelle, *La comédie de Charleroi* (1932; reprint, Paris: Gallimard, 1982), p. 48; Joseph Kessel, *L'équipage* (Paris: Gallimard, 1969; text completed in 1923), pp. 93–95; Jean Bernier and Léon Werth quoted and analyzed in Cru, *Témoins,* pp. 575–577, 655, and a discussion of the subject in Cru, *Du témoignage,* pp. 109–112; Evelyne Desbois, "Paroles de soldats, entre images et écrits," *Mots* 24 (1990), pp. 41–42, 48, 51–52; Jean-Jacques Becker, "Préface" to Maurice Genevoix, *Ceux de 14* (Paris:

Omnibus, 1998), p. v; Marilène Patten Henry, *Monumental Accusations: The Monuments aux Morts as Expressions of Popular Resentment* (New York: Peter Lang, 1996), pp. 190, 196–198. Compare Mary Louise Roberts, *Civilization without Sexes: Reconstructing Gender in Postwar France, 1917–1921* (Chicago: University of Chicago Press, 1994), p. 15, and Samuel Hynes, *The Soldiers' Tale: Bearing Witness to Modern War* (New York: Penguin Books, 1997), pp. 72–73.

43. Matsuda, *Memory.*

CHAPTER 1. SATIRE AND CENSORSHIP

1. There were other war-related meanings to which the weekly apparently never made reference. A *canard,* for example, was an instrument used to introduce food into the mouths of soldiers with severe facial wounds; see Sophie Delaporte, *Les gueules cassées, les blessés de la face de la Grande Guerre* (Paris: Editions Noêsis, 1996), p. 62. Another example is the verb *canarder,* which means to fire on someone or something from a covered position (as in a duck hunt). Though it was apparently not used during the first decade of the *Canard,* it has been used in more recent years, in the form of "Canardages," as the title of a multipage column.

2. See, for example, Claude Bellanger et al., *Histoire générale de la presse française,* vol. 3, *De 1871 à 1940* (Paris: Presses Universitaires de France, 1972), p. 424. The connection is made quasi-explicit in a cartoon by H. P. Gassier, "Résurrection," *CE,* No. 1, 8 July 1916, p. 1.

3. See chapter 3 and the introduction.

4. "Re-présentation!" *CE,* No. 1, 8 July 1916, p. 1.

5. See, for example, chapter 3.

6. Jean-Jacques Becker, *La France en guerre, 1914–1918, la grande mutation* (Paris: Editions Complexe, 1988), pp. 70–71.

7. See Christian Delporte, " 'Anastasie': L'imaginaire de la censure dans le dessin satirique (XIXe–XXe siècles)," in Pascal Ory, *La censure en France à l'ère démocratique (1848– . . .)* (Paris: Editions Complexe, 1997), pp. 89–99.

8. H. P. Gassier, "Pour faire un journal en 1915," *CE,* No. 1, 10 September 1915, p. 1.

9. Victor Snell, "De l'utilisation des blancs," *CE,* No. 33, 14 February 1917, p. 1.

10. See, for example, "Sur le nez de la censure," *CE,* No. 28, 10 January 1917, p. 1; "Pouvons-nous laisser lire Jules Verne à nos enfants," *CE,* No. 36, 7 March 1917, p. 3; Bellanger et al., *Histoire,* pp. 3:417–419; Delporte, "'Anastasie,'" p. 94.

11. "D'un tour de Canard que nous avons joué à un censeur bête comme une oie," *CE,* No. 24, 13 December 1916, p. 1; "Le Canard et le censeur," *CE,* No. 37, 14 March 1917, p. 1; "Encore un tour de Canard," *CE,* No. 39, 28 March 1917, pp. 3–4. See also Georges de la Fouchardière, "Pour l'histoire," *L'Heure,* 11 March 1917, p. 1; "Petit poulet du 'Canard Enchaîné' à sa vieille tante Anastasie," *CE,* No. 38, 21 March 1917, p. 1.

12. "Sur Maurice Maréchal," in *Documentation,* prepared and provided by the *Canard Enchaîné,* p. 1.

13. AN F7 13981, " 'Le Canard Enchaîné' (Rapport 1929 complété à 1932)," p. 3.

14. See, for example, SHAT: 5N 348, Liste des principales revues et périodiques, January 1918; 5N 332, Cabinet du Ministre de la Guerre (Section Presse), 29 September 1915; 5N 378, Censure et saisies, 1914–1918. In the BDIC, see F. Res. 270 SPE, t. 2–10; F. Res. 270 C.G., t. 2 Instructions et consignes; F. Res. 270 CNS, nos. 1–2; F. Res. 270 C, t. 2 Journaux . . . observations; F. Res. 270 Avis, t. 1 Avis, t. 2 Consignes, t. 5 Avis. See also the participants' account by Marcel Berger and Paul Allard, *Les secrets de la censure pendant la guerre* (Paris: Edition des Portiques, 1932), pp. 86–94. Compare the similar results in Françoise Navet-Bouron, "Censure et dessin de presse en France pendant la Grande Guerre," *Guerres mondiales et conflits contemporains* 197 (2000), pp. 14–15, though these are based exclusively on the censorship of cartoons.

15. See the documents in SHAT cartons 16N 10, 16N 1561, and 19N 1205, and especially, for example, 16N, D-59 Rapport secret, and reports dated 30 January, 11 April, and 10 May 1918; 16N 1561, IVe Armée, Etat-Major, No. 2208/S.R., 11 May 1918; Grand Quartier Général des Armées du Nord et du Nord-Est, No. 84/S.R.A. 2, 16 March 1918; 1/10/17 Journaux que le Bureau des Services Spéciaux (Affaires Politiques) désirait recevoir; 19N 1205, 40e C.A., Etat-Major, No. 428, 1 July 1918; 16N 10, au Grand Quartier Général, No. 3302, 2 July 1919; Jean-Jacques Becker, "Les débuts du 'Canard Enchaîné,' " in *L'histoire, 14–18 mourir pour la patrie* (Paris: Editions du Seuil, 1992), pp. 224–226.

16. See chapter 10.

17. In AN: F7 13.349, "La propagande pacifiste," 1 January 1917; F7 13.372, "Rapports sur la propagande pacifiste de 1914 à 1918"; F7 13413, folder "Campagne du Maroc 4 extraits de presse," and also F7 9951, Paris, "D'un correspondent," July 1925, F7 13981, " 'Le Canard Enchaîné' (Rapport 1929 complété à 1932)."

18. In the BDIC: F. Res. 270 SPE, "Echoppages du Service des Périodiques" and similar titles: t. 2, 23 July 1915 to 27 December 1915; t. 4, 5 May 1916 to 19 July 1916; t. 5, 20 July 1916 to 13 October 1916; t. 6, 14 October 1916 to 10 January 1917; t. 7, 11 January 1917 to 18 April 1917; t. 8, 19 April 1917 to 2 August 1917; t. 9, 3 August 1917 to 26 November 1917; t. 10, 27 November 1917 to 17 July 1918. Compare the table in Navet-Bouron, "Censure," p. 19, though, again, this is based only on cartoons.

19. Since the systems of recording cuts were not consistent, I am counting effective objections to a unit of content.

20. Vale, "Le Canard Enchaîné à mon censeur qui l'enchaîne," *CE,* No. 24, 13 December 1916, p. 3; Charles Rearick, *The French in Love and War: Popular Culture in the Era of the World Wars* (New Haven, Conn.: Yale University Press, 1977), p. 9.

21. See, for example, Ludwig Wolff, "La guerre aérienne," and "Sur le pas de la Porte," both in *CE,* No. 1, 10 September 1915, p. 3. See also chapter 10.

22. See chapter 3.

23. Zette, "Ménageons nos réserves," *CE,* No. 4, 22 July 1916, p. 1. See also Stéphane Audoin-Rouzeau, *La guerre des enfants: Essai d'histoire culturelle* (Paris: Armand Colin, 1993), pp. 129ff.

24. See chapter 7.

25. Henry Bordelaux, "La classe heureuse," *CE,* Nos. 1–10, 5 July–10 September 1916, pp. 2–3.

26. Alfred Jarry, *Ubu roi* (Paris: Bordas, 1986).

27. Bordelaux, "La classe heureuse," *CE,* No. 5, 1 August 1916, p. 3.

28. Bordelaux, "La classe heureuse," *CE,* No. 6, 8 August 1916, p. 3.

29. For more on de la Fouchardière, see chapter 6.

30. Georges de la Fouchardière, "La divine tragédie," *CE,* Nos. 43–49, 25 April–6 June 1917, p. 2.

31. Georges de la Fouchardière, "La divine tragédie, chant septième," *CE,* No. 49, 6 June 1917, p. 2.

32. See, for example, Jacqueline Lalouette, *La libre pensée en France 1848–1940* (Paris: Albin Michel, 1997), pp. 31, 87.

33. Anatole France, *La révolte des anges* (Paris: Calmann-Lévy, 1986); Anatole France, *Les dieux ont soif* (1912; reprint, Paris: Flammarion, 1989); Georges de la Fouchardière, "La divine tragédie, chant premièr," *CE,* No. 43, 25 April 1917, p. 2. The similarity of de la Fouchardière's account to that of A. France becomes clearer when both are compared with other anticlerical rehabilitations of Satan; Lalouette, *La libre pensée,* pp. 157–158.

34. "Le journal que lit Anatole France," *CE,* No. 33, 14 February 1917, p. 2; L'Horloger, "L'heure qui passe," *L'Heure,* 10 February 1917, p. 3.

35. Curiously, there is nothing on this series in the *échoppages* register for the period, though the May 15 entry includes an objection to irony in an installment of the "divine tragedy" series; BDIC, F. Res. 270 SPE 1917, t. 8. Nor do the available registers of telephone interventions or warnings contain any reference to the series, but these are incomplete. On the censorship of reporting on strike activity, see BDIC, F. Res. 270 C, Relevé des consignes 1917—for example, June 6, June 9.

36. M. Prométhée, "Regards littéraires," *CE,* No. 25, 28 February 1917, p. 3.

37. See, for example, René Rémond, *L'anticléricalisme en France de 1815 à nos jours* (Paris: Fayard, 1999), pp. 243–247.

38. "A travers la presse sérieuse," *CE,* No. 7, 15 August 1916, p. 4.

39. G. de Pawlowski, "Dans le 'No Man's Land,' " *CE,* No. 85, 13 February 1918, p. 2.

40. See, for example, Whip, "Contes du Canard: Kromaryas," *CE,* No. 62, 5 September 1917, p. 3, and "La mare aux Canards," *CE,* No. 12, 20 September 1916, p. 2.

41. "Chanson de route," *CE,* No. 76, 12 December 1917, p. 2.

42. "Les lignes de la main," *CE,* No. 24, 13 December 1916.

43. Becker, *La France en guerre,* pp. 121–122. Compare, however, Stéphane Audoin-Rouzeau and Annette Becker, *14–18 Retrouver la guerre* (Paris: Gallimard, 2000), p. 125.

44. Ernest Hemingway, *A Farewell to Arms* (1929; reprint, New York: Scribner, 1995), p. 118; Fussell, *The Great War,* pp. 71ff.

45. H. P. Gassier, "Pendant la Guerre de Cent Ans," *CE,* No. 4, 28 July 1916, p. 1; "La mare aux Canards," *CE,* No. 66, 3 October 1917, p. 2.

46. Roger Brindolphe, "Les contes du Canard, pas de paix!" *CE,* No. 25, 20 December 1916, p. 3; H. P. Gassier, "T'en fais pas!" *CE,* No. 29, 17 January 1917, p. 1; "Une opinion," *CE,* No. 85, 13 February 1918, p. 1.

47. "L'oiseau de la paix," *CE,* No. 30, 24 January 1917, p. 2.

48. PAB, "Conte de Pâques, c'était un rêve," *CE,* No. 40, 4 April 1917, p. 3.

49. "Nos buts de guerre," *CE,* No. 26, 27 December 1916, p. 1; "Le conte incomplet," *CE,* No. 26, 27 December 1916, p. 3.

50. Lucien Laforge, untitled cartoon, *CE,* No. 72, 14 November 1917, p. 1.

51. "Le perroquet mort," *CE,* No. 13, 27 September 1916, p. 4. See also, for example, Roger Brindolphe, "Contes du Canard, pas de paix," *CE,* No. 24, 13 December 1916, p. 3; "Le péril blanc," *CE,* No. 29, 17 January 1917, p. 4; also, BDIC, F. Res. 270 SPE, t. 5, Echoppages du Service des Périodiques, 20 July 1916–13 October 1916.

52. Rousselle Cadet, "Machins et choses du jour, défaitiste," *CE,* No. 54, 11 July 1917, pp. 1–2.

53. *CE,* No. 100, 29 May 1918, p. 1.

54. *CE,* No. 101, 4 June 1918, p. 1.

55. "Déplacements et villégiatures," *CE,* No. 101, 4 June 1918, p. 3; Henri Béraud, "Epitre," *CE,* No. 111, 14 August 1918, p. 2.

56. "Dans les bégonias," *CE,* No. 113, 28 August 1918, p. 4.

57. "Le billet de Junia," *CE,* No. 117, 25 September 1918, p. 1.

58. "Regards littéraires," *CE,* No. 35, 28 February 1917, p. 3; Q, "Enfin! La fin!" *CE,* No. 117, 25 September 1918, p. 1.

59. Julius, "Le billet de Julius," *CE,* No. 123, 6 November 1918, p. 1; H. P. Gassier, "La colombe," *CE,* No. 123, 6 November 1918, p. 1.

60. Lucien Laforge, "Il y a tout de même progrès," and "Honneur!" and headline in *CE,* No. 124, 13 November 1918, p. 1.

CHAPTER 2. VERBAL AND VISUAL, HUMOR AND POLITICS

1. "Coin! Coin! Coin!" *CE,* No. 1, 10 September 1915, pp. 1 and 2.

2. "Dernière heure," and H. P. Gassier, "Cocorico," both in *CE,* No. 1, 10 September 1915, p. 3.

3. "Peut-on le dire," *La Guerre Sociale,* No. 203, 23 January 1915, p. 2, in SHAT, 5N 338; Claude Bellanger et al., *Histoire générale de la presse française,* vol. 3, *De 1871 à 1940* (Paris: Presses Universitaires de France, 1972), p. 437. See also chapter 3.

4. On this general problem, see, for example, Pierre Fresnault-Deruelle, *L'éloquence des images*, vol. 3, *Images fixes* (Paris: Presses Universitaires de France, 1993), pp. 12–13; Allen Douglas and Fedwa Malti-Douglas, *Arab Comic Strips: Politics of an Emerging Mass Culture* (Bloomington: Indiana University Press, 1994), pp. 161–163.

5. *CE:* No. 79, 2 January 1918, p. 1; "Vive la Russie libérée," No. 35, 21 March 1917, p. 1; "Honneur!" No. 124, 13 November 1918, p. 1.

6. "La mare aux canards," *CE*, No. 1, 5 July 1916, pp. 1–2; "La mare aux canards," *CE*, No. 118, 2 October 1918, p. 3.

7. See, for example, "Conte du Canard," *CE*, No. 79, 2 January 1918, p. 3; "Les livres," *CE*, No. 79, 2 January 1918, p. 4; "Les canards aux champs," *CE*, No. 101, 4 June 1918, p. 4.

8. See, for example, *CE*, No. 7, 16 August 1916, p. 2; No. 27, 3 January 1917, p. 2.

9. *CE*, No. 80, 9 January 1918.

10. Fresnault-Deruelle, *L'éloquence*, p. 3:1.

11. See, for example, Christian Delporte, *Les crayons de la propagande, dessinateurs et dessin politique sous l'occupation* (Paris: CNRS Editions, 1993), pp. 1–16; Henri Monier, *A baton rompu* (Paris: Editions Pierre Horay, 1953), pp. 53–55. A typical number of *L'Assiette au Beurre* would be "Vos papiers" of 4 August 1906.

12. Jean-Jacques Becker, *The Great War and the French People*, trans. Arnold Pomerans (New York: St. Martin's Press, 1986), p. 53; BDIC, F. Res. 270 C.G., t. 2, Instructions et consignes, 16 August 1915–15 June 1916, note of 27 September.

13. "L'ex-poilu en soirée," *CE*, No. 27, 3 January 1917, p. 1; "On ne sait jamais," *CE*, No. 84, 6 February 1918, p. 1.

14. See, for example, Gustave Téry, "Vite et tout!" *L'Oeuvre*, 8 September 1917, p. 1; Gustave Téry, "Enquête et huis-clos ou lentement et rien," *L'Oeuvre*, 7 January 1918, p. 1.

15. See also "Hors d'oeuvre," *L'Oeuvre*, 3 January 1918, p. 2.

16. See chapter 1.

17. Charles-Henry Hirsch, "Zulaïna, conte persan en neuf tableaux," *CE*, No. 88, 6 March 1918, pp. 2–3, and subsequent issues.

18. Bellanger et al., *Histoire*, p. 3:299.

19. Panthéon Courcelle, "Le flacon de gaz, Chapitre IX, Epilogue prématuré," *CE*, No. 82, 23 January 1918, pp. 2–3; "Le masque aux dents gâtées," *CE*, No. 31, 31 January 1917, pp. 2–3; Yves Pourcher, *Les jours de guerre, la vie des français au jour le jour 1914–1918* (Paris: Plon, 1994), p. 374.

20. "Nos feuilletons," *CE*, No. 113, 28 August 1918, p. 1.

21. See, for example, "La presse sérieuse," *CE*, No. 1, 5 July 1916, p. 4; "A travers la presse sérieuse," *CE*, No. 3 January 1917, p. 2.

22. See, for example, G. de Pawlowski, "Le lit de plume," *La Baïonnette*, No. 132, 10 January 1918, pp. 19, 22; G. de Pawlowski, "Inventions nouvelles et

dernières nouveautés," *Le Rire Rouge,* No. 209, 16 November 1918, n.p; *L'Oeuvre,* 23 January 1917, p. 4.

23. See chapter 1 and "Tadeblag Zeitung," *Fantasio,* No. 233, 1 October 1916, p. 185. In addition to *Le Ruy Blas,* see, for this period, *Le Strapontin* and *Le Sourire.*

24. Sigmund Freud, *Jokes and Their Relation to the Unconscious,* trans. James Strachey (1905; New York: Norton, 1963), pp. 120–123; Téry quoted in Bellanger et al., *Histoire,* p. 3:438; "Re-présentation," *CE,* No. 1, 5 July 1916, p. 1.

25. *CE,* No. 55, 18 July 1917, p. 4.

26. See the introduction.

27. *CE,* No. 16, 18 October 1916, p. 1; *CE,* No. 76, 12 December 1917, p. 2.

CHAPTER 3. UNSTUFFING SKULLS

1. See the introduction and R. Manévy, *Histoire de presse 1914–1939* (Paris: Editions Corréa, 1945), pp. 49–51.

2. H. P. Gassier, "La carte que n'a pas prévue M. Herriot," *CE,* No. 36, 7 March 1917, p. 3.

3. Maurice Maréchal, "Les bourreurs de crânes," *CE,* 2 May 1917, p. 3; Maurice Maréchal, "Chez les bourreurs de crânes," *CE,* No. 45, 9 May 1917, p. 3; Maurice Maréchal, "Les bourreurs de crânes," *CE,* No. 50, 13 June 1917, pp. 1–2.

4. "Union sacrée," *CE,* No. 3, 19 July 1916, p. 2; "Les beaux titres," *CE,* No. 5, 2 August 1916, p. 1.

5. "Dans les bégonias," *CE,* No. 89, 13 March 1918, p. 3.

6. "Concours," *CE,* No. 1, 5 July 1916, p. 3; Henry de la Ville d'Avray, "Sur les sentiers de l'arrière," *CE,* No. 22, 29 November 1916, p. 1; "Plébiscite national pour la désignation du grand chef des bourreurs de crâne," *CE,* No. 23, 6 December 1916, p. 4; Jean-Jacques Becker, "Les débuts du 'Canard Enchaîné,' " in *L'histoire, 14–18 mourir pour la patrie* (Paris: Editions du Seuil, 1992), p. 225.

7. "Notre referendum," *CE,* No. 51, 20 June 1917, p. 1; Maurice Maréchal, "Après l'élection," *CE,* No. 51, 20 June 1917, p. 4.

8. "Petit jeu," *CE,* No. 9, August 30, 1916, p. 1; "Le petit jeu," *CE,* No. 10, 6 September 1916, p. 2.

9. "Sur Maurice Maréchal," in *Documentation,* prepared and provided by the *Canard Enchaîné,* p. 1. For combatant hostility to Barrès, see Jean Norton Cru, *Témoins, essai d'analyse et de critique des souvenirs de combattants édités en français de 1915 à 1928* (1929; reprint, Nancy: Presses Universitaires de Nancy, 1993), pp. 275, 423.

10. The censor frequently objected to attempts to refer to this phrase, apparently to protect the dignity of the flag, not of Hervé. See, for example, BDIC, F. Res. 270 SPE, t. 5, August 15 and 27, 1915.

11. Claude Bellanger, *Histoire générale de la presse française,* vol. 3, *De 1871 à 1940* (Paris: Presses Universitaires de France, 1972), p. 437; Jean De-

frasne, *Le pacifisme en France* (Paris: Presses Universitaires de France, 1994), pp. 54–56. On Hervé, see Gilles Heuré, *Gustave Hervé, itinéraire d'un provocateur* (Paris: Editions La Découverte, 1997), especially pp. 205–246; Raoul Villette, ed., *La guerre sociale, un journal "contre"* (Paris: Les Nuits Rouges, 1999).

12. On Maurice Barrès, see C. Stewart Doty, *From Cultural Rebellion to Counterrevolution: The Politics of Maurice Barrès* (Athens: Ohio University Press, 1976); Robert Soucy, *Fascism in France: The Case of Maurice Barrès* (Berkeley: University of California Press, 1972); Zeev Sternhell, *Maurice Barrès et le nationalisme français* (Paris: Armand Colin, 1972).

13. "Un point d'histoire," *CE,* No. 52, 27 June 1917, p. 4; "Conseil au Wattman," *CE,* No. 115, 2 October 1918, p. 2; André Dahl, "Poème de guerre," *CE,* No. 124, 13 November 1918, p. 2; Henri Lavedan, "Courrier de Paris, les grandes heures," *L'Illustration,* 8 August 1914, p. 107. The *Canard* took the occasion in 1919 to reprint the article on Barrès and his *mouvement de menton*: "Chez les bourreurs de crâne, une étrange disparition," *CE,* No. 160, 23 July 1919, pp. 1–2.

14. "Echos," *CE,* No. 1, 10 September 1915, p. 2.

15. Henry de la Ville d'Avray, "Un point d'histoire," *CE,* No. 17, 26 October 1916, p. 4.

16. "Dernière heure, un raid sur Strasbourg," *CE,* No. 112, 21 August 1918, p. 3.

17. H. P. Gassier, "Faites donner l'Académie!" *CE,* No. 2, 12 July 1916, p. 1; [H. P. Gassier?], "L'Echo de Paris . . . et de l'Académie," *CE,* No. 4, 15 October 1915, p. 3.

18. H. P. Gassier, "Les imprécations de Maurice," *CE,* No. 8, 22 August 1916, p. 1.

19. See, for example, Allen Douglas, *From Fascism to Libertarian Communism: Georges Valois against the Third Republic* (Berkeley: University of California Press, 1992), pp. 78–79, 224.

20. "Le cas Barrès," *CE,* No. 7, 15 August 1916, p. 3. See also Maurice Barrès, "Les rumeurs infâmes," *L'Echo de Paris,* 6 August 1916, p. 1.

21. Henry Bordeleaux, "La classe heureuse," *CE,* No. 1, 5 July 1916, p. 3. See also chapter 1.

22. "La mare aux canards," *CE,* No. 5, 2 August 1916, p. 2; headline, *L'Oeuvre,* 27 July 1916, p. 1.

23. Gustave Hervé, "Les tombes de la Marne," *La Victoire,* 11 September 1916, p. 1; "Survivant!" *CE,* No. 12, 20 September 1916, p. 3.

24. Gustave Hervé, "De la Somme à la Meuse," *La Victoire,* 15 September 1916, p. 1; "A travers la presse déchaînée," *CE,* No. 117, 25 September 1918, p. 4.

25. "A travers la presse déchaînée," *CE,* No. 34, 21 February 1917, p. 4.

26. "Le point de vue du fumiste," *CE,* No. 84, 6 February 1918, p. 3; "A travers la presse déchaînée," *CE,* No. 85, 13 February 1918, p. 4.

27. G. de la Fouchardière, "Gustave en redemande," *CE,* No. 85, 13 February 1918, p. 1; compare Heuré, *Hervé,* pp. 245–246.

28. G. de la Fouchardière, "Lettre familière à M. Gustave Hervé, patriote," *CE,* No. 32, 7 February 1917, p. 1.

29. See, for example, Gustave Hervé, "Ce qui se passe en Russie," *La Victoire,* 16 March 1917, p. 1; Gustave Hervé, "La Russie est libre!" and E. Tap, "Le jour de gloire . . . ," both in *La Victoire,* 17 March 1917, p. 1; "Et ceci n'est plus de la rigolade," *CE,* No. 38, 21 March 1917, p. 4.

30. See, for example, "Le point de vue du fumiste," *CE,* No. 1, 5 July 1916, p. 1; "Le petit jeu," *CE,* No. 10, 6 September 1916, p. 2; "Le point de vue du plombier," *La Victoire,* 15 and 17 September 1916, p. 1.

31. See, for example, G. de la Fouchardière, "J'ai dit," *CE,* No. 84, 6 February 1918, p. 3.

32. Rodolphe Bringer, "Une bonne oeuvre," *CE,* No. 79, 2 January 1918, p. 2.

33. "Notre enquête sur les propositions de paix," *CE,* No. 120, 16 October 1918, p. 1.

34. H. P. Gassier, "Décidément, c'est bien la fin," *CE,* No. 121, 23 October 1918, p. 1.

35. H. P. Gassier, "La colombe," *CE,* No. 123, 6 November 1918, p. 1.

36. H. P. Gassier, "Citations à l'ordre du jour," *CE,* No. 5, 4 November 1915, p. 1. On the *Action Française,* see, for example, Eugen Weber, *Action Française* (Stanford, Calif.: Stanford University Press, 1962), pp. 89–112.

37. "Revue de la presse," *CE,* No. 2, 20 September 1915, p. 4; "La mare aux canards," *CE,* No. 7, 15 August 1916, p. 2.

38. "La mare aux canards," *CE,* No. 67, 10 October 1917, p. 3; G. de Pawlowski, "Dans le 'No Man's Land,' " *CE,* No. 73, 21 November 1917, p. 1; *CE,* Nos. 176–177, 12 and 19 November 1919, p. 2.

39. "Echos et nouvelles," *CE,* No. 2, 4 November 1915, p. 2.

40. Ch. M., "Les trois millions du Canard Enchaîné," *CE,* No. 80, 9 January 1918, p. 2.

41. Quoted in H. B., "Nouveau style," *CE,* No. 111, 14 August 1918, p. 1.

42. "A travers la presse déchaînée," *CE,* No. 8, 22 August 1916, p. 3.

43. See chapter 1.

44. "Ils en ont aussi," *CE,* No. 94, 17 April 1918, p. 1; Whip, "Nivelés," *CE,* No. 105, 2 July 1918, p. 1; "Plein aux as," *CE,* No. 113, 28 August 1918, p. 3.

45. "Maintenant, il marche . . . ," *CE,* No. 55, 18 July 1917, p. 3.

46. "La revanche," *CE,* No. 19, 8 November 1916, p. 1.

47. Capitaine Hurluret, "Nos grands stratèges," *CE,* No. 13, 27 September 1916, p. 1; Capitaine Hurluret, "Nos grands stratèges," *CE,* No. 16, 18 October 1916, pp. 1–2; Colonel Poucet, "La situation militaire," *CE,* No. 32, 7 February 1917, p. 4.

48. Capitaine Hurluret, "Nos grands stratèges," *CE,* No. 13, 27 September 1916, pp. 1–2; A. des Enganes, "Un prophète," *CE,* No. 19, 8 November 1916, p. 1.

49. See, for example, Jean-Jacques Becker, *La France en guerre, 1914–1918, la grande mutation* (Paris: Editions Complexe, 1988), pp. 30–31, 88. One of the few exceptions would appear to have been Jacques Bainville of the *Action Française;* Weber, *Action Française,* p. 97.

50. Rodolphe Bringer, "Plaidoyer," *CE*, No. 40, 4 April 1917, pp. 1–2.

51. André Dahl, "Heures de gloire!" *CE*, No. 36, 7 March 1917, p. 4.

52. H. de la Ville d'Avray, "Sur les sentiers de l'arrière," *CE*, No. 31, 31 January 1917, p. 1; "Une injustice," *CE*, No. 109, 31 July 1918, p. 2.

53. G. de la Fouchardière, "Quelques recettes de cuisine," *CE*, No. 3, 19 July 1916, p. 2.

54. "A travers la presse déchaînée," *CE*, No. 19, 8 November 1916, p. 4; Raymond Lefebvre, "Interview du Dr. Obnubile," *CE*, No. 30, 24 January 1917, p. 3. Compare Stéphane Audoin-Rouzeau and Annette Becker, *14–18 Retrouver la guerre* (Paris: Gallimard, 2000), p. 124.

55. On the *Canard*'s brushes with racism and xenophobia, see chapters 10 and 13.

56. "On nous écrit," *CE*, No. 45, 9 May 1917, p. 3; Maurice Maréchal, "Trois ans après, l'homme qui voulait qu'on assassinat," No. 58, 8 August 1917, p. 4; "Le ruban rouge de Kartoffel," *CE*, No. 127, 4 December 1918, p. 4. See also Becker, *La France en guerre*, p. 10.

57. "Au Mont Athos," *CE*, No. 30, 24 January 1917, p. 1.

58. "La quinzaine de Nénette et de Rintintin," *CE*, No. 107, 17 July 1918, p. 1.

59. H. P. Gassier, "Passeront pas," *CE*, No. 102, 12 June 1918, p. 2.

60. See, for example, Francesco Siccardo, "1917. La guerre, la paix et le pape dans un sermon du père Sertillanges," *Mots* 24 (1990), pp. 108ff.

61. "La main coupée," *CE*, No. 4, 15 October 1915, p. 4. The *Canard* was quite precocious in this analysis, preceding, for example, the work done by Marc Bloch after the war on the subject of atrocity rumors. See, for example, the discussion in Audoin-Rouzeau and Becker, *Retrouver*, pp. 64–66.

62. "La force du matelot," *CE*, No. 85, 13 February 1918, p. 4.

63. "Étrange! Étrange!" *CE*, No. 82, 23 January 1918, p. 3.

64. "A travers la presse déchaînée," *CE*, No. 104, 26 June 1918, p. 4; "Echos," *La Presse*, 20 June 1918, p. 2.

65. Ph. Berthelier, "La fin d'un bluff," *CE*, No. 4, 28 July 1916; "Ils ne marchent pas. Ils courent!" *CE*, No. 6, 8 August 1916, p. 1; "Le sous-marin démontable," *CE*, No. 6, 8 August 1916, p. 3; "Le 'Deutschland' et le 'Bremen,' " *La Liberté*, 2 August 1916, p. 1; Georges de la Fouchardière, "Les bourreurs de crâne," *L'Oeuvre*, 5 August 1916, p. 1.

66. "Les bourreurs de crâne," *CE*, No. 18, 1 November 1916, p. 4.

67. "118e semaine de la guerre, communiqués de l'arrière," *CE*, No. 20, 15 November 1916, p. 1.

68. Pierre Mac-Orlan, "Un album de Gus Bofa," *CE*, No. 84, 6 February 1918.

69. Henry de la Ville d'Avray, "Chez les bourreurs de crâne," *CE*, No. 22, 29 November 1916, p. 3.

70. "118e semaine de la guerre, communiqués de l'arrière," and "L'article à faire," both in *CE*, No. 20, 15 November 1916, p. 1.

71. "Soyons renseignés," *CE*, No. 95, 24 April 1918, p. 4. For the newspaper coverage, see "Bolo a été fusillé hier," *Le Journal*, 18 April 1918, pp. 1–2; "Bolo

est mort courageusement," *Le Populaire de Paris,* 18 April 1918, pp. 1–2; "La fin d'un traître," *Le Matin,* 18 April 1918, p. 1; "La justice passe," *L'Echo de Paris,* 18 April 1918, pp. 1–2.

72. "A travers la presse déchaînée," *CE,* No. 115, 11 September 1918, p. 4; "A travers la presse déchaînée," *CE,* No. 106, 10 July 1918, p. 4; Commandant de Civrieux, "La défaite autrichienne" and "La victoire italienne sur la Piave," *Le Matin,* 25 June 1918, pp. 1, 3.

73. Pierre Meudon, "A messieurs les censeurs," *CE,* No. 18, 1 November 1916, pp. 1–2; "La mare aux canards," *CE,* No. 89, 13 March 1918, p. 2.

74. Bellanger et al., *Histoire,* p. 3:410.

75. See, for example, *CE,* No. 62, 5 September 1917, p. 4, and chapters 5 and 7 in this book.

76. Victor Snell, "De l'utilisation des blancs," *CE,* No. 33, 14 February 1917, p. 1.

77. J. J. Brousson, "L'impot scélérat," *CE,* No. 32, 7 February 1917, p. 1.

78. See, for example, Bellanger et al., *Histoire,* pp. 3:258–275, and, for the quote, p. 3:270.

79. Maurice Maréchal, "Une maison de crystal," and Roger Brindolphe, "D'où vient l'argent?," both in *CE,* No. 54, 11 July 1917, p. 1.

80. "La mare aux canards," *CE,* No. 17, 25 October 1916, p. 2.

81. See, for example, No. 154, 11 June 1919, p. 2; "La mare aux canards," *CE,* No. 290, 18 January 1922, p. 2.

CHAPTER 4. THE TEARS OF *L'INTRAN*

1. See, for example, Yves Pourcher, *Les jours de guerre, la vie des français au jour le jour 1914–1918* (Paris: Plon, 1994), pp. 14–18, 29–32, 72, 88, 267–328, 403; Jean-Jacques Becker and Serge Berstein, *Victoire et frustrations, 1914–1929* (Paris: Editions du Seuil, 1990), p. 26; Jean-Baptiste Duroselle, *La Grande Guerre des français* (Paris: Librairie Académique Perrin, 1994), p. 63; Daniel Halévy, *L'Europe brisée, journal et lettres 1914–1918* (Paris: Editions de Fallois, 1998), pp. 29–31.

2. Roland Dorgelès, *Les croix de bois* (1919; reprint, Paris: Albin Michel, 1931), pp. 260–262, 274–278; see, for example, Roland Dorgelès, "L'alcool tue!" *CE,* No. 145, 9 April 1919, p. 1.

3. Claude Bellanger et al., *Histoire générale de la presse française,* vol. 3, *De 1871 à 1940* (Paris: Presses Universitaires de France, 1972), pp. 341–342.

4. "Dans les bégonias," *CE,* No. 104, 26 June 1918, p. 4.

5. Bellanger et al., *Histoire,* pp. 3:416, 3:442; "Des échos de '*L'Intran,*' " *CE,* No. 106, 10 July 1918, p. 4; Le Puisatier, "Chose vue à la manière de," *La Vérité,* 6 July 1918, p. 2.

6. See chapter 2.

7. "Des échos de '*L'Intran,*' " *CE,* No. 106, 10 July 1918, p. 4.

8. "Echos," *Le Petit Journal,* 9 July 1918, p. 2; "Petite histoire bien parisienne," *CE,* No. 108, 24 July 1918, p. 2; Bellanger et al., *Histoire,* p. 3:430.

9. "Dans les bégonias," *CE*, No. 111, 14 August 1918, pp. 3–4.

10. "Petite histoire bien parisienne," *CE*, No. 108, 24 July 1918, p. 2.

11. "A travers la presse déchaînée," *CE*, No. 120, 16 October 1918, p. 4.

12. "Dans les bégonias," *CE*, No. 125, 20 November 1918, p. 4.

13. Marel Cahon, in "Concours d'échos pour *'L'Intran,'* " *CE*, No. 108, 24 July 1918, p. 2.

14. "Concours d'échos pour *'L'Intran,'* " *CE*, No. 109, 31 July 1918, p. 3. See, for example, "Aux enfers, la crise du charbon," *CE*, No. 45, 9 May 1917, p. 4.

15. "Concours d'échos pour *'L'Intran,'* " *CE*, No. 111, 14 August 1918, p. 3.

16. "Concours d'échos pour *'L'Intran,'* " *CE*, No. 115, 11 September 1918, p. 3.

17. See chapter 5.

18. "Concours d'échos pour *'L'Intran,'* " *CE*, No. 115, 11 September 1918, p. 3.

19. "Concours d'échos pour *'L'Intran,'* " *CE*, No. 108, 24 July 1918, p. 3.

20. "Concours d'échos pour *'L'Intran,'* " *CE*, No. 112, 21 August 1918, p. 3.

21. H. P. Gassier, untitled cartoon, *CE*, No. 89, 13 March 1918, p. 1. See also Mary Louise Roberts, *Civilization without Sexes: Reconstructing Gender in Postwar France, 1917–1927* (Chicago: University of Chicago Press, 1994), pp. 37–41, and chapters 5 and 11 of this book for other male-female issues.

22. See, for example, "Coups de pointe" and "L'esprit des autres," in *La Baïonnette*, No. 128, 13 December 1917, pp. 794, 798. On the existence of such anxieties nevertheless, see, for example, Charles Rearick, *The French in Love and War: Popular Culture in the Era of the World Wars* (New Haven, Conn.: Yale University Press, 1977), p. 29.

23. "Concours d'échos pour *'L'Intran,'* " *CE*, No. 109, 31 July 1918, p. 3. On cross-dressing and its gender politics, see Marjorie Garber, *Vested Interests: Cross-Dressing and Cultural Anxiety* (New York: HarperCollins, 1992).

24. "Concours d'échos pour *'L'Intran,'* " *CE*, No. 115, 11 September 1918, p. 3.

25. "Concours d'échos pour *'L'Intran,'* " *CE*, No. 118, 2 October 1918, p. 4.

26. The *Canard* also repeated from the conservative *Gaulois* an anecdote about an officer who collected his cigarette butts in a box for future distribution to common soldiers; "L'inépuisable charité," *CE*, No. 94, 17 April 1918, p. 2.

27. "Concours d'échos pour *'L'Intran,'* " *CE*, No. 117, 25 September 1918, pp. 3–4.

28. See, for example, Dorgelès, *Les croix*, p. 129; Henri Barbusse, *Le feu, journal d'un escouade* (1916; reprint, Paris: Flammarion, 1965), pp. 104–107.

29. "Concours d'échos pour *'L'Intran,'* " *CE*, No. 111, 14 August, 1918, p. 3, and No. 119, 9 October 1918, p. 3.

30. SHAT, 19N 868, No. 26,204, Grand Quartier Général des Armées du Nord et du Nord-Est, 23 August 1917, signed "Pétain."

31. Maurice Agulhon, *Marianne into Battle: Republican Imagery and Symbolism in France, 1789–1880*, trans. Janet Lloyd (Cambridge: Cambridge University Press, 1981), p. 83.

32. Marina Warner, *Monuments and Maidens: The Allegory of the Female Form* (New York: Atheneum, 1985), e.g., pp. 277ff.

33. "Concours d'échos pour *'L'Intran,'* " *CE*, No. 110, 7 August 1918, p. 3.

34. "Concours d'échos pour *'L'Intran,'* " *CE*, No. 113, 28 August 1918, p. 4.

35. "Concours d'échos pour *'L'Intran,'* " *CE*, No. 114, 4 September 1918, p. 3; Marilène Patten Henry, *Monumental Accusations: The Monuments aux Morts as Expressions of Popular Resentment* (New York: Peter Lang, 1996), p. 130.

36. "Concours d'échos pour *'L'Intran,'* " *CE*, No. 119, 9 October 1918, p. 3.

37. See, for example, Angus McLaren, *The Trials of Masculinity: Policing Sexual Boundaries 1870–1930* (Chicago: University of Chicago Press, 1997), p. 236.

38. "Les grandes heures," *CE*, No. 245, 9 March 1921, p. 1.

39. "L'âme populaire," *CE*, No. 241, 9 February 1921, p. 1; "L'instant solennel," *CE*, No. 333, 15 November 1922, p. 1.

40. "La mare aux canards," *CE*, No. 389, 12 December 1923, p. 2.

41. "Un tournoi d'émotion bien française," *CE*, No. 278, 26 October 1921, p. 2; "Des dépêches pour 'Le Matin,' " *CE*, No. 289, 11 January 1922, p. 4.

42. "Nos échos," *L'Intransigeant*, 26 January 1924, p. 2; "Les échos de *'L'Intran'* (nouvelle série)," *CE*, No. 396, 30 January 1924, p. 2.

43. Jules Rivet, "Une émouvante cérémonie," *CE*, No. 419, 9 July 1924, p. 3; "Lettre non-affranchie à M. François Coty," *CE*, No. 459, 15 April 1925, p. 1.

CHAPTER 5. SOLDIERS VERSUS PROFITEERS

1. Allen Douglas, *From Fascism to Libertarian Communism: Georges Valois against the Third Republic* (Berkeley: University of California Press, 1992), p. 72.

2. On the image of the profiteer in the political cartoons of a selection of French, German, and British periodicals, see the brief but provocative study by Jean-Louis Robert, "The Image of the Profiteer," in Jay Winter and Jean-Louis Robert, *Capital Cities at War: Paris, London, Berlin 1914–1919* (Cambridge, England: Cambridge University Press, 1997), pp. 104–132.

3. Thierry Bonzon, "Des tranchées au Palais-Bourbon (des pacifistes au temps de Verdun)," *Mots* 24 (1990), pp. 61–64.

4. "Les embusqués," *CE*, No. 2, 20 September 1915, p. 1.

5. *CE*, No. 20, 15 November 1916, p. 2.

6. J. Dépaquit, "La mauvaise prière d'un bon père," *CE*, No. 50, 13 June 1917, p. 1.

7. "Revue de la presse," *CE*, No. 2, 20 September 1915, p. 4.

8. G. de Pawlowski, "Dialogue des morts," *CE*, No. 68, 17 October 1917, pp. 1–2.

9. Roger Brindolphe, "Les contes du Canard, pas de paix!" *CE*, No. 25, 20 December 1916, p. 3; compare Robert, "Image," pp. 108–109.

10. "Notre enquête sur les propositions de paix," *CE*, No. 120, 16 October 1918, p. 1; "La mare aux canards," *CE*, No. 122, 30 October 1918, p. 4; Ph. Berthelier, "Les 'bénéfices de guerre,' " *CE*, No. 7, 15 August 1916, p. 1; "126e semaine de la guerre, communiqués de l'arrière," *CE*, No. 28, 10 January 1917,

p. 4. Compare Charles Rearick, *The French in Love and War: Popular Culture in the Era of the World Wars* (New Haven, Conn.: Yale University Press, 1977), pp. 20, 60. Rearick's discussion would suggest that popular songs were censored more aggressively than was the *Canard.*

11. [Zour?], "Après fortune faite," *CE,* No. 47, 23 May 1917, p. 4; René Goscinny and Albert Uderzo, *Le bouclier arverne* (Paris: Dargaud, 1968). Halévy also accuses Auvergnat merchants of returning to their region after getting rich on the war; Daniel Halévy, *L'Europe brisée, journal et lettres 1914–1918* (Paris: Editions de Fallois, 1998), p. 209. For other *Canard* humor on the coal shortage, see, for example, Lucien Laforge, "Profiteuse," *CE,* No. 34, 21 February 1917, p. 1.

12. See chapter 12.

13. Junon de Larfin, "Le saint de la semaine, Saint Pothin," *CE,* No. 48, 30 May 1918, p. 3; Pierre Guiral, *Clemenceau en son temps* (Paris: Grasset, 1994), p. 261.

14. Kahn-Aranche, "D'une certaine susceptibilité professionnelle," *CE,* No. 123, 6 November 1918, p. 3.

15. Whip, "Contes du Canard: Kromaryas," *CE,* No. 62, 5 September 1917, p. 3. See, for example, the Oriental tales in Voltaire, *Romans et contes* (Paris: Flammarion, 1966).

16. "L'héroïque mercanti," *CE,* No. 19, 8 November 1916, p. 2.

17. See, for example, Henri Barbusse, *Clarté* (1919; reprint, Paris: Flammarion, 1978), p. 128; Henri Barbusse, *Le feu, journal d'un escouade* (1916; reprint, Paris: Flammarion, 1965), pp. 105–106.

18. [Zour?], "Risques et brisques," *CE,* No. 61, 29 August 1917, p. 1.

19. Jean Giono, *Le grand troupeau* (1931; reprint, Paris: Gallimard, 1995), p. 141.

20. Barbusse, *Le feu,* pp. 110–111. See also Maurice Genevoix, *Ceux de 14* (1916–1923; reprint, Paris: Omnibus, 1998), pp. 129, 512.

21. In *CE,* No. 3, 30 September 1915: "Les malheurs de l'heureux M. Vautour," p. 1; "Le probloc s'apitoie," p. 1; "Les commandements du proprio," p. 1; "Les grands reportages," p. 2; Robert, "Image," pp. 122–123.

22. "Les deux écoles," *CE,* No. 3, 30 September 1915, p. 1.

23. "Est-ce bien vrai?" *CE,* No. 3, 30 September 1915, p. 3; Dupont-Durand, "Une loi d'espoir," *CE,* No. 5, 1 August 1916, p. 1; Victor Snell, "L'autre question," *CE,* No. 55, 18 July 1917, p. 1.

24. Victor Snell, "Le double poison," *CE,* No. 3, 19 July 1916, p. 1; "Nos buts de guerre," *CE,* No. 26, 27 December 1916, p. 1. See chapter 1.

25. "Qu'est-ce que je risque?" *CE,* No. 25, 20 December 1916, p. 2.

26. "120e semaine de la guerre, communiqués de l'arrière," *CE,* No. 22, 29 November 1916, p. 1.

27. "Chez les patissiers," *CE,* No. 46, 16 May 1917, p. 2; H. P. Gassier, "Le mauvais français," *CE,* No. 32, 7 February 1917, p. 1; "Considérations philosophiques," *CE,* No. 46, 16 May 1917, p. 3.

28. "Au troisème plat," *CE*, No. 32, 7 February 1917, p. 4; "Petites correspondances," *CE*, No. 33, 14 February 1917, p. 4.

29. H. de la Ville d'Avray, "Durand, le nouveau riche," *CE*, No. 34, 21 February 1917, p. 2.

30. Victor Snell, "Les restrictions restreintes," *CE*, No. 44, 2 May 1917, p. 1; "Restrictions," *CE*, No. 100, 29 May 1918, p. 1; compare Robert, "Image," pp. 112–113.

31. André Dahl, "Le civil," *CE*, No. 20, 15 November 1916, p. 1.

32. On these newspapers, which were produced by front-line soldiers, and about this one in particular, see Stéphane Audoin-Rouzeau, *14–18, La très grande guerre* (Paris: Le Monde Editions, 1994), and Stéphane Audoin-Rouzeau, *Les combattants des tranchées* (Paris: Armand Colin, 1986), p. 33.

33. "A travers la presse déchaînée," *CE*, No. 36, 7 March 1917, p. 4; Raymond Lefebvre, "Dans le secteur de la Côte-d'Azur," *CE*, No. 32, 7 February 1917, p. 2; Jean Norton Cru, *Témoins, essai d'analyse et de critique des souvenirs de combattants édités en français de 1915 à 1928* (1929; reprint, Nancy: Presses Universitaires de Nancy, 1993), p. 625.

34. See Audoin-Rouzeau, *Les combattants*, and Audoin-Rouzeau, " 'Le Canard' s'envole des champs de bataille," in *14–18*, p. 189.

35. Henri Béraud, "Lettre anonyme," *CE*, No. 106, 10 July 1918, p. 3.

36. Henri Béraud, "Lettre aux civils qui veulent nous écrire," *CE*, No. 100, 29 May 1918, pp. 1–2.

37. "Le soldat," *CE*, No. 27, 3 January 1917, p. 1; "Le 'Canard' va devenir parrain d'un 75," *CE*, No. 105, 2 July 1918, p. 4.

38. "Citation," *CE*, No. 107, 17 July 1918, p. 2.

39. Dahl, "Le civil," p. 1.

40. "Convalescent," *CE*, No. 33, 14 February 1917, p. 4; H. P. Gassier, "Ne faisons-pas ça," *CE*, No. 46, 16 May 1917, p. 3; Lucien Laforge, "Les bourreuses de crâne," *CE*, No. 51, 20 June 1917, p. 1. Compare Margaret H. Darrow, "French Volunteer Nursing and the Myth of War Experience in World War I," *American Historical Review* 101 (1996), pp. 80–106.

41. See chapter 4.

42. Madeleine Delarue-Le Peletier, "Un succès féministe," *CE*, No. 32, 7 February 1917, p. 1. The *Canard* author burlesqued the French feminist Madeleine Pelletier. See Darrow, "French Volunteer Nursing," p. 85.

43. See the excellent work by Stéphane Audoin-Rouzeau, *L'enfant de l'ennemi 1914–1918* (Paris: Aubier, 1995), pp. 33–98.

44. Lucien Laforge, "Elle retarde!" *CE*, No. 28, 10 January 1917, p. 3; H. P. Gassier, "A quoi rêvent les vieilles filles?" *CE*, No. 14, 4 October 1916, p. 3.

45. See chapter 3 and Audoin-Rouzeau, *L'enfant*, p. 69. For the distinctiveness of the *Canard*'s position, see also Margaret Randolph Higonnet, Jane Jenson, Sonya Michel, and Margaret Collins Weitz, "Introduction," in *Behind the Lines: Gender and the Two World Wars* (New Haven, Conn.: Yale University Press, 1987), p. 11.

46. "Scènes de la Grande Guerre," *CE,* No. 29, 17 January 1917, p. 2. See, for example, Roland Dorgelès, *Au beau temps de la butte* (Paris: Albin Michel, 1963), pp. 251, 266–270, 294, 309; Roland Dorgelès, *Les croix de bois* (1919; reprint, Paris: Albin Michel, 1931), pp. 303–304: Roland Dorgelès, *Le Cabaret de la belle femme* (1920; reprint, Paris: Albin Michel, 1928), pp. 67–68. On the image of women during the conflict, see Mary Louise Roberts, *Civilization without Sexes: Reconstructing Gender in Postwar France, 1917–1921* (Chicago: University of Chicago Press, 1994), pp. 24–45. See also chapters 4 and 11 of this book.

47. See, for example, "La différence," *CE,* No. 9, 30 August 1916, p. 2.

48. [Zour?], "Terre sacrée," *CE,* No. 16, 18 October 1916, p. 3.

49. "A la recherche d'une filleule," *CE,* No. 99, 22 May 1918, p. 2; Lucien Laforge, "Tristesse," *CE,* No. 16, 18 October 1916, p. 2.

50. Henry de la Ville d'Avray, "En plein vingtième siècle," *CE,* No. 10, 6 September 1916, p. 4.

51. "Leçon de gastronomie," *CE,* No. 64, 19 September 1917, p. 1; "Approximation," *CE,* No. 70, 31 October 1917, p. 4.

52. Roland Catenoy, "Le poilu et la belle dame," *CE,* No. 92, 3 April 1918, pp. 1–2; "On écrit au 'Canard,' " *CE,* No. 96, 1 May 1918, p. 4. Compare Rearick, *The French in Love and War,* p. 33: "When German Gothas bombed the capital in late 1917 and 1918, the Casino de Paris produced a morale-serving revue bearing the defiant title 'Laisse-les tomber' (Let 'em fall). In fact, many Parisians responded to the bombing by fleeing in a mass exodus to the south. But what echoed in French memory was the courageous, cocky response." Unless, of course, one read the *Canard Enchaîné.*

53. "Pour les vacances," *CE,* No. 94, 17 April 1918, p. 1; "La mare aux canards," *CE,* No. 100, 29 May 1918, p. 2; Lucien Laforge, "Juin 1918," *CE,* No. 104, 26 June 1918, p. 1.

54. Pierre Meudon, "La grande offensive de Deauville," *CE,* No. 56, 25 July 1917, p. 1.

55. "Déplacements et villégiatures," *CE,* No. 93, 10 April 1918, p. 2.

56. "Communiqués de Paris," *CE,* No. 106, 10 July 1918, p. 2. The *Canard* did not give a source, but a similar version of this joke appeared earlier in *L'Intransigeant* ("Nos échos," 25 June 1918, p. 2), where it was attributed to "a *poilu.*"

57. J. Dépaquit, "Il y a la guerre . . . et la guéguerre," *CE,* No. 3, 19 July 1916, p. 4.

58. G. de Pawlowski, "Dans le 'No Man's Land,' " *CE,* No. 82, January 23, 1918, p. 2; Alain [Emile Chartier], *Mars ou la guerre jugée* (1921; reprint, Paris: Gallimard, 1995), p. 179.

CHAPTER 6. *IN VINO VERITAS*

1. C. E., "Savoir attendre," *CE,* No. 120, 16 October 1918, p. 1.

2. See chapter 5.

3. Lucien Laforge, "Restrictions," *CE*, No. 101, 4 June 1918, p. 1; and, for example, "La carte du tabac," *CE*, No. 100, 29 May 1918, p. 1.

4. Compare Didier Nourrisson, "Les crayons de la morale: Alcool et caricature," *Sociétés & Représentations* (November 1995), pp. 125ff.

5. Maurice Barrès, *Colette Baudoche* (Paris: Plon, 1968), pp. 70–74.

6. G. de la Fouchardière, "La voix dans les ténèbres," *CE*, No. 89, 13 March 1918, pp. 1–2.

7. Lucien Laforge, "A la cave," *CE*, No. 94, 17 April 1918, p. 4.

8. Headline and "Honneur!" in *CE*, No. 124, 13 November 1918, p. 1; "Ordre et tradition," *CE*, No. 159, 16 July 1919, p. 2.

9. *CE*, No. 263, 13 July 1921, p. 2; V. S. [Victor Snell], "La fête nationale a permis aux apéritifs français de prouver leur heureuse vitalité," *CE*, No. 316, 19 July 1922, p. 1.

10. Pedro, "Les grandes journées," *CE*, No. 420, 16 July 1924, p. 1; J. Prouvost, "Cas de conscience," *CE*, No. 420, 16 July 1924, p. 1.

11. "L'ennemi de l'alcool," *CE*, No. 25, 20 December 1916, p. 3.

12. Roland Dorgelès, "L'alcool tue!" *CE*, No. 145, 9 April 1919, p. 1; "Protestation," *CE*, No. 457, 1 April 1925, p. 4; "Petite correspondance," *CE*, No. 457, 1 April 1925, p. 4.

13. Roland Barthes, *Mythologies*, trans. Annette Lavers (New York: Hill & Wang, 1995), pp. 58–59.

14. "Sembat paiera une tournée," *CE*, No. 101, 4 [sic] June 1918, p. 1; "Sommation avec frais," *CE*, No. 102, 12 June 1918, p. 3; "Une fête intime," *CE*, No. 103, 19 June 1918, p. 3.

15. See, for example, "Une souveraine de plus," *CE*, No. 294, 15 February 1922, p. 1; "Un concours finit . . . un autre commence!" *CE*, No. 300, 29 March 1922, p. 1; "Légion et noix d'honneur," *CE*, No. 310, 7 June 1922, pp. 3–4; "La mare aux canards," *CE*, No. 323, 6 September 1922, p. 2; "Nos feuilletons," *CE*, No. 325, 20 September 1922, p. 2; I. R., "Chez les 'Canetons,' " *CE*, No. 325, 20 September 1922, p. 4.

16. "Un concours finit . . . un autre commence!" *CE*, No. 300, 29 March 1922, p. 1.

17. G. de la Fouchardière, "Du Vouvray à Vouvray," *CE*, No. 524, 14 July 1926, p. 1.

18. Maurice Marchand, "Contes du Canard, le coup des Ilotes," *CE*, No. 323, 6 September 1922, p. 4.

19. Jules Rivet, "Contes du Canard, mise au point," *CE*, No. 336, 6 December 1922, p. 4. Bicard [de la Fouchardière], "Les propos du Bouif," *CE*, No. 47, 23 May 1917, p. 4; "On nous écrit," *CE*, No. 48, 30 May 1917, p. 4.

20. "Le prix du paté," *CE*, No. 29, 17 January 1917, p. 1.

21. AN F7 13981, " 'Le Canard Enchaîné' (Rapport 1929 complété à 1932)," pp. 11–13.

22. See chapter 1.

23. Bicard [de la Fouchardière], "Des cadeaux à nos lecteurs," *CE*, No. 45, 9 May 1917, p. 1; Bicard [de la Fouchardière], "Les propos du Bouif," *CE*, No. 46

16 May 1917, p. 1; G. de la Fouchardière, "La grande pitié de M. Barrès, " *CE*, No. 49, 6 June 1917, p. 1; Georges de la Fouchardière, "Le crime du Bouif," *L'Heure*, 3 February 1917, p. 2.

24. See, for example, de la Fouchardière, "La grande pitié de M. Barrès, " p. 1; Georges de la Fouchardière, "Les propos du Bouif," *CE*, No. 54, 11 July 1917, p. 1.

25. G. de la Fouchardière, "La lanterne du Bouif," *CE*, No. 235, 29 December 1920, p. 2; G. de la Fouchardière, "Chronique de l'oeil-de-Bouif: Souvenirs de chasse," *CE*, No. 323, 6 September 1922, pp. 3–4; AN F7 13981, " 'Le Canard Enchaîné' (Rapport 1929 complété à 1932)," p. 11.

26. "Des nouvelles de G. de la Fouchardière," *CE*, No. 452, 25 February 1925, p. 1; "Bicard et son ami," *CE*, No. 522, 30 June 1926, p. 1; "La santé du Bouif," *CE*, No. 600, 28 December 1927, p. 1.

27. See, for example, G. de la Fouchardière, "Chronique de l'oeil-de-Bouif: Le coup du rajah," CE, No. 440, 3 December 1924, p. 2.

28. See, for example, G. de la Fouchardière, "La lanterne du Bouif: Le scandale de Tours," *CE*, No. 237, 12 January 1921, p. 2.

29. G. de la Fouchardière, "Chronique de l'oeil-de-Bouif: Un type dans le genre du Duc d'Uzès," *CE*, No. 514, 5 May 1926, p. 3.

30. G. de la Fouchardière, "Chronique de l'oeil-de-Bouif," *CE*, No. 591, 26 October 1927, p. 2.

31. See, for example, Caumery [Maurice Languereau] and J. P. Pinchon, *Bécassine pendant la Grande Guerre* (1915; reprint, Paris: Gautier-Languereau, 1993), p. 35.

32. BDIC, F. Res. 270 SPE, t. 7, Service des Périodiques, Echoppages, 11 January 1917–18 April 1917; "Les caprices de la dame," *CE*, No. 35, 28 February 1917, p. 2; G. de la Fouchardière, "Les flics de luxe," *CE*, No. 29, 17 January 1917, p. 1; "Enfin! Enfin!" *CE*, No. 111, 14 August 1918, p. 1.

33. Pierre Bénard, "Les bagarres du 23 Août," *CE*, No. 583, 31 August 1927, p. 1.

34. "La vague d'économie," *CE*, No. 399, 20 February 1924, p. 2.

35. Roland Dorgelès, "L'armée policière," *CE*, No. 149, 7 May 1919, p. 1.

36. "Gloire de la gendarmerie," *CE*, No. 322, 30 August 1922, p. 1; "Une nouvelle reine," *CE*, No. 503, 17 February 1926, p. 2. See also, for example, Henri Barbusse, *Le feu, journal d'un escouade* (1916; reprint, Paris: Flammarion, 1965), pp. 158–159; John Dos Passos, *One Man's Initiation: 1917* (1920; reprint, Lanham, Md.: University Press of America, 1986), pp. 31–32; Blaise Cendrars, *La main coupée* (1946; reprint, Paris: Editions Denoël, 1997), which deals almost exclusively with the First World War, pp. 347–350; Joseph Kessel, *L'équipage* (Paris: Gallimard, 1969; text completed in 1923), pp. 147–149; Maurice Genevoix, *Ceux de 14* (1916–1923; reprint, Paris: Omnibus, 1998), p. 667.

37. Barthes, *Mythologies*, pp. 58–60; G. de la Fouchardière, "Chronique de l'oeil-de-Bouif: L'execution de M. Malvy," *CE*, No. 420, 16 July 1924, p. 2; Evelyne Desbois, "Paroles de soldats, entre images et écrits," *Mots* 24 (1990), p. 43. Compare Richard Kuisel, *Seducing the French* (Berkeley: University of California Press, 1993), pp. 58–69.

38. Compare Véronique Nahoum-Grappe, "Jusqu'à plus soif: Le boire comme système de communication," *Sociétés & Représentations* (November 1995), p. 116.

39. G. de la Fouchardière, "Chronique de l'oeil-de-Bouif: C'est la faute à Christophe Colomb," *CE*, No. 583, 31 August 1927, p. 3. See chapters 10 and 13 of this book.

40. "Petite correspondance," *CE*, No. 576, 13 July 1927, p. 4.

41. G. de la Fouchardière, "Chronique de l'oeil-de-Bouif: L'amélioration de la race électorale," *CE*, No. 461, 29 April 1925, p. 2.

42. G. de la Fouchardière, "Chronique de l'oeil-de-Bouif: Quelques erreurs regrettables," *CE*, No. 422, 30 July 1924, p. 2. Compare the prewar example of this line of argument in Nourrisson, "Les crayons," p. 133.

43. Victor Snell, "Vraiment, c'est trop facile!" *CE*, No. 452, 25 February 1925, p. 1.

44. [G. de la Fouchardière], "Présentation du Bouif," *CE*, No. 281, 16 November 1921, p. 2; Charles Dickens, *The Pickwick Papers* (Oxford: Oxford University Press, 1992).

45. Henri Barbusse, *Clarté* (1919; reprint, Paris: Flammarion, 1978), pp. 76–77. See, for example, "Le point de vue du plombier," and Albert Turpain, "Briand! L'alcool!" both in *La Victoire*, 15 September 1916, p. 1; Hermann-Paul, "Propos de la guerre . . . à l'alcool," *La Victoire*, 30 January 1917, p. 1. For prewar attacks from both the right and the anarchist left, see Nourrisson, "Les crayons," pp. 139–142.

46. See chapters 10 and 13.

47. G. de la Fouchardière, "Intelligences avec l'ennemi," *CE*, No. 90, 20 March 1918, pp. 1–2; see also Stéphan Valot, "Notre frère le Canard," *CE*, No. 307, 17 May 1922, pp. 2–3, which reproduces an article from the *Progrès Civique*.

48. General Edouard de Castelnau never became a marshal.

49. G. de la Fouchardière, "Chronique de l'oeil-de-Bouif: La réhabilitation du maréchal," *CE*, No. 435, 29 October 1924, p. 2.

50. G. de la Fouchardière, "Chronique de l'oeil-de-Bouif: La descente de la courtine," *CE*, No. 412, 21 May 1924, p. 2.

51. G. de la Fouchardière, "Chronique de l'oeil-de-Bouif: Où Bicard trouve un excellent moyen d'empêcher les guerres," *CE*, No. 386, 21 November 1923, pp. 1–2.

52. See chapter 8.

53. G. de la Fouchardière, "Chronique de l'oeil-de-Bouif: Féminisme," *CE*, No. 334, 22 November 1922, p. 2.

54. G. de la Fouchardière, "Chronique de l'oeil-de-Bouif: Fumées," *CE*, No. 329, 18 October 1922, p. 3.

55. G. de la Fouchardière, "Chronique de l'oeil-de-Bouif: Le nouveau locataire de l'Elysée," *CE*, No. 416, 18 June 1924, p. 2.

56. G. de la Fouchardière, "Chronique de l'oeil-de-Bouif: Eloquence parlementaire," *CE*, No. 364, 20 June 1923, p. 2.

57. De la Fouchardière, "La lanterne du Bouif: Le scandale de Tours."

58. De la Fouchardière, "Chronique de l'oeil-de-Bouif: Le coup du rajah," p. 2.

59. [De la Fouchardière], "Présentation du Bouif," p. 2.

60. G. de la Fouchardière, "Chronique de l'oeil-de-Bouif: Opinions politiques," *CE*, No. 492, 2 December 1925, p. 3.

61. G. de la Fouchardière, "La lanterne du Bouif: Dans le lit de Millerand," *CE*, No. 285, 14 December 1921, p. 3.

CHAPTER 7. PEACE OR POSTWAR

1. Jean Renoir, *Grande Illusion* (1937).

2. Samuel Hynes, *A War Imagined: The First World War and English Culture* (London: Bodley Head, 1990), p. 20; Henri Barbusse, *Le feu, journal d'un escouade* (1916; reprint, Paris: Flammarion, 1965), p. 421. See also Charles Rearick, *The French in Love and War: Popular Culture in the Era of the World Wars* (New Haven, Conn.: Yale University Press, 1977), p. 59. Some were more pessimistic even during the war. See, for example, Daniel Halévy, *L'Europe brisée, journal et lettres 1914–1918* (Paris: Editions de Fallois, 1998), pp. 237–238.

3. R. Guérin, "Le grand chagrin de la classe 30," *CE*, No. 121, 23 October 1918, p. 4.

4. Roland Dorgelès, *Les croix de bois* (1919; reprint, Paris: Albin Michel, 1931), p. 262.

5. Mat, untitled cartoon, *CE*, No. 305, 3 May 1922, p. 2.

6. Maurice Morice, "Dans l'attente du 31 Mai," *CE*, No. 305, 3 May 1922, p. 1; V. S., "La Re-Madelon de la Re-Victoire," *CE*, No. 305, 3 May 1922, p. 1; "Les grandes heures," *CE*, No. 245, 9 March 1921, p. 1. On the politics of the *Madelon de la Victoire*, see Rearick, *The French in Love and War*, pp. 35–36.

7. "Petite correspondance," *CE*, No. 20, 15 November 1916, p. 4.

8. "L'armée de demain," *CE*, No. 127, 4 December 1918, p. 1.

9. "Convocations," *CE*, No. 135, 29 January 1919, p. 3.

10. See, for example, Roger Brindolphe, "Pour fixer la date du prochain armistice," *CE*, No. 386, 21 November 1923, p. 1; "Opinions, nouveaux principes," *CE*, No. 470, 1 July 1925, p. 1.

11. "Convocations," p. 3.

12. On the ostensible apoliticism of the veterans' movements, which could carry anti-Republican ideas, see Antoine Prost, *Les anciens combattants et la sociéte française 1914–1939* (Paris: Fondation Nationale des Sciences Politiques, 1977), especially vols. 1 and 2.

13. Henri Béraud, "Une conférence de la guerre," *CE*, No. 135, 29 January 1919, p. 1.

14. "Pour le traité de paix," *CE*, No. 153, 4 June 1919, p. 2; "La mare aux canards," *CE*, No. 160, 23 July 1919, p. 2; Maurice Maréchal, "Pourquoi pas?" *CE*, No. 161, 30 July 1919, p. 1.

15. "Honneur!" *CE,* No. 124, 13 November 1918, p. 1.

16. Headline and illustration, *CE,* No. 128, 11 December 1918, p. 1; Lucien Laforge, "La femme enchaînée," *CE,* No. 129, 18 December 1918, p. 1; "Mauvais exemple," *CE,* No. 132, 8 January 1919, p. 1.

17. "Wilson est parti," *CE,* No. 157, 2 July 1919, p. 2. The position was echoed by Romain Rolland; see Pierre Sipriot, *Guerre et paix autour de Romain Rolland, le désastre de l'Europe 1914–1918* (Paris: Editions Bartillat, 1997), p. 376.

18. "A travers la presse enchaînée," *CE,* No. 188, 4 February 1920, p. 3; "Après l'exécution de Landru," *CE,* No. 296, 1 March 1922, p. 1.

19. "La mare aux canards," *CE,* No. 361, 30 Mai 1923, p. 2; "Le *'Canard'* avait raison," *CE,* No. 368, 18 July 1923, p. 1; "La paix par le droit," *CE,* No. 430, 24 September 1924, p. 1; "La mare aux canards," *CE,* No. 430, 24 September 1924, p. 3; G. de la Fourchardière, "Chronique de l'oeil-de-Bouif: Paris fête avec enthousiasme," *CE,* No. 586, 21 September 1927, p. 3.

20. Victor Snell, "Remettre ça," *CE,* No. 190, 18 February 1920, p. 1; Maurice Maréchal, "Bordeaux d'abord! Le premier voyage du président," *CE,* No. 191, 25 February 1920, p. 3.

21. Whip, "Probabilités," *CE,* No. 337, 13 December 1922, pp. 3–4. The *Canard* here brought together the issues that Gubar attributes to the Second World War: "consciousness of the infinite sequentiality of world wars, technological advances in destructive capabilities, the obliteration of a safe homefront"; Susan Gubar, " 'This Is My Rifle, This Is My Gun': World War II and the Blitz on Women," in Margaret Randolph Higonnet et al., *Behind the Lines: Gender and the Two World Wars* (New Haven, Conn.: Yale University Press, 1987), p. 230. There are, of course, some similarities between the *Canard*'s vision and the apocalyptic strain so well described by Jay Winter, *Sites of Memory, Sites of Mourning: The Great War in European Cultural History* (Cambridge: Cambridge University Press, 1995), pp. 145–203.

22. René Virad, "Une redoutable découverte, si la prochaine dernière éclatait," *CE,* No. 450, 11 February 1925, p. 1.

23. Maurice Maréchal, "Une erreur judiciaire," *CE,* No. 242, 16 February 1921, p. 3.

24. Roger Brindolphe, "Pour fixer la date du prochain armistice," p. 1.

25. "La mare aux canards," *CE,* No. 372, 15 August 1923, p. 2; "Le budget militaire," *CE,* No. 451, 18 February 1925, p. 1; Pierre Bénard, "Après la loi Paul Boncour," *CE,* No. 558, 9 March 1927, p. 1.

26. Lucien Laforge, untitled cartoon, and headline, *CE,* No. 159, 16 July 1919, p. 1.

27. *Anthologie de la chanson française: La chanson traditionnelle, l'histoire de France,* CD and text, EPM, 1996.

28. "En r'venant d'la revue," *CE,* No. 159, 16 July 1919, p. 2; Rodolphe Bringer, "Contes du Canard, la fenêtre," *CE,* No. 159, 16 July 1919, p. 3.

29. Henri Guilac, "Retraites militaires," *CE,* No. 369, 25 July 1923, p. 3.

30. "Leçon des choses," *CE*, No. 369, 25 July 1923, p. 1.

31. "Le temps qu'il fait," *CE*, No. 254, 11 May 1921, p. 4; "Petite correspondance," *CE*, No. 131, 1 January 1919, p. 3; G. de la Fouchardière, "La lanterne du Bouif, histoire et géographie," *CE*, No. 254, 11 May 1921, pp. 1–2.

32. G. de la Fouchardière, "Quand même!" *CE*, No. 207, 16 June 1920.

33. "Les Boches préparent ouvertement une guerre de revanche," *CE*, No. 229, 17 November 1920, p. 3.

34. Pierre Miquel, *La paix de Versailles et l'opinion française* (Paris: Flammarion, 1972), pp. 304–308.

35. Simon Hégésippe, "Progrès et adaptation," *CE*, No. 133, 15 January 1919, p. 1.

36. Maurice Coriem, "Les travaux de la paix," *CE*, No. 278, 26 October 1921, p. 1.

37. "Contre le militarisme allemand," *CE*, No. 376, 12 September 1923, p. 1.

38. "La paix par le droit," *CE*, Nos. 385, 386, and 387, 14, 21, and 28 November 1923, p. 1.

39. "Pour la paix du monde," *CE*, No. 403, 19 March 1924, p. 1; "La paix du droit," *CE*, No. 406, 9 April 1924, p. 1; "La paix par le droit," *CE*, No. 430, 24 September 1924, p. 1; "Pour la paix," *CE*, No. 582, 24 August 1927, p. 3.

40. "A travers la presse déchaînée," *CE*, No. 281, 16 November 1921, p. 3.

41. "Notre flotte s'est accrue d'une nouvelle unité pacifique" and "Pour la paix du monde," both in *CE*, No. 373, 22 August 1923, p. 3.

42. "A nous le Nordstern," *CE*, No. 259, 15 June 1921, p. 1; "Le désarmement naval," *CE*, No. 381, 17 October 1923, p. 1; "Pour la paix du monde," *CE*, No. 422, 30 July 1924, p. 1.

43. "Le désarmement n'est pas chose facile," *CE*, No. 264, 20 July 1921, p. 1.

44. "Sécurité et désarmement," *CE*, No. 499, 20 January 1926, p. 1.

45. "Avant la conférence," *CE*, No. 277, 19 October 1921, p. 1; René Buzelin, "La conférence de Vassingueton," *CE*, No. 281, 16 November 1921, p. 3.

46. See, for example, "Pour la paix du monde, de belles maneuvres du désarmement ont eu lieu en Angleterre," *CE*, No. 421, 30 July 1924, p. 1.

47. Ibid.

48. *CE*, No. 480, 9 September 1925, p. 1.

49. "La mare aux canards," *CE*, No. 561, 30 March 1927, p. 2.

50. "La mare aux canards," *CE*, No. 564, 20 April 1927, p. 2.

51. "Après Spithead et Toulon la Sociéte des Nations organise la revue navale de la paix," *CE*, No. 430, 24 September 1924, p. 1.

52. "Un coup de théâtre à la S.D.N. la flotte anglaise devra-t-elle bombarder l'Angleterre," *CE*, No. 432, 29 October 1924, p. 1.

53. "La paix règne sur le monde grâce aux efforts de la Société des Nations," *CE*, No. 555, 16 February 1927, p. 1.

54. Pierre Scize, "Quelques considérations sur la S.D.N.," *CE*, No. 559, 16 March 1927, pp. 1–2.

55. For examples, see chapter 11.

56. "En lisant," *CE*, No. 485, 14 October 1925, p. 4.

57. Gustave Hervé [sic], "La trahison de Locarno," and Jules Rivet, "Le traité de Locarno, M. Poincaré nous donne son avis," both in *CE*, No. 486, 21 October 1925, p. 1.

58. Drégerin, "Une belle réponse de M. Poincaré à M. Briand," *CE*, No. 535, 29 September 1926, p. 3.

59. "Propos," *CE*, No. 535, 29 September 1926, p. 1, paragraphing in original.

60. See, for example, *CE*, No. 513, 28 April 1926, p. 3; *CE*, No. 540, 3 November 1926, p. 3.

61. G. de la Fouchardière, "Chronique de l'oeil-de-Bouif: Le pacte de sécurité," *CE*, No. 485, 14 October 1925, p. 3. On the natalist arguments here burlesqued, see Mary Louise Roberts, *Civilization without Sexes: Reconstructing Gender in Postwar France, 1917–1921* (Chicago: University of Chicago Press, 1994), pp. 89–147.

62. "L'esprit de Locarno," *CE*, No. 496, 30 December 1925, p. 3.

63. See, for example, "Après Locarno" and "L'esprit de Locarno," both in *CE*, No. 507, 17 March 1926, p. 3; "L'esprit de Locarno souffle sur le monde," *CE*, No. 508, 24 March 1926, pp. 1–2.

64. Franklin-Bouillon [sic], "Pas de paix perpétuelle avec l'Amérique," *CE*, No. 581, 17 August 1927, p. 1.

65. "Depuis deux jours la guerre est hors la loi," *CE*, No. 586, 21 September 1927, p. 2.

66. G. de la Fouchardière, "Chronique de l'oeil-de-Bouif: Une formule de guerre pacifique," *CE*, No. 468, 17 June 1925, p. 1.

67. Pierre Scize, "Dans ma boîte aux lettres," *CE*, No. 552, 26 January 1927, p. 1.

68. Pierre Scize, "Considérations sur les étrennes," *CE*, No. 598, 14 December 1927, p. 1; Alain [Emile Chartier], *Mars ou la guerre jugée* (1921; reprint, Paris: Gallimard, 1995). Compare the similar position of Romain Rolland quoted in Sipriot, *Guerre*, p. 352. On the motif of maternal opposition to war toys in popular song, see Rearick, *The French in Love and War*, p. 59.

69. "Notre devise," *CE*, No. 557, 2 March 1927, p. 4.

CHAPTER 8. WEB OF MEMORY

1. Pierre Nora, "Présentation" and "Entre mémoire et histoire," in Pierre Nora, ed., *Les lieux de mémoire*, vol. 1, *La République* (Paris: Gallimard, 1984), pp. vii–xlii.

2. Henri Barbusse, *Clarté* (1919; Paris: Flammarion, 1978), p. 260.

3. "Un grand anniversaire sportif," *CE*, No. 153, 4 June 1919, p. 3; "Dimanche, la capitale a célébré le 5e anniversaire," *CE*, No. 173, 22 October 1919, p. 1; "Des échos sur M. Poincaré," *CE*, 291, 25 January 1922, p. 4; and chapter 11 of this book.

4. "Les grands anniversaires, Paris a fêté le 15 Août," *CE*, No. 164, 20 August 1919, p. 1. See also chapter 5 of this book.

5. "La mare aux canards," *CE*, No. 269, 24 August 1921, p. 2; "Six ans après," *CE*, No. 213, 28 July 1920, p. 1; "Les Cosaques à cinq étapes de Berlin," *Le*

Matin, 24 August 1914, p. 1; Maurice Morice, "Dans l'attente du 31 Mai la France se prépare," *CE*, No. 305, 3 May 1922, p. 1; "Suspects préparatifs russes," *CE*, No. 307, 17 May 1922, p. 3. See chapter 3 of this book.

6. "Le musée de guerre des B.D.C.," *CE*, No. 163, 13 August 1919, p. 4. See chapter 10 of this book.

7. Pierre Lafitte, "Nos blessés," *Excelsior*, 22 August 1914, p. 2; "La mare aux canards," *CE*, No. 269, 24 August 1921, p. 2; "La mare aux canards," *CE*, No. 271, 7 September 1921, p. 2.

8. Maurice Coriem, "Offensives," *CE*, No. 299, 20 March 1922, p. 1; J. Pruvost, "A la terrasse," *CE*, No. 299, 20 March 1922, p. 2.

9. "L'anniversaire de la bataille de Morhange," *CE*, No. 530, 25 August 1926, p. 1; "La mare aux canards," *CE*, No. 511, 14 April 1926, p. 2.

10. "Honneur!" *CE*, No. 124, 13 November 1918, p. 1.

11. See chapter 3.

12. "A travers la presse déchaînée," *CE*, No. 130, 25 December 1918, p. 4; and see, for example, "La journée," *La Croix*, 1 October 1918, p. 1.

13. Rodolphe Bringer, "Sainte Geneviève n'a pas été gentille," *CE*, No. 445, 7 January 1925, p. 1.

14. "A travers la presse déchaînée," *CE*, No. 143, 26 March 1919, pp. 3–4; "Les grands prédicateurs du carême," *L'Echo de Paris*, 23 March 1919, p. 1. See also chapter 1 of this book; "La noix d'honneur appartient à M. Eugène Langevin," *CE*, No. 319, 9 August 1922, p. 1.

15. "Dans les bégonias," *CE*, No. 128, 11 December 1918, p. 4.

16. "A travers la presse déchaînée," *CE*, No. 255, 18 May 1921, p. 3.

17. "La mare aux canards," *CE*, No. 328, 11 October 1922, p. 2.

18. "Le démobilisé," *CE*, No. 139, 26 February 1919, p. 2; "Notre enquête sur la crise de la production," *La Journée Industrielle*, 8 January 1920, p. 1; "A travers la presse déchaînée," *CE*, No. 188, 4 February 1920, p. 3.

19. " 'La hausse est certainement enrayée,' " *L'Intransigeant*, 21 October 1920, p. 1; "A travers la presse déchaînée," *CE*, No. 226, 27 October 1920, p. 4. See also chapter 12 of this book and, for example, Jean-Jacques Becker and Serge Berstein, *Victoire et frustrations, 1914–1929* (Paris: Editions du Seuil, 1990), p. 347; Matt K. Matsuda, *The Memory of the Modern* (New York: Oxford University Press, 1996), p. 127.

20. Roland Catenoy, "Et nos 28 jours?" *CE*, No. 192, 3 March 1920, pp. 1–2; Allen Douglas, *From Fascism to Libertarian Communism: Georges Valois against the Third Republic* (Berkeley: University of California Press, 1992), p. 34.

21. Georges de la Fouchardière, "Chronique de l'oeil-de-Bouif: Souvenirs du bon temps," *CE*, No. 401, 5 March 1924, p. 1; "Pourquoi hésiter?" *CE*, No. 335, 29 November 1922, p. 1; "Lettres," *CE*, No. 474, 29 July 1925, p. 4.

22. Roland Dorgelès, *Les croix de bois* (1919; reprint, Paris: Albin Michel, 1931), pp. 148–149, 376.

23. Blaise Cendrars, *La main coupée* (1946; reprint, Paris: Editions Denoël, 1997), p. 132.

24. G. de la Fouchardière, "Chronique de l'oeil-de-Bouif: L'offensive posthume du Général Percin," *CE*, No. 598, 14 December 1927, p. 3.

25. Pierre Scize, "Sur deux aspects de la sculpture militaire," *CE*, No. 570, 1 June 1927, p. 2; Abel Gance, *J'accuse* (1937). In Gance's film this argument is introduced along with the faces of disfigured veterans. The series of shots is all the more ideologically telling in that it is narratively inappropriate since these men, whose wounds have healed, are intercalated in a sequence of the risen dead. On the Gueules Cassées, see Sophie Delaporte, *Les Gueules Cassées, les blessés de la face de la Grande Guerre* (Paris: Editions Noêsis, 1996), especially pp. 171–218. See also chapter 9 of this book. See the incident described in Marilène Patten Henry, *Monumental Accusations: The Monuments aux Morts as Expressions of Popular Resentment* (New York: Peter Lang, 1996), p. 89, and Antoine Prost, *Les anciens combattants et la société française 1914–1939*, vol. 3, *Mentalités et idéologies* (Paris: Presses de la Fondation Nationale des Sciences Politiques, 1977), pp. 103–104.

26. Pierre Scize, "En lisant 'L'Officiel,' " *CE*, No. 541, 10 November 1926, p. 1. Scize's argument uses the facially wounded as indices of the war's brutality. Though many men were understandably frightened about the loss of female companionship, Delaporte's study suggests that most were able to marry, many wedding their nurses; Delaporte, *Les Gueules Cassées*, pp. 161–163.

27. See, for example, Stéphane Audoin-Rouzeau, "Préface," in Delaporte, *Les Gueules Cassées*, pp. 24–26, and in the main work, p. 161. Delaporte's work deals with the medical, social, and physical experiences of the facially wounded.

28. "Les crânes qu'on bourrait (suite)," *CE*, No. 359, 16 May 1923, p. 4.

29. "Les belles annonces," *CE*, No. 551, 19 January 1927, p. 1. See also, for example, Dorgelès, *Les croix*, p. 305.

30. For attitudes toward police and gendarmes, see chapter 6.

31. "La série continue!" *CE*, No. 534, 22 September 1926, p. 2.

32. On the mutinies, see Guy Pédroncini, *Les mutineries de l'armée française, 1917* (Paris: Presses Universitaires de France, 1967).

33. Pierre Scize, "A la façon de . . . ," *CE*, No. 544, 1 December 1926, p. 2; "La mare aux canards," *CE*, No. 243, 23 February 1921, p. 2; Jules Rivet, "Oui, mais . . . et les fusilleurs de Vingré," *CE*, No. 368, 18 July 1923, p. 1; "Epilogue de l'affaire Bersot," *CE*, No. 395, 23 January 1924, p. 1; "Inauguration du monument aux six fusillés de Vingré," *CE*, No. 458, 8 April 1925, p. 3; Pédroncini, *Les mutineries*, p. 23. See also Nicolas Offenstadt, *Les fusillés de la Grande Guerre et la mémoire collective (1914–1999)* (Paris: Editions Odile Jacob, 1999).

34. Henri Barbusse, "Faits divers," *CE*, No. 614, 4 April 1928, p. 2.

35. "En lisant," *CE*, No. 498, 13 January 1926, p. 4; John Dos Passos, *One Man's Initiation: 1917* (1920; reprint, Lanham, Md.: University Press of America, 1986), pp. 58, 60.

36. "Epidémie," *CE*, No. 404, 26 March 1924, p. 2.

37. "L'écho incomplet," *CE*, No. 334, 22 November 1922, p. 2.

38. G. de la Fouchardière, "Chronique de l'oeil-de-Bouif: Stratégie," *CE*, No. 377, 19 September 1923, p. 2; John Keegan, *The First World War* (New York: Vintage Books, 2000), pp. 315–316.

39. "La mare aux canards," *CE*, No. 307, 17 May 1922, p. 2; G. de la Fouchardière, "Chronique de l'oeil-de-Bouif," *CE*, No. 435, 29 October 1924, p. 2. See also chapter 6 of this book. Compare the article quoted in Blanche Maupas, *Le fusillé* (Cherbourg: Editions Isoète, 1994), pp. 151–152, where the idea of French responsibility appears without the softening of the *Canard*'s irony.

40. For Mangin and the colonial army, see chapter 10; for "the butcher," see, for example, Service Historique de l'Armée de Terre, *1916 année de Verdun* (Paris: Lavauzelle, 1996), p. 72. "Regards littéraires," *CE*, No. 252, 27 April 1921, p. 4; "A travers la presse déchaînée," *CE*, No. 345, 7 February 1923, p. 3; René Buzelin, "A chacun son quartier!" *CE*, No. 392, 2 January 1924, pp. 3–4; "Héroique retour de Mangin," *CE*, No. 284, 7 December 1921, p. 1; "La grande séance," *CE*, No. 180, 10 December 1919, p. 2; Jules Rivet, "Décentralisation patriotique," *CE*, No. 310, 7 June 1922, p. 3; "Insinuations tendancieuses," *CE*, No. 311, 14 June 1922, p. 1; "La mare aux canards," *CE*, No. 322, 30 August 1922, p. 2.

41. Henri Béraud, "Ces messieurs du balcon," *CE*, No. 149, 7 May 1919, p. 1; Henri Béraud, "La ligue des civils de 2e classe," *CE*, No. 146, 16 April 1919, p. 1.

42. "Petite correspondance," *CE*, No. 301, 5 April 1922, p. 4; "Petite correspondance," *CE*, No. 335, 29 November 1922, p. 4; Jean Norton Cru, *Témoins, essai d'analyse et de critique des souvenirs de combattants édités en français de 1915 à 1928* (1929; reprint, Nancy: Presses Universitaires de Nancy, 1993), pp. 274–275.

43. "Dans les bégonias," *CE*, No. 157, 2 July 1919, p. 4; Rodolphe Bringer, "Encore une ligue!" *CE*, No. 156, 25 June 1919, p. 1.

44. Pierre Scize, "Ceux qui exagèrent," *CE*, No. 572, 15 June 1927, pp. 1–2.

45. See chapter 11.

46. Pierre Scize, "Les Etats-Généraux ou trop tard le tonnerre," *CE*, No. 593, 9 November 1927, pp. 1–2; Pierre Scize, "Amende honorable Maginot! Maginot!" *CE*, No. 594, 16 November 1927, pp. 1–2.

47. See Robert Wohl, *The Generation of 1914* (Cambridge: Harvard University Press, 1979).

48. "Et les réparateurs?" *CE*, No. 152, 28 May 1919, p. 1; Maurice Maréchal, "Le rajeunissement des cadres," *CE*, No. 146, 16 April 1919, p. 1.

49. See chapter 6.

50. Roland Dorgelès, "Dernière heure," *CE*, No. 148, 30 April 1919, p. 3. "Le grand concours du plus vieux vieillard de France," *CE*, No. 246, 16 March 1921, pp. 1–2.

51. "La mare aux canards," *CE*, No. 488, 4 November 1925, p. 2.

52. See chapter 13.

53. Pierre Scize, "Les belles promotions de la victoire," *CE*, No. 519, 9 June 1926, pp. 1–2; Henri Guilac, "La Gare de l'Est en 192 . . . ," *CE*, No. 519, 9 June 1926, p. 1. A black-and-white copy of the painting, by Albert Herter, is in An-

thony Livesey, *Great Battles of World War I* (London: Marshall Editions, 1989), pp. 8–9. Henri Barbusse's position was similar in *Paroles d'un combattant* (Paris: Flammarion, 1920), p. 107. See also Jay Winter, *Sites of Memory, Sites of Mourning: The Great War in European Cultural History* (Cambridge: Cambridge University Press, 1995), p. 182.

54. Pierre Scize, "Atrocités?" *CE*, No. 608, 22 February 1928, pp. 1–2; Daniel Halévy, *L'Europe brisée, journal et lettres 1914–1918* (Paris: Editions de Fallois, 1998), p. 179, and Sébastian Laurent, "Notes," in Halévy, *L'Europe*, p. 362; Annette Becker, "Edith Cavell, résistante executée," in Stéphane Audoin-Rouzeau, *14–18, La très grande guerre* (Paris: Le Monde Editions, 1994), pp. 115–119; Stéphane Audoin-Rouzeau and Annette Becker, *14–18 Retrouver la guerre* (Paris: Gallimard, 2000), p. 162.

55. "La mare aux canards," *CE*, No. 148, 30 April 1919, p. 2; "La mare aux canards," *CE*, No. 193, 10 March 1920, p. 2; "La mare aux canards," *CE*, No. 293, 8 February 1922, p. 2.

56. "La mare aux canards," *CE*, No. 453, 4 March 1925, p. 3.

57. "Dans les bégonias," *CE*, No. 214, 4 August 1920, p. 4.

58. "Un festin à tout casser," *CE*, No. 424, 13 August 1924, p. 2.

59. André Charpentier, "Contes du Canard, anticipation," *CE*, No. 67, 10 October 1917, p. 3.

60. "Petite correspondance," *CE*, No. 150, 14 May 1919, p. 4; "On n'est jamais trop prudent," *CE*, No. 151, 21 May 1919, p. 1.

61. Roland Dorgelès, "Les pèlerins doivent payer," *CE*, No. 170, 1 October 1919, p. 1. See chapter 5 of this book.

62. André Dahl, "La victime," *CE*, No. 164, 20 August 1919, pp. 1–2.

63. Rodolphe Bringer, "La vie renaît dans les régions dévastées," *CE*, No. 321, 23 August 1922, p. 1.

64. "Cinéma, pour ne pas oublier," *CE*, No. 582, 24 August 1927, p. 4; Boisyvon, "La vie du cinéma," *L'Intransigeant*, 20 August 1927, p. 4.

65. "La mare aux canards," *CE*, No. 392, 2 January 1924, p. 2.

66. "Embellisons Paris," *CE*, No. 137, 12 February 1919, p. 2; "Le projet bonnefous," *CE*, No. 136, 5 February 1919, p. 1.

67. Maurice Coriem, "Le wagon historique aux invalides," *CE*, No. 253, 4 May 1921, p. 3; G. de la Fouchardière, "La lanterne du Bouif, à propos du wagon," *CE*, No. 253, 4 May 1921, p. 4. On railroad accidents, see, for example, "Les chemins de fer d'Alsace sont désormais bien à nous," *CE*, No. 330, 25 October 1922, p. 1, and "M. Le Trocquer institue la catastrophe permanente et intégrale," *CE*, No. 331, 1 November 1922, p. 3.

68. See chapter 7.

69. "La mare aux canards," *CE*, No. 376, 12 September 1923, p. 2; Mat, "Le taxi de la Marne," *CE*, No. 339, 27 December 1922, p. 2.

70. G. de la Fouchardière, "Histoire du petit Chapeauléon," *CE*, No. 220, 15 September 1920, p. 1.

71. "Un hommage national à l'inventrice du camembert," *CE*, No. 562, 6 April 1927, p. 1.

72. See, for example, Antoine Prost, "Les monuments aux morts," in Nora, *Les lieux*, pp. 1:195–225; Winter, *Sites*, pp. 78–98; Daniel J. Sherman, "Art, Commerce, and the Production of Memory in France after World War I," in John R. Gillis, ed., *Commemorations: The Politics of National Identity* (Princeton, N.J.: Princeton University Press, 1994), pp. 186–193; Daniel J. Sherman, *The Construction of Memory in Interwar France* (Chicago: University of Chicago Press, 1999); Annette Becker, *Les monuments aux morts: Patrimoine et mémoire de la Grande Guerre* (Paris: Editions Errance, 1988).

73. "La mare aux canards," *CE*, No. 292, 1 February 1922, p. 2; "A travers la presse déchaînée," *CE*, No. 300, 29 March 1922, p. 3; "A cette occasion," *CE*, No. 261, 29 June 1921, p. 1; "Et gai gai! La faridondon," *CE*, No. 329, 18 October 1922, p. 2.

74. "A travers la presse déchaînée," *CE*, No. 325, 20 September 1922, p. 3.

75. "La mare aux canards," *CE*, No. 455, 18 March 1925, p. 3; Barbusse, *Paroles*, pp. 106–107. Barbusse translated and discussed in Winter, *Sites*, p. 182.

76. "La mare aux canards," *CE*, No. 265, 27 July 1921, p. 2; "Morts pour la patrie dormez en paix!" *CE*, No. 342, 17 January 1923, p. 1.

77. "M. Vel-Durand maire de Joinville reçoit la noix dorée d'honneur," *CE*, No. 333, 15 November 1922, p. 2.

78. Pierre Scize, "Voyage autour d'un monument aux morts," *CE*, No. 542, 17 November 1926, pp. 1–2. See also Prost, "Les monuments," p. 1:206.

79. "La leçon de Levallois," *CE*, No. 562, 6 April 1927, p. 1. For a discussion of the politics of the Levallois-Perret monument, see Sherman, *Construction*, p. 111, and for a photo, p. 84.

80. "La mare aux canards," *CE*, No. 450, 11 February 1925, p. 3.

81. "La mare aux canards," *CE*, No. 608, 22 February 1928, p. 2; G. de la Fouchardière, "Chronique de l'oeil-de-Bouif: Toujours du même au même," *CE*, No. 610, 7 March 1928, p. 3. See also Priscilla Parkhurst Clark, *Literary France: The Making of a Culture* (Berkeley: University of California Press, 1987), pp. 1–7.

82. "Bravo!" *CE*, No. 124, 13 November 1918, p. 1; V. S. [Victor Snell], "A l'instar de l'ordre des avocats," *CE*, No. 232, 8 December 1920, p. 3.

83. See, for example, "Au temps pour le zouave!" *CE*, No. 436, 5 November 1924, p. 1; "Toujours le zouave," *CE*, No. 438, 19 November 1924, p. 2; "La Bourse," *CE*, No. 507, 17 March 1926, p. 4.

84. "La mare aux canards," *CE*, No. 329, 18 October 1922, p. 2; "Rompez, les poètes!" *CE*, No. 445, 7 January 1925, p. 1; Roland Dorgelès, "Une croix volée," *CE*, No. 212, 21 July 1920, p. 1; "La mare aux canards," *CE*, No. 212, 21 July 1920, p. 2; "M. Victor Margueritte et la Légion d'Honneur," *CE*, No. 340, 3 January 1923, p. 1. The risqué novelist was Victor Margueritte. On the scandal of his novel, *La garçonne*, see Mary Louise Roberts, *Civilization without Sexes: Reconstructing Gender in Postwar France, 1917–1921* (Chicago: University of Chicago Press, 1994), pp. 46–62.

85. Whip, "Passementeries," *CE*, No. 161, 30 July 1919, p. 4; V. S. [Victor Snell], "Dans l'ordre national," *CE*, No. 377, 19 September 1923, p. 1; Jules

Rivet, "Petits papiers, la promotion Léon Bérard," *CE,* No. 401, 5 March 1924, p. 1; Henri Guilac, "Le Musée de la Légion d'Honneur," *CE,* No. 437, 12 November 1924, p. 3.

86. "M. Gaston Chéraux refuse la croix," *CE,* No. 422, 30 July 1924, p. 4; "Lettres ou pas lettres," *CE,* No. 373, 22 August 1923, p. 4.

87. Mat, "La promotion Ronsard," *CE,* No. 427, 3 September 1924, p. 2; Jules Rivet, "Une grande manifestation sportive," *CE,* No. 298, 15 March 1922, p. 1; "Légion d'Honneur," *CE,* No. 355, 18 April 1923, p. 3; "Légion d'Honneur," *CE,* No. 360, 23 May 1923, p. 1; "Dans la Légion d'Honneur," *CE,* No. 360, 23 May 1923, p. 3; Jules Rivet, "Les fêtes de la mi-carême," *CE,* No. 404, 25 March 1924, p. 3.

88. See, for example, Pierre Renouvin, *L'armistice de Rethondes* (Paris: Gallimard, 1969), pp. 255–275; Pierre Miquel, *La paix de Versailles et l'opinion française* (Paris: Flammarion, 1972), pp. 224–228.

89. On the armistice debate, see chapters 1 and 3.

90. See, for example, "Deux anniversaires," *CE,* No. 281, 16 November 1921, p. 1; V. S. [Victor Snell], "Aspects," *CE,* No. 330, 25 October 1922, p. 1; Jules Rivet, "La cérémonie du 11 Novembre," *CE,* No. 332, 8 November 1922, p. 1; Victor Snell, "Anniversaire," *CE,* No. 384, 7 November 1923, p. 1; "Anniversaire," *CE,* No. 436, 5 November 1924, p. 1.

91. See, for example, Prost, "Les monuments," pp. 1:208–210.

92. Rodolphe Bringer, "De ma fenêtre," *CE,* No. 542, 17 November 1926, p. 2. See also, for example, "Deux anniversaires," *CE,* No. 281, 16 November 1921, p. 1.

93. "Deux anniversaires," *CE,* No. 281, 16 November 1921, p. 1; Varé, "L'anniversaire," *CE,* No. 281, 16 November 1921, p. 4; V. S., "Aspects," p. 1; de la Fouchardière, "Chronique de l'oeil-de-Bouif: Lendemain d'anniversaire," *CE,* No. 333, 15 November 1922, p. 2. See chapter 4 of this book.

94. Varé, "Le président de la République a inauguré respectueusement le monument du Matin," and "L'instant solennel," in *CE,* No. 333, 15 November 1922, p. 1.

95. "La mare aux canards," *CE,* No. 384, 7 November 1924, p. 2.

96. René Virard, "Armistice conte maigre," *CE,* No. 541, 10 November 1926, p. 4.

97. Whip, "Dialogue ingénu," *CE,* No. 594, 16 November 1927, p. 2.

CHAPTER 9. BETWEEN CANNIBALISM AND RESURRECTION

1. Claude Lévi-Strauss, *Tristes Tropiques,* trans. John and Doreen Weightman (New York: Penguin Books, 1992), pp. 232–233.

2. Ibid., pp. 233–234. On the cult of the unknown soldier, see Daniel J. Sherman, "Bodies and Names: The Emergence of Commemoration in Interwar France," *American Historical Review* 103 (1998), pp. 463–466.

3. Benedict Anderson, *Imagined Communities: Reflections on the Origin and Spread of Nationalism* (New York: Verso, 1991), p. 9.

4. René Buzelin, "Le civil inconnu," *CE,* No. 227, 3 November 1920, pp. 1–2; V. S. [Victor Snell], "Réflexes," *CE,* No. 322, 30 August 1922, p. 1; Pierre Bénard, "Une belle journée historique," *CE,* No. 400, 27 February 1924, p. 3.

5. "La mare aux canards," *CE,* No. 234, 22 December 1920, p. 2; G. de la Fouchardière, "Chronique de l'oeil-de-Bouif: Où M. Doumergue plante un clou," *CE,* No. 473, 22 July 1925, p. 2. On Citroën, see, for example, "Petite correspondance," *CE,* No. 222, 29 September 1920, p. 4.

6. "La tombe du député inconnu," *CE,* No. 353, 4 April 1923, p. 1; Jean de Pierrefeu, "Le retour triomphal des capitaux évadés," *CE,* No. 524, 14 July 1926, p. 3.

7. Maréchal Pétain [sic], "Bonne feuilles, 'Le soldat,' " *CE,* No. 540, 3 November 1926, pp. 1–2.

8. "L'inconnu no. 2," *CE,* No. 256, 25 May 1921, p. 1; G. de la Fouchardière, "L'art d'utiliser les restes," *CE,* No. 232, 8 December 1920, p. 1. See also Sherman, "Bodies," pp. 464–465.

9. "Le 'culte nouveau,' " *CE,* No. 244, 2 March 1921, p. 1.

10. G. de la Fouchardière, "Chronique de l'oeil-de-Bouif: Où Bicard utilise l'Arc de Triomphe et le Métro," *CE,* No. 385, 14 November 1923, pp. 3–4.

11. Headline, *CE,* No. 383, 31 October 1923, p. 1; P. S., "Laisse flotter les rubans," *CE,* No. 540, 3 November 1926, p. 1.

12. P. S., "Laisse flotter les rubans," p. 1; P. S., "Un succès pour le 'Canard,' " *CE,* No. 593, 9 November 1927, p. 1; Jacqueline Lalouette, *La libre penseé en France 1848–1940* (Paris: Albin Michel, 1997), pp. 189–193.

13. "La mare aux canards," *CE,* No. 389, 12 December 1923, p. 2.

14. "Fleurs et couronnes, la manière de s'en servir: Un ouvrage patriotique nous enseigne l'exploitation rationelle et intensive du poilu," *CE,* No. 327, 4 October 1922, p. 1.

15. "La course du flambeau," *CE,* No. 456, 25 March 1925, p. 1; Gaston Vidal, "Le relai sacré," *Le Journal,* 18 March 1925, p. 1.

16. "Dans les bégonias," *CE,* No. 230, 24 November 1920, p. 3.

17. See chapters 6 and 10.

18. De la Fouchardière, "L'art d'utiliser les restes," p. 1; G. de la Fouchardière, "Chronique de l'oeil-de-Bouif: A titre posthume," *CE,* No. 400, 27 February 1924, p. 3; Jean Defrasne, *Le pacifisme en France* (Paris: Presses Universitaires de France, 1994), pp. 94–95. See also M. D., "Le matin," *La Vérité,* 2 July 1918, p. 1.

19. G. de la Fouchardière, "Chronique de l'oeil-de-Bouif: Un filon," *CE,* No. 317, 26 July 1922, p. 2.

20. Lalouette, *La libre pensée,* p. 344.

21. De la Fouchardière, "Chronique de l'oeil-de-Bouif: A titre posthume," p. 3; Le Poète Inconnu, "Jusqu'au bout du symbole," *CE,* No. 229, 17 November 1920, p. 2. On the political maneuverings that surrounded the choice of location, see Marilène Patten Henry, *Monumental Accusations: The Monuments aux Morts as Expressions of Popular Resentment* (New York: Peter Lang, 1996), p. 106.

22. De la Fouchardière, "L'art d'utiliser les restes," p. 1.

23. Fanny Clab, "Le laurier," *CE*, No. 271, 7 September 1921, p. 2.

24. "Leçon de gastronomie," *CE*, No. 64, 19 September 1917, p. 1; Victor Snell, "Vive le Sologne! L'offensive victorieuse de nos troupes," *CE*, No. 218, 1 September 1920, p. 1; Blaise Cendrars, *La main coupée* (1946; reprint, Paris: Editions Denoël, 1997), pp. 55–57.

25. P. S., "Un succès pour le 'Canard,' " p. 1.

26. See chapter 1.

27. Maggie Kilgour, *From Communion to Cannibalism* (Princeton, N.J.: Princeton University Press, 1990).

28. G. de la Fouchardière, "Chronique de l'oeil-de-Bouif," *CE*, No. 327, 4 October 1922, p. 3.

29. See, for example, Jay Winter, *Sites of Memory, Sites of Mourning: The Great War in European Cultural History* (Cambridge: Cambridge University Press, 1995), pp. 161–164, 186; Joanna Bourke, *Dismembering the Male: Men's Bodies, Britain, and the Great War* (Chicago: University of Chicago Press, 1996), pp. 212–213, 249; Stéphane Audoin-Rouzeau and Annette Becker, *14–18 Retrouver la guerre* (Paris: Gallimard, 2000), pp. 146–149.

30. Sauvegeot, "Pâques 1925," *Le Nouveau Siècle*, No. 8, 16 April 1925, p. 1.

31. Lob, Gotlib, Alexis, *Superdupont—Oui nide iou* (Paris: J'ai Lu, 1992), pp. 4–28.

32. Abel Gance, *J'accuse* (1938). See the discussion in Winter, *Sites*, pp. 133–144.

33. Roger Brindolphe, "Si j'étais," *CE*, No. 245, 9 March 1921, p. 2; Pol Ferjac, "Le pauvre bougre," *CE*, No. 400, 27 February 1924, p. 3. Compare the cover of *Le Crapouillot*, 15 November 1919, edited by the occasional *Canard* contributor Jean Galtier-Boissière, in which the dead ask to be left alone by the politicians of various stripes who evoke them in their electoral propaganda.

34. See, for example, Winter, *Sites*, pp. 205–207; Jean Norton Cru, *Témoins, essai d'analyse et de critique des souvenirs de combattants édités en français de 1915 à 1928* (1929; reprint, Nancy: Presses Universitaires de Nancy, 1993), pp. 32–33, 379–382. And see Henri Monier, "Mots historiques," *CE*, No. 466, 3 June 1925, p. 1.

35. "La mare aux canards," *CE*, No. 256, 25 May 1921, p. 2; "Eventualité d'une promenade," *CE*, No. 271, 7 September 1921, p. 1.

36. This crucial distinction is elided, for example, by Anderson when he links the cult of the unknown soldiers with "ghostly *national* imaginings," which are actually of the mass of military dead rising from their white-crossed cemeteries; Anderson, *Imagined*, pp. 9–10.

37. Paul Ory, "Réflexes: Ce n'est qu'un rêve," *CE*, No. 385, 14 November 1923, p. 4.

38. G. de la Fouchardière, "Chronique de l'oeil-de-Bouif: Inter pocula," *CE*, No. 546, 15 December 1926, p. 3.

39. Pedro, "La classe!" *CE*, No. 584, 7 September 1927, p. 2. Compare Marilène Patten Henry's discussion of the flat tombstone of the unknown soldier,

which she links to Philippe Ariès's conclusion that flat gravestones marked the absence of fear of the returning dead; Henry, *Monumental Accusations,* pp. 109–110.

40. See, for example, Matt K. Matsuda, *The Memory of the Modern* (New York: Oxford University Press, 1996), p. 29. During the war, a positive idea of resurrection was present through the notion of the rebirth of the country (not, as with the *Canard,* physical rising from a tomb). See Audoin-Rouzeau and Becker, *Retrouver,* pp. 145–146.

41. On begonias, see chapter 3.

42. G. de la Fouchardière, "Chronique de l'oeil-de-Bouif: Dans les bégonias," *CE,* No. 542, 17 November 1926, p. 2.

43. Jacques Leclerc, "Soliloque du poilu inconnu," *CE,* No. 385, 14 November 1923, p. 1.

44. Roland Dorgelès, *Les croix de bois* (1919; reprint, Paris: Albin Michel, 1931); Henri Barbusse, *Le feu, journal d'un escouade* (1916; reprint, Paris: Flammarion, 1965).

45. Pierre Scize, "Après la 'réparation': Paroles entendues sous l'Arc de Triomphe," *CE,* No. 585, 14 September 1927, pp. 1–2.

46. Winter, *Sites,* pp. 133ff.; Henry, *Monumental Accusations,* p. 150.

47. See chapter 7.

48. "La mare aux canards," *CE,* No. 583, 31 August 1927, p. 2.

49. "Deauville s'est magnifiquement associé à la cérémonie de réparation nationale," *CE,* No. 584, 7 September 1927, p. 3; "Après les bagarres révolutionnaires, cérémonie expiatoire," *CE,* No. 583, 31 August 1927, p. 3.

50. G. de la Fouchardière, "Chronique de l'oeil-de-Bouif: La manière de s'en servir," *CE,* No. 594, 16 November 1927, p. 3.

51. See chapter 8.

CHAPTER 10. ANTI-IMPERIALISM AND ITS STEREOTYPES

1. See, for example, Edward Said, *Orientalism* (New York: Pantheon Books, 1978), and his more recent *Culture and Imperialism* (New York: Pantheon Books, 1994).

2. W., "Le vrai bonheur," *CE,* No. 373, 22 August 1923, p. 2; G. de la Fouchardière, "Hors d'oeuvre, d'une république heureuse," *L'Oeuvre,* 11 August 1923, p. 2; G. de la Fouchardière, "Hors d'oeuvre, dois-je m'excuser?" *L'Oeuvre,* 20 August 1923, p. 2.

3. See, for example, Jules Rivet, "Evviva Italia," *CE,* No. 337, 13 December 1922, p. 2; "Cinéma éducateur," No. 337, 13 December 1922, p. 4; "La mare aux canards," *CE,* No. 378, 26 September 1923, p. 2; "Au jour le jour," *CE,* No. 491, 25 November 1925, p. 2.

4. On the Rif war, see *Abd el-Krim et la république du Rif, actes du Colloque International d'Etudes Historiques et Sociologiques 18–10 Janvier 1923* (Paris: Maspéro, 1976). On other press coverage of the war, see Charles-Robert Ageron, "La presse parisienne devant la guerre du Rif (Avril 1925–Mai 1926),"

Presse et politique, actes du Colloque de Nanterre (Mars 1973): Les Cahiers du CEREP, No. 1 (1975), pp. 1–25.

5. "La mare aux canards," *CE,* No. 420, 16 July 1924, p. 3; "La joie est intense au Sénégal," *CE,* No. 327, 4 October 1922, p. 3; "Recrutement," *CE,* No. 352, 28 March 1923, p. 1.

6. "Les bonnes méthodes," *CE,* No. 354, 11 April 1923, p. 3; see chapter 7 of this book.

7. "Recrutement," *CE,* No. 352, 28 March 1923, p. 1.

8. See, for example, Jules Rivet, "Décentralisation patriotique," *CE,* No. 310, 7 June 1922, p. 3; "Recrutement," *CE,* No. 352, 28 March 1923, p. 1; "Respect aux hommes de couleur," *CE,* No. 371, 8 August 1923, p. 1; A. des Enganes, "Une trahison," *CE,* No. 440, 3 December 1924, p. 1.

9. "Respect aux hommes de couleur," *CE,* No. 371, 8 August 1923, p. 1; Alain [Emile Chartier], *Mars ou la guerre jugée* (1921; reprint, Paris: Gallimard, 1995), p. 238, Henri Barbusse, *Le feu, journal d'un escouade* (1916; reprint, Paris: Flammarion, 1965), pp. 74–75, 343–344. See also Tyler Stovall, *Paris Noir: African Americans in the City of Light* (Boston: Houghton Mifflin, 1996), p. 19.

10. Henri Guilac, "L'Américain qui se noie," and "Respect aux hommes de couleur," both in *CE,* No. 371, 8 August 1923, p. 1; Maurice Morice, "Après l'affaire du Bar 'El Garon,' " *CE,* No. 375, 5 September 1923, p. 3; "Mystère et publicité," *CE,* No. 382, 24 October 1923, p. 1; "Canetons," *CE,* No. 373, 22 August 1923, p. 4. See also chapter 13 of this book, and René Goscinny and Albert Uderzo, *Astérix et le chaudron* (Paris: Dargaud, 1972), pp. 15–16. On the conflicts created by the racist attitudes of Americans in France, see, for example, Stovall, *Paris,* pp. 15, 41, 72–74.

11. "Carnets de la bonne ménagère, enfin voici des servantes, madame," *CE,* No. 351, 21 March 1923, p. 4; R. Bz. [René Buzelin], "Un poing noir à l'horizon," *CE,* No. 267, 10 August 1921, pp. 1–2; Jules Rivet, "Le péril noir: Les palabres de la rue Blanche," *CE,* No. 271, 7 September 1921, p. 3.

12. "Chronique industrielle," *CE,* No. 306, 10 May 1922, p. 2; Morice, "Après l'affaire du Bar 'El Garon,' " p. 3.

13. Mat, "Grande exposition de blanc," *CE,* No. 395, 23 January 1924, p. 4; Jules Rivet, "Contes du Canard, les festins du roi Bamboula," *CE,* No. 529, 18 August 1926, p. 4; Noré Brunel, "Contes du Canard," *CE,* No. 460, 22 April 1925, p. 4; René Dubosc [?], "Musique et cuisine," *CE,* No. 467, 10 June 1925, p. 2; BDIC, F. Res. 270 SPE, t. 8, 3 July 1917; Caumery [Maurice Languereau] and J. P. Pinchon, *Bécassine pendant la Grande Guerre* (1915; reprint, Paris: Gautier-Languereau, 1993), pp. 56–57. For an example of French wartime racist exploitation of this idea, see Stéphane Audoin-Rouzeau and Annette Becker, *14–18 Retrouver la guerre* (Paris: Gallimard, 2000), pp. 176–177.

14. See chapter 6.

15. Jules Rivet, "Mes mémoires (fragments) par Joséphine Baker," *CE,* No. 544, 1 December 1926, p. 3; J. Pruvost, "Nouvelles de Chine et d'Albanie," *CE,* No. 561, 30 March 1927, p. 3; "Comme Joséphine," *CE,* No. 575, 6 July 1927,

p. 3; Rodolphe Bringer, "De ma fenêtre," *CE,* No. 595, 23 November 1927, p. 3; Rodolphe Bringer, "De ma fenêtre," *CE,* No. 615, 11 April 1928, p. 2. On Baker's brilliant career in the Paris of the twenties, see Stovall, *Paris,* pp. 49–56.

16. "Sur le pas de la Porte," *CE,* No. 1, 10 September 1915, p. 3.

17. For a discussion of wartime censorship, see chapter 1; SHAT, 5N 347, Consigne, Rappel du Gouverneur Général de l'Algérie, 18 July 1915. The BDIC registers do not record any cuts related to anti-Islamic material in the *Canard.*

18. Georges de la Fouchardière, "Chronique de l'oeil-de-Bouif: La neuvième croisade," *CE,* No. 327, 4 October 1922, pp. 3–4; Whip, "Le gouverneur général de l'Algérie est désigné," *CE,* No. 260, 22 June 1921, p. 1.

19. "Les opérations en Tripolitaine," *CE,* No. 359, 16 May 1923, p. 3.

20. See, for example, "La mare aux canards," *CE,* No. 184, 7 January 1920, p. 2.

21. "Les peuples ont le droit de disposer d'eux-mêmes," *CE,* No. 333, 15 November 1922, p. 3.

22. "Mise au point," *CE,* No. 365, 27 June 1923, p. 1.

23. Georges de la Fouchardière, "Chronique de l'oeil-de-Bouif: On remet ça," *CE,* No. 363, 13 June 1923, p. 2.

24. "Réflexes" and "La situation au Maroc," both in *CE,* No. 425, 20 August 1924, pp. 2 and 4.

25. "Les espagnols au Maroc," *CE,* No. 429, 17 September 1924, p. 1; "La victoire espagnole" and "Le repli," both in *CE,* No. 439, 26 November 1924, p. 2.

26. Blasco Ibanez, "Alphonse XIII," *CE,* No. 446, 14 January 1925, p. 4.

27. "Pour le Maroc," *CE,* No. 462, 6 May 1925, p. 2.

28. Daniel Say, "Les riffains devenaient trop turbulents," *L'Intransigeant,* 8 May 1925, p. 1. See also chapter 4 of this book.

29. Georges Duhamel, *Civilisation 1914–1917* (1918; reprint, Monaco: Les Editions de l'Imprimerie Nationale de Monaco, 1950), especially pp. 197–207; Jean Norton Cru, *Témoins, essai d'analyse et de critique des souvenirs de combattants édités en français de 1915 à 1928* (1929; reprint, Nancy: Presses Universitaires de Nancy, 1993), p. 596.

30. "Le 'Canard' ouvre une enquête, à quels signes reconnaît-on la civilisation?" *CE,* No. 463, 13 May 1925, pp. 1–2; "Notre enquête, à quels signes reconnaît-on la civilisation?" *CE,* No. 464, 20 May 1925, p. 1; Pierre Bouillette, "Opinions, les signes de la barbarie," *CE,* No. 465, 27 May 1925, p. 1, and on p. 2, "Notre enquête, les signes de la civilisation."

31. Pedro, "Quelques signes indiscutables," *CE,* No. 464, 20 May 1925, p. 4.

32. J. R. [Jules Rivet], "Petits papiers, propos sur le Rif," *CE,* No. 464, 20 May 1925, p. 1; "Une grande victoire," *CE,* No. 484, 7 October 1925, p. 2; "La mare aux canards," *CE,* No. 484, 7 October 1925, p. 3.

33. David H. Slavin, "The French Left and the Rif War, 1924–1925: Racism and the Limits of Internationalism," *Journal of Contemporary History* 26 (1991), pp. 11–13; "La mare aux canards," *CE,* 13 May 1925, p. 3.

34. Georges de la Fouchardière, "Pour le droit et la civilisation" and "Chronique de l'oeil-de-Bouif: Le prince des Galles plume une autruche," both in *CE,* No. 463, 13 May 1925, pp. 1 and 2.

35. "La guerre au Maroc, les espagnols à cinq étapes d'Ajdir," *CE,* No. 481, 16 September 1925, p. 1. See also, for example, Maurice Morice, "Les opérations au Maroc," *CE,* No. 463, 13 May 1925, p. 1.

36. Pedro, "Vieilles connaissances," *CE,* No. 466, 3 June 1925, p. 1.

37. "En Orient, ils remettent ça," *CE,* No. 210, 7 July 1920, p. 1.

38. Jules Rivet, "Une émouvante cérémonie," *CE,* No. 468, 17 June 1925, p. 1.

39. Pedro, "Comme de juste," *CE,* No. 465, 27 May 1925, p. 2; Pedro, "Vieilles connaissances," p. 1; René B., "Victoire," *CE,* No. 472, 15 July 1925, p. 1; J. R. [Jules Rivet], "Savez-vous planter les clous?" *CE,* No. 473, 22 July 1925, p. 1; "Printemps du Rif," *CE,* No. 505, 3 March 1926, p. 1.

40. "Réflexes sur la guerre," *CE,* No. 474, 29 July 1925, p. 1; "Succès espagnol au Maroc," *CE,* No. 483, 30 September 1925, p. 1.

41. Jules Rivet, "Mauvais propos," *CE,* No. 481, 16 September 1925, p. 1.

42. "Un piège grossier," *CE,* No. 474, 29 July 1925, p. 1; D. H., " 'Pas de paix blanche au Maroc,' nous déclare M. Painlevé," *CE,* No. 509, 31 March 1926, p. 3; "Cela ne sera pas!" *CE,* No. 511, 14 April 1926, p. 1.

43. "Fidèles à l'attache," *CE,* No. 525, 21 July 1926, p. 3; "Petite correspondance," *CE,* No. 526, 26 July 1926, p. 4; "La mare aux canards," *CE,* No. 527, 4 August 1926, p. 2.

44. J. R., "Petits papiers, propos sur le Rif," p. 1.

45. "L'offensif contre le Maroc Français," *L'Illustration,* 16 May 1925, pp. 478–481; [Pedro,] "Les deux marocains," *CE,* No. 465, 27 May 1925, p. 2.

46. J. Prouvost, "La guerre du Rif," and Henri Monier, "Ne pas confondre," both in *CE,* No. 465, 27 May 1925; Henri Monier, "Incidence," *CE,* No. 473, 22 July 1925, p. 3; W. N. Grove, "Du pain sur la planche," *CE,* No. 476, 12 August 1925, p. 1; W. N. Grove, "Le gouvernement," *CE,* No. 482, 23 September 1925, p. 1; W. N. Grove, "Queue de colonne au Maroc," *CE,* No. 463, 13 May 1925, p. 3.

47. Monier, "Ne pas confondre," p. 1. A similar argument was used, in an essentially racist way, in German attacks on French claims to be champions of civilization; see Audoin-Rouzeau and Becker, *Retrouver,* p. 176.

48. "La guerre au Maroc, les espagnols à cinq étapes d'Ajdir," *CE,* No. 481, 16 September 1925, p. 1.

49. Pierre Bénard, "Tout le Maroc célèbre les fêtes de la victoire," *CE,* No. 518, 2 June 1926, p. 1; "Paris a enfin une mosquée," *CE,* No. 525, 21 July 1926, p. 1; "Le sort d'Abd-el-Krim," *CE,* No. 519, 9 June 1926, p. 3.

50. "Le problème syrien," *CE,* No. 488, 4 November 1925, p. 2.

51. "De la décision" and PR. B., "Chez les sauvages," both in *CE,* No. 476, 12 August 1925, p. 1.

52. See chapter 11.

53. "Un nouveau roi du Cambodge est monté sur le trône," *CE,* No. 581, 17 August 1927, p. 1.

54. "La question de Syrie" and "Le droit des peuples," both in *CE,* No. 169, 24 September 1919, p. 3.

55. Grove, "Du pain sur la planche," p. 1.

56. See, for example, E. R., "Dettes, autour de la conférence," and "Cinéma," both in *CE,* No. 483, 30 September 1925, p. 4; Pierre Bénard, "Un document inédit, la déclaration ministérielle," *CE,* No. 492, 2 December 1925, p. 2; "Les gestes symboliques," *CE,* No. 508, 24 March 1926, p. 1.

57. Ernest Raynaud, "Le prix de la paix," *CE,* No. 508, 24 March 1926, p. 1; "Conseil des ministres," *CE,* No. 502, 10 February 1926, p. 2; Albert Londres, *Marseille, porte du Sud* (1927; reprint, Paris: Le Serpent à Plumes, 1994), p. 19.

58. See, for example, "Les nouvelles de Syrie sont bonnes," *CE,* No. 479, 2 September 1925, p. 4; "La situation en Syrie," *CE,* No. 480, 9 September 1925, p. 3; Ernest Raynaud, "Propos," *CE,* No. 514, 5 May 1926, p. 1; "L'esprit de Locarno, les négociations avec les druses se poursuivent victorieusement," *CE,* No. 507, 17 March 1926, p. 3.

59. "La paix syrienne," *CE,* No. 515, 12 May 1926, p. 1.

60. J. Kessel, "Le 'Journal' en Syrie, comment j'ai bombardé Soueida," *Le Journal,* 15 May 1926, p. 1. On Kessel, see Ivan Stephen, Alain da Cunha, and Arlette Moreau, *Kessel* (Paris: Plon, 1985); Cru, *Témoins,* p. 624; Joseph Kessel, *L'équipage* (Paris: Gallimard, 1969; text completed in 1923); Joseph Kessel, *Témoin parmi les hommes,* vol. 1, *Le temps de l'espérance* (Paris: del Duca, 1956), p. 231.

61. Jules Rivet, "Divertissements d'intellectuels," *CE,* No. 517, 26 May 1926, p. 2.

62. Not surprisingly, these attacks have excited indignation from the Syrians, who commemorate them in patriotic children's literature. See, for example, Allen Douglas and Fedwa Malti-Douglas, *Arab Comic Strips: Politics of an Emerging Mass Culture* (Bloomington: Indiana University Press, 1994), pp. 111–112. Interestingly, Kessel himself seems not too proud of the escapade, which is omitted from his memoirs, just as the reportage is absent from a book of tribute; Kessel, *Témoin,* pp. 1:231–266, and Stephen, da Cunha, and Moreau, *Kessel.*

63. See Jan Karl Tanenbaum, *General Maurice Sarrail 1856–1929: The French Army and Left-Wing Politics* (Chapel Hill: University of North Carolina Press, 1974), and, on Syria, pp. 185–214.

64. "La mare aux canards," *CE,* No. 490, 18 November 1925, p. 2.

65. See, for example, "La Bourse," *CE,* No. 476, 12 August 1925, p. 4; "La situation en Syrie," *CE,* No. 480, 9 September 1925, p. 3.

66. Slavin, "The French Left," pp. 5–32.

CHAPTER 11. POLITICS AS USUAL

1. Pierre Miquel, *La paix de Versailles et l'opinion française* (Paris: Flammarion, 1972), pp. 11, 21–22; Jean-Jacques Becker, *La France en guerre, 1914–1918, la grande mutation* (Paris: Editions Complexe, 1988), p. 71.

2. See, for example, "A travers la presse déchaînée," *CE,* No. 133, 15 January 1919, p. 4; "Bien renseignés" and "La mare aux canards," both in *CE,* No. 128, 11 December 1918, p. 2; "L'état de siège," *CE,* No. 161, 30 July 1919, p. 1.

3. "Tant d'Alliés que nous avons," *CE*, No. 134, 22 January 1919, p. 1; H. P. Gassier, "Chut! Chut! Chut!" *CE*, No. 135, 29 January 1919, p. 1.

4. *CE*, No. 127, 4 December 1918, and No. 128, 11 December 1918.

5. André Dahl, "Autre conte," *CE*, No. 132, 8 January 1919, p. 3.

6. See, for example, "La mare aux canards," *CE*, No. 134, 22 January 1919, p. 2.

7. See, for example, "Dernière heure, la première sortie," *CE*, No. 128, 11 December 1918, p. 3; "Nos feuilletons," *CE*, No. 154, 11 June 1919, p. 4.

8. Miquel, *La paix de Versailles*, pp. 62–112.

9. Headline and p. 1 in *CE*, No. 148, 30 April 1919.

10. "Souvenez-vous!" *CE*, No. 132, 8 January 1919, p. 4.

11. "Dans leurs petits souliers," *CE*, No. 130, 25 December 1918, p. 1.

12. "Ohé! Les démobilisés!" *CE*, No. 143, 26 March 1919, p. 1.

13. H. P. Gassier, "Le démobilisé à l'exercice," *CE*, No. 147, 23 April 1919, p. 2.

14. "La mare aux canards," *CE*, No. 161, 30 July 1919, p. 2; *CE*, No. 166, 3 September 1919, p. 1.

15. "La mare aux canards," *CE*, No. 165, 27 August 1919, p. 2; "Encore un baiser," *CE*, No. 168, 17 September 1919, p. 1.

16. "La campagne électorale est ouverte," *CE*, No. 173, 22 October 1919, p. 1.

17. "Le bloc enfariné," *CE*, No. 171, 8 October 1919, pp. 1–2; "Chronique électorale," *CE*, No. 173, 22 October 1919, p. 4.

18. *CE*, No. 163, 13 August 1919, p. 2; *CE*, No. 174, 29 October 1919, p. 1.

19. See, for example, Jean-Jacques Becker and Serge Berstein, *Victoire et frustrations, 1914–1929* (Paris: Editions du Seuil, 1990), pp. 191–194.

20. See chapter 10.

21. "Pour combattre le bolchévisme," *CE*, No. 180, 10 December 1919, p. 4.

22. "Banquet du Bloc National," *CE*, No. 181, 17 December 1919, p. 3.

23. Leygues-Boulide, "Une escroquerie," *CE*, No. 196, 31 March 1920, p. 1.

24. H. P. Gassier, "Petite histoire des bons petits tsars," *CE*, No. 109, 31 July 1918, pp. 1–4.

25. See, for example, "En Russie? Jamais!" *CE*, No. 139, 26 February 1919, p. 1; Miquel, *La paix de Versailles*, pp. 109–110.

26. See, for example, Maurice Coriem, "Les rescapés de Russie," *CE*, No. 226, 27 October 1920, p. 1; "A travers la presse déchaînée," *CE*, No. 266, 3 August 1921, p. 3.

27. Jules Rivet, "La fiancée du bolchevik ou le couteau sanglant," *CE*, Nos. 191–194, 25 February–17 March 1920.

28. Legrand-Mézet, "Phrases extraites de mon prochain livre," *CE*, No. 196, 31 March 1920, p. 4.

29. "Les flics à la C.G.T.," *CE*, No. 201, 5 May 1920, p. 2.

30. "Dernière heure, après le discours d'Evreux," *CE*, No. 382, 24 October 1923, p. 3.

31. See chapter 10.

32. Pierre Scize, "En zig-zag," *CE*, No. 602, 11 January 1928, pp. 1–2.

33. *CE*, No. 312, 21 June 1922; "Le 'Canard' avait raison," *CE*, No. 187, 28 January 1922, p. 1; Victor Snell, "Pour surmonter la vague de la baisse," *CE*,

No. 208, 23 June 1922, p. 1; "Démenti catégorique," *CE,* No. 210, 7 July 1922, p. 2.

34. Lucien Laforge, "Basse-cour," *CE,* No. 111, 14 August 1918, p. 1.

35. See, for example, "Dernière heure, frappant activité parlementaire," *CE,* No. 343, 24 January 1923, p. 3; "Dernière heure, il n'y en a pas qu'en Angleterre," *CE,* No. 355, 18 April 1923, p. 3; Mat, "Et cette santé," *CE,* No. 372, 15 August 1923, p. 4; "Une aimable et traditionnelle cérémonie," *CE,* No. 394, 16 January 1924, p. 1.

36. "Dernière heure, après le discours d'Evreux," *CE,* No. 382, 24 October 1923, p. 3.

37. "Quel est l'homme le plus propre de France?" *CE,* No. 346, 14 February 1923, p. 1.

38. "Les lecteurs du 'Canard' ont voté," *CE,* No. 360, 23 May 1923, p. 3.

39. See, for example, BDIC, F. Res. 270 SPE, t. 6 Service des Périodiques, Echoppages, 14 October 1916–10 January 1917, note of 31 October.

40. "Carnet," *CE,* No. 499, 20 January 1926, p. 2. See, for example, Pierre Miquel, *Poincaré* (Paris: Fayard, 1961), p. 452; Max Gallo, *Le grand Jaurès* (Paris: Editions Robert Laffont, 1984), p. 528; Stanislas Jeannesson, *Poincaré, la France et la Ruhr (1922–1924): Histoire d'une occupation* (Strasbourg: Presses Universitaires de Strasbourg, 1998), p. 132; introduction to Raymond Poincaré, "Au service de la France," *La Revue de France* 2 (1926), p. 225; headline, *CE,* No. 294, 15 February 1922; "La mare aux canards," *CE,* No. 538, 20 October 1926, p. 2; Charles Lussy, "Est-ce le cabinet de la prochaine guerre," *L'Humanité,* 16 January 1922, p. 1.

41. Maurice Maréchal, "Dernière heure, une erreur judiciaire?" *CE,* No. 242, 16 February 1921, p. 3.

42. Rodolphe Bringer, "Poincaré-pas-la-guerre," *CE,* No. 309, 31 May 1922; "Nouvelles preuves," *CE,* No. 325, 20 September 1922, p. 1.

43. See chapter 1.

44. "L'homme qui rit," *CE,* No. 310, 7 June 1922, p. 1; "Un homme vraiment sérieux," *CE,* No. 315, 12 July 1922, p. 1; Blaise Cendrars, *La main coupée* (1946; reprint, Paris: Editions Denoël, 1997), pp. 254–255. And see, for example, "Poincaré chez ses morts," *L'Humanité,* 6 June 1922, p. 1, and "L'homme qui rit," *L'Humanité,* 19 June 1922, p. 2.

45. Robert Henne, "M. Poincaré voyage dans l'Est," *CE,* No. 316, 19 July 1922, p. 3. Varé, "On annonce la fin du monde," *CE,* No. 322, 30 August 1922, p. 4. See chapter 7 of this book.

46. Miquel, *Poincaré,* pp. 450–454; Jules Rivet, "Marche Lorraine," *CE,* No. 378, 26 September 1923, p. 1.

47. "Un homme vraiment sérieux," *CE,* No. 315, 12 July 1922, p. 1; Jacques Leclerc, "Solilique du poilu inconnu," *CE,* No. 385, 14 November 1923, p. 1. "Cinés," *CE,* No. 298, 13 March 1922, p. 4; "Un exemple," *CE,* No. 384, 7 November 1923, p. 1; J. Pruvost, "Lendemain de Mardi Gras," *CE,* No. 296, 1 March 1922, p. 1.

48. "Excès intolérables," *CE,* No. 334, 22 November 1922, p. 1.

49. *CE,* No. 318, 2 August 1922.

50. René Buzelin, "Le ministère Poincaré," *CE,* No. 290, 18 January 1922, p. 1.

51. *CE,* No. 393, 9 January 1924, p. 4, bottom. For the Ruhr occupation, see Jeannesson, *Poincaré,* entire, and for the epithet, p. 382.

52. See chapter 4. The importance of foreign occupation is indicated by Audoin-Rouzeau's point that rapes occurred virtually everywhere troops invaded an enemy country; Stéphane Audoin-Rouzeau, *L'enfant de l'ennemi 1914–1918* (Paris: Aubier, 1995), pp. 33–54. On women as the booty of war, see, for example, Margaret Randolph Higonnet et al., "Introduction," in *Behind the Lines: Gender and the Two World Wars* (New Haven, Conn.: Yale University Press, 1987), p. 11.

53. Jules Rivet, "Dernière heure, apprenons à connaître nos richesses nationales," *CE,* No. 338, 20 December 1922, p. 3; "Heureux augure," *CE,* No. 340, 3 January 1923, p. 1.

54. G. de la Fouchardière, "Chronique de l'oeil-de-Bouif: Occupations dangereuses," *CE,* No. 342, 17 January 1923, pp. 1–2. And see, for example, Becker and Berstein, *Victoire,* pp. 151–161; Mary Louise Roberts, *Civilization without Sexes: Reconstructing Gender in Postwar France, 1917–1921* (Chicago: University of Chicago Press, 1994), pp. 89ff.

55. "Une grande victoire," *CE,* No. 475, 5 August 1925, p. 1.

56. Christian Delporte, "Méfions-nous du sourire de Germania! L'Allemagne dans la caricature française (1919–1939)," *Mots* 48 (1996), p. 38; Pierre Scize, "Benda, Plunkett et nous," *CE,* No. 605, 1 February 1928, pp. 1–2; Roland Dorgelès, *Le Cabaret de la Belle Femme* (1920; reprint, Paris: Albin Michel, 1928), p. 11. See also the examples (though these are of desire for rape rather than of sexual possession generally) noted in Audoin-Rouzeau, *L'enfant,* pp. 81–83.

57. See chapter 5.

58. Compare Audoin-Rouzeau, *L'enfant,* pp. 33–77, and see chapter 4 of this book.

59. "Heureux augure," *CE,* No. 340, 3 January 1923, p. 1.

60. "Communiqués officiels," *CE,* No. 341, 10 January 1923, p. 1.

61. Varé, "L'hiver dans la Ruhr," CE, No. 17 January 1923, p. 1; Mat, "Dans la Ruhr," *CE,* No. 370, 1 August 1923, p. 1.

62. "Dernière heure, l'occupation porte d'admirables fruits," *CE,* No. 342, 17 January 1923, p. 3.

63. "Dernière heure, la Ruhr productrice," *CE,* No. 374, 29 August 1923, p. 3; headline, *CE,* No. 378, 26 September 1923; "La revanche de la victoire," *CE,* No. 379, 3 October 1923, p. 1; "La bonne méthode," *CE,* No. 361, 30 May 1923, p. 1.

64. "Bonne affaire," *CE,* No. 371, 8 August 1923, p. 2; "A travers la presse déchaînée," *CE,* No. 381, 17 October 1923, p. 3.

65. "Réflexes," *CE,* No. 371, 8 August 1923, p. 2.

66. "M. De Lasteyrie dénonce un grave péril," *CE,* No. 372, 15 August 1923, p. 2.

67. "La mare aux canards," *CE*, No. 223, 6 October 1920, p. 2; "La révolution en Allemagne," *CE*, No. 385, 14 November 1923, p. 1.

68. "La mare aux canards," *CE*, No. 393, 9 January 1924, p. 2.

69. "Tout le pays," *CE*, No. 384, 7 November 1923, p. 1; Mat, "Une bonne année se présage," *CE*, No. 391, 26 December 1923, p. 1; Mat, "Le coup de balai," *CE*, No. 393, 9 January 1924, p. 2; headline, *CE*, No. 407, 16 April 1924.

70. "Le 'Canard' entre dans sa 9me année," *CE*, No. 392, 2 January 1924, p. 1.

71. "La feuille d'impôts et des Alpes-Maritimes," *CE*, No. 406, 9 April 1924, p. 4; Pierre Bénard, "Le petit Girond," *CE*, No. 407, 16 April 1924, p. 4; "La croix de mamers," *CE*, No. 408, 23 April 1924, p. 4; "Le petit électeur illustré," *CE*, No. 410, 7 May 1924, p. 4.

72. "Promesses," *CE*, No. 410, 7 May 1924, p. 1.

73. "Petite chronique électorale," *CE*, No. 402, 12 March 1924, p. 1; "Chronique électorale, préparez vos balais!" *CE*, No. 404, 26 March 1924, p. 1; "Petite chronique électorale," *CE*, No. 408, 23 April 1924, p. 1; Rodolphe Bringer, "Notre politique," *CE*, No. 345, 7 February 1923, p. 1; Pierre Bénard, "Les radicaux et le ministère," *CE*, No. 368, 18 July 1923, pp. 1–2.

74. "Après le scrutin" and "Un grand succès," both in *CE*, No. 411, 14 May 1924, p. 1.

75. "La mare aux canards," *CE*, No. 411, 14 May 1924, p. 3; Maurice Morice, "Rendons à César," *CE*, No. 413, 18 May 1924, p. 1.

76. Rodolphe Bringer, "La chambre du 11 Mai," *CE*, No. 411, 14 May 1924, pp. 1–2.

77. *CE*, No. 412, 21 May 1924.

78. "La mort de Marie-Stuart, M. Herriot n'en est-il pas responsable," *CE*, No. 417, 25 June 1924, p. 1; "Après Raymond, Edouard," *CE*, No. 419, 9 July 1924, p. 1; Henri Guilac, untitled cartoon, *CE*, No. 426, 27 August 1924, p. 1.

79. "La mare aux canards," *CE*, No. 420, 16 July 1924, p. 3; "Ohé M. Herriot," *CE*, No. 423, 6 August 1924, p. 1.

80. "Un fou," *CE*, No. 422, 30 July 1924, p. 1.

81. Maurice Morice, "Soyons justes," *CE*, No. 423, 6 August 1924, p. 1.

82. "Craintes injustifiées," *CE*, No. 432, 8 October 1924, p. 2.

83. Maurice Maréchal, "Trop de demi-mesures," *CE*, No. 454, 11 March 1925, p. 1.

84. Pierre Bénard, "Le scandale des autocars," *CE*, No. 483, 30 September 1925, pp. 3–4.

85. Maurice Morice, "Les symboliques, Q.D.M.," *CE*, No. 500, 27 January 1926, p. 1.

86. Jules Rivet, "Opinions, les quarante mille," *CE*, No. 501, 3 February 1926, p. 1; Ernest Raynaud, "Propos," *CE*, No. 504, 24 February 1926, p. 1.

87. "Un grand parti," *CE*, No. 467, 10 June 1925, p. 1.

88. See chapter 10 of this book and Becker and Berstein, *Victoire*, pp. 269ff.

89. "Feuilleton du Canard Enchaîné, les survies mystérieuses," *CE*, No. 486, 21 October 1925, p. 3.

90. Drégerin, "Les chambres sont rentrées hier," *CE*, No. 498, 13 January 1926, p. 1.

91. Henri Guilac, "Pâques 1925," *CE*, No. 459, 15 April 1925, p. 1.

92. Jean de Pierrefeu, "Lettres anticipées, de Miss Kate G. . . . à Miss W., à Boston (Etats-Unis)," *CE*, No. 494, 16 December 1925, p. 1.

93. Allen Douglas, *From Fascism to Libertarian Communism: Georges Valois against the Third Republic* (Berkeley: University of California Press, 1992), pp. 121–125.

94. "Signe des temps" and Pierre Bénard, "Un chic type," both in *CE*, No. 504, 24 February 1926, p. 2.

95. "La minute attendue," *CE*, No. 521, 23 June 1926, p. 1; Mat, "Si Poincaré revient," *CE*, No. 525, 21 July 1926, p. 2; "Propos," *CE*, No. 526, 28 July 1926, p. 2.

96. Pedro, "Le coq et le renard (fable)," *CE*, No. 526, 28 July 1926, p. 1; "La mare aux canards," *CE*, No. 526, 28 July 1926, p. 2.

97. "Certitudes et espoirs," *CE*, No. 526, 28 July 1926, p. 1; S., "Opinions," *CE*, No. 532, 8 September 1926, p. 1.

98. Léon Archambaud, "Le Congrès Radical va définir irrévocablement la politique du parti," *CE*, No. 537, 13 October 1926, p. 3.

99. William Napoleon Grove, "Dispositions," *CE*, No. 542, 17 November 1926, p. 2.

100. "Une belle fête républicaine à la Sorbonne," *CE*, No. 576, 13 July 1927, p. 3; "La mare aux canards," *CE*, No. 551, 19 January 1927, p. 2.

101. "Certitudes et espoirs," *CE*, No. 526, 28 July 1926, p. 1; Pierre Bénard, "La loi d'abord," *CE*, 23 February 1927, p. 1.

102. Rodolphe Bringer, "De ma fenêtre," *CE*, No. 542, 17 November 1926, p. 2.

103. Henri Monier, "Le mauvais exemple," p. 1, and "La mare aux canards," p. 2, both in *CE*, No. 527, 4 August 1926.

104. *CE*, No. 527, 4 August 1926.

105. See, for example, Maurice Morice, "Le discours de Lunéville," *CE*, No. 573, 22 June 1927, p. 1.

106. "Propos," *CE*, No. 556, 23 February 1927, p. 1; Drégerin, "Le budget de l'armée," *CE*, No. 597, 7 December 1927, p. 1; Henri Monier, "Convictions," *CE*, No. 573, 22 June 1927, p. 1.

107. "Au seuil de l'année," *CE*, No. 600, 28 December 1927, p. 1.

108. "Prévision pour l'année 1928," *CE*, No. 610, 4 January 1928, p. 1.

109. [Rodolphe Bringer,] "De ma fenêtre," *CE*, No. 613, 28 March 1928, p. 3; Ernest Raynaud, "La main de Moscou," *CE*, No. 585, 14 September 1927, p. 3.

110. "Petit dictionnaire à l'usage de M. Kérillis," *CE*, No. 578, 27 July 1927, p. 3.

111. Henri Barbusse, "Faits divers," *CE*, No. 614, 4 April 1928, p. 2; Jules Rivet, "Les heures nouvelles, un parti paysan va se constituer," *CE*, No. 604, 25 January 1928, p. 2.

112. See, for example, "Curieuse initiative," *CE*, No. 604, 25 January 1928, p. 4; headline, *CE*, No. 605, 1 February 1928.

113. "La Bourse," *CE,* No. 614, 4 April 1928, p. 4.
114. Ernest Raynaud, "La leçon d'un incident," *CE,* No. 618, 2 May 1928, p. 2.
115. "M. Ubu, électeur," *CE,* No. 618, 2 May 1928, p. 1.

CHAPTER 12. *CANARD* ECONOMICS, OR THE COSTS OF THE WAR

1. Lucien Laforge, "M. et Mme. Mercanti se retirent des affaires," *CE,* No. 125, 20 November 1918, p. 1; "Le scruple du nouveau riche," *CE,* No. 124, 13 November 1918, p. 3.
2. Henri Béraud, "Feux d'armistice," *CE,* No. 125, 20 November 1918, p. 1; Whip, "En attendant mieux," *CE,* No. 124, 13 November 1918, p. 1. For a more pessimistic version of the *mercanti*-war relationship, see Charles Rearick, *The French in Love and War: Popular Culture in the Era of the World Wars* (New Haven, Conn.: Yale University Press, 1977), p. 60.
3. "Une bien bonne," *CE,* No. 128, 11 December 1918, p. 3, and see "Un noble geste," *CE,* No. 152, 28 May 1919, p. 4; "Simple question," *CE,* No. 396, 30 January 1924, p. 1.
4. See, for example, Henri Béraud, "Une conférence de la guerre," *CE,* No. 135, 29 January 1919, p. 1; "Les bonnes élections," *CE,* No. 178, 26 November 1919, p. 3; Whip, "Brelan de rois," *CE,* No. 132, 8 January 1919, pp. 1–2; "La mare aux canards," *CE,* No. 138, 19 February 1919, p. 2.
5. "Ce que vous ne verrez jamais," *CE,* No. 335, 29 November 1922, p. 2.
6. René Dubosc, "Savoir comprendre," *CE,* No. 503, 17 February 1926, p. 1; "Une affaire d'accaparement de blés en Angoulême," *CE,* No. 525, 21 July 1926, p. 1.
7. "Questions écrites," *CE,* No. 401, 5 March 1924, p. 2; "La mare aux canards," *CE,* No. 179, 3 December 1919, p. 2.
8. André Dahl, "La victime," *CE,* No. 164, 20 August 1919, pp. 1–2.
9. "Compensation nécessaire," *CE,* No. 205, 2 June 1920, p. 1; "Amnistie," *CE,* No. 315, 12 July 1922, p. 1.
10. Roland Catenoy, "L'ouverture de la chasse," *CE,* No. 164, 20 August 1919, p. 1; "L'opinion de M. Mercanti," *CE,* No. 164, 20 August 1919, p. 1.
11. "Signe des temps," *CE,* No. 129, 18 December 1918, p. 2.
12. See, for example, "L'accident rêvé," *CE,* No. 179, 3 December 1919, p. 1; G. de la Fouchardière, "Quand même!" *CE,* No. 207, 16 June 1920, p. 1.
13. Coty [sic], "En marge des deux décimes," *CE,* No. 398, 13 February 1924, p. 1; "Le lait va diminuer," *CE,* No. 296, 1 March 1922, p. 1.
14. "La mare aux canards," *CE,* No. 264, 20 July 1921, p. 2; "Infraction aux lois de spéculation licite," *CE,* No. 440, 3 December 1924, p. 4; "La mare aux canards," *CE,* No. 563, 13 April 1927, p. 2.
15. "La lutte pour l'émancipation patronale," *CE,* No. 336, 6 December 1922, p. 3.
16. "La mare aux canards," *CE,* No. 372, 15 August 1923, p. 2; "On écrit au Canard, le prix d'une boulangerie," *CE,* No. 374, 29 August 1923, p. 4; L. Bel-

lot, "Le pain à 23 sous," *CE*, No. 372, 15 August 1923, p. 4; "La baisse du pain," *CE*, No. 457, 1 April 1925, p. 2; "La liberté du travail," *CE*, No. 484, 7 October 1925, p. 2.

17. "Un office national de l'augmentation du prix du pain," *CE*, No. 448, 26 January 1925, p. 2; "Le prix du pain," *CE*, No. 453, 4 March 1925, p. 1; "Le prix du pain, une enquête s'impose," *CE*, No. 456, 25 March 1925, p. 1; "Le prix du pain," *CE*, No. 495, 23 December 1925, p. 1; "Ça ne prend plus!" *CE*, No. 505, 3 March 1926, p. 1.

18. "Le prix du pain," *CE*, No. 550, 12 January 1927, p. 2.

19. "Le prix du pain," *CE*, No. 615, 11 April 1928, p. 3.

20. "Les belles initiatives" and "Contes du Canard, un fin repas," both in *CE*, No. 344, 31 January 1923, p. 4; Arsène Brivot, "A la manière de l'Évangile," *CE*, No. 345, 7 February 1923, p. 2; "Relativité des injures," *CE*, No. 352, 28 March 1923, p. 1; "La mare aux canards," *CE*, No. 365, 27 June 1923, p. 2. See also chapter 9 of this book.

21. "Un office national de l'augmentation du prix du pain," *CE*, No. 448, 26 January 1925, p. 2; "Le prix du pain," *CE*, No. 453, 4 March 1925, p. 1.

22. "Un office national de l'augmentation du prix du pain," *CE*, No. 448, 26 January 1925, p. 2.

23. Jules Rivet, "Pour que le pain n'ait pas le goût amer," *CE*, No. 567, 11 May 1927, p. 9.

24. "Une belle initiative de M. Chéron," *CE*, No. 376, 12 September 1923, pp. 1–2; "Une cérémonie franco-britannique," *CE*, No. 517, 26 May 1926, p. 1; Pol Ferjac, "Petite chanson bretonne," *CE*, No. 570, 1 June 1927, p. 1.

25. "Un office national de l'augmentation du prix du pain," *CE*, No. 448, 26 January 1925, p. 2.

26. See, for example, W. A. Hoisington Jr., "Taxation: Governmental Policies Concerning," and A. Sedgewick, "Méline, Jules," in Patrick H. Hutton, ed., *Historical Dictionary of the French Third Republic* (New York: Greenwood Press, 1986), pp. 2:997–998 and 2:631–632, respectively.

27. Pol Ferjac, "L'inegalité fiscale," *CE*, No. 492, 2 December 1925, p. 4.

28. Pol Ferjac, "L'inégalité fiscale, les cultivateurs sont des contribuables incompris," *CE*, No. 494, 16 December 1925, p. 4; "Enthousiasme général," *CE*, No. 495, 23 December 1925, p. 3; W[illiam] N[apoleon] Grove, "Pas si bête," *CE*, No. 499, 20 January 1926, p. 1.

29. For the *Canard*'s attitude toward alcohol, see chapter 6.

30. "La récolte de 1922," *CE*, No. 326, 27 September 1922, p. 3; "Le prix du vin, M. Barthe va aviser," *CE*, No. 585, 14 September 1927, p. 3; "Le vin cher, le véritable responsable c'est le consommateur," p. 3, Pol Ferjac, "Le vin cher," p. 3, and Henri Monier, "Le viticulteur mécontent," p. 4, all in *CE*, No. 569, 25 May 1927.

31. See, for example, André Dahl and Lucien Laforge, "Conseil," *CE*, No. 148, 30 April 1919, p. 1; Victor Snell, "Le jour de demain," *CE*, No. 148, 30 April 1919, p. 1; "Toujours des dilapidations," *CE*, No. 251, 20 April 1921, p. 1. For wartime attitudes, see chapter 3 of this book.

32. "La mare aux canards," *CE*, No. 158, 9 July 1919, p. 3; "L'opinion de M. Mercanti," *CE*, No. 164, 20 August 1919, p. 1.

33. "La mare aux canards," *CE*, No. 597, 7 December 1927, p. 2.

34. Lucien Laforge, untitled cartoon, *CE*, No. 159, 16 July 1919, p. 1; "Pour faire baisser le prix de la vie," *CE*, No. 160, 23 July 1919, p. 1.

35. Victor Snell, "Réflexion et modération," *CE*, No. 161, 30 July 1919, p. 1.

36. Victor Snell, "Le miracle des farines," *CE*, No. 351, 21 March 1923, p. 1.

37. Headline and Henri Guilac, "La corde sauvera le franc!" *CE*, No. 398, 13 February 1924, p. 1.

38. "Le coût du pain," *CE*, No. 489, 11 November 1925, p. 4.

39. "Le prix du pain, un nouveau succès de la commission et de M. Queuille," *CE*, No. 447, 21 January 1925, p. 2; Henri Guilac, "Les maneuvres contre le franc," *CE*, No. 487, 28 October 1925, p. 2; "Aux halles centrales," *CE*, No. 595, 23 November 1927, p. 3.

40. Henri Guilac, "A la manière de . . . ," *CE*, No. 433, 15 October 1924, p. 1; "Evidences," *CE*, No. 449, 4 February 1925, p. 1.

41. "La baisse du franc, un agent de change suspendu pour un mois," *CE*, No. 452, 25 February 1925, p. 2.

42. Henri Guilac, "Reconstitutions historiques," *CE*, No. 449, 4 February 1925, pp. 1, 4. The July 14 issue of 1924, however, did show a guillotine in a French revolutionary scene. Though this cartoon did not verbally describe the victims, it showed them with the wigs of aristocrats; Henri Guilac, "Le 14 Juillet, l'origine de quelques réjouissances d'usage," *CE*, No. 419, 9 July 1924, p. 1.

43. See, for example, Jules Rivet, "Le pendu de Chicago," *CE*, No. 297, 8 March 1922, p. 2.

44. "Les grands voyages, le journal d'un polynésien à Paris," *CE*, No. 537, 13 October 1926, p. 3.

45. "Petite correspondance," *CE*, No. 312, 21 June 1922, p. 4; "Petite correspondance," *CE*, No. 450, 11 February 1925, p. 4; note, *CE*, No. 399, 20 February 1924, p. 1; "C'est un commencement," *CE*, No. 401, 5 March 1924, p. 4.

46. "Un démenti," *CE*, No. 209, 30 June 1920, p. 1; Jules Rivet, "Nos grands enquêtes, pourquoi le franc baisse," *CE*, No. 494, 16 December 1925, p. 3; note, *CE*, No. 359, 16 May 1923, p. 3.

47. P. Lenoy-Beaulieu [sic], "Les finances de la France," and headline, both in *CE*, No. 90, 20 March 1918, p. 4.

48. Pierre Miquel, *La paix de Versailles et l'opinion française* (Paris: Flammarion, 1972), pp. 195, 212.

49. Roger Brindolphe, "Les suites d'une interview," *CE*, No. 138, 19 February 1919, p. 4.

50. Lucien Laforge, untitled cartoon, *CE*, No. 159, 16 July 1919, p. 1; "La canonisation municipale des artisans de la victoire," *CE*, No. 206, 9 June 1920, p. 3.

51. Whip, "Anticipations," *CE*, No. 237, 12 January 1921, p. 1.

52. Henri Guilac, "Dialogue d'anniversaire," *CE*, No. 423, 6 August 1924, p. 1.

53. Pedro, "Le français moyen à travers les âges," *CE*, No. 530, 25 August 1926, p. 1.

54. "J'étais trop gros," *CE,* No. 538, 20 October 1926, p. 4; and see, for example, Angus McLaren, *The Trials of Masculinity: Policing Sexual Boundaries 1870–1930* (Chicago: University of Chicago Press, 1997), p. vii.

55. See, for example, *CE,* No. 163, 13 August 1919, p. 4; Georges de la Fouchardière, "La récolteuse," *CE,* No. 211, 14 July 1920, pp. 1–2.

56. "En r'venant de la revue," *CE,* No. 159, 16 July 1919, p. 2; "Etrennes! Etrennes!" *CE,* No. 338, 20 December 1922, p. 1.

57. "Contre l'obésité," *CE,* No. 150, 14 May 1919, p. 4.

58. Jules Rivet, "Anniversaire," *CE,* No. 318, 2 August 1922, p. 1; Mat, "Une minute de recueillement," *CE,* No. 332, 8 November 1922, p. 1; "On plante des arbres," *CE,* No. 233, 15 December 1920, p. 1.

59. "L'heure attendue," *CE,* No. 525, 21 July 1926, p. 1.

60. Charles Humbert [sic], "Pour la prochaine, sommes-nous prêts," *CE,* No. 297, 8 March 1922, p. 1; Ernest Raynaud, "Propos," *CE,* No. 552, 26 January 1927, p. 1.

61. Pierre Bénard, "Tout le Maroc célèbre les fêtes de la victoire," *CE,* No. 518, 2 June 1926, p. 1.

62. Rodolphe Bringer, "De ma fenêtre," *CE,* No. 591, 26 October 1927, p. 2.

63. Miquel, *La paix de Versailles,* pp. 433–455; Jean-Jacques Becker and Serge Berstein, *Victoire et frustrations, 1914–1929* (Paris: Editions du Seuil, 1990), pp. 225–226.

64. Victor Snell, "Fausses nouvelles," *CE,* No. 295, 22 February 1922, p. 1; Ph. Bertheller, "Visite à l'exposition d'art fiscal," *CE,* No. 504, 24 February 1926.

65. See, for example, "Reprise des hostilités au Maroc," *CE,* No. 515, 12 May 1926, p. 2.

66. "Petite correspondance," *CE,* No. 127, 4 December 1918, p. 4; "Petite correspondance," *CE,* No. 128, 11 December 1918, p. 4.

67. "Tant mieux, tant mieux!" *CE,* No. 130, 25 December 1918, p. 4.

68. "Le partage du butin," *CE,* No. 151, 21 May 1919, p. 2.

69. "Une heureuse surprise," *CE,* No. 307, 17 May 1922, p. 1; "La mare aux canards," *CE,* No. 307, 17 May 1922, p. 2; "La mare aux canards," *CE,* No. 312, 21 June 1921, p. 2.

70. "Plus un sou," *CE,* No. 140, 5 March 1919, p. 2; "Ne pas se frapper," *CE,* No. 210, 7 July 1920, p. 1.

71. See, for example, Roland Catenoy, "Les fruits de la victoire, comment l'Allemagne va nous payer," *CE,* No. 168, 17 September 1919, p. 1; R. Guérin, "Tête de pont," *CE,* No. 246, 16 March 1921, p. 4.

72. "Le sarcophage est ouvert," *CE,* No. 345, 7 February 1923, p. 1.

73. Henri Guilac, "Chacun son tour," *CE,* No. 451, 18 February 1925, p. 2. On French caricatures of Germania, see Christian Delporte, "Méfions-nous du sourire de Germania! L'Allemagne dans la caricature française (1919–1939)," *Mots* 48 (1996), pp. 35–40.

74. Pedro, "Chanson patriotique," *CE,* No. 396, 30 January 1924, p. 3; "Le rêve passe," in *Anthologie de la chanson française, 1900–1920: Les chansons patriotiques,* CD, EPM, 1997.

75. On this banquet, see chapter 8 of this book; "Un festin à tout casser," *CE,* No. 424, 13 August 1924, p. 2.

76. See, for example, "Pourquoi ces complications," *CE,* No. 241, 9 February 1921, p. 2.

77. Rodolphe Bringer, "Ce qu'aurait pu être l'année mil neuf cent vingt-deux," *CE,* No. 339, 27 December 1922, p. 1.

78. Pierre Bénard, "Si les Boches payaient," *CE,* Nos. 401–405, 5 March–2 April 1924, pp. 2–3. See, for example, Allen Douglas, *From Fascism to Libertarian Communism: Georges Valois against the Third Republic* (Berkeley: University of California Press, 1992), pp. 136–137.

79. "La Bourse," *CE,* No. 504, 24 February 1926, p. 4; "Mesures contre les spéculateurs," *CE,* No. 512, 21 April 1926, p. 2.

80. "La baisse artificielle du franc," *CE,* No. 334, 22 November 1922, p. 1.

81. "L'an qui nait et l'an qui meurt, ce que dit la voyante," *CE,* No. 392, 2 January 1924, p. 1.

82. See chapter 11 of this book; "Enfoncez-vous bien dans la tête," *CE,* No. 393, 9 January 1924, p. 2; Georges de la Fouchardière, "Chronique de l'oeil-de-Bouif: Questions financières," *CE,* No. 396, 30 January 1924, p. 3.

83. "Réflexes," *CE,* No. 404, 26 March 1924, p. 1; "Petite correspondance," *CE,* No. 352, 28 March 1923, p. 4.

84. See, for example, "Occasion ratée," *CE,* No. 404, 26 March 1924, p. 1.

85. See, for example, "La Bourse," *CE,* No. 517, 26 May 1926; No. 518, 2 June 1926; No. 520, 16 June 1926; No. 496, 30 December 1926, all on p. 4.

86. See, for example, "Bourse de Paris," *CE,* No. 309, 31 May 1922, p. 4; Noll Grove, "Pour donner le change, parlons franc," *CE,* No. 348, 28 February 1923, p. 1; Rodolphe Bringer, "Calendrier, la semaine prochaine," *CE,* No. 401, 5 March 1924, p. 2; "La livre baisse sérieusement," *CE,* No. 402, 12 March 1924, p. 3; "Occasion ratée," *CE,* No. 404, 26 March 1924, p. 1.

87. Rodolphe Bringer, "M. Poincaré a ses nerfs," *CE,* No. 402, 12 March 1924, p. 1.

88. Victor Snell, "En regardant monter le franc," *CE,* No. 416, 18 June 1924, p. 3; headline, *CE,* No. 443, 24 December 1924, p. 1; "Réflexes," *CE,* No. 460, 22 April 1925, p. 1.

89. See, for example, Victor Snell, "Un bon filon," *CE,* No. 459, 15 April 1925, p. 1.

90. See, for example, "Rompez, les poètes," *CE,* No. 445, 7 January 1925, p. 1; "La Bourse," *CE,* No. 469, 24 June 1925, p. 4; "Le 'Canard' a toujours raison," *CE,* No. 520, 16 June 1926, pp. 3–4.

91. Drégerin, "Les victimes du cartel vont recevoir de justes réparations," *CE,* No. 531, 1 September 1926, p. 3; "La Bourse," *CE,* No. 606, 8 February 1928, p. 4.

92. See, for example, Douglas, *From Fascism,* pp. 136–137.

93. Ernest Raynaud, "Un faux bruit," *CE,* No. 551, 19 January 1927, p. 1; Pierre Bénard, "Il faut maintenant stabiliser la livre," *CE,* No. 529, 18 August

1926, p. 1; "La Bourse," *CE*, No. 532, 8 September 1926, p. 3; "La Bourse," *CE*, No. 542, 17 November 1926, p. 4; "Le péril présent," *CE*, No. 539, 29 October 1926, p. 1; "La victoire du franc prend les proportions d'un désastre," *CE*, No. 543, 24 November 1926, p. 1; "Petite correspondance," *CE*, No. 527, 4 August 1926, p. 4.

94. Drégerin, "L'état de M. Poincaré s'améliore de jour en jour," *CE*, No. 545, 8 December 1926, p. 1; "Le péril présent," *CE*, No. 539, 29 October 1926, p. 1; "La Bourse," *CE*, No. 612, 21 March 1928, p. 4; "Situation nette," *CE*, No. 613, 28 March 1928, p. 1.

95. "Juste récompense aux patriotes," *CE*, No. 535, 29 September 1926, p. 1.

96. "Une solennité triomphale," *CE*, No. 184, 7 January 1920, p. 3.

97. Roland Dorgelès, "Le sang et l'argent," *CE*, No. 194, 17 March 1920, p. 1. The same point was made by Alain [Emile Chartier], *Mars ou la guerre jugée* (1921; reprint, Paris: Gallimard, 1995), pp. 41–43.

98. See, for example, "M. Queuille visite l'exposition des poires," *CE*, No. 431, 1 October 1924, p. 1; Pedro, "On ne paie qu'en sortant," *CE*, No. 493, 9 December 1925, p. 1.

99. Victor Snell, "Vraiment c'est trop facile," *CE*, No. 425, 25 February 1925, p. 1.

CHAPTER 13. THE WEALTH OF NATIONS

1. J. Pruvost, "L'invasion," *CE*, No. 510, 7 April 1926, p. 1.

2. Henri Guilac, "Gare du Nord, le jour de Pâques," *CE*, No. 510, 7 April 1926, p. 1.

3. J. Pruvost, "Sur les grand boulevards," *CE*, No. 488, 4 November 1925, p. 1; and see, for example, Victor Snell, "Feuilleton du Canard Enchaîné, lettres d'Angleterre," *CE*, No. 299, 20 March 1922, p. 2; Pol Ferjac, "On peut s'arranger," *CE*, No. 544, 1 December 1926, p. 1.

4. René Buzelin, "La taxe de séjour, laissons faire les hôteliers," *CE*, No. 375, 5 September 1923, p. 1.

5. "Les auto-cars, cordiales manifestations," *CE*, No. 526, 26 July 1926, p. 4; Jean de Pierrefeu, "Petit drame (par correspondance)," *CE*, No. 526, 26 July 1926, pp. 1–2.

6. G. de la Fouchardière, "Chronique de l'oeil-de-Bouif: L'autocar," *CE*, No. 527, 4 August 1926, pp. 1–2.

7. Pol Ferjac, "La colère populaire," *CE*, No. 527, 4 August 1926, p. 4.

8. J. Pruvost, "C'est bien différent," *CE*, No. 533, 15 September 1926, p. 1.

9. "Questions coloniales," *CE*, No. 539, 27 October 1926, p. 4. See chapter 10 in this book for a discussion of the *Canard*'s stand on imperialism.

10. Mat, "Le retour du parisien," *CE*, No. 528, 11 August 1926, p. 1.

11. Pierre Bénard, "Une anticipation sûre et certaine, quand le franc sera à 150 livres," *CE*, No. 515, 12 May 1926, p. 1.

12. G. de la Fouchardière, "Chronique de l'oeil-de-Bouif: Bicard enrichit son vocabulaire," *CE,* No. 552, 26 January 1927, p. 3.

13. "Le change, les dettes, les étrangers et le 'Canard Enchaîné,' " *CE,* No. 530, 25 August 1926, pp. 3–4.

14. "Autres amis lecteurs, M. Jean Armand a ouvert une controverse," *CE,* No. 531, 1 September 1926, pp. 3–4; "Entre amis lecteurs, réponses à Armand," *CE,* No. 532, 8 September 1926, pp. 3–4; "Nouvelles réponses à Armand," *CE,* No. 533, 15 September 1926, pp. 3–4.

15. See chapter 10.

16. "Entre amis lecteurs, réponses à Armand," *CE,* No. 532, 8 September 1926, p. 3. For the context of these debt disagreements, see, for example, Melvyn P. Leffler, *The Elusive Quest: America's Pursuit of European Stability and French Security 1919–1933* (Chapel Hill: University of North Carolina Press, 1979), pp. 121–193.

17. "Le change, les dettes, les étrangers et le 'Canard Enchaîné,' " *CE,* No. 530, 25 August 1926, p. 4.

18. "Toujours 'payer,' " *CE,* No. 373, 22 August 1923, p. 1.

19. G. de la Fouchardière, "Chronique de l'oeil-de-Bouif: Manifestations," *CE,* No. 390, 19 December 1923, p. 3.

20. G. de la Fouchardière, "Chronique de l'oeil-de-Bouif: Pour régler la dette anglaise," *CE,* No. 478, 26 August 1925, p. 1; G. de la Fouchardière, "Chronique de l'oeil-de-Bouif: De Mlle Suzanne Lenglen au maharadjah de Patiala," *CE,* No. 479, 2 September 1925, p. 2.

21. Pierre Bénard, "Feuilletons du Canard Enchaîné, un voyage au pays de la troisième république," *CE,* No. 482, 23 September 1925, p. 2; "Un geste de mauvais goût," *CE,* No. 321, 23 August 1921, p. 1.

22. "La mare aux canards," *CE,* No. 528, 11 August 1926, p. 2; "La question des dettes, M. Coolidge répond enfin à M. Clemenceau," *CE,* No. 530, 25 August 1926, p. 3. See chapter 12 of this book.

23. E. R., "Dettes, autour de la conférence," *CE,* No. 483, 30 September 1926, p. 4.

24. "Impérialisme," *CE,* No. 529, 18 August 1926, p. 2; "Utilisations," *CE,* No. 565, 25 April 1927, p. 1.

25. See, for example, Leffler, *The Elusive Quest,* p. 180.

26. Mat, "American Legion," *CE,* No. 582, 24 August 1927, p. 3.

27. Jules Rivet, "Opinions, Borah . . . pro nobis," *CE,* No. 448, 26 January 1925, p. 1; Pedro, "Un seul coup," *CE,* No. 484, 7 October 1925, p. 3.

28. Rodolphe Bringer, "L'espoir renait!" *CE,* No. 408, 23 April 1924, p. 1.

29. René Virard, "Nos oncles d'Amérique," *CE,* No. 522, 30 June 1926, p. 1; Pierre Bénard, "Les américains nous envoient une auto de la Federal Bank," *CE,* No. 544, 1 December 1926, p. 3.

30. See, for example, "A propos des paiements," *CE,* No. 557, 2 March 1927, p. 1; Pedro, "Payez toujours," *CE,* No. 558, 9 March 1927, p. 1.

31. "Pour Uncle Shylock, Sacco, Vanzetti et le goût du sport," *CE,* No. 580, 10 August 1927, p. 1.

32. "A la votre!" *CE,* No. 530, 25 August 1926, p. 1; G. de la Fouchardière, "Chronique de l'oeil-de-Bouif: Paris fête avec enthousiasme," *CE,* No. 586, 21 September 1927, p. 3.

33. Pierre Scize, "Lettre à M. l'Ambassadeur de France à Washington," *CE,* No. 545, 8 December 1926, pp. 1–2.

34. G. de la Fouchardière, "Chronique de l'oeil-de-Bouif," *CE,* No. 567, 11 May 1927, pp. 1, 3. The act was the same one that Monica Lewinsky became famous for performing on President Bill Clinton.

35. Pierre Scize, "Charlot," *CE,* No. 557, 2 March 1927, pp. 1–2. Charles Rearick in *The French in Love and War: Popular Culture in the Era of the World Wars* (New Haven, Conn.: Yale University Press, 1977), pp. 20–21, notes Chaplin's popularity with French soldiers.

36. Pierre Scize, "Un peuple sportif, pour un homme qui nous connaît bien," *CE,* No. 568, 18 May 1927, p. 2; "L'épreuve des faits," *CE,* No. 568, 18 May 1927, p. 1.

37. Headline and W., "Réflexions entre le ciel et l'eau," *CE,* No. 569, 25 May 1927, p. 1; "Un message de Lindbergh," *CE,* No. 571, 8 June 1927, p. 2. For a vivid account of the pro-Lindbergh hysteria, see Modris Eksteins, *Rites of Spring: The Great War and the Birth of the Modern Age* (New York: Anchor Books, 1990), pp. 242–274.

38. Pierre Scize, "Lettre familière à Charles Lindbergh," *CE,* No. 569, 25 May 1927, pp. 1–2.

39. Pierre Scize, "Pourquoi Lindbergh est parti ou l'aigle en proie aux brises," *CE,* No. 571, 8 June 1927, pp. 1–2.

40. Headline, *CE,* No. 580, 10 August 1927, p. 1.

41. Henri Guilac, untitled cartoon, *CE,* No. 580, 10 August 1927, p. 1; headline, *CE,* No. 581, 17 August 1927, p. 1; William Napoleon Grove, "Injustice est faite," *CE,* No. 582, 24 August 1927, p. 1.

42. "Pour Uncle Shylock, Sacco, Vanzetti et le goût du sport," *CE,* No. 580, 10 August 1927, p. 1.

43. "La mare aux canards," *CE,* No. 580, 10 August 1927, p. 2; "Une bonne leçon," *CE,* No. 580, 10 August 1927, p. 3.

44. Maurice Morice, "La grande fête nationale d'automne," *CE,* No. 586, 21 September 1927.

45. Headline, *CE,* No. 586, 21 September 1927, p. 1; Drégerin, "Mais notre enthousiasme généreux n'est-il pas une gaffe?" *CE,* No. 586, 21 September 1927, p. 4.

46. "Welcome," *CE,* No. 586, 21 September 1927, p. 1.

47. Pierre Scize, "Sous le signe de l'hypocrisie," *CE,* No. 587, 28 September 1927, p. 1.

48. Henri Guilac, untitled cartoon, *CE,* No. 586, 21 September 1927, p. 4.

49. Pierre Scize, "Propos désabusés," *CE,* No. 589, 12 October 1927, pp. 1–2.

50. François Furet, *Le passé d'une illusion* (Paris: Robert Laffont, 1995).

51. See chapters 7 and 11.

CHAPTER 14. CONCLUSION

1. Headline, *CE*, No. 437, 12 November 1924.

2. "Une lettre," *CE*, No. 438, 19 November 1924, p. 4.

3. See, for example, "Note," *CE*, No. 361, 30 May 1923, p. 1; headline and Maurice Maréchal, "Pour notre 'Canard' ami," *CE*, No. 379, 3 October 1923, p. 1; Maurice Maréchal, "Pour notre 'Canard,' " and "Abonnez-vous," both in *CE*, No. 382, 24 October 1923, p. 1; headline, *CE*, No. 564, 20 April 1927.

4. "Note," *CE*, No. 376, 12 September 1923, p. 1; headline, *CE*, No. 306, 10 May 1922; "Du sucre sans ticket à 2 frs. le kilo," *CE*, No. 171, 8 October 1919, p. 1.

5. See chapter 2.

6. Untitled article, *CE*, No. 38, 21 March 1917, p. 1; "Et ceci n'est plus de la rigolade," *CE*, No. 38, 21 March 1917, p. 4.

7. Roland Dorgelès, "A la manière de Louis XIV," *CE*, No. 208, 23 June 1920, p. 1.

8. See chapters 8 and 9.

9. See chapter 8.

10. "La grande force des petites histoires," *CE*, No. 583, 31 August 1927, p. 4.

11. "Concours du 'CE,' " *CE*, No. 134, 22 January 1919, p. 4; "Concours du 'CE,' " *CE*, No. 135, 29 January 1919, p. 2; "Concours," *CE*, No. 137, 12 February 1919, p. 4; "Les résultats du concours," *CE*, No. 140, 5 March 1919, p. 4.

12. "Mise au point," *CE*, No. 567, 11 May 1927, p. 4.

13. *CE*, No. 367, 11 July 1923, p. 4; "Un bel acte d'énergie, M. Léon Daudet part enfin pour le front," *CE*, No. 449, 4 February 1925, p. 1.

14. From Horace, as quoted in the note in Roland Barthes, *Mythologies*, trans. Annette Lavers (New York: Hill & Wang, 1995), p. 12.

15. Pedro, "Une vieille connaissance," *CE*, No. 565, 27 April 1927, p. 3.

16. See, for example, "S.A.I. le Kronprinz," *CE*, No. 1, 10 September 1915, p. 2; "Dernière heure," *CE*, No. 5, 1 August 1916, p. 4.

17. See Stéphane Audoin-Rouzeau and Annette Becker, *14–18 Retrouver la guerre* (Paris: Gallimard, 2000), p. 122. See also Christian Delporte, "Méfions-nous du sourire de Germania! L'Allemagne dans la caricature française (1919–1939)," *Mots* 48 (1996), pp. 38–40.

18. Henri Guilac, "Au paradis du fascisme," *CE*, No. 363, 13 June 1923, p. 1.

19. See, for example, Victor Snell, "L'anglais qu'il faut parler," *CE*, No. 106, 10 July 1918, p. 1; "Petite correspondance," *CE*, No. 106, 10 July 1918, p. 4; Whip, "French Lessons," *CE*, No. 107, 17 July 1918, p. 1 (English in original).

20. Louis Vorest [sic], "Brobos d'un barisien," *CE*, No. 258, 8 June 1921, p. 2; "La mare aux canards," *CE*, No. 497, 6 January 1926, p. 2.

21. On German terms, see chapter 3 of this book and "Plein aux as," *CE*, No. 113, 28 August 1918, p. 3; "Merveilleuse adaptation," *CE*, 114, 4 September 1918, p. 4; "Les merveilles de la science, le savant Einstein sera bientôt un grand français," *CE*, No. 300, 29 March 1922, p. 1; see also Rodolphe Bringer, "Emouvante manifestation franco-française," and accompanying illustration, *CE*, No. 300, 29 March 1922, p. 3.

22. "Théâtres," *CE,* No. 257, 1 June 1921, p. 4.

23. Henri Guilac, "Alphabet moderne: À l'usage des petits canards," *CE,* No. 431, 1 October 1924, p. 4; Robert J. Courtine, "Curnonsky prince des gastronomes," in Curnonsky, *Cuisine et vins de France* (Paris: Larousse, 1974), pp. 5–8.

24. Nori Brunel, "Les contes du Canard, les mémoires de Cancrelat par l'amant de sa femme," *CE,* No. 438, 19 November 1924, p. 4. And see, for example, Whip, "Le pétard prohibé," *CE,* No. 398, 13 February 1924, p. 2; Whip, "Justice distributive," *CE,* No. 443, 24 December 1924, pp. 1–2.

25. Jean-Louis Robert, "The Image of the Profiteer," in Jay Winter and Jean-Louis Robert, eds., *Capital Cities at War: Paris, London, Berlin 1914–1919* (Cambridge, England: Cambridge University Press, 1997), pp. 112–113, 131; Didier Nourrisson, "Les crayons de la morale: Alcool et caricature," *Sociétés & Représentations* (November 1995), pp. 140–142; and chapters 5 and 6 of this book.

26. On such war-induced corporality in a British context, see Joanna Bourke, *Dismembering the Male: Men's Bodies, Britain, and the Great War* (Chicago: University of Chicago Press, 1996).

27. See, for example, the incident described in William R. Keylor, *Jacques Bainville and the Renaissance of Royalist History in Twentieth-Century France* (Baton Rouge: Louisiana State University Press, 1979), pp. 78–79.

28. Jay Winter, *Sites of Memory, Sites of Mourning: The Great War in European Cultural History* (Cambridge: Cambridge University Press, 1995); Jacqueline Lalouette, *La libre pensée en France 1848–1940* (Paris: Albin Michel, 1997), pp. 68ff.; René Rémond, *L'anticléricalisme en France de 1815 à nos jours* (Paris: Fayard, 1999), pp. 225ff. and especially pp. 260–263, 286–293, 323–329. On the relationship between *joie de vivre* and anticlericalism in general, see Maurice Agulhon, *De Gaulle, histoire, symbole, mythe* (Paris: Plon, 2000), p. 117.

29. Lalouette, *La libre pensée,* p. 162. See also chapters 7, 8, and 10 of this book.

30. Georges Duhamel, *Civilisation 1914–1917* (1918; reprint, Monaco: Les Editions de l'Imprimerie Nationale de Monaco, 1950), p. 197.

31. François Furet, *Le passé d'une illusion* (Paris: Robert Laffont, 1995).

32. Quoted in Jean-Jacques Becker and Stéphane Audoin-Rouzeau, *La France, la nation, la guerre: 1850–1920* (Paris: Sedes, 1995), p. 187.

33. Margaret Randolph Higonnet and Patrice L.-R. Higonnet, "The Double Helix," in Margaret Randolph Higonnet et al., *Behind the Lines: Gender and the Two World Wars* (New Haven, Conn.: Yale University Press, 1987), pp. 31–47.

34. Guilac, "Au paradis du fascisme," p. 1.

35. Alain [Emile Chartier], *Mars ou la guerre jugée* (1921; reprint, Paris: Gallimard, 1995), pp. 204–210.

36. See, for example, Mary Louise Roberts, *Civilization without Sexes: Reconstructing Gender in Postwar France, 1917–1921* (Chicago: University of Chicago Press, 1994), pp. 103–107.

37. Alain, *Mars*, pp. 256–260.

38. Samuel Hynes, *The Soldier's Tale: Bearing Witness to Modern War* (New York: Penguin Books, 1997), pp. 109–111, and see also the discussion in Barbara Ehrenreich, "Once upon a Wartime," *The Nation* 264/18 (May 12, 1997), p. 21.

39. Tzvetan Todorov, *Les abus de la mémoire* (Paris: Arléa, 1998), entire, and, for example, p. 33; Martin Jay, "Against Consolation: Walter Benjamin and the Refusal to Mourn," in Jay Winter and Emmanuel Sivan, *War and Remembrance in the Twentieth Century* (Cambridge: Cambridge University Press, 1999), pp. 221–239.

40. Winter, *Sites.*

41. Modris Eksteins, *Rites of Spring: The Great War and the Birth of the Modern Age* (New York: Anchor Books, 1990); Paul Fussell, *The Great War and Modern Memory* (London: Oxford University Press, 1975).

42. Compare Charles Rearick, *The French in Love and War: Popular Culture in the Era of the World Wars* (New Haven, Conn.: Yale University Press, 1977), p. 278.

Index

Page numbers in italics indicate figures.

Text: 10/13 Aldus
Display: Aldus
Compositor: Impressions Book & Journal Services
Printer and Binder: Sheridan Books, Inc.